WORLD OF CRICKET 1979

GW00644779

Edited by
TREVOR BAILEY

Compiled by
BILL FRINDALL

MACDONALD AND JANE'S, LONDON

Unless otherwise credited, all pictures were supplied by Patrick Eagar

Editing and design by Graeme Wright

Front cover: England all-rounder Ian Botham of Somerset appeals successfully for yet another wicket in the Test series against New Zealand.
Back cover: Mark Burgess, the New Zealand captain, on the defensive against aggressive England close-fielding. Edmonds lunges, wicket-keeper Taylor and Botham watch, and Gower views proceedings from his patrol in the covers.

© Macdonald and Jane's Publishers Ltd 1979
Published by
The Queen Anne Press Division, Macdonald and Jane's Publishers Ltd,
Paulton House, 8 Shepherdess Walk, London N1 7LW
Photoset in Times, Printed and bound by Redwood Burn Limited
Trowbridge & Esher

CONTENTS

FOREWORD FROM SCHWEPPES LIMITED

Schweppes are delighted to be associated with a second year of *World of Cricket*. It is particularly pleasing to know that every copy of last year's edition has been sold.

The 1979 season promises to be an eventful one, especially with the staging of the second World Cup tournament. For the first time, all the newer cricket-playing countries have been invited to participate, and we welcome to England the many entrants. Hopefully we shall have a warm, hot summer as we had the last time the World Cup was contested.

The Schweppes Championship increased in popularity in 1978, and yet again there was an exciting finish. With increased prize-money it increases in importance and prestige, and, equally importantly, it remains the essential breeding-ground for a successful England side.

We wish everyone, players, umpires, and spectators alike, a happy and enjoyable season.

Geoffrey Darby
Managing Director
Schweppes Limited

EDITORIAL

The summer of 1978, which began with an English monsoon, contained many interesting events, some of which were not concerned directly with the playing of the game. The Packer pirates returned from the first WSC season in Australia to a very mixed reception from both the counties and the players. Many of the clubs would not have re-engaged them had they not been compelled to do so by law; others warmly welcomed them. A high percentage of the members of the Professional Cricketers' Association was worried by what was happening. Should the players under contract to WSC take part in county cricket when WSC was clearly having an adverse effect on the revenue from Test cricket, on which the clubs who paid their wages were so dependent? There was talk of a strike and a new-found militancy was seen, indicating a marked increase in 'player power'. I believe this could be a good thing, but only if it is used sensibly for the benefit *both* of the game and of the players. Cricket, because of its particular financial problems, could not afford the almost entirely mercenary approach of professional tennis which stemmed directly from the big increase of 'player power'.

What will be the views of the majority of professional players about playing with, and against, those from WSC in 1979? Some could be influenced by the extra money they make because Packer men in their team can help win honours. In contrast, those on the Warwickshire staff were prepared to see Amiss depart. One thing is certain: if the players' association members decide not to take part in games containing WSC players, then the Prudential World Cup will either be reduced in importance or be killed.

The good things of 1978, in no order of merit, included the boisterous all-round performances of Ian Botham, the elegance of Gower, and the seam bowling, the very high standard of fielding, and the wicket-keeping in the England team. On the domestic scene Kent, Essex, Middlesex, Yorkshire, Somerset, Leicestershire, Nottinghamshire, Hampshire, Derbyshire, and Sussex, again in no order of merit, all had causes for satisfaction. Individually there were numerous outstanding performances. My choice for the best bowler must go to Underwood, who was the chief reason why Kent won the Schweppes Championship. My batting place would unquestionably go to Greenidge, who played such a tremendous part in Hampshire, against all the odds, walking off with the John Player League. My most difficult task was trying to choose between Clive Rice and Botham as the best all-rounder. Rice was clearly ahead on points with the bat; Botham with the ball. Many of Botham's most spectacular efforts were reserved for Test cricket, from which Rice is barred. Both are match-winners, fine fielders and real fighters; I will call it a tie.

In 1978, England captain Mike Brearley and the helmet came in for their share of adverse comment. Brearley was soon to hang up his helmet, but its absence did nothing to ensure a return to form.

Perhaps 1978 will best be remembered as the year when the crash helmet became fashionable. From a distance, Sadiq Mohammad going out to bat in his 'skid lid' looked like a white-clad skate-boarder. Apart from its novelty, one of the main reasons for the crash helmet becoming fashionable has been the over-employment of the bouncer by quick bowlers combined with the inability of so many batsmen to cope with them. I should hate to see the bouncer banned completely, but I would like to see the number reduced to one every other over, or at most one an over. It is plainly unsatisfactory to give immunity to the tail, because the number 11 of one side could well be a better batsman than number 7 in another. Moreover, it would give undeserved protection to those who send them down, and I have always enjoyed the pained expression that appears on the face of a fast bowler with an impressive record of direct hits on opposing batsmen when he himself is struck by a bouncer! More positive action by captains and umpires is required to reduce the number of bouncers. Both ought to be able to discern the difference between the deliberate bumper and the fast ball that lifts unpleasantly from just short of a length.

Two of the unhappy features of 1978 concerned Yorkshire: the much publicised Boycott affair and the banning of Geoffrey Cope for throwing. This is the second time in his career that Cope has been outlawed for his faulty action. He showed considerable determination and patience when he amended it on the first occasion, and his bowling was then judged legitimate. What is rather difficult to understand is why the umpires, the Yorkshire cricket committee, and the England selectors, who took him on tour overseas where he was never called, took such a long time to realise that he was still jerking in his delivery.

SUMMER OF '78

April

19   Botham celebrates the start of the first-class season with a hat-trick, all clean bowled, for MCC v Middlesex.

20   Nottinghamshire County CC sack their newly appointed captain, and best player, Rice, when he announces he has signed for WSC.

21   Sarfraz Nawaz, a member of the Pakistan touring party, calls a one-man strike because he feels he is being inadequately paid.

22   Benson and Hedges Cup competition starts. Wayne Daniel takes 7–12 in 12 overs for Middlesex against Minor Counties East, who go west as expected.

24   Glamorgan panic when 187–5 against Somerset and fail to score the 197 required, finishing level but losing on the more wickets lost rule. Their South African, Swart, makes an impressive début with a half-century.

25   WSC lawyers seek a High Court injunction declaring Clive Rice's contract with Nottinghamshire to be still valid. An unprecedented move in the cricket world. The county sign Richard Hadlee as Rice's replacement.

26   Pakistan start their first-class fixtures at Worcester. The weather was totally unsuitable, and indicates that the beginning of May, rather than the middle of April, would be a more sensible date for the tourists to arrive.

29   Derbyshire show, with an impressive win over Lancashire in the Benson and Hedges Cup, that they are a side to watch.

30   The John Player League has a very damp start; five matches abandoned, two completed, and one adjudicated on a faster scoring-rate.

May

2   Two Benson and Hedges matches abandoned; Yorkshire beat Essex in a 10-over slog.

3   Charlie Palmer, chairman and former captain of Leicester, nominated the new MCC president.

4   Clive Lloyd hits 114 for Lancashire against Sussex, although Arnold picks up 7–44 for his new county.

5   Nottinghamshire, realising they have no case in Law, agree to take Rice back on their staff, but not as captain. A classic case of act in haste, repent at leisure. John Snow not re-engaged by Sussex, which did not appear to surprise anybody other than Snow.

6   FA Cup final in the sun, but cricket possible in only one Benson and Hedges match, Glamorgan beating Hampshire at Swansea.

7   Kent crash to Somerset in the John Player League after being shot out for 86.

8   Imran, with 65 and 5–8 in the Benson and Hedges Cup against Northamptonshire, underlines his all-round skill and his loss to the Pakistan team.

9   Minor Counties East almost cause a major upset in the Benson and Hedges Cup as Leicestershire scrape home by one wicket in the final over.

10   Mike Brearley appointed captain of England for the one-day internationals and the three Tests against Pakistan.

11   Geoff Boycott makes a characteristic – and appropriate – century against Warwickshire.

12   The two counties which have never won a major title, Essex and Somerset, start with convincing wins in the Schweppes Championship. Essex beat reigning champions Middlesex by 109 runs; Somerset thrash Glamorgan by nine wickets. Could 1978 be their year?

13   Norbert Phillip makes a dramatic début for Essex, taking 6–37 as Pakistan are shot out for 80.

14   Derbyshire win their third successive

John Player League match with an easy victory over Yorkshire.

15   Combined Universities fail by one run to beat Glamorgan.

17   Hignell scores 108 out of 213 for Combined Universities against Surrey.

18   Pakistan struggle to 149-9 declared against MCC as Old takes 6-36.

19   David Gower's attractive 71 against Pakistan rewarded by a place in the England squad for the Prudential one-day internationals.

20   A fine century by Kallicharran paves the way for Warwickshire's 36-run win over Gloucestershire.

21   An impressive 65 not out by new Lancashire skipper Hayes, in the gloom, guides his team to victory over Middlesex.

22   Brearley withdraws from the Prudential international, thus leaving Boycott as captain.

23   West Indies want the ICC to re-open talks with Kerry Packer, and are prepared to act as intermediary. J. Bailey (TCCB secretary) says the matter needs to be discussed with other countries.
    WIBC cable WSC to find out if any West Indies players (with Packer contracts) are available for the Indian tour.

24   The start of the limited-overs Prudential internationals. England take control.

25   England beat Pakistan. Willis, with 4-15, the most successful bowler in the rout.
    Lancashire fined £500 and have six Championship points taken away by the TCCB for failing to register Clive Lloyd and Croft in time. In the circumstances, a heavy-handed justice; only the previous year few clubs bothered over-much about registration.

26   Gower hits an impressive century to spearhead England to an easy second win in the second Prudential international.
    Bishan Bedi and Mushtaq Mohammad to sue Northamptonshire for wrongful dismissal. Is industrial law either suitable for or relevant to the requirements of an essentially aesthetic game?

27   A remarkable century by Carrick in the low-scoring Roses Match puts Yorkshire into a winning position on a doubtful Headingley pitch.

28   A black day for Sussex at The Oval in the John Player League; their first five batsmen registering ducks. Young Thomas did most of the damage (4-13 in eight overs) and Surrey won by seven wickets.

29   After 16 seasons in county cricket, Cumbes awarded his cap; by Worcestershire. Davison strikes a spectacular 180 not out for Leicestershire against Northants, who must surely possess the most insipid attack in domestic cricket.

30   Notts continue to show form with an impressive victory over Derbyshire by eight wickets, suggesting that 1978 could be their best season for a very long time. But what will happen when Hadlee joins the New Zealanders?

31   Geoff Boycott withdraws from the first Test against Pakistan with a bruised left thumb and Barry Wood is brought in; a selection lacking in originality. Gooch, now opening for Essex, hits a century against Kent; a useful reminder for the selectors.

June
1   Old takes four wickets in five balls in the Pakistan rout. Somewhat ironically, Imran Khan strikes a spectacular 167 for Sussex, the fastest century of the season to date.

2   David Gower hooks the first ball he receives in Test cricket to the boundary, and strokes a half-century glittering with excitement and promise.
    Zaheer Abbas, another of Pakistan's ineligible Packer men, scores 213 out of 381 for Gloucestershire against Sussex.

3   Ian Botham plunders a boisterous century off the fragile Pakistan attack.
    Three men seeking England places display good form; Hayes 136 not out, Willey 112, and Lever 7-56.

4   Leicestershire, the holders, achieve their fifth successive victory in the Sunday League with a convincing eight-wicket win over Glamorgan and so remain top of the table. Hampshire continue to challenge strongly by coming back against the odds to beat Lancashire.

5   England beat Pakistan by an innings and 57 runs. After Iqbal Qasim was hit in the face by a Willis bouncer, the Pakistan manager described the bowling as unfair and said he would complain to the TCCB. His view that bouncers should not be bowled at non-recognised batsmen was valid in respect of the note on playing conditions (Law 46), but Iqbal Qasim is such a limited player against pace that it could be argued he should never have been sent in as a night-watchman.
    Kent beat Middlesex on a pig of a pitch at Lord's. McEwan and Gooch establish a county

The unhappiest moment of the summer. Iqbal Qasim receives treatment after being hit in the face by a Willis bouncer. The accident fired yet more controversy about short-pitched bowling.

record second wicket stand for Essex by putting on 321 against Northants.

6   Somerset and Essex achieve convincing victories to take them second and third in the table behind Notts.

7   Kent go through to the semi-final of the Benson and Hedges Cup by beating Notts, who played below their recent form.

8   Somerset, Derbyshire, and Warwickshire become the other semi-finalists.

Predictably, the TCCB declared that Iqbal Qasim, having been promoted up the order, should have been able to defend himself adequately against short-pitched fast bowling. However, this does not disguise the fact that too many bouncers have been, and are being, bowled in international and domestic cricket. Although Croft has been warned this summer, the umpires are still too tolerant.

9   The TCCB issue a new statement about bouncers. Their first statement had been mis-interpreted; not surprisingly, as it was lament-ably inadequate. The new statement empha-sised the need to observe existing regulations and bitterly regretted the injury to Iqbal. There should also be a meeting between the two captains to sort out the bouncer and the matter of non-recognised batsmen situation.

Before the start of the series would have been better.

10   South Africans in the runs. Kirsten makes an unbeaten 206 against Glamorgan, Procter 203 against Essex.

11   Gooch recalled to the Test squad; Boycott still unfit to open.

Sussex achieve an unlikely victory over Kent in the Sunday League, scoring 71 in the last 10 overs with only four wickets left and making 11 in the last over.

12   Russell, fielding in his crash helmet in a suicidal position, is hit in the visor, where the ball lodges. The 'catch' is disallowed, but the fielder goes to hospital with a fractured cheek-bone. Would he have moved quicker, in taking evasive action, if not protected in this fashion, and would he have stood quite so close?

13   Phillip strikes a remarkable maiden first-class century for Essex with 7 sixes and 12 fours (his previous best score was 99 for Windward Isles). As a result, Essex eventually won by two wickets, having been set 313 in 200 minutes and still needing 185 when the final 20 overs began!

15   No play in the Lord's Test, but Brearley and Wasim Bari agree not to bowl bouncers at tailenders. This somewhat ironic decision means that Willis, who is a useful tailender, a forward lunger, and the chief culprit, receives protection.

16   Botham hits a spectacular century and Roope, Gooch, and Gower strike attractive fifties. England reach 309–8 in a shortened day memorable for the unusual number of strokes played. It must be admitted that the Pakistan attack was indifferently handled, and generally insipid.

17   Pakistan humiliated by England and shot out for 105.
  Greig returns to county cricket in a crash helmet, is out first ball, and Sussex are dismissed for 77, to which Hampshire manage 301–2 in reply.

18   Brearley hangs up his helmet, having been out lbw three times to left-arm bowlers while wearing it.
  Worcestershire beat Leicestershire with a six in the last over by Holder and reach 231. Illingworth's men pay the penalty for indifferent fielding and missed catches.

19   Magnificent swing bowling by Botham (8–34) as Pakistan surrender abjectly.
  Bedi's claim for unfair dismissal by Northamptonshire is turned down by an Industrial

New Zealand opener Robert Anderson views the English summer with some pessimism.

Tribunal on technical grounds, but he is allowed to submit a fresh claim on the following day.

20   Spectator cruelty at Cardiff after Gloucestershire set Glamorgan 294 to win in 105 minutes, having declared their second innings at 369–2! Both teams must accept some of the responsibility: Procter's negative approach was influenced by the opposition batting too long in their first innings.
  Kent beat Middlesex by 39 runs, their fourth successive victory, and move to the top of the table.

21   Pakistan embassy deny that pressure has been brought on the Pakistan team to include Packer men. This followed an address by their ambassador to the players.
  Benson and Hedges semi-finals commence. Kent, having been put in by Somerset, reach 149–5 in 41.2 overs.
  The Industrial Tribunal at Bedford rejects Bedi's claim of unfair dismissal by Northants. County clubs are very relieved by the verdict, which established their right to dispense with the services of a player at the end of his contract.

22   Derbyshire reach their first Benson and Hedges final with a 21-runs victory. Hendrick, with 2–14 in 11 overs, ensures that Warwickshire fail to make 203, despite a brave innings from Humpage.

23   Kent in the Benson and Hedges final for the third year in succession. Somerset must have regretted inserting the opposition, for they struggled to 163 in conditions that were far more helpful to bowlers than they had been on the opening day.

24   New Zealand impress in their first county match against Sussex.
  Athey scores a splendid century against Somerset.
  Illingworth dropped by Leicestershire.

25   A great race for the John Player League developing. Hampshire, Somerset, Worcestershire, Lancashire, Leicestershire, Derbyshire, and Essex all in with a good chance.

26   Miller, batting at number 6, hits an impressive 77 as Derbyshire are bundled out for 167 by Leicestershire. Clive Lloyd savages a fragile Glamorgan attack to the fastest hundred (91 minutes) while Lancashire scamper to 401–4 in 100 overs.

27   The Schweppes Championship race hots up: Middlesex demolish Nottinghamshire, Essex slaughter Hampshire. There are now five obvious contenders: Kent, Somerset, Essex, Middlesex, and Yorkshire, with Kent favourites.

New Zealand win their first county match. Pakistan also win their first county match, *which was also their last*, beating Surrey in a contrived finish.

28   Randall makes a spectacular 157 not out against Sussex.

In the University Match, Cambridge are bowled out for 92 and Oxford gain a lead of 100 on a turning pitch.

New Zealand Cricket Council suspend Turner, one of their few truly world-class players, from playing in New Zealand. A sad end to a row which had been simmering for a long time with faults on both sides. Cricket administrators have an inclination towards being tactless and over-righteous.

29   Pakistan make a reasonable start in the final Test; 65–0 in a rain-shortened day.

David Steele follows up his 130 by taking six wickets against Derbyshire, who are heading for an innings defeat.

30   Kent beat Surrey by an innings; Underwood's 9–32 is the best bowling performance of the season.

Steele picks up another five wickets against Derbyshire to complete his finest all-round performance; 11–75 and a century.

Zaheer Abbas becomes the first batsman to score 1,000 runs in first-class cricket, going from 15 not out to 121 not out before lunch for Gloucestershire against the New Zealanders.

July
1   No play in the Test because of antiquated covering arrangements. For the third successive day, spectators wait, but on this occasion there is no cricket to compensate for their boredom. Some may well think twice before going to another Test at Headingley.

2   Despite injuries, Hampshire retain their place at the top of the Sunday League table, scoring 212 to beat Nottinghamshire by seven wickets.

3   Old returns a remarkable 41.1–22–41–4 in the Test, and Brearley secures a second-ball nought in front of a crowd who think 'Our Geoffrey' should be leading England.

Procter, on a slow pitch, slams 143 in 113 minutes against Surrey, his third century of the season. Another South African, McEwan, reaches his fourth and adds 201 in 41 overs with the Essex captain, Fletcher, for the third wicket against Yorkshire.

4   Further rain makes sure the third Test ends as a draw. Brearley is appointed as skipper against New Zealand, despite a most unproductive spell with the bat.

5   Vivian Richards hits 139 not out in the Gillette Cup as Somerset pass Warwickshire's 293. This was the highest score ever made by a county batting second in the competition, and was obtained for the loss of only four wickets and with 19 balls to spare!

6   Derbyshire come back from what looked like certain defeat to beat Worcestershire by five runs. Worcestershire, requiring only 159 runs to win in 60 overs, were 120–3 at one stage. Barlow not only handled his attack with skill but also took 5–30.

7   Yorkshire, with the aid of another century from John Hampshire, gain revenge for their 1973 Gillette Cup defeat by Durham in a 45 overs match.

Hampshire surrender to Gloucestershire: Childs follows up his 4–24 in the first innings with 8–34, emphasising that he might become an outstanding slow left-armer with more bowling potential than his colleague, Graveney.

8   Hampshire scores a masterly 132 for Yorkshire against Warwickshire to become the first Englishman to reach 1,000 runs, and to suggest he could be the experienced batsman needed for Australia. He has the added advantage of having played much cricket in Tasmania.

9   A brilliant 107 not out by Larkins, containing eight sixes and eight fours and lasting 74 minutes! He came to the crease when Northamptonshire were 57–4 and completely shattered Surrey.

Boycott not included in the 13-man squad for the two Prudential internationals against New Zealand. Randall, who has been having a good season for Nottinghamshire, is brought back – a logical decision as Brearley and Boycott could hardly be described as the ideal opening pair for a limited-overs match.

10   Glenn Turner, with 155 not out, makes his first century for Worcestershire in what is proving his least successful season for a long time. Impressive début by the slow left-armer Mellor; 5–52 for Derbyshire against Kent.

11   New Zealand show their power with an innings victory over Middlesex.

Kent retain their place at the top of the Championship table after beating Derbyshire by eight wickets, thanks largely to Underwood picking up 11 victims in the match. Essex move into second place with Lever, unlucky not to command a regular place in the England XI, taking 7–32 against Sussex.

Tony Greig ends his contract with Sussex, due to expire in September, by mutual consent with the county. He had not been successful with either bat or ball since his resumption after suspension. A sad anti-climax to a 12-

year career in English cricket.

12   The TCCB remind umpires and players of the need to get the game going whenever possible and to play fair with the paying public. These sentiments are excellent, but the statement really means nothing; what the umpires and players consider possible is usually very different from the public's view.

July

13   Congdon and Parker complete undefeated centuries as New Zealand power their way to 414 for four declared and take command against Warwickshire.

14   Essex achieve their seventh Championship victory, beating Somerset, and move into second place in the Schweppes Championship. Yorkshire go to third as a result of a win against Surrey in the penultimate over of a slow, low-scoring contest that never came alive until the last day. Middlesex beat Leicestershire by one wicket on yet another very poor pitch at Lord's.

15   England have trouble beating New Zealand in the first one-day international. Play held up for poor, but far from impossible, light. It must be less than a week since the TCCB reminded umpires and players of their duty to spectators!

Rice scores 213 not out, out of 370 for four, after the first two Nottinghamshire wickets had gone cheaply.

16   The Sunday when it paid to bat second and the favourites fell. Glamorgan beat Middlesex, Surrey beat Hampshire (they had to score 239 to win), Derbyshire beat Worcestershire, Somerset beat Leicestershire, and Warwickshire beat Essex with overs to spare.

17   A dashing century from Radley sets England up for an easy win over New Zealand in the second Prudential one-day international.

Boycott scores an ultra-laboured century against Northamptonshire, who do not possess the most formidable of attacks. Athey's hundred is a more attractive one. In the last 10 overs, Hampshire and Johnson added 11 runs, which cost Yorkshire a bonus batting point and a first innings lead that was there for the taking. Presumably, the length of Boycott's innings irritated the later batsmen, who failed to see why they should be called on to sacrifice their wickets in a wild slog after he had occupied the crease for hour upon hour. An official enquiry is to be held by the Yorkshire cricket committee.

18   Denness continues his Colchester run-spree with 126 in the first and another innings to follow his 70 in the first; Essex win to close up on Kent, despite a masterly 120 not out from Woolmer, who carried his bat.

Sussex win their first Championship match of the season at their 13th attempt.

19   Kent move into the quarter-finals of the Gillette Cup with a last-over win against Northamptonshire, despite having to score 249 in the 60 overs. Denning makes 146 not out in Somerset's massive 330 total against Glamorgan.

20   D. J. Insole appointed manager for the Australian tour, with Barrington as his number two.

In the Gillette Cup second day, Staffordshire fail by only three runs to beat Sussex, and Yorkshire scramble home against Nottinghamshire by one wicket with three balls remaining.

The Lloyds hit remarkable not out centuries in a record Gillette partnership of 234 which took Lancashire to victory over Gloucestershire, even though Lancashire had to make a formidable 267 and were 33 for three in the 15th over!

The Yorkshire cricket committee issue a somewhat nebulous statement following their enquiry into the reasons for the uncharacteristic go-slow batting by Hampshire against Northamptonshire: "The selection committee have considered all aspects of the incident at Northampton, and have conveyed their findings to the players concerned, and now consider the matter closed."

The Kent committee predictably change their mind and offer contracts to their Packer men for next summer.

22   Kent beat Derbyshire comfortably in a disappointing Benson and Hedges Cup final.

Cope banned from bowling for Yorkshire for the second time in his career. The TCCB adjudicating committee came to this decision after studying a film of his action taken against Surrey earlier in the week. Everybody in cricket knew that he had a suspect action, yet he was still chosen to tour India, Pakistan, and New Zealand, where he was *not* called. Moreover, he was *not* called in England this summer, or last. All in all, rather odd!

23   Worcestershire storm to the top of the Sunday League by beating Essex by one run in the last over.

Boycott not included in the squad for the first Test v New Zealand.

D. G. Clark, MCC president and chairman of ICC, resigns from the Kent committee because they have re-engaged their Packer men.

24   Boycott meanders to a typical Boycott century against the New Zealanders, and Hampshire hammers a spectacular 90 while his captain makes 34.

25   ICC meet at Lord's to hear report on a

secret meeting between J. A. Bailey and D. G. Clark and Packer representatives Andrew Caro and Lynton Taylor in New York. The West Indies, who have lost the best side in the world to Packer, are desperate for a compromise, whereas both England and Australia can afford to sit back and wait. Their top players are now able to earn so much through sponsorship that the Packer contracts have lost much of their appeal. Although Caro and Taylor were in London, they were not invited to the meeting.

26 The Packer proposals unanimously rejected by the ICC including the West Indies. These proposals were pitched too high, and were also impracticable cricket-wise. Had they been adopted, it would have meant 10 months of Packer-motivated cricket in a calender year, all with approval of ICC. To have accepted them in their entirety would have been tantamount to handing over the control of the game to an organisation, the length of whose interest in cricket was unknown and whose policy might change dramatically if Kerry Packer died, or changed his mind.

Somerset, with a century from Rose (122) and an eighty from Richards, power themselves to 364 in their 100 overs against Worcestershire.

27 New Zealand struggle to 274 for seven against England at The Oval. Boycott taps out a reminder to the selectors with a masterly century against Glamorgan which puts his team in control. The South African, Allan Lamb, hits maiden century for Northamptonshire against Essex. At Hove, the Surrey opener, Butcher, produces the type of knock his county have been hoping for; 188, which included 7 sixes and 26 fours and took less than four and a half hours!

The ICC agree by a majority vote to examine multi-racial cricket being played in South Africa. Predictably, the following countries voted against sending a delegation to South Africa: West Indies, India, Pakistan, East Africa, Bangladesh, Sri Lanka and Malaysia. The conference refused to hear Mr Varachia explain his Board's work in introducing non-racial cricket in South Africa. One gains the impression that many members of the ICC are uninterested in cricket in South Africa for purely political reasons. Dictatorships, military governments and make-believe emperors are all acceptable and respectable, but South Africa is beyond the pail.

28 Gower's first Test century is more than adequate compensation for much indifferent batting by England.

The Schweppes Championship continues to bring out the best in those teams at the top of the table. Kent beat Leicestershire with seven balls to spare, despite needing 137 at the start

Extensive, and sensible, covering at The Oval during the first England-New Zealand Test.

of the last 20 overs. East, with eight for 41, sets up the Essex victory over Northamptonshire, while another left-armer, Breakwell, plays a big part in Somerset's success, taking six vital wickets. Yorkshire crush Glamorgan by an innings. A career best of five for 32 by second-choice off-spinner Featherstone speeds Middlesex home.

At Hove, a hat-trick for 20-year-old Sussex fast bowler Pigott bring his first wickets in first-class cricket.

The Packer representatives hastily convene a press conference at the Dorchester in the evening. There, Andrew Caro explains that the original Packer proposals were only intended to be taken as a starting point for negotiations. Their main objective was to establish a knock-out world cup between England, West Indies, Australia, and another country to be decided by a previous tournament. This competition would be staged in Australia and last for about six weeks in February and March, thus avoiding the key dates in the Australian international cricket programme. The national teams would be chosen by their respective authorities to give authenticity and Test match status. The eventual winner would be prepared to go on a short tour to other countries, if this was requested. In addition, WSC would continue to operate in Australia during the other months, presumably with an emphasis on night cricket. It is noticeable how, during the

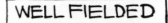

SSSCHWICKET-KEEPER SSSCHOUTS

SSSCHILLY SSSCHORT LEG

SSSCHAMBLES!

Another ssschambles. Collinge swoops, Gower is stranded, and Radley escapes to continue his record-breaking innings in the Prudential Trophy match at Manchester.

1978–79 Anglo–Australian series, they have carefully avoided clashing with the Test matches; not, one assumes, to accommodate the Australian Board but because genuine Tests have so much more appeal, both live and on television, than friendlies, whatever the size of the prizemoney or the calibre of the players.

29 Steady graft from the England tail, followed by tight, accurate bowling, push New Zealand towards a heavy defeat.

Essex, thanks largely to yet another century from McEwan, race to 379 and then shoot out four Lancashire batsmen to sustain their challenge for the Schweppes Championship. While New Zealand flounder, their most accomplished batsman, Turner, hits 150 for his adopted county, including a hundred before lunch.

30 Rain devastates the Sunday League with no play possible in three matches and the other four reduced to shortened slogs, including one 10 overs biff-bang at Edgbaston. Worcestershire increase their lead at the top of the table in a 13 overs game in which their remarkable 127 proves far too much for Surrey; the type of uninhibited and inspired hitting which wins titles.

31 No play in the Test match at The Oval. Essex take over as leaders of the Schweppes Championship with an easy two-day innings defeat of Lancashire, who were shot out for 70 by Lever and Phillip.

August

1 Despite a fine fightback by Congdon and Cairns, England win the first Test comfortably and Gooch, with an undefeated ninety, makes sure of his place at Trent Bridge.

Rain washes out three county matches and prevents any of the others from achieving a definite result.

2 The quarter-finals of the Gillette Cup, which would have produced very large attendance figures, sum up the summer. No play at Canterbury and Leicester, Yorkshire reach 174 in 52 overs, and a splendid 131 by Kennedy helps Lancashire to a massive 279 total, which should prove too much for Middlesex. Only twice in the 16 years of this competition have the team batting second scored more runs.

3 Somerset beat Kent to reach the Gillette Cup semi-final after a low-scoring game at Canterbury. Little play at Old Trafford; completely rained off at Headingley and Leicester.

Minor Counties beat New Zealand by three

Sartorial elegance. Phil Edmonds and umpire David Constant in contrasting head-gear.

younger and more adventurous. The TCCB confirm the principle of setting a proper wages target as from 1979. This had the full support of the Cricketers' Association, and the target for a capped player was £4,000. It was decided that a batsman could not be caught out in a visor, or off a rebound from a crash helmet worn by a fielder.

5 Barry Richards walks out on Hampshire, six weeks after agreeing to assist them in the one-day matches. Only his batting will be missed. The club players will be happier without Richards and Roberts, who has often appeared disinterested and reluctant to bowl for his adopted county.

Parker scores a century for the New Zealanders against Lancashire, and hundreds by both Woolmer and Asif emphasise just what the Packer men mean to Kent.

6 Boycott recalled to the Test twelve, Brearley drops down the order to accommodate him, and Lever comes in for the injured Old.

Sussex, with the aid of spin, trounce the John Player League leaders, Worcestershire, by eight wickets; Somerset maintain their challenge with a nine-wicket win over Warwickshire, Viv Richards supplying 76 out of the 108 required.

7 Clifford, a 36-year-old off-spinner from the Yorkshire League, takes six for 74 in an unbroken spell of 35 overs to make Somerset struggle. Glamorgan gain their second Championship victory, beating Northamptonshire by an innings, despite an impressive century from Allan Lamb.

Sussex fined £100 and lose six bonus points for not registering Miandad when he joined them from the Pakistan touring party. Championship contenders Kent and Essex both fined for falling below the required 19 per hour over-rate in the first 11 matches of the season; other culprits are Lancashire, Nottinghamshire and Worcestershire.

8 Sharp of Yorkshire hits 260 not out for England Under 19 against West Indies Under 19 to suggest it will not be long before he establishes himself in the national side; he clearly possesses ability, temperament, and pedigree.

Kent return to the top of the table with a convincing win over Leicestershire; Somerset keep going for a possible, though improbable, treble with an easy victory over Warwickshire.

9 For the fourth consecutive day, not a ball is bowled at Cheltenham and the county faces a heavy financial loss.

10 Boycott celebrates yet another return to Test cricket by grafting his way to a typical

wickets in the final over after three declarations in a rain-affected two-day match.

Fast bowlers to be limited to one bouncer per over under a new experimental law by the ICC. This should have been introduced several years ago. The ICC will not bar Packer players from the Prudential World Cup to be played next year between 9 and 23 June. The associate member countries joining the elite six will take part in three pre-qualifying groups of matches in the Midlands after 22 May. The winners of each group and the best runner-up have a play-off to decide who goes forward; Sri Lanka, Canada, and Bangladesh appear to be the strongest.

4 Middlesex, chasing that formidable Lancashire 279, fail by only 21 runs with 13 balls remaining. Essex beat Leicestershire by three runs in their 10 overs frolic. Yorkshire fail by nine runs to reach a Sussex total of 68 in 10 overs. Although Hampshire was unable to play, Boycott still held himself back until number 9, an odd decision as class must always tell.

The establishment get their man – George Mann elected chairman of TCCB rather than O. S. Wheatley or R. Subba Row, both much century. Although dropped at two and surviving some narrow escapes, including a couple of close lbw decisions early on, he was still there at stumps, 108 not out. England, at 252 for two, looked to be in an almost unassailable position.

11   England move into a match-winning position with a first innings of 429 – Brearley ended his bad patch with a somewhat laboured fifty – and then hit the weary tourists, who finish at 35 for three, and with Howarth retired hurt. Ironically, at the same time, Turner produces a masterly century for Worcestershire to prevent an Essex win on a difficult pitch.

The Warwickshire players issue a statement to the effect that they do not want Amiss to be offered a contract for 1979 because of his association with Packer and also deprecating the steps taken by other counties, such as Kent and Gloucestershire, who have re-engaged their Packer players. The wording of the pronouncement is very reminiscent of a trade union statement on an off day.

Kallicharran to captain the West Indies in India. Their Packer players were not considered – for the very good reason that they were not available.

Pakistan have announced that they will welcome back their Packer contingent for the coming Tests against India, New Zealand, and Australia, but there must be some doubts as to whether these players will be in a position to accept.

13   Worcestershire's expected slip occurs; well beaten by Kent, they drop to second in the John Player League. Hampshire move into top place, but the powerful Somerset, level on points, have that champions' look.

14   England win the Cornhill Test series 2–0, beating New Zealand by an innings and 119 runs despite some spirited resistance, especially from Edgar.

Rice, comfortably topping the first-class batting averages, follows up his 120 not out against Glamorgan on Sunday with 213 in 205 minutes against them, illustrating a distinct partiality for St Helens and Welsh bowling.

15   Kent storm to the top of the Schweppes Championship table with a 10-wicket win over Worcestershire, while Essex are robbed by the weather at Chelmsford and drop further behind.

16   Somerset win the match of the season to beat Essex in their Gillette Cup semi-final, and Sussex, somewhat surprisingly, crush a disappointing Lancashire in the other semi-final.

Gower, captaining Young England against the New Zealanders, scores an impressive century and Gatting, with 88, reveals the type of form he showed in the previous summer.

17   Impressive bowling by Emburey against the New Zealanders indicates that he is likely to replace Miller for the third Test.

The two umpires for the Lord's Test to carry light meters. They will not be used to decide whether or not it is fit to play, but merely to determine whether the light has improved or deteriorated.

19   Kent continue to make the running by scoring 347 for four and removing one Gloucestershire batsman. Asif and Tavaré star.

Warwickshire confirm they will not be renewing the contract of Dennis Amiss, who thus becomes the first Packer player to be exiled by his own colleagues.

20   Emburey comes into the England squad for Miller.

Somerset, with the help of a typical Richards' special – 62 in only 25 overs – demolish Middlesex and take over at the top of the John Player League from Hampshire, who go down rather surprisingly to Northamptonshire. Leicestershire make a late bid to retain their title and move into second place as the result of the only significant stand, between Gower and Tolchard, of their match against Lancashire.

21   Kent capture 19 Gloucestershire wickets in a day to win by 10 wickets and so add a further 20 points to their considerable lead at the top of the Schweppes Championship. Splendid swing bowling by Selvey scuttles out Somerset for 118 and he then destroys a threatened revival in their second innings. This ended Somerset's Championship aspirations.

22   No play at Derby as rain washes out the fast-fading hopes of Essex for the title.

23   Essex, with Gooch and Lever required by England, meet Kent at Folkestone. D'Oliveira hits a century in only 107 minutes, a nostalgic reminder.

24   Howarth hits a century and New Zealand finish the first day of the Lord's Test at 260 for five. Emburey captures his first Test wicket in his first over.

Essex overcome the disadvantage of being behind on the first innings and finish the day with a lead of 57, eight wickets in hand and with Kent having to bat last on a pitch giving encouragement to spin.

25   Another six wickets for Botham. Radley and Gower dominate the New Zealand attack.

Kent, needing 175 to beat Essex, not surprisingly settle for a draw, which basically gives them the title. They finished with 111 for five, and possibly Essex should have set an easier and more tempting target. Still, they might have won had they held their catches.

26   England stagger from 175 for two to 289 all out, and then Botham and Willis send the tourists reeling to 37 for seven and certain defeat.

Essex, refusing to give up hope, shoot out Surrey for fewer than 100 and plunder 224 for four, including a fine century from Hardie.

Pakistan invite their Packer players to play against India in the Tests this winter and again in the World Cup next summer. Will England players refuse to play against them in the World Cup? It would be sensible if the Cricketers' Association decided what action they want to take before next April, by which time it will be too late.

27   Somerset destroy Gloucestershire by eight wickets to go clear at the top of the Sunday League and are now poised to complete a Cup and League double the next weekend. Hampshire keep in the race with a Greenidge-inspired victory over Kent.

28   Burgess and Howarth fail to supply the stand required were England to be set a formidable total in their second innings. In a fiery opening spell, Hadlee bowled Boycott and Radley with successive balls, but he lacked adequate support, and Gooch and Gower batted impressively. As a result, England won the third Test by seven wickets.

Greenidge blasts a century off Kent. Essex just remain in the Schweppes Championship race by slaughtering a spineless Surrey by an innings and 107 runs.

29   Hampshire crush an astonised Kent by seven wickets as a result of Greenidge's second century of the match, supported by a fine hundred from Jesty. This leaves Essex with a mathematical, though highly improbable, chance of still achieving their first major honour.

Edgbaston provides an example of the wicket so good that it is bad. A travesty of a pitch produced runs galore and the expected draw. Warwickshire lost only two wickets in making 303 in their 100 overs first innings, and then amassed 390 for four declared in their second. Amiss scored a century in each. Worcestershire replied with 395 for two in their first innings (Turner 202 not out) and 84 without loss in their second, Turner undefeated for 45. This meant that the New Zealander his country had missed so much was actually on the field for every moment of a distinctly pointless contest.

30   Essex, desperately seeking batting bonus points, are shot out by Hendrick for 141 at Southend. Amiss acquires his third successive hundred to suggest that his scoring qualities will be much missed by Warwickshire next summer. However, he would obviously be a big acquisition for any county; a bigger one than many of the other Packer players from overseas! If his registration was refused, it might seem to suggest that only overseas Packer players were welcome.

31   Essex, who have had very bad luck with weather, suffer yet another setback in their Championship bid, losing four hours play.

September
1   Essex fail to capture the last Derbyshire wicket in the final over, which would have given them victory, and Kent become the Schweppes champions. With three Packer players available throughout the season and no Test calls, this always seemed the logical outcome. Put Underwood, Woolmer and Asif Iqbal in any county side, let them play in all the games, and the club must stand a good chance of carrying off the title, especially in a wet summer. However, Ealham led his side cheerfully and competently, and he also had at his disposal a highly talented group of young, up-and-coming cricketers, all products of the Kent nursery.

2   Sussex win the Gillette Cup, beating the favourites, Somerset, by five wickets in a better-than-average final.

3   Somerset, after the disappointment of losing the previous day's final, are beaten in the final over by Essex at Taunton, only two runs short of the tie that would have given them the John Player League. At Bournemouth, Hampshire, thanks to another superlative century from Greenidge, are able to hold off Middlesex's challenge to make 221, despite an insipid attack and some uncharacteristically lax fielding. As a result, Hampshire finish as champions; although having the same number of points as luckless Somerset, they had a fractionally higher scoring-rate over the season. A great performance by Hampshire, considering they lost both Richards and Roberts during the summer. Illingworth marks his retirement by leading Leicestershire, the holders, to victory over Derbyshire to finish equal on points with both Hampshire and Somerset, but with a lower scoring-rate.

4   The England 16-strong party announced to tour Australia under Brearley. Few surprises, but Willis is given the vice-captaincy instead of Boycott. Two off-spinners, Emburey and Miller, are included rather than another batsman with class, such as Tavaré, especially as there is a very good chance of England going into the Tests with four seamers. Tolchard, by no stretch of the imagination the second-best 'keeper in the country and over thirty, is taken as the reserve 'keeper, though he could prove more successful with the bat than some of the six pure batsmen included in the group.

5   Clive Rice logically named the Bonusplan's Cricketer of the Year.

Willey takes seven for 73 as T. N. Pearce's XI beat the New Zealanders, a reminder that this talented all-rounder, who had the misfortune to make his international debut against West Indies, might have done well for England in less demanding times.

6   In their final match, Surrey display the same uncertain batting form which has characterised their play throughout the summer and are removed for 122 by Middlesex. K. B. Smith makes a promising 43 for the Gillette champions against the Schweppes champions at Hove to suggest that he might

have been a more imaginative choice for the Gillette final than Storey.

7   Greenidge scores the fastest century of the season, in 82 minutes, to beat the previous fastest, held jointly by Clive Lloyd and himself, by nine minutes. The runs would probably have come even faster against an amiable Glamorgan attack if he had not been limping from an injury received at the weekend and therefore was unable to take any quick singles.

8   Sussex end the season with a five runs victory over the Schweppes county champions, something which would have seemed inconceivable two months earlier and which bodes well for the future. Essex, the runners-up, finish on a high note with a nine-wicket win over Nottinghamshire in a run-chase in which the very promising Lilley scores a century on his Championship debut. Amiss ended his long association with Warwickshire by becoming the only batsman to score more than 2,000 runs in the summer '78.

Happy days in Hampshire. Eight minutes past seven and the crowd at Bournemouth hears the news that Essex have beaten Somerset to give Hampshire the John Player League title.

A memorable innings of 116 by Viv Richards set alight the thrilling Gillette Cup semi-final at Taunton where Somerset won a tied match from Essex by losing fewer wickets.

MATCH OF THE SEASON

It was more than just the best match of the season, it was one of the great games of cricket. Those who were lucky enough to be at Taunton for the Gillette Cup semi-final between Somerset and Essex will never forget the occasion and will treasure the many magic moments for the rest of their lives. It was the perfect limited-overs contest, containing a century from the finest batsman in the world, Viv Richards, a number of high-quality innings from players in both teams, ever-changing situations, brilliant fielding, moments of panic, and finally the last over with its storybook finish.

When Dredge, a respectable seamer and a little sharper than he might appear, ran up for that last over, Essex, with numbers 9 and 10 at the crease, required 12 runs to win. With all the fielders strategically guarding the boundary, there was no way they were going to reach their target, provided the bowler obeyed the fundamental rules of his trade.

The first delivery produced a single. Somerset looked almost home. The second delivery. East plays the ideal shot, the unintentional snick that beats fine third man to the boundary. Seven runs are now needed in four balls; odds are now even, perhaps slightly with Essex.

The third delivery. East clean-bowled; Somerset back on top.

The fourth delivery. A no ball. Lever scrambles a single and the batting side are presented with the unexpected bonus of two panic-inspired overthrows. Essex back in the driving seat; four runs in three balls.

The fifth delivery. Smith fails to make contact. Somerset breathe again; four runs in two balls. Even money.

The sixth delivery. One run taken, leaving Essex needing three off the last ball for victory. Two would produce a tie, but as Essex had lost more wickets than Somerset that was not enough to get them to the final. It should be Somerset, but it still could be Essex.

The seventh delivery. This broth of a match ends with the scores level at 287, Smith just run out going for that third run. What an over, what a match!

The ground was uncomfortably full when Rose won the toss and was left with the problem of batting, or inserting the opposition, on a pitch that was slightly damp and likely to give some assistance in the early stages. Only recently he had put Kent in, and his team, batting second in much more difficult conditions, had been eliminated from the Benson and Hedges Cup.

He decided to bat, and lost Slocombe in the second over. Richards celebrated his arrival by dispatching the second ball he received from Phillip – it was only fractionally short – to the mid-wicket boundary. It is doubtful whether any other current player would have even considered that shot, let alone played it! In the following over from Phillip, Richards played and missed on a couple of occasions, but it was Lever, in a splendid spell, who really troubled the great man. When he had reached 22, Richards was put down at first slip, and an over later the unlucky Lever had Rose also dropped at slip. This was really the turning-point of the match. At this stage the pitch was still giving the seamers some encouragement, and if both Richards and Rose had departed with only some 40 runs on the board, Somerset would have been hard-pushed to reach 200.

At 86, Rose was caught for 24, but by this time Richards was in full cry with a range of probable and improbable strokes that were a joy to watch. The fact that Roebuck became becalmed did not matter; runs were flowing so freely at the other end. Richards reached his hundred, and was eventually out for 116 with the score 189 for three. Among his many unforgettable shots were the three successive lofted drives to the boundary off Pont, so knocking him from the firing line; the two fours, one off the front foot and one off the back when he savaged Turner on his return, having first given himself room and hitting the ball so hard that even the fielders in the deep did not have time to move; and the six off East over extra cover.

After the departure of Richards, Roebuck began to accelerate and looked a real England prospect. Botham failed, but Marks hit well and crisply, and when Roebuck was well caught for 57 he found another forthright partner in Breakwell. In the final onslaught the Essex bowling lost some of its edge, even Lever coming in for some unexpectedly heavy punishment. The final total of 287 for six looked well beyond their grasp, even though the ground was comparatively small, the pitch had improved, and the outfield had quickened.

The visitors set out on their journey towards that formidable 288 against Garner, because of his exceptional height able to make the ball lift on any wicket, and Dredge, who might be termed a typical county seamer. Denness soon departed, but Gooch and McEwan kept the score moving along sufficiently quickly to maintain the basic asking-rate until the latter, over-ambitious, was bowled. Gooch was then joined by his captain, Fletcher, who initially encountered numerous problems against Botham. At tea they were still together with 119 off 25 overs, including a disastrous one immediately before tea from which Marks conceded 13 runs without either batsman having to take the slightest chance.

When Gooch went for a splendid 61, Fletcher and Hardie found runs difficult to acquire against the less demanding of the Somerset bowlers and there were few, even among the most ardent Essex supporters, who really fancied their chances. It was the arrival of Pont, who began to pick up Richards – and did deposit him over the boundary for six – that changed the whole complexion of the game. Fletcher, scenting a whiff of victory, provided the perfect support. These two continued to storm their way towards that unlikely target, despite the recall of the main bowlers, Garner and Botham. The latter was treated especially roughly, but he had his revenge in the 55th over when he ran out Pont from third man with 42 runs still required, caught and bowled Fletcher for an admirably judged 67, and bowled the always dangerous Turner for 12.

In retrospect, possibly Essex should have begun their assault a shade earlier against the not-unfriendly medium-pace of Burgess and Richards, for they could not have expected Botham and Garner to be quite so loose in the closing stages. But who can blame any team who, chasing 287, finishes with the scores level. All credit to both teams for a marvellous game of cricket, and let us not forget the umpires who did their difficult job smoothly and efficiently.

GILLETTE CUP 1978
SEMI-FINAL
SOMERSET v ESSEX at Taunton on 16 August
Somerset won by losing fewer wickets in a tied match
Toss: Somerset
Man of the Match: I. V. A. Richards

* *captain*
† *wicket-keeper*

SOMERSET

B. C. Rose*	c East b Pont	24
P. A. Slocombe	lbw b Phillip	0
I. V. A. Richards	c Denness b Gooch	116
P. M. Roebuck	c Lever b Phillip	57
I. T. Botham	b East	7
V. J. Marks	not out	33
G. I. Burgess	b Lever	5
D. Breakwell	not out	17
D. J. S. Taylor†		
J. Garner	did not bat	
C. H. Dredge		
Extras	(b 10, lb 14, nb 3, w 1)	28
TOTAL	(6 wickets – 60 overs)	287

ESSEX	O	M	R	W
Lever	12	0	61	1
Phillip	11	1	56	2
Turner	8	6	22	0
Pont	6	1	35	1
Gooch	12	0	42	1
East	11	1	43	1

SOMERSET	O	M	R	W
Garner	12	1	46	1
Dredge	12	0	60	2
Botham	12	1	48	2
Burgess	12	1	43	1
Breakwell	2	0	11	0
Marks	1	0	13	0
Richards	9	1	41	0

ESSEX

M. H. Denness	c Marks b Dredge	3
G. A. Gooch	c Taylor b Garner	61
K. S. McEwan	b Burgess	37
K. W. R. Fletcher*	c and b Botham	67
B. R. Hardie	run out	21
K. R. Pont	run out	39
N. Phillip	run out	1
S. Turner	b Botham	12
R. E. East	b Dredge	10
N. Smith†	run out	6
J. K. Lever	not out	5
Extras	(b 14, lb 9, nb 2)	25
TOTAL	(60 overs)	287

FALL OF WICKETS

Wkt	Sm	E
1st	2	9
2nd	86	70
3rd	189	127
4th	208	166
5th	247	246
6th	255	248
7th		248
8th		266
9th		281
10th		287

Umpires: D. G. L. Evans and A. Jepson

For the second year in succession Trent Bridge welcomed the return of Geoff Boycott to the England team, and again he obliged the faithful with a characteristic hundred.

ENGLAND AND THE TOURISTS

England's selectors had every reason to be well satisfied with the events of last summer. Pakistan were thrashed with almost embarrassing ease; New Zealand were crushed. Yet both these beaten opponents had more than held their own on home ground against England in the previous winter. Against opposition which from time to time became demoralised and dejected, Brearley and company showed themselves to be a well-balanced team, efficient and confident. They set out for Australia in defence of the Ashes with high expectations, especially as Australia were unlikely to have recovered from the twin handicaps of reaching the end of an era and the Packer defections.

What must have given Alec Bedser and his fellow selectors special pleasure was the number of their choices who came off. They picked a very high percentage of winners, with several outsiders in addition to the obvious favourites.

From the outset, Gower looked a thoroughbred, the most exciting young home-bred batsman for more than a decade. He collects his runs with an eloquence and grace that automatically make him a major attraction. Gooch suggested, especially in his second innings at The Oval and Lord's, that he could become the aggressive opener England have not possessed since the Milburn era; somebody who not only is able to see off the new ball, but is prepared to counter-attack.

Boycott celebrated another return to the international scene by grinding out a typical Boycott century. He may be a little past his prime, but he remained easily the most consistent English batsman in the country, and once he had settled there was an air of inevitability about the hundred. His business is runs, and he runs a very successful business.

Radley continued to accumulate in his own highly individual way with the same profusion he has displayed since making his début as an emergency replacement in New Zealand. Although he has certain technical limitations, which cannot be entirely hidden by his obvious application and dedication, he has, of course, always been a much-respected county batsman. What remained something of a mystery was why neither visiting captain seriously tried to reduce the effectiveness of his two most productive scoring strokes; the push off his legs through mid-wicket, and the cut. Radley must have had difficulty in believing his good luck when he found himself confronted by a medium-paced inswinger bowling over the wicket with only three fielders on the leg side.

Brearley experienced a horrid patch. Even if he is not a batsman of genuine international calibre, he had the ability to score more against

Pakistan and New Zealand than he did. On the other hand, he is an astute skipper, has yet to lose a Test match, and has played a not-inconsiderable part in welding together England into a team. Where he could count himself fortunate was leading the present side against limited opposition. Had England been confronted by the West Indies of 1976, the odds are they would not only have been well beaten, but would have been unable to afford the luxury of a captain who was, comparatively speaking, unproductive with the bat.

The real strength of Brearley's team lay in their seam attack which, in English conditions, had quality, depth, and variety. Willis, the fastest, a straightforward quickie with height and an unpleasant bounce; Old, a class seamer, very accurate, who gave nothing away; Hendrick, even tighter than Old but on Test pitches not quite so penetrative; Lever, who never played in last summer's Tests but has the advantage of being left-handed, and captured over 100 wickets in the first-class season; and Botham, who swings the ball considerably either way and is full of aggression.

In addition to his prowess as a match-winning bowler, Botham proved himself to be a match-winning batsman who hit with rare zest and could develop into probably the best all-rounder England has ever produced. In addition to his prowess with bat and ball, he is a splendid all-purpose fieldsman. Old is also a good striker with the bat, especially against slow bowling, and a brilliant fieldsman. Hendrick has a marvellous pair of hands and is an outstanding slip with remarkable agility for such a big person, while Lever is a great outfielder and a determined number 11.

England did not miss their Packer men – Greig, Amiss, Woolmer, Knott, and Underwood – nearly as much as had been feared. Botham proved a far better all-rounder than Greig, and the runs that Woolmer and Amiss would probably have acquired against the tourists were never essential. What was much more surprising was that neither Knott nor Underwood, both world-class performers, proved indispensable. Taylor demonstrated what everybody in the game already knew; that he was a brilliant, yet undemonstrative, 'keeper of genuine international calibre. The added bonus of runs that Knott brought to the side was no longer essential, as it had been against Australia the previous summer. Edmonds improved as a slow left-arm bowler, and he is also a distinctly useful batsman and fine field. He can never hope to be so deadly on a helpful pitch as Underwood, but on many Test wickets he may well prove to have as much, if not more, penetration, particularly against lefthanders.

The one player, apart from Brearley, who might be termed fortunate to have been picked so often was Miller, who did not really impress with either bat or ball. As an off-spinner, he did not receive that number of opportunities, but he did appear to lack the ability to get the ball past the outside of a righthander's bat. This is essential on good wickets, and it was noticeable that Emburey, when he was brought into the England eleven, immediately showed he was able to drift the ball away from the bat.

The England batting was unexceptional, though the promise of Gower, Gooch, and Botham, plus a number of very good young players to be found among the counties, suggested that good days are coming. However, backed

Middlesex to the fore at Lord's as Phil Edmonds' superb catch at leg slip gives John Emburey (arms raised) his first Test wicket. New Zealand's Bruce Edgar is the victim.

by such formidable bowling and excellent fielding, the England line-up proved sufficient for the limited opposition.

It may be that, within a year or two, England will at long last be in a position to lay claim to being the unofficial world champions, something she cannot have boasted for more than 20 years. However, before being swept away on a wave of euphoria, it would be as well to take into account the standard of the opposition encountered since West Indies routed England in 1976. England have destroyed the weakest Australian team to tour this country since the 1914–18 war, Pakistan without their Packer men, and New Zealand, who have never won a single Test over here.

Some 300 wickets have fallen in the last three series in England; but apart from Chappell, Boycott, the promising Gower, and possibly Amiss, how many quality batsmen were to be found in the four Test teams? Certainly, any international fast bowler would have fancied his chances against the majority in England during 1977 and 1978. There have been occasions when Fred Trueman's mouth positively watered at the prospect; hardly to be wondered at when one considers these batting line-ups against which Fred was expected to, and did, take wickets:

Australia: Hassett, Morris, Miller, Harvey, Hole, de Courcy, Archer, Lindwall, Langley, Johnstone; or Lawry, McDonald, Harvey, O'Neill, Burge, Mackay, Simpson.

West Indies: Hunte, McMorris, Kanhai, Sobers, Worrell, Butcher; or Holt, Stollmeyer, Weekes, Worrell, Walcott, Atkinson, Gomez.

The Pakistan tour was expected to be successful, entertaining, and to produce a close Test series. Their strongest team should have been more formidable than the 1977 Australians and the 'Rubber' wide open. Yet their visit proved to be little short of a disaster. They not only crumpled before England, but also failed to do themselves justice in the other matches. By the end, they were so dispirited that it was almost impossible to believe these were virtually the same players who had enjoyed the better of a drawn series with England in the previous winter. What went wrong?

First, the tourists arrived in April to discover, to their dismay, a monsoon that continued throughout that month and for the whole of May. In consequence they never obtained sufficient practice, and the conditions encountered were even further removed from those at home. The slow, sodden pitches did not suit either their wrist-spinners or their natural strokemakers, while their finger-spinners found difficulty in gripping a ball that was perpetually shiny and was seldom worn.

The truth is that no touring team should arrive in this country before May, and that short, three-Test tours are never really satisfactory, even if they do have the financial advantage of providing six Tests and allow the crowd-drawing West Indians to visit more frequently. This second aspect means less these days, because most of the Caribbean players are currently playing in county cricket, though, of course, as a national side they draw a large immigrant following who turn up in large numbers only when they are over here as such.

Second, the Pakistan Board of Control decided not to include their Packer men in the party, so excluding Imran Khan, Majid Khan, Zaheer Abbas, Asif Iqbal, and Mushtaq Mohammad from consideration. All five would have been a considerable asset, for not only are they exceptional cricketers, but they know English conditions and the bowlers. They would have provided the batting line-up with the class, the experience, and the backbone it so palpably lacked, while Imran would have caused problems for the opposing batsmen that only Sarfraz posed; and he was fit for only one Test.

Third, once things started to go sour, nobody appeared capable of stopping the rot, let alone of leading a revival rally. Their play steadily worsened as they lost faith in themselves.

Very few members of the Pakistan team were able to do themselves justice. One exception was Mudassar Nazar, an opening batsman with more strokes than is sometimes appreciated and a correct technique; in addition, he was an enthusiastic medium-paced seamer. His obvious zest for the game, combined with his considerable promise, should mean he will be of great service to his country for years to come.

Sikander Bakht, a young beanpole of a quick bowler, is another to note for the future. At the moment he is sharp, rather than fast, but when he fills out his pace should increase; already his height and high action enable him to achieve lift. Mohsin Khan showed consistency in the Tests, which bodes well for the future. He repeatedly steadied the innings, but his inexperience showed when he was unable to turn his hard-fought thirties into big scores.

Sadiq Mohammad, the youngest of that most distinguished cricket-playing family, is a neat, diminutive left-handed opener with great knowledge of English conditions after his years with Gloucestershire, and from previous tours. Although he looked vulnerable against the pace and extra bounce of Willis – to be expected considering his lack of inches – he did provide Pakistan with some solidarity and two good innings.

The big disappointment for tourists and spectators alike was that the three spectacular strokemakers in the middle order, Haroon Rashid, Javed Miandad, and Wasim Raja, never came off; either collectively or individually. Although the ball did move, sometimes a great deal – some of the shots they attempted were over-ambitious – one feels they should have done better. After all Javed Miandad has often demonstrated his considerable skill for Sussex, and many good judges reckoned that Haroon in Pakistan looked a batsman of exceptional class; a Vivian Richards in the making.

Another big disappointment was Abdul Qadir, whom many reckoned to be among the finest wrist-spinners in the world; he was unable to command a regular place in the Test team. Their two slow left-armers, Naeem Ahmed and Iqbal Qasim, never learned to exploit conditions that could have been helpful to them. To overcome the problems of controlling a ball with a shiny cover, as distinct from the roughened covers encountered in Pakistan, they even practised bowling with a new ball.

The one outstanding attacking bowler in the Pakistan party was Sarfraz Nawaz, whose one-man strike over insufficient wages at the start of the tour can hardly have assisted team spirit. Once the matter was settled, he was often over-bowled in county matches, broke down early in the first Test, missed the second, and in the third indicated just how much, when he was in the mood and interested, he would have worried the English batsmen.

A wicket-keeper, especially in Test cricket, should have more than enough on his plate without also being entrusted with the captaincy, and the extra responsibilities appeared to have an adverse effect on Wasim Bari's performances behind the stumps. He found himself leading a side that became progressively more disheartened as their batsmen were repeatedly mown down by the England bowlers and their bowlers (often indifferently handled) unable to inflict the damage needed. Their fielders, sometimes found in distinctly odd positions, tended to be individually brilliant but unreliable and prone to expensive lapses. An out-of-form side, under an out-of-form captain who was repeatedly out-thought, as well as out-fought, by Brearley, not surprisingly proved a disaster. It was not that they were beaten that hurt; more that they performed so far below their capabilities.

Our second visitors were lucky to arrive in the second half of a distinctly unpleasant summer. They were able to practise in their opening matches against the counties, whereas the Pakistanis had spent much of their time peering out of dressing-rooms as the rain streamed down. Moreover, the difference between our pitches and those found in New Zealand is less than between those in Pakistan. This is one of the reasons why there has always been a shortage of spinners in New Zealand, and an abundance of seamers.

With the New Zealanders having at last achieved that elusive victory and drawn the series in the previous winter, it was hoped that the 1978 Kiwis would provide England with the challenge required after the disappointing performance by Pakistan. The tourists began very well against the counties, and suggested that there might be a repeat of the excitement of the two close, hard-fought Tests that occurred on their last visit, under Bevan Congdon. Unfortunately, the demands of five-day international matches quickly exposed their limitations. They were overwhelmed in all three Tests, as well as in the two Prudential limited-overs games.

The New Zealand batting, though it lacked top-quality players – Congdon, now an individual member of the party, was past his peak – was, in fact, similar in ability to that of England, except that the home side had Boycott and a rather more resilient tail.

The big difference between the two contestants lay in the respective attacks. The tourists possessed only one major strike bowler, Richard Hadlee, and he was completely fit only for the last Test. In sharp contrast, Brearley had under his command Willis, Botham, Hendrick, and Edmonds, who had the happy knack of breaking through the New Zealand batting whenever the visitors appeared to have established a satisfactory position. One gains the impression that the same would have happened to the England batting had it been confronted by a bowling line-up as formidable as its own.

The New Zealand attack, apart from Hadlee, was built around the speed of Brendon Bracewell, a most promising novice fast bowler who should have an outstanding future if carefully and sensibly handled; the medium-paced inswingers of Cairns; the gentle swerve of Congdon; and the accurate spin of Boock who, despite a rather ugly action, is a talented operator likely to do well in first-class cricket for many years. In the last Test, there was the pace of that great trier, Collinge, who still possessed a run-up of marathon proportions but had lost his incisive edge. Although this attack was clearly not as formidable as England's, the gap was widened still further by indifferent support in the field. Too many chances were put down in the slips, which understandably discouraged Hadlee, the main sufferer, and the home side made them pay dearly for those mistakes.

Before the tour started, the Kiwi selectors chose to ignore one of the game's unwritten fundamental rules: Always pick the best wicket-keeper available, irrespective of anything else. This is never more true than in England where, with the ball often moving about and some irregularity of bounce expected, chances must inevitably come his way. There are some pitches abroad where the bat is beaten so rarely that a team will make do with a 'keeper who is no more than adequate. However, it is doubtful whether even that constitutes a sensible gamble, because over a period of time he will have more opportunities to effect a dismissal than any of the fielders; and one error can easily cost a hundred runs. In addition, the 'keeper should be the hub around which the whole tone of the fielding revolves.

Yet, knowing this, the selectors chose Edwards, a cheerful, well-rounded, avuncular figure who lacked the experience to do the job at the highest level.

Bruce Edgar – neat, stylish, and an exciting prospect for New Zealand in the future.

It was neither fair on him nor on the team. To make matters worse, his colourful hitting, which had proved so attractive and effective in New Zealand, was unsuccessful, probably because he was worried by the problems he was discovering as stumper.

It was somewhat ironic that while the tourists repeatedly failed to score sufficient runs, easily their most accomplished player, Glenn Turner, was playing for Worcestershire in the County Championship. This cannot have been in the best interests of the game as a whole. Turner's ability might have made a considerable difference, and, if he had been on hand to give advice, some of the more naive field placings must surely have been avoided. It was bad enough that the Pakistan tour should lose its bite because Packer had removed five important teeth, but Turner was not even a member of World Series Cricket. It underlined the dangers of having overseas cricketers in domestic cricket. Imagine the last visit of West Indies if all those players under contract to different counties had turned out for them instead of for the tourists. It would have inevitably reduced interest in the Tests and the gate-takings would have suffered. This in turn would have been felt by the county clubs, who rely so much on that revenue.

Although New Zealand lost all three Tests heavily, they have reason to be well satisfied with certain aspects of their tour. Howarth has made a considerable advance as a batsman and demonstrated that those two centuries in New Zealand were not a flash in the pan. For the first time, the promise he displayed when he first arrived in England – and before he joined Surrey and became just another competent county cricketer – has come to fruition.

The best way to appreciate the potential of Bracewell is to think that he could have been playing in his last year of school cricket rather than in Tests. Another exciting prospect for the future was Edgar, a lefthander with a style not unreminiscent of Neil Harvey's, especially in the way he forced the ball off his legs with a straight bat and in his timing. Although he was pressed into service as wicket-keeper in the final Test and did all that can have been expected of him, indeed rather more, his future clearly lies as a batsman with plenty of flowing strokes and a most impressive basic technique. It could well be that he is destined to become one of the finest players his country has yet produced. Boock, unlike most left-arm bowlers, did not possess a graceful action. There was too much arm and not enough body, but his control was excellent and he spun the ball sufficiently to beat the bat from time to time on good pitches.

In his first season with Derbyshire, John Wright had impressed as a conscientious left-handed opener, and with the tourists there were indications, though these were not really backed up by the runs, that he possessed the ability to become more than an efficient county performer. This is also how one would rate his more experienced and very determined colleague, Parker.

The captain, Burgess, like his opposite number, Brearley, although a naturally more fluent strokemaker, ran into a bad patch and only occasionally did himself justice. His lack of confidence stemmed to some extent, one feels, from the responsibility of skippering a team which, in the Tests, was palpably outgunned and frequently outmanoeuvred. Had he played throughout the series as he did in the first innings of the Lord's Test, it would have made a considerable difference.

Probably the biggest disappointment in the New Zealand party was the burly Anderson, a belligerent opener who, at his best, is not unreminiscent of Stackpole. He scored runs away from the Test arena but was unable to strike any form against England.

Right: Sadiq Mohammad, the Pakistan opener, was one of the few Pakistani tourists to approach true form in the Test series.

THE 1978 PAKISTANIS

David Gower, whose pulled four off his first ball in Test cricket heralded a series of uninhibited innings that warmed England's supporters throughout the summer.

ENGLAND GO ONE UP

First Test, Edgbaston

England won the opening Test against Pakistan by an innings and 57 runs to go one up in the Cornhill Test series. If one ignores the Rest of the World series, this was the first Test match to be sponsored in England. The size of the victory accurately sums up the enormous difference between the two teams on this occasion, for Pakistan were outclassed in all departments. Their attack, handicapped by the loss of Sarfraz with a pulled muscle after only a few overs, was considerably weaker than that of most county teams.

England omitted Hendrick from their original selection. Pakistan, having won the toss, elected to bat on a good pitch with a certain amount of pace, although when the sun departed behind the clouds, the bowlers were able to move the ball about in the air and off the seam. The tourists began reasonably well, helped by a certain waywardness from Botham, but in the afternoon Old, who bowled splendidly throughout, destroyed them by taking four wickets in five balls. A couple of Willis's bouncers accounted for Mohsin Khan, who had promised much before making the mistake of taking his eye off the ball, and Haroon Rashid, who received a nasty one that rose sharply before he had time to become acclimatised. When bad light stopped play, Pakistan, despite a brave last-wicket stand, were 162 for nine and heading for a heavy defeat well within the distance.

Old, who finished with his best-ever international figures of seven for 50, correctly secured the last Pakistan wicket and England then proceeded to lumber quietly along against a mediocre attack to a satisfactory 256 for three at the close. Radley was undefeated on a workmanlike 97; Gower, in his first Test, had lifted the whole occasion with a brief and enchanting cameo which produced 58 runs, marvellous entertainment, and several shots not normally associated with English players.

On the Saturday Radley completed his century and then Botham bludgeoned his way to a spectacular 100 before England declared at 452 for eight. Long before this the opposition had appeared to be going through the motions, waiting for the closure, although Sikander did stick nobly to his task. However, he was grossly over-bowled. Sadiq and Mudassar provided Pakistan with a good start to their second innings, but the latter was bowled by Edmonds just before the weekend break.

Hopes that the visitors would make a serious fight on the Monday never materialised once Sadiq was lbw to Old for an excellent 79. The only other serious resistance came in a belligerent 39 from Miandad, whose innings ended with an injudicious sweep, and a sensible 38 from Mohsin Khan, who looks to have the makings of a very good player. The England bowlers gradually chipped away, with the spinners, Edmonds and Miller, capturing six wickets between them. The one sour note to this convincing victory was the Willis bouncer that hit the unfortunate Qasim in the mouth and sent him back to the pavilion for treatment and stitches in his lip.

There were several extremely satisfactory features about this game from England's point of view. Old again showed that he has developed in the past year or so from a good opening bowler into an outstanding seamer with exceptional command of line and length and with sufficient movement to worry all batsmen. Willis has become a high-class fast bowler, while Botham, although not at his best with the ball in this match, batted in the manner of a fine and exciting all-rounder. Taylor kept wicket beautifully, making a couple of brilliant catches, Edmonds began to look as if he had,

Sadiq, from a distance looking like some white-flannelled skateboarder, despatches a Bob Willis bouncer to the boundary during his plucky innings of 79 at Edgbaston.

during the winter in Pakistan, learned that extra control which is essential if a spinner is to reach the top, and Gower's promise was both obvious and refreshing. The fielding was first-class, and with Old coming in at number nine the batting had exceptional depth. Nevertheless, it must also be admitted that it would have been perfectly feasible to have picked at least one, probably two, more English elevens that would have beaten Pakistan in this particular match.

ENGLAND v PAKISTAN 1978—1st Test

Played at Edgbaston, Birmingham, 1, 2, 3, 5 June
Toss: Pakistan   Result: **England** won by an innings and 57 runs

*captain
†wicket-keeper

PAKISTAN

Batsman	Dismissal		Score		Dismissal	Score
Mudassar Nazar	c and b Botham		14		b Edmonds	30
Sadiq Mohammad	c Radley b Old		23		lbw b Old	79
Mohsin Khan	b Willis		35	(4)	c Old b Miller	38
Javed Miandad	c Taylor b Old		15	(5)	c Brearley b Edmonds	39
Haroon Rashid	c Roope b Willis		3	(6)	b Willis	4
Wasim Raja	c Taylor b Old		17	(7)	b Edmonds	9
Sarfraz Nawaz	not out		32	(8)	not out	6
Wasim Bari*†	b Old		0	(9)	c Miller b Edmonds	3
Iqbal Qasim	c Taylor b Old		0	(3)	retired hurt	5
Sikander Bakht	c Roope b Old		0		c Roope b Miller	2
Liaquat Ali	c Brearley b Old		9		b Willis	3
Extras	(lb 3, nb 13)		16		(b 4, lb 4, w 1, nb 4)	13
TOTAL			**164**			**231**

ENGLAND

Batsman	Dismissal	Score
J. M. Brearley*	run out (Mohsin/Bari)	38
B. Wood	lbw b Sikander	14
C. T. Radley	lbw b Sikander	106
D. I. Gower	c Miandad b Sikander	58
G. R. J. Roope	b Sikander	32
G. Miller	c Wasim Bari b Mudassar	48
I. T. Botham	c Qasim b Liaquat	100
C. M. Old	c Mudassar b Qasim	5
P. H. Edmonds	not out	4
R. W. Taylor†	} did not bat	
R. G. D. Willis		
Extras	(lb 26, w 5, nb 16)	47
TOTAL	(8 wickets declared)	**452**

ENGLAND	O	M	R	W	O	M	R	W
Willis	16	2	42	2	23.4	3	70	2
Old	22.4	6	50	7	25	12	38	1
Botham	15	4	52	1	17	3	47	0
Wood	3	2	2	0				
Edmonds	4	2	2	0	26	10	44	4
Miller					12	4	19	2

PAKISTAN	O	M	R	W
Sarfraz	6	1	12	0
Liaquat	42	9	114	1
Sikander	45	13	132	4
Mudassar	27	7	59	1
Qasim	14	2	56	1
Wasim Raja	10	1	32	0

FALL OF WICKETS

Wkt	Pakistan 1st	2nd	England 1st	2nd
1st	20	94	36	
2nd	56	123	101	
3rd	91	176	190	
4th	94	193	275	
5th	103	214	276	
6th	125	220	399	
7th	125	224	448	
8th	126	227	452	
9th	126	231		
10th	164			

Umpires: H. D. Bird and K. E. Palmer
Attendance: 28,500 (17,059 paid). Receipts: £38,438.

THE HUMILIATION

Second Test, Lord's

No play was possible on the first day of the Lord's Test, the match started 45 minutes late on the Friday, and yet before lunch on the Monday England had won by an innings and 120 runs. Pakistan were not just easily beaten, they were publicly executed and humiliated. Their surrender was so complete and abject that it was hard to credit that the same players had enjoyed the better of the three drawn Tests in Pakistan only the previous winter, although it does emphasise the enormous difference that pitches make to the game.

Having won the toss, Brearley came out to bat in a crash helmet – surely unnecessary against a Pakistan attack weakened still further by the absence of the injured Sarfraz! Although their captain quickly departed, it was to prove a memorable day for England batsmanship. It contained more strokes and entertainment than had been seen from our national team for a very long time, beginning in a most exciting manner with an attractive partnership between Gooch and Gower which took the score to 120 before both departed with somewhat undistinguished shots. Miller hung around uncertainly before being caught bat and pad and, at 134 for five, England looked to be in some trouble. But Botham and Roope immediately launched a satisfying and effective counter-attack, both hitting a six early on. Roope, who has probably never played better for England, was first to go for a most attractive 69, but Botham, with the bowling and fielding becoming increasingly ragged and receiving practical assistance from Taylor, continued to savage the Pakistan attack. Despite the fielders being dispersed around the boundary, he managed to complete a boisterous hundred before stumps, when the total was 309 for eight.

Botham added only six runs to his overnight score and then dragged a ball on to his stumps, leaving Edmonds and Willis to plunder bowling that would have been more appropriate in Minor County cricket than in a Test match. On an easy paced pitch, Pakistan began their reply to a total of 364 and by lunch, Mudassar (mis-hooking), Sadiq (sparring uncertainly at a shortish ball outside off stump), and Haroon (bowled after he had produced a couple of spectacular strokes) were back in the pavilion.

In the afternoon the remaining batsmen surrendered. Miandad attempted to hook Willis and was caught behind, Raja, attempting a stroke suitable only for the concluding overs of a one-day game, was bowled by Edmonds, Talat was completely out of touch, and the long, vulnerable tail could not cope with the pace of Willis. Only Mohsin suggested permanence and character until he rather tamely lofted an intended drive and was out for 31.

Geoff Miller is caught by Javed Miandad off the bowling of Iqbal Qasim for 0 at Lord's. The crash-helmeted close-leg fieldsman was an unwelcome innovation in 1978.

The tourists' first innings score of 105 was due as much to spineless batting as to some very good bowling by England. The pace of Willis on a wicket that gave him no encouragement was the decisive factor in the rout, but Edmonds exploited the situation intelligently to return the remarkable figures of 8-6-6-4. With four of those runs coming from a hopeful slog, those figures really underline a performance of near-immaculate control.

The general feeling was that Pakistan had to bat better in their second innings; it was hard to imagine them batting worse. Yet their start was far from encouraging. Sadiq predictably edged a ball outside his off stump from Willis, and after some sensible resistance Mudassar was superbly caught by Taylor. Fortunately, and without undue difficulty, Mohsin and Talat stayed together until the close of play, when the score was 96 for two, Mohsin 45 and Talat 36. Unless rain fell it was obvious that England would clock up their second victory, but this stand had suggested that the match might last until after tea on the Monday. It did not happen. When play was resumed, the last eight wickets went down before lunch for only 43 runs, a collapse due more to an inspired spell of swing bowling by Botham than to the Pakistan batting. On a cloudless morning he found he was able to curve the ball prodigiously – it was by no means unusual for him to beat the bat three times in an over – and he would have worried any batsmen. In 13.5 overs he took seven wickets for 14 runs, to finish with the astonishing figures of eight for 34. Ironically, had Willis not wanted to change ends after only one over, Botham might never have had the opportunity to acquire such a rich haul. Apart from a brave, and hopeless, 22 by Miandad, the Pakistan players had no idea how to cope with such high-quality swing bowling.

ENGLAND v PAKISTAN 1978—2nd Test
Played at Lord's, London, 15 *no play*, 16, 17, 19 June
Toss: England   Result: **England** won by an innings and 120 runs   *captain
    †wicket-keeper

ENGLAND

J. M. Brearley*	*lbw b* Liaquat	2
G. A. Gooch	*lbw b* Wasim Raja	54
C. T. Radley	*c* Mohsin *b* Liaquat	8
D. I. Gower	*b* Qasim	56
G. R. J. Roope	*c* Mohsin *b* Qasim	69
G. Miller	*c* Miandad *b* Qasim	0
I. T. Botham	*b* Liaquat	108
R. W. Taylor†	*c* Mudassar *b* Sikander	10
C. M. Old	*c* Mohsin *b* Sikander	0
P. H. Edmonds	*not out*	36
R. G. D. Willis	*b* Mudassar	18
Extras	(*lb* 2, *nb* 1)	3
TOTAL		**364**

PAKISTAN

Mudassar Nazar	*c* Edmonds *b* Willis	1		*c* Taylor *b* Botham	10
Sadiq Mohammad	*c* Botham *b* Willis	11		*c* Taylor *b* Willis	0
Mohsin Khan	*c* Willis *b* Edmonds	31		*c* Roope *b* Willis	46
Haroon Rashid	*b* Old	15	(5)	*b* Botham	4
Javed Miandad	*c* Taylor *b* Willis	0	(6)	*c* Gooch *b* Botham	22
Wasim Raja	*b* Edmonds	28	(7)	*c and b* Botham	1
Talat Ali	*c* Radley *b* Edmonds	2	(4)	*c* Roope *b* Botham	40
Wasim Bari*†	*c* Brearley *b* Willis	0		*c* Taylor *b* Botham	2
Iqbal Qasim	*b* Willis	0	(10)	*b* Botham	0
Sikander Bakht	*c* Brearley *b* Edmonds	4	(9)	*c* Roope *b* Botham	1
Liaquat Ali	*not out*	4		*not out*	0
Extras	(*nb* 9)	9		(*b* 1, *lb* 3, *w* 5, *nb* 4)	13
TOTAL		**105**			**139**

PAKISTAN	O	M	R	W	O	M	R	W
Sikander	27	3	115	2				
Liaquat	18	1	80	3				
Mudassar	4.2	0	16	1				
Qasim	30	5	101	3				
Wasim Raja	12	3	49	1				

ENGLAND	O	M	R	W	O	M	R	W
Willis	13	1	47	5	10	2	26	2
Old	10	3	26	1	15	4	36	0
Botham	5	2	17	0	20.5	8	34	8
Edmonds	8	6	6	4	12	4	21	0
Miller					9	3	9	0

FALL OF WICKETS

	England		Pakistan	
Wkt	1st	2nd	1st	2nd
1st	5		11	1
2nd	19		22	45
3rd	120		40	100
4th	120		41	108
5th	134		84	114
6th	252		96	119
7th	290		97	121
8th	290		97	130
9th	324		97	130
10th	364		105	139

Umpires: D. J. Constant and W. L. Budd
Attendance: 48,055 (44,955 paid). Receipts: £124,652.

A BAD TEST

Third Test, Headingley

The third Test at Headingley was a financial disaster, a cricket disaster, and a spectator disaster. After five rain-ruined days it ended – thankfully and appropriately – early on the Tuesday with the heavens opening and England still to complete the first innings. Although it was essentially a match to forget, it did draw attention to several weaknesses in staging Tests in this country when the weather turns really mean.

Firstly, the covers available at Leeds were sadly inadequate. For hours no play took place, not because the pitch or outfield was unplayable but because most of the square and the bowlers' run-ups had become boggy. This could have been prevented if more covering had been available, and could have meant that another six more hours of play would have been possible.

Secondly, cricket spectators are amazingly patient, tolerant, and eternally optimistic. Nowhere is this more apparent than at Headingley, where this year they sat uncomplaining for hours and, with no rain falling, gazed out hopefully at a covered pitch while the umpires made periodic inspections and the players did exercises and practised fielding in the outfield. It might, perhaps, be worth investigating whether it would not be possible to provide these long-suffering spectators with some entertainment when it is fine.

Thirdly, is it not time that the umpires and the players began to rethink about what constitutes playable conditions? There is no doubt that on numerous occasions the umpires, almost invariably supported by the players, suspend play, not because it is, strictly speaking, unplayable but because the conditions are far from ideal. Provided the batsmen and bowlers are not unduly handicapped, does it really matter if a fielder occasionally slips over? It has been suggested that he might hurt himself, but this is a minor risk which thousands of club cricketers take each week without giving it a thought. It is much less a hazard than standing in a suicidal, close-fielding position! And it is worth remembering that none of the players appeared over-worried about safety when they went on playing in that tropical thunderstorm at The Oval in the 1977 Prudential Trophy international. On that occasion it happened to suit them.

Spectators would get more value for money if the umpires were prepared to interpret 'playable' more literally, and to accept conditions that were less than perfect. This also applies to that other, and even bigger, robber of play, 'bad light'. Umpires come off for bad light, with the full approval of the players, when it is unpleasant, rather than when it is strictly dangerous, sometimes even when slow bowlers are operating. The umpire may claim, 'I

Chris Old, destroyer of Pakistan's first innings at Edgbaston, again illustrated his deadly accuracy during the playing intervals of the Headingley Test.

came off because I was afraid that a batsman might be hurt'. It is easy to understand his concern, but it overlooks one factor: although batting in poor light against a fast bowler is unpleasant, it is not nearly as dangerous as facing the same bowler in brilliant sunshine on a really bad pitch from which the ball lifts off a length!

However, it must be appreciated that the umpires, who are the sole judges of ground, weather, and light, depend on reports by the captains to secure the high marks in county matches which ultimately lead to an appointment in the very well paid Tests. In these circumstances it is inevitable that umpires will try not to offend the players, whose own judgment of playing conditions has always tended to be selfish, conservative, and with little, if any, thought for the spectators who help to pay their wages.

As to this Test match itself, the first two truncated days saw Pakistan advance cautiously on a docile pitch to 163 for three, with Sadiq 73 not out and Mohsin, with 41, once again demonstrating his consistency and promise. Towards the close on the Friday, Willis breathed some life back into a game which was already beginning to die by taking two wickets in two balls.

There was a full programme of League cricket in Leeds and surrounding districts on the Saturday, but not a ball was bowled at Headingley; a matter which was not appreciated by those who had paid admission to see nothing. Monday's resumption, in conditions which gave the bowlers some assistance, saw the last seven Pakistan wickets fall quickly, and the tourists were all out for 201. Sadiq was unfortunate not to reach a century and was easily the top scorer with 97. Old returned the remarkable figures of 41.4-22-41-4, and Botham also picked up four wickets.

England did not find batting easy and at stumps had lost five wickets for only 106 runs. Brearley's unhappy patch continued, departing second ball to Sarfraz, and apart from Gower, who hit an impressively mature 39 before being adjudged lbw, none of the batsmen was convincing. More delays and frustrations occurred on the final day, until a heavy downpour put everybody out of their misery. England were 119 for seven, five of those falling to Sarfraz. Miller played sensibly and impressed rather more with the bat than he had done with the ball.

ENGLAND v PAKISTAN 1978—3rd Test
Played at Headingley, Leeds, 29, 30 June, 1 (*no play*), 3, 4 July
Toss: Pakistan   Result: **Match drawn**

*captain
†wicket-keeper

PAKISTAN

Mudassar Nazar	c Botham b Old	31
Sadiq Mohammad	c Brearley b Botham	97
Mohsin Khan	lbw b Willis	41
Talat Ali	c Gooch b Willis	0
Haroon Rashid	c Brearley b Botham	7
Javed Miandad	b Old	1
Wasim Raja	lbw b Botham	0
Sarfraz Nawaz	c Taylor b Botham	4
Wasim Bari*†	not out	7
Sikander Bakht	b Old	4
Iqbal Qasim	lbw b Old	0
Extras	(lb 8, nb 1)	9
TOTAL		**201**

ENGLAND

J. M. Brearley*	c Wasim Bari b Sarfraz	0
G. A. Gooch	lbw b Sarfraz	20
C. T. Radley	b Sikander	7
D. I. Gower	lbw b Sarfraz	39
G. R. J. Roope	c Sadiq b Miandad	11
G. Miller	not out	18
R. W. Taylor†	c Wasim Bari b Sarfraz	2
I. T. Botham	lbw b Sarfraz	4
P. H. Edmonds	not out	1
C. M. Old	} did not bat	
R. G. D. Willis		
Extras	(b 1, lb 5, w 1, nb 10)	17
TOTAL	(7 wickets)	**119**

ENGLAND	O	M	R	W	O	M	R	W
Willis	26	8	48	2				
Old	41.4	22	41	4				
Botham	18	2	59	4				
Edmonds	11	2	22	0				
Miller	9	3	22	0				

PAKISTAN	O	M	R	W
Sarfraz	20	6	39	5
Sikander	15	4	26	1
Mudassar	5	2	12	0
Qasim	11	8	11	0
Miandad	3	0	14	1

FALL OF WICKETS

Wkt	Pakistan 1st	2nd	England 1st	2nd
1st	75		0	
2nd	147		24	
3rd	147		51	
4th	169		77	
5th	182		102	
6th	183		110	
7th	189		116	
8th	190			
9th	201			
10th	201			

Umpires: H. D. Bird and K. E. Palmer
Attendance: 26,250 (16,546 paid). Receipts: £58,263.

STATISTICAL SURVEY OF THE SERIES

ENGLAND – BATTING AND FIELDING

*Not out

	Tests	I	NO	HS	Runs	Av	Mins	Balls	Runs/100b	100	50	6s	4s	Ct
I. T. Botham	3	3	0	108	212	70.66	368	256	83	2	—	1	24	4
D. I. Gower	3	3	0	58	153	51.00	325	277	55	—	2	—	24	—
P. H. Edmonds	3	3	3	36*	41	—	82	65	63	—	—	—	3	1
C. T. Radley	3	3	0	106	121	40.33	370	277	44	1	—	—	12	2
G. R. J. Roope	3	3	0	69	112	37.33	302	246	46	—	1	1	11	6
G. A. Gooch	2	2	0	54	74	37.00	222	158	47	—	—	—	6	2
G. Miller	3	2	0	48	66	33.00	258	195	34	—	1	—	5	1
R. G. D. Willis	3	1	1	18	18	18.00	39	29	62	—	—	—	1	—
B. Wood	1	1	0	14	14	14.00	64	52	27	—	—	—	—	—
J. M. Brearley	3	3	0	38	40	13.33	179	134	30	—	—	—	2	6
R. W. Taylor	3	2	0	10	12	6.00	66	59	20	—	—	—	—	8
C. M. Old	3	2	0	5	5	2.50	41	23	22	—	—	—	—	1
TOTALS	33	29	4	(108)	868	34.72	2,316	1,771	49	3	4	3	89	32

PAKISTAN – BATTING AND FIELDING

*Not out

	Tests	I	NO	HS	Runs	Av	Mins	Balls	Runs/100b	100	50	6s	4s	Ct
Sadiq Mohammad	3	5	0	97	210	42.00	645	476	44	—	2	—	21	1
Sarfraz Nawaz	2	3	2	32*	42	42.00	160	124	34	—	—	—	6	—
Mohsin Khan	3	5	0	46	191	38.20	656	539	35	—	—	1	17	3
Mudassar Nazar	3	5	0	31	86	17.20	348	299	29	—	—	—	7	2
Javed Miandad	3	5	0	39	77	15.40	232	217	35	—	—	—	9	2
Talat Ali	2	3	0	40	42	14.00	157	147	29	—	—	—	5	—
Wasim Raja	3	5	0	28	55	11.00	118	90	61	—	—	—	7	—
Liaquat Ali	2	4	2	9	16	8.00	82	83	19	—	—	—	2	—
Haroon Rashid	3	5	0	15	33	6.60	155	137	24	—	—	1	2	—
Wasim Bari	3	5	1	7*	12	3.00	46	51	24	—	—	—	—	3
Sikander Bakht	3	5	0	4	11	2.20	74	69	16	—	—	—	1	—
Iqbal Qasim	3	5	1	5*	5	1.25	61	46	11	—	—	—	—	1
TOTALS	33	55	6	(97)	780	15.91	2,734	2,278	34	—	2	2	77	12

COMPARATIVE SCORING RATES
ENGLAND   52.8 runs per 100 balls (935 runs, including 67 extras, off 1,771 balls)
PAKISTAN   36.9 runs per 100 balls (840 runs, including 60 extras, off 2,278 balls)

ENGLAND – BOWLING

	O	M	R	W	Av	BB	5wI	Balls/Wkt	Runs/100b	NB	Wides
P. H. Edmonds	61	24	95	8	11.87	4-6	—	46	26	—	—
C. M. Old	114.2	47	191	13	14.69	7-50	1	53	28	12	—
I. T. Botham	75.5	19	209	13	16.07	8-34	1	35	46	8	4
R. G. D. Willis	88.4	16	233	13	17.92	5-47	1	41	44	21	2
G. Miller	30	10	50	2	25.00	2-19	—	90	28	—	—
B. Wood	3	2	2	0	—	—	—	—	11	—	—
TOTALS	372.5	118	780	49	15.91	(8-34)	3	46	35	41	6

PAKISTAN – BOWLING

	O	M	R	W	Av	BB	5wI	Balls/Wkt	Runs/100b	NB	Wides
Sarfraz Nawaz	26	7	51	5	10.20	5-39	1	31	33	6	—
Javed Miandad	3	0	14	1	14.00	1-14	—	18	78	8	—
Sikander Bakht	87	20	273	7	39.00	4-132	—	75	52	12	2
Iqbal Qasim	55	15	168	4	42.00	3-101	—	83	51	—	—
Mudassar Nazar	36.2	9	87	2	43.50	1-16	—	109	40	—	4
Liaquat Ali	60	10	194	4	48.50	3-80	—	90	54	6	—
Wasim Raja	22	4	81	1	81.00	1-49	—	132	61	3	—
TOTALS	289.2	65	868	24	36.16	(5-39)	1	72	50	35	6

COMPARATIVE BOWLING RATES
ENGLAND   15 overs 5 balls per hour (372.5 overs in 1,409 minutes)
PAKISTAN   14 overs 4 balls per hour (289.2 overs in 1,177 minutes)

TIME LOST DURING SERIES   Unfit playing conditions: 28 hours 56 minutes

TOTAL ATTENDANCE FOR THE SERIES: 102,805 (78,560 paid).Receipts: £221,353.

PRUDENTIAL TROPHY

England beat Pakistan in both the Prudential Trophy one-day internationals with an ease which was almost embarrassing. The tourists were short of practice, confidence, and the tactical requirements and experience needed for this type of cricket. As a result they were outclassed in all departments and never seriously threatened their opponents at any stage in either match.

Having won the toss, Boycott, captaining the side in place of the injured Brearley, elected to bat at Old Trafford on a very dark, overcast day, and fell an early victim to Sarfraz, thus continuing his run of low scores – 4, 9, 2, 0, and 13. Undeterred by this setback, Radley, fighting to retain the place in the national eleven that he had gained when brought in as a tour replacement, contributed a well-judged 79. He found useful partners in Wood and the exciting Gower, while towards the end there was a little gem of an innings from Botham. Bad light prematurely ended play for the day with England comfortably poised for victory, having scored 217 for seven in their 55 overs and having Pakistan, at 12 for two in 11 overs, deep in trouble. There was no escape on the following morning. Willis, Old, Botham, Wood, and Edmonds proved too much and the visitors were shot out for a miserable 85 in conditions far more conducive to batting than they had been on the previous day.

PRUDENTIAL TROPHY 1978
ENGLAND v PAKISTAN—1st Match
Played at Old Trafford, Manchester, 24, 25 May
Toss: England   Result: **England** won by 132 runs
Man of the Match: R. G. D. Willis

*captain
†wicket-keeper

ENGLAND			FALL OF WICKETS	
B. Wood	*c* Miandad *b* Wasim Raja	26	1st	3
G. Boycott*	*c* Wasim Bari *b* Sarfraz	3	2nd	86
C. T. Radley	*c and b* Mudassar	79	3rd	157
D. I. Gower	*c* Miandad *b* Mudassar	33	4th	158
G. R. J. Roope	*c* Wasim Bari *b* Sikander	10	5th	176
I. T. Botham	*c* Haroon *b* Sikander	31	6th	185
G. Miller	*b* Sikander	0	7th	209
C. M. Old	*not out*	6		
P. H. Edmonds	*not out*	4		
R. W. Taylor†	} *did not bat*			
R. G. D. Willis				
Extras	(*b* 2, *lb* 15, *w* 3, *nb* 5)	25		
TOTAL	(7 wickets – 55 overs)	**217**		

PAKISTAN					FALL OF WICKETS	
Mudassar Nazar	*c* Wood *b* Botham			8	1st	3
Sadiq Mohammad	*b* Willis			3	2nd	7
Haroon Rashid	*b* Old			1	3rd	20
Javed Miandad	*lbw b* Willis			9	4th	21
Mohsin Khan	*c* Roope *b* Willis			1	5th	21
Wasim Raja	*lbw b* Willis			0	6th	31
Sarfraz Nawaz	*c* Taylor *b* Botham			7	7th	31
Wasim Bari*†	*b* Wood			19	8th	60
Iqbal Qasim	*b* Wood			9	9th	61
Sikander Bakht	*not out*			16	10th	85
Liaquat Ali	*b* Old			7		
Extras	(*lb* 3, *w* 1, *nb* 1)			5		
TOTAL	(47 overs)			**85**		

PAKISTAN	O	M	R	W	ENGLAND	O	M	R	W
Sarfraz	11	6	13	1	Willis	11	5	15	4
Liaquat	11	3	20	0	Old	7	4	6	2
Sikander	11	0	56	3	Botham	8	1	17	2
Mudassar	11	1	52	2	Wood	11	3	25	2
Qasim	4	1	24	0	Edmonds	10	4	17	0
Wasim Raja	7	1	27	1					

Umpires: D. J. Constant and K. E. Palmer
Attendance: 8,133 (4,133 paid). Receipts: £11,375.

Warwickshire's Bob Willis, Man of the Match for his remarkable bowling performance in the first Prudential Trophy match against Pakistan.

Willis, leading England in the second international at The Oval – Boycott also was not fit – won the toss and batted. His team responded with 248 for six in the 55 overs, a total which was far beyond the capabilities of Pakistan and one which they never looked like even approaching. The England innings was built around a spectacular century from their young recruit, Gower, who hit a splendid, undefeated 114. He came to the wicket with the score at 60 for two, and immediately began to stroke the ball around the ground. When Lloyd departed for a pleasing 34, Gower found another helpful partner in Roope, who was prepared to take singles and give him most of the strike, and he was still plundering an unimpressive attack and some indifferently set fields when England ran out of overs.

Mudassar Nazar gained some useful batting practice as Pakistan wickets fell steadily, and Wasim Raja contributed a colourful 44. But at the end of the permitted number of overs Pakistan had managed to reach only 154, or 94 runs short of their target. Their defeat would have been even heavier had England, with victory a certainty, not relaxed and used some of their second-line bowlers.

PRUDENTIAL TROPHY 1978
ENGLAND v PAKISTAN—2nd Match
Played at Kennington Oval, London, 26 May
Toss: Pakistan   Result: **England** won by 94 runs
Man of the Match: D. I. Gower
Men of the Series: D. I. Gower (E) and Mudassar Nazar (P)

*captain
†wicket-keeper

ENGLAND			FALL OF WICKETS	
D. Lloyd	*b* Wasim Raja	34	1st	27
B. Wood	*b* Sarfraz	8	2nd	60
C. T. Radley	*b* Liaquat	13	3rd	83
D. I. Gower	*not out*	114	4th	188
G. R. J. Roope	*c* Naeem *b* Mudassar	35	5th	194
I. T. Botham	*b* Mudassar	1	6th	195
G. Miller	*lbw b* Sikander	0		
C. M. Old	*not out*	25		
R. W. Taylor†				
J. K. Lever	*did not bat*			
R. G. D. Willis*				
Extras	(*b* 5, *lb* 9, *nb* 4)	18		
TOTAL	(6 wickets – 55 overs)	**248**		

PAKISTAN			FALL OF WICKETS	
Mudassar Nazar	*c* Willis *b* Botham	56	1st	27
Sadiq Mohammad	*c and b* Old	9	2nd	38
Arshad Pervaiz	*lbw b* Miller	3	3rd	39
Javed Miandad	*b* Old	0	4th	80
Haroon Rashid	*st* Taylor *b* Miller	20	5th	117
Wasim Raja	*c* sub (P. H. Edmonds) *b* Lloyd	44	6th	130
Wasim Bari*†	*c* Taylor *b* Wood	1	7th	154
Sarfraz Nawaz	*c* Gower *b* Wood	12	8th	154
Naeem Ahmed	*not out*	0		
Sikander Bakht	*not out*	0		
Liaquat Ali	*did not bat*			
Extras	(*b* 1, *lb* 7, *w* 1)	9		
TOTAL	(8 wickets – 55 overs)	**154**		

England opener Barry Wood is effectively removed by Sarfraz at The Oval.

PAKISTAN	O	M	R	W		ENGLAND	O	M	R	W
Sarfraz	11	2	48	1		Willis	9	1	25	0
Liaquat	11	1	41	1		Old	11	1	26	2
Sikander	11	0	53	1		Miller	11	3	24	2
Wasim Raja	6	0	14	1		Botham	11	2	36	1
Naeem	10	0	43	0		Lever	7	1	17	0
Mudassar	6	0	31	2		Wood	4	0	14	2
						Lloyd	2	1	3	1

Umpires: H. D. Bird and W. L. Budd
Attendance: 7,535 (5,035 paid). Receipts: £16,100.

The mixed fortunes of close fielders: a quiet life for Sadiq with Warwickshire's Whitehouse on the defensive for MCC; danger for Miandad from the belligerent Botham.

TOURISTS' FIRST-CLASS MATCHES AND AVERAGES

RESULTS
Played 13   Won 1   Drew 10   Lost 2   (Abandoned 1)

WORCESTERSHIRE at Worcester, 25, 26 (no play), 27 (no play) April. Match drawn. Pakistanis 31—0.

LEICESTERSHIRE at Leicester, 29 April, 1, 2 (no play) May. Match drawn. Leicestershire 269 (J. F. Steele 62). Pakistanis 90—4.

NOTTINGHAMSHIRE at Nottingham, 3, 4, 5 (no play) May. Match drawn. Pakistanis 212—5 (Wasim Raja 56*).

YORKSHIRE at Bradford, 6, 7, 8 May. Match abandoned without a ball being bowled.

NORTHAMPTONSHIRE at Northampton, 10, 11, 12 May. Match drawn. Pakistanis 190 (Mudassar Nazar 80, G. Sharp held five catches) and 217—9. Northamptonshire 205—8d (D. S. Steele 86).

ESSEX at Chelmsford, 13, 15 (no play), 16 (no play) May. Match drawn. Pakistanis 80 (N. Phillip 6—33). Essex 8—0.
Phillip was making his first-class début for Essex.

MCC at Lord's, 17, 18, 19 May. Match drawn. MCC 193 and 149—6d (D. I. Gower 71). Pakistanis 149—9d (C. M. Old 6—36) and 75—4.

DERBYSHIRE at Chesterfield, 20, 21, 22 May. Match drawn. Derbyshire 333—3d (J. G. Wright 164, A. Hill 58, P. N. Kirsten 58) and 101—5d. Pakistanis 182 (Mudassar Nazar 78, P. E. Russell held five catches) and 115—3.

KENT at Canterbury, 27, 28, 29 May. Match drawn. Pakistanis 420—7d (Sadiq Mohammad 161, Talat Ali 60, Javed Miandad 59, Wasim Raja 56*) and 245—7 (Mudassar Nazar 68). Kent 342—7d (A. G. E. Ealham 95, C. J. Tavaré 90, C. J. C. Rowe 85).

ENGLAND (1st Test) at Birmingham, 1, 2, 3, 5 June. England won by an innings and 57 runs. (See match report for full scorecard.)

HAMPSHIRE at Southampton, 10, 11, 12 June. Match drawn. Hampshire 246 (T. E. Jesty 77, J. M. Rice 55) and 307—3d (D. R. Turner 111, T. E. Jesty 102*, C. G. Greenidge 60). Pakistanis 258 (Sadiq Mohammad 56, M. N. S. Taylor 5—67) and 217—5 (Mudassar Nazar 107, Mohsin Khan 79).

ENGLAND (2nd Test) at Lord's, 15 (no play), 16, 17, 19 June. England won by an innings and 120 runs. (See match report for full scorecard.)

SURREY at The Oval, 24 (no play), 26, 27 June. Pakistanis won by 7 wickets. Surrey 178—3d (M. A. Lynch 101, G. R. J. Roope 64*) and 97—5d. Pakistanis 158—6d (Haroon Rashid 78) and 121—3 (Javed Miandad 55*).

ENGLAND (3rd Test) at Leeds, 29, 30 June, 1 (no play), 3, 4 July. Match drawn. (See match report for full scorecard.)

The tour also included three non-first-class matches—a two-day match against Combined Universities, and two limited-overs internationals. Losses (2): England (2 Prudential Trophy matches). Draw (1): Combined Universities.

BATTING AND FIELDING   *Not out

	M	I	NO	HS	Runs	Av	100	50	Ct	St
Sadiq Mohammad	13	20	2	161	675	37.50	1	3	6	—
Mudassar Nazar	13	21	1	107	677	33.85	1	3	5	—
Wasim Raja	12	17	5	56*	324	27.00	—	2	3	—
Talat Ali	8	14	3	60	278	25.27	—	1	1	—
Javad Miandad	13	20	4	59	397	24.81	—	2	5	—
Mohsin Khan	11	16	0	79	386	24.12	—	1	4	—
Sarfraz Nawaz	8	8	4	32*	90	22.50	—	—	3	—
Haroon Rashid	10	15	0	78	268	17.86	—	1	2	—
Wasim Bari	12	11	2	38*	123	13.66	—	—	13	—
Aamer Hameed	6	3	1	13	26	13.00	—	—	—	—
Arshad Pervaiz	3	5	0	30	59	11.80	—	—	1	—
Liaquat Ali	8	7	5	9	18	9.00	—	—	—	—
Hasan Jamil	1	2	1	7	9	9.00	—	—	—	—
Masood Iqbal	1	1	0	8	8	8.00	—	—	3	—
Abdul Qadir	7	6	0	9	16	2.66	—	—	4	—
Iqbal Qasim	9	9	2	8*	16	2.28	—	—	4	—
Sikander Bakht	6	6	1	4	11	2.20	—	—	—	—
Naeem Ahmed	2	1	0	2	2	2.00	—	—	—	—
TOTALS	143	182	31	(161)	3,383	22.40	2	13	54	—

BOWLING

	O	M	R	W	Av	BB	5wI	10wM	Balls/ wkt	Runs/ 100b
Sarfraz Nawaz	147.3	35	330	18	18.33	5–39	1	—	49	37
Sadiq Mohammad	12	4	25	1	25.00	1–13	—	—	72	35
Liaquat Ali	188	45	510	18	28.33	3–26	—	—	63	45
Mudassar Nazar	100.1	23	253	8	31.62	2–28	—	—	75	42
Wasim Raja	89.2	15	258	8	32.25	2–15	—	—	67	48
Sikander Bakht	149	31	450	12	37.50	4–132	—	—	75	50
Hasan Jamil	24	3	77	2	38.50	2–32	—	—	72	53
Aamer Hameed	95	28	237	6	39.50	3–71	—	—	95	42
Iqbal Qasim	115.4	34	310	7	44.28	3–101	—	—	99	45
Abdul Qadir	123	22	396	6	66.00	2–29	—	—	123	54
Naeem Ahmed	47	7	136	2	68.00	1–45	—	—	141	48
Javed Miandad	43	4	137	2	68.50	1–14	—	—	129	53
TOTALS	1,133.4	251	3,119	90	34.65	(5–39)	1	—	76	46

Right: New Zealand fast bowler Richard Hadlee. The agony of the appeal might have been inspired by Lee Strasberg or Dennis Lillee; his pace and hostility were genuine enough and troubled all the England batsmen.

THE 1978 NEW ZEALANDERS

*Approaching a maiden Test century the Gower way. Kiwi spinner Stephen Boock and his
fielders look resigned; non-striker Botham and umpire Meyer follow the ball with interest.*

ENGLAND SHOW SUPREMACY

First Test, The Oval

England retained the same team that had annihilated Pakistan at Lord's for their first Test against New Zealand at The Oval. The pitch that has depressed so many international bowlers in recent years was still too slow, but it did provide some encouragement to the spinners in the later stages. As a result, the tourists were fortunate to win the toss and bat in conditions which should have produced a substantial total.

After losing Anderson to an injudicious stroke early on, Howarth and Wright, who have reasonable if far from outstanding records in county cricket, took the score to 130 by sensible batting and without many problems, although both were uncharacteristically put down by Roope at second slip. For the first time in the summer the England side looked no more than competent.

The departure of Wright was followed by that of young Edgar, who allowed himself to be hypnotised by Miller for an unhappy duck. Nevertheless, Howarth was now playing well and he found a sound accomplice in Burgess. At tea, a score of around 250 for four at the close seemed more than possible, but the tourists lost the initiative in the final session and were never to recover it completely. Howarth was superbly caught at square-leg off a long hop – six short of his third successive hundred against England – Congdon was brilliantly run out, and Edwards departed swinging across the line. Although the new ball was available, Brearley was able to delay taking it until the morning, when his bowlers were completely fresh, because Burgess and the tail were content with a largely runless survival operation for the final 45 minutes. Almost predictably, New Zealand managed to lose their captain in the final over.

On the following morning Willis quickly gobbled up the last three wickets and England went in facing a moderate 234, only to lose both Gooch and Brearley cheaply to the 18-year-old quickie, Bracewell. Radley and Gower quickly put the task into its true perspective with a pleasing stand that ended with the former running himself out. Gower, aided by a couple of lives – both easy chances to mid-on – went on to reach his first Test century. It contained many delightful strokes and was proof that the most promising English batsman for more than a decade had come of age. His innings was eventually ended when he sacrificed his wicket in a misunderstanding with Botham.

In almost the identical situation as the opposition had been in on the first day, the England rearguard also settled on survival for the final hour; and lost their best batsman, Botham. But on the following morning they coped

Geoff Howarth – at The Oval, just six short of three successive hundreds against England.

better with the new ball and, thanks mainly to Edmonds, acquired a useful lead of 45.

The respectable start that was so essential if the tourists were to come back into the game failed to materialise, and their first three were soon back in the pavilion, victims of the swing of Botham and the pace of Willis. Edgar showed considerable promise until he was bowled by Edmonds, from over the wicket making the ball turn unpleasantly from the considerable rough just outside the lefthander's off stump, and the same fate later befell Hadlee. At stumps the visitors were only 78 runs ahead with three wickets standing, including that of Congdon, who had coped with the increasing vagaries of the wicket with more ease than any of his colleagues. One could not help feeling he should have gone in earlier in this situation.

The umpires eventually called off play on Monday without a ball being bowled. By that time the heavy rain had turned the ground into a lake, and the fact that it was possible to start on time the following day was a considerable tribute to the efforts of the groundstaff. Congdon and Cairns immediately settled in a splendid fighting stand in which they saw off the two spinners and then dealt efficiently with the new ball before, with the spinners back again, Cairns was bowled by Miller. Bracewell departed without addition, and finally the gallant Congdon was bowled by Edmonds for 36 with probably the best ball of the match.

This left England with the comparatively simple task of making 138 against a team with one recognised spinner, Boock. Things were made even easier for them when the young left-armer was not used at the end from which Edmonds had returned his remarkable figures – 34.1-23-20-4 – until it was much too late and his fingers were tired. At tea England were 41 runs short of their target with seven wickets in hand, and the only threat at this stage was rain. This possibility caused Gooch to cut loose with a barrage of fierce attacking strokes that sped his team to victory and left him with 91 not out in a total of 138, plus the comforting knowledge that he was assured of a place in the next contest.

ENGLAND v NEW ZEALAND 1978—1st Test

Played at Kennington Oval, London, 27, 28, 29, 31 (*no play*) July, 1 August
Toss: New Zealand   Result: **England** won by 7 wickets

*captain
†wicket-keeper

NEW ZEALAND

Batsman	Dismissal 1	Score	Dismissal 2	Score
J. G. Wright	*c* Radley *b* Willis	62	*lbw b* Botham	25
R. W. Anderson	*b* Old	4	*c* Taylor *b* Botham	2
G. P. Howarth	*c* Edmonds *b* Botham	94	*b* Willis	0
B. A. Edgar	*c and b* Miller	0	*b* Edmonds	38
M. G. Burgess*	*lbw b* Willis	34	*lbw b* Botham	7
B. E. Congdon	*run out* (*Gower*)	2	*b* Edmonds	36
G. N. Edwards†	*b* Miller	6	*c* Brearley *b* Edmonds	11
R. J. Hadlee	*c* Brearley *b* Willis	5	*b* Edmonds	7
B. L. Cairns	*lbw b* Willis	5	*b* Miller	27
B. P. Bracewell	*c* Taylor *b* Willis	0	*b* Miller	0
S. L. Boock	*not out*	3	*not out*	0
Extras	(*b* 1, *lb* 7, *nb* 11)	19	(*b* 8, *lb* 10, *nb* 11)	29
TOTAL		**234**		**182**

ENGLAND

Batsman	Dismissal 1	Score	Dismissal 2	Score
J. M. Brearley*	*c* Edwards *b* Bracewell	2	*lbw b* Boock	11
G. A. Gooch	*lbw b* Bracewell	0	*not out*	91
C. T. Radley	*run out* (*Anderson*)	49	*lbw b* Bracewell	2
D. I. Gower	*run out* (*Anderson/Boock*)	111	*c* Howarth *b* Cairns	11
G. R. J. Roope	*b* Boock	14	*not out*	10
G. Miller	*lbw b* Cairns	0		
I. T. Botham	*c* Bracewell *b* Boock	22		
R. W. Taylor†	*c* Edwards *b* Hadlee	8		
P. H. Edmonds	*lbw b* Hadlee	28		
C. M. Old	*c* Edwards *b* Cairns	16		
R. G. D. Willis	*not out*	3		
Extras	(*b* 15, *lb* 8, *nb* 3)	26	(*b* 2, *lb* 3, *nb* 8)	13
TOTAL		**279**	(3 wickets)	**138**

ENGLAND	O	M	R	W	O	M	R	W
Willis	20.2	9	42	5	13	2	39	1
Old	20	7	43	1	5	2	13	0
Botham	22	7	58	1	19	2	46	3
Miller	25	10	31	2	34	19	35	2
Edmonds	17	2	41	0	34.1	23	20	4

NEW ZEALAND	O	M	R	W	O	M	R	W
Hadlee	21.5	6	43	2	11.3	3	18	0
Bracewell	17	8	46	2	13	3	26	1
Cairns	40	16	65	2	7	0	21	1
Boock	35	18	61	2	20	6	55	1
Congdon	21	6	38	0	1	0	5	0

FALL OF WICKETS

	New Zealand		England	
Wkt	1st	2nd	1st	2nd
1st	7	15	2	26
2nd	130	19	7	51
3rd	131	30	123	82
4th	191	70	165	
5th	197	86	166	
6th	207	105	208	
7th	224	113	212	
8th	230	182	232	
9th	230	182	257	
10th	234	182	279	

Umpires: D. J. Constant and B. J. Meyer
Attendance: 36,900 (27,842 paid). Receipts: £71,719.

A MISLEADING MARGIN

Second Test, Trent Bridge

At six o'clock on the fourth day of the Trent Bridge Test, Edmonds bowled Boock to give England a substantial victory by an innings and 119 runs and also the series. They won because they had a much more formidable attack, caught far better, had a high-class 'keeper, and, in Boycott, possessed the one batsman in either team whom one expected to score a century. It came as no surprise when he obliged. What was misleading was the extent of New Zealand's defeat. If they had caught Boycott, when he was 2, or Gooch, or Radley – and a more athletic wicket-keeper might well have had Brearley down the leg-side before he opened his account – the outcome would have been much closer. After all, only the previous winter the Kiwis had held England to a drawn series.

As so often happens with a side lacking in confidence, luck, in the matter of decisions and situations, tended to go against them. On the other hand, good teams make their own luck, and the tourists had only themselves to blame that at the end of the first day England had meandered to a respectable 252 for two, with Boycott 108 not out. On the first morning there was considerable assistance to be had from the pitch, but only Hadlee of the New Zealand bowlers took advantage of it; and his efforts were frustrated by disheartening, indifferent catching and unsympathetic umpires. In the same circumstances, England would have expected to pick up four or five wickets, and their opponents would have been heading for a small total.

Having survived with some difficulty the first session, Boycott predictably celebrated yet another return to the international arena with a solid, carefully grafted century which provided his side with the substance they required. In the early part of the innings, Gooch looked the more confident and competent, but gradually the Yorkshireman found his touch, helped, it must be admitted, by the naivety of much of the field placing. Once established, he played and missed less often than his three partners, Gooch, Radley, and Gower, all of whom got themselves out with casual strokes when well set and a big score was there for the taking.

With wickets in hand and runs already in the book, the pattern for the second day was easy to predict. England would pile up a substantial score and then the New Zealanders, after some 10 hours in the field, would collapse. Thus it turned out, although the England batting was not as impressive as had been hoped. Their bowling, however, was distinctly hostile, and the tourists were sent reeling towards defeat; 35 for three and Howarth retired hurt.

Boycott took his score to 131, including a fine hook off Hadlee, but trying to repeat the shot he was caught and bowled. Gower, without ever quite suggesting permanence, played most of the memorable strokes in a pleasing 46 and Brearley, who had relegated himself down the order and was in the unenviable position of being unable to justify his place as a batsman, put together a workmanlike 50 to end a very lean spell. The remainder of the batting was undistinguished and laboured, but 429 was enough to make sure that England could not lose. The three wickets picked up by Botham and Hendrick before the close were sufficient to suggest a handsome victory.

The next morning, the umpires, well aware of the instructions to provide as much play as possible for the long-suffering spectator, went out in light that was far from good. Although it was unpleasant, any club game would have started and the umpires' decision could be upheld on the grounds that it was playable, but whether a Test match should be played in such conditions is a different matter. Where the umpires made their mistake was coming in again after only two deliveries. The light was certainly no worse, and their decision meant that the pitch was then open to the elements until stumps. As expected, rain did fall, and in a foreshortened day New Zealand were removed for 120 on a pitch that had been freshened, though was never made difficult by the rain that had fallen on its uncovered surface. With three of their best batsmen already back in the pavilion, slightly demoralised and convinced they had been harshly treated by the umpires, the New Zealanders found the England attack, and Botham in particular with six wickets, too much for their limited resources.

The miss that mattered. Howarth puts down Boycott off Hadlee early in the day. Predictably the Yorkshireman went on to amass his fifteenth Test century.

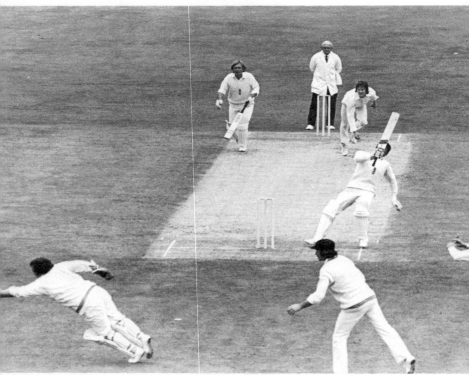

Another lucky break for Boycott at Trent Bridge. Edwards fails to move fast and far enough to make the England opener pay for a mis-hook off young Brendon Bracewell.

Although there was no chance of New Zealand saving the match without intervention from the weather, it was hoped that they would prolong the proceedings until the final day. Had it not been for two needless run-outs, this would have almost certainly occurred. Just before tea, with the score at 148 for three the cricket press had already started booking back into their hotels. In the event, the running out of Anderson and Parker, and the combination of Edmonds' spin and control and Botham's ebullience in the final session, proved too much. Both bowled well, especially the former, but they were assisted by batting that became dispirited and lacked real determination. One gained the impression that some surrendered unconditionally.

Before the decline and fall, Edgar had emphasised his potential with a most impressive 60 in which he never appeared in much trouble against any of the England bowlers. Howarth looked equally at home, until Hendrick, the most menacing member of the attack, found his edge with a fine delivery. The young lefthander, reminding one of Neil Harvey in style and technique, was then joined by the knowledgeable Parker. This pair batted with such authority that by mid-afternoon one began to wonder whether the menace of the English bowlers had not been exaggerated. It was at this point that the tourists experienced one of those unlucky breaks; 15 minutes off for a light shower. Not only did this break the rhythm, but Parker, still wearing crepes, slipped over and was run out. And, just before the delayed tea interval, Edgar's concentration wavered after the England fielders had prematurely set off for tea and were recalled by the umpires, correctly making allowance for the stoppage. In the final session the remaining New Zealand batsmen went quickly from, and back to, the pavilion like dejected men who knew their fate and had given up hope.

ENGLAND v NEW ZEALAND 1978—2nd Test

Played at Trent Bridge, Nottingham, 10, 11, 12, 14 August
Toss: England   Result: **England** won by an innings and 119 runs   *captain
†wicket-keeper

ENGLAND

G. A. Gooch	*c* Burgess *b* Bracewell	55
G. Boycott	*c and b* Hadlee	131
C. T. Radley	*lbw b* Hadlee	59
D. I. Gower	*c* Cairns *b* Boock	46
J. M. Brearley*	*c* Parker *b* Bracewell	50
I. T. Botham	*c* Hadlee *b* Boock	8
G. Miller	*c* Howarth *b* Hadlee	4
P. H. Edmonds	*b* Cairns	6
R. W. Taylor†	*b* Hadlee	22
M. Hendrick	*c* Edwards *b* Bracewell	7
R. G. D. Willis	*not out*	1
Extras	(*b* 16, *lb* 12, *w* 1, *nb* 11)	40
TOTAL		**429**

NEW ZEALAND

R. W. Anderson	*lbw b* Botham	19		*run out (Gower)*	0
B. A. Edgar	*c* Taylor *b* Botham	6		*c* Botham *b* Edmonds	60
G. P. Howarth	*not out*	31		*c* Botham *b* Hendrick	34
S. L. Boock	*c* Taylor *b* Willis	8	(10)	*b* Edmonds	2
J. M. Parker	*c* Taylor *b* Hendrick	0	(4)	*run out (Miller/Edmonds)*	38
M. G. Burgess*	*c* Taylor *b* Botham	5	(5)	*c* Brearley *b* Edmonds	7
B. E. Congdon	*c* Hendrick *b* Botham	27	(6)	*c* Brearley *b* Botham	4
G. N. Edwards†	*c* Taylor *b* Botham	0	(7)	*c and b* Edmonds	18
B. L. Cairns	*b* Edmonds	9	(8)	*lbw b* Botham	0
R. J. Hadlee	*c* Gooch *b* Botham	4	(9)	*c* Taylor *b* Botham	11
B. P. Bracewell	*b* Edmonds	0		*not out*	0
Extras	(*lb* 1, *w* 1, *nb* 9)	11		(*lb* 6, *w* 1, *nb* 9)	16
TOTAL		**120**			**190**

NEW ZEALAND

	O	M	R	W	O	M	R	W
Hadlee	42	11	94	4				
Bracewell	33.5	2	110	3				
Cairns	38	7	85	1				
Congdon	39	15	71	0				
Boock	28	18	29	2				

ENGLAND

	O	M	R	W	O	M	R	W
Willis	12	5	22	1	9	0	31	0
Hendrick	15	9	18	1	20	7	30	1
Botham	21	9	34	6	24	7	59	3
Edmonds	15.4	5	21	2	33.1	15	44	4
Miller	6	1	14	0	6	3	10	0

FALL OF WICKETS

England   New Zealand

Wkt	1st	2nd	1st	2nd
1st	111		22	5
2nd	240		27	63
3rd	301		35	127
4th	342		47	148
5th	350		49	152
6th	364		99	164
7th	374		99	168
8th	419		110	180
9th	427		115	190
10th	429		120	190

Umpires: D. J. Constant and T. W. Spencer
Attendance: 38,500 (28,761 paid). Receipts: £80,975.

OUTGUNNED AGAIN

Third Test, Lord's
England recovered from the disadvantage of losing the toss and a deficit on
the first innings to beat New Zealand by seven wickets in their third and final
meeting. They owed their victory to some splendid bowling from Willis and
Botham which routed the tourists in their second innings. Once again, it
might have been a closer contest: if Hadlee had had a bowler of similar
penetration at the other end; if Howarth had been fit to bat on the Saturday;
if the tourists could have limped to 150 in their second innings; if their one
international-class batsman had been playing for them instead of for
Worcestershire. So many ifs.

The first day belonged to Howarth, who completed an undefeated
century on an easy paced pitch against an attack in which Willis and, until
later in the day, Botham were not at their best. Emburey had the satisfaction
of capturing a wicket in his first over of Test cricket when Edgar was caught
at leg slip off a ball that went with the arm.

After the departure of Parker, Howarth and Burgess engaged in a fine
stand of 130 which suggested that a total of about 400 was possible. But
typically, Botham, with two wickets in nine balls when he dismissed both
Burgess and Congdon, changed the whole outlook and the tourists were
forced to settle for 280 for five at stumps. The last five wickets produced only
a further 59 runs on the Friday, and took until 10 minutes after lunch. The
redoubtable Botham picked up a further three wickets to finish with six for
the innings.

The English batsmen also struggled. Gooch departed in Hadlee's first
over. The latter bowled with pace and hostility, but Boycott played him with
commendable skill. Radley existed with rather more difficulty, and indeed
should have been caught in the slips early on. After tea, Boycott, for once,
erred and was caught, which set the scene for a joyous partnership between
Radley and Gower. They prospered as the New Zealand bowling wavered in
line and length and no attempt was made to block Radley's partiality for the
push through mid-wicket or the square cut. Indeed, the out-cricket lost
direction. In the last half-hour Gower was driving exquisitely, and his half-
century of elegance and charm sent the spectators home well content.

The excitement of the previous evening did not carry over into Saturday,
when a full six hours produced a miserly 151 runs, the lowest ever recorded
in England. Fortunately the suffering watchers quickly forgot the
somnolent hours in the excitement of seeing New Zealand dissipate their
advantage of a substantial lead by crashing to 37 for seven before the pace of
Willis and the swing of Botham.

In the morning, Radley, who never looks comfortable against the fast lifting ball, received one from Hadlee and departed. Gower, unable to find the flow of the previous evening, became tied down against the accurate Boock and holed out sweeping. There looked to be an increasing unevenness in the bounce, which understandably worried the batsmen and encouraged the bowlers, and of the last seven England batsmen only Brearley ever suggested any permanence. He was made to work very hard for his 33 before being caught behind off Hadlee, easily the best of the bowlers. It was also difficult to envisage Taylor as a number 7 in an international side.

England were eventually out for 289, and as they had started the day at 175 for two, Burgess must have been well pleased with his bowlers, the lead, and the situation. Moreover, with the pitch likely to become increasingly untrustworthy, the first ever New Zealand victory in this country seemed a possibility. Until, that is, Willis and Botham took over with the new ball. At stumps Burgess came in 8 not out and the innings in ruins, Willis having taken four for seven and Botham three for 23.

When play restarted on Monday morning, New Zealand's one faint hope was that their captain, Burgess, and Howarth, who had been ill and unable to bat on Saturday, could repeat their first innings' partnership. The odds were strongly against it. Burgess was superbly caught very low down at slip by Hendrick; Hadlee was run out for no good reason (Botham again!); Collinge was bowled off his pad by a Botham inswinger, leaving Howarth 14 not out and the total a miserable 67.

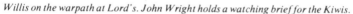

Willis on the warpath at Lord's. John Wright holds a watching brief for the Kiwis.

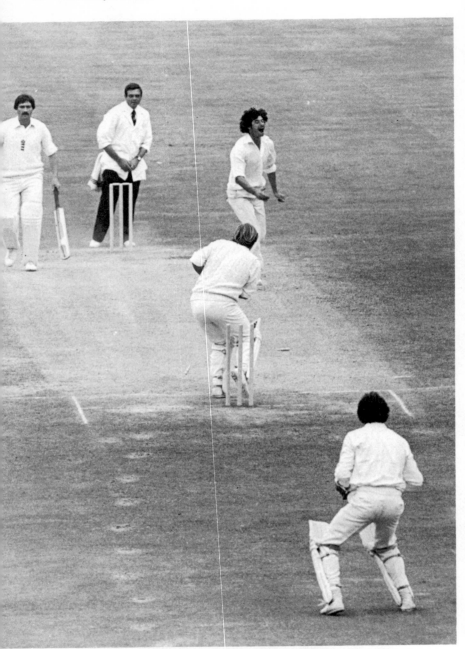

Radley is bowled first ball by Hadlee, who had skittled Boycott with his previous delivery. However, Gooch, with Gower and then Brearley, ensured England's victory.

Once again Hadlee produced several fast and fiery overs in the course of which he bowled both Boycott and Radley with successive deliveries. But he did not have enough runs to play with, and there was not the same venom at the other end. Gooch was unperturbed by these two setbacks, and his new partner, Gower, launched a spectacular counter-attack before being caught in the gulley for an exhilarating 46 with the total at 84. Gooch and Brearley then proceeded to steer England quietly and soberly home.

ENGLAND v NEW ZEALAND 1978—3rd Test
Played at Lord's, London, 24, 25, 26, 28 August
Toss: New Zealand   Result: **England** won by 7 wickets

*captain
†wicket-keeper

NEW ZEALAND

J. G. Wright	c Edmonds b Botham	17		b Botham	12
B. A. Edgar†	c Edmonds b Emburey	39		b Botham	4
G. P. Howarth	c Taylor b Botham	123	(9)	not out	14
J. M. Parker	lbw b Hendrick	14		c Taylor b Botham	3
M. G. Burgess*	lbw b Botham	68		c Hendrick b Botham	14
B. E. Congdon	c Emburey b Botham	2		c Taylor b Willis	3
R. W. Anderson	b Botham	16	(3)	c Taylor b Willis	1
R. J. Hadlee	c Brearley b Botham	0	(10)	run out (Botham)	5
R. O. Collinge	c Emburey b Willis	19	(11)	b Botham	0
S. L. Boock	not out	4	(7)	c Radley b Willis	0
B. P. Bracewell	st Taylor b Emburey	4	(8)	c Hendrick b Willis	0
Extras	(b 4, lb 18, w 4, nb 7)	33		(lb 3, nb 8)	11
TOTAL		**339**			**67**

ENGLAND

G. A. Gooch	c Boock b Hadlee	2		not out	42
G. Boycott	c Hadlee b Bracewell	24		b Hadlee	4
C. T. Radley	c Congdon b Hadlee	77		b Hadlee	0
D. I. Gower	c Wright b Boock	71		c Congdon b Bracewell	46
J. M. Brearley*	c Edgar b Hadlee	33		not out	8
I. T. Botham	c Edgar b Collinge	21			
R. W. Taylor†	lbw b Hadlee	1			
P. H. Edmonds	c Edgar b Hadlee	5			
J. E. Emburey	b Collinge	2			
M. Hendrick	b Bracewell	12			
R. G. D. Willis	not out	7			
Extras	(b 7, lb 5, nb 22)	34		(lb 3, w 4, nb 11)	18
TOTAL		**289**		(3 wickets)	**118**

ENGLAND	O	M	R	W	O	M	R	W
Willis	29	9	79	1	16	8	16	4
Hendrick	28	14	39	1				
Botham	38	13	101	6	18.1	4	39	5
Edmonds	12	3	19	0				
Emburey	26.1	12	39	2	3	2	1	0
Gooch	10	0	29	0				

NEW ZEALAND	O	M	R	W	O	M	R	W
Hadlee	32	9	84	5	13.5	2	31	2
Collinge	30	9	58	2	6	1	26	0
Bracewell	19.3	1	68	2	6	0	32	1
Boock	25	10	33	1	5	1	11	0
Congdon	6	1	12	0				

FALL OF WICKETS

	New Zealand		England	
Wkt	1st	2nd	1st	2nd
1st	65	10	2	14
2nd	70	14	66	14
3rd	117	20	180	84
4th	247	29	211	
5th	253	33	249	
6th	290	37	255	
7th	290	37	258	
8th	321	43	263	
9th	333	57	274	
10th	339	67	289	

Umpires: H. D. Bird and B. J. Meyer
Attendance: 65,334 (55,334 paid). Receipts: £142,549.

STATISTICAL SURVEY OF THE SERIES

†Plus one 'five'   *Not out

ENGLAND – BATTING AND FIELDING

	Tests	I	NO	HS	Runs	Av	Mins	Balls	Runs/100b	100	50	6s	4s	Ct/St
G. A. Gooch	3	5	2	91*	190	63.33	495	403	47	1	2	—	24	1
D. I. Gower	3	5	0	111	285	57.00	666	608	47	1	1	1	30	—
G. Boycott	2	3	0	131	159	53.00	540	461	34	—	—	—	13†	—
C. T. Radley	3	5	0	77	187	37.40	582	521	36	—	2	—	14	2
J. M. Brearley	3	5	1	50	104	26.00	440	351	30	—	1	—	8	5
G. R. J. Roope	1	2	—	14	24	24.00	102	95	25	—	—	—	—	—
I. T. Botham	3	3	0	22	51	17.00	185	174	29	—	—	1	6	2
C. M. Old	1	1	0	16	16	16.00	68	54	30	—	—	—	3	—
P. H. Edmonds	3	3	0	28	39	13.00	185	164	24	—	—	—	4	4
R. G. D. Willis	3	3	3	7*	11	—	61	47	23	—	—	—	—	—
R. W. Taylor	3	3	0	22	31	10.33	148	146	21	—	—	—	2	12/1
M. Hendrick	2	2	0	12	19	9.50	72	40	48	—	—	—	1	3
G. Miller	2	2	0	4	4	2.00	42	39	10	—	—	—	—	1
J. E. Emburey	1	1	0	2	2	2.00	50	34	6	—	—	—	—	2
TOTALS	33	43	7	(131)	1,122	31.16	3,636	3,137	36	2	6	2	105†	32/1

NEW ZEALAND – BATTING AND FIELDING

	Tests	I	NO	HS	Runs	Av	Mins	Balls	Runs/100b	100	50	6s	4s	Ct
G. P. Howarth	3	6	2	123	296	74.00	899	769	38	1	1	—	28	2
J. G. Wright	2	4	0	62	116	29.00	417	348	33	—	1	—	11	1
B. A. Edgar	3	6	0	60	147	24.50	570	465	32	—	1	—	13	3
M. G. Burgess	3	6	0	68	135	22.50	503	449	30	—	1	—	15	1
J. M. Parker	2	4	0	38	55	13.75	193	185	30	—	—	—	3	1
B. E. Congdon	3	6	0	41	74	12.33	401	388	19	—	—	—	6	2
B. L. Cairns	2	4	0	27	41	10.25	172	162	25	—	—	—	2	1
R. O. Collinge	1	2	0	19	19	9.50	106	87	22	—	—	—	2	—
G. N. Edwards	2	4	0	18	35	8.75	84	90	39	—	—	—	2	4
R. W. Anderson	3	6	0	19	42	7.00	168	144	29	—	—	—	4	—
S. L. Boock	3	6	3	8	17	5.66	139	115	15	—	—	—	1	1
R. J. Hadlee	3	6	0	11	32	5.33	137	124	26	—	—	—	5	3
B. P. Bracewell	3	6	1	4	4	0.80	44	53	8	—	—	—	1	1
TOTALS	33	66	6	(123)	1,013	16.88	3,833	3,379	30	1	4	—	93	20

COMPARATIVE SCORING RATES
ENGLAND   39.9 runs per 100 balls (1,253 runs, including 131 extras, off 3,137 balls)
NEW ZEALAND   33.5 runs per 100 balls (1,132 runs, including 119 extras, off 3,379 balls)

ENGLAND – BOWLING

	O	M	R	W	Av	BB	5wI	Balls/Wkt	Runs/100b	NB	Wides
I. T. Botham	142.1	42	337	24	14.04	6-34	3	36	40	21	2
P. H. Edmonds	112	48	145	10	14.50	4-20	—	67	22	—	—
R. G. D. Willis	99.2	33	229	12	19.08	5-42	1	50	38	39	1
J. E. Emburey	29.1	14	40	2	20.00	2-39	—	88	23	—	—
G. Miller	71	33	90	4	22.50	2-31	—	107	21	—	—
M. Hendrick	63	30	87	3	29.00	1-18	—	126	23	—	2
C. M. Old	25	9	56	1	56.00	1-43	—	150	37	9	1
G. A. Gooch	10	0	29	0	—	—	—	—	48	—	—
TOTALS	551.4	209	1,013	56	18.08	(6-34)	4	59	31	69	6

NEW ZEALAND – BOWLING

	O	M	R	W	Av	BB	5wI	Balls/Wkt	Runs/100b	NB	Wides
R. J. Hadlee	121.1	31	270	13	20.76	5-84	1	56	37	34	5
B. P. Bracewell	89.2	14	282	9	31.33	3-110	—	60	53	26	—
S. L. Boock	113	53	189	6	31.50	2-29	—	113	28	—	—
R. O. Collinge	36	10	84	2	42.00	2-58	—	108	39	8	—
B. L. Cairns	85	23	171	4	42.75	2-65	—	128	34	—	—
B. E. Congdon	67	22	126	0	—	—	—	—	31	—	—
TOTALS	511.3	153	1,122	34	33.00	(5-84)	1	90	37	68	5

COMPARATIVE BOWLING RATES
ENGLAND   16 overs 5 balls per hour (551.4 overs in 1,971 minutes)
NEW ZEALAND   16 overs 3 balls per hour (511.3 overs in 1,845 minutes)

TIME LOST DURING SERIES   Unfit playing conditions: 9 hours 14 minutes

TOTAL ATTENDANCE FOR THE SERIES: 140,734 (111,937 paid).   Receipts: £295,243.

PRUDENTIAL TROPHY

The first Prudential limited-overs international between England and New Zealand was played at Scarborough, though why it should have been staged there on a Saturday simply illustrated a lack of thought, and a disregard for money. Everybody has known for more than 50 years that this is change-over day and that this well-appointed seaside ground invariably gets its biggest gates midweek. The weekend obviously should have gone to Old Trafford, and the Monday to Scarborough; a little matter that might just about have been realised by the TCCB!

Having been inserted by New Zealand on a slow pitch, but in conditions that enabled the seam bowlers to achieve a certain amount of movement both in the air and off the wicket, England found runs hard to acquire in the morning session. Brearley, who was never convincing and survived a couple of half-chances, managed with Gooch to put on 67 for the first wicket before he mis-drove Boock. Gooch, who played some impressive strokes, and his new partner, the busy Radley, were still together at lunch and, with nine wickets in hand, were ideally placed to increase the three runs per over tempo achieved at that stage. Accelerating, they were especially severe on Boock, who lacked the experience and control needed in these circumstances. The third fifty of the innings took only eight overs. A big total now seemed assured, but Gooch (94) and Radley (41) departed in the same over to Cairns and England simply collapsed. They eventually struggled to 206 for eight, and provided a perfect example of how wickets in hand do not always guarantee runs in the book.

Against some good, accurate seam bowling brilliantly supported in the field, New Zealand failed by 19 runs to reach a total that was feasible, but which they never seemed capable of reaching. After a spectacular first over by Wright, their two openers struggled to survive and to score fast enough. Wright and Howarth were beginning to look menacing until the former was superbly run out by Botham, and though Howarth continued to bat with distinction, he received little support until the arrival of Edwards.

Brearley, after one unimpressive over from Miller, and perhaps remembering the earlier savaging of Boock, turned to Gooch, a medium-paced, phantom seamer, as fifth bowler. It proved a wise decision; the Essex man was economical, had Edwards splendidly caught, and Hadlee well stumped down the leg-side.

At 5.30pm, with Howarth still batting well and just joined by Congdon, who had been held back, New Zealand decided to go off for bad light. As well as irritating the crowd, this could have been a mistake, because immediately on resumption, after a delay of nearly 45 minutes, Howarth mis-hooked and departed. With New Zealand well behind the scoring rate, the outcome now looked settled, but such thinking failed to take into account a somewhat improbable stand between Congdon and Cairns. Although this pair never quite promised victory, until Cairns was run out at 173 they did suggest it was almost possible. Congdon was left with time to reach an admirable fifty, which made one question the wisdom of his lowness in the order.

At Manchester on the Monday, England won the second international with ease and by the considerable margin of 126 runs. This handsome victory contained several records and gave England the Prudential series, although the justification for calling two single-innings games a series is hard to fathom. Perhaps it sounds impressive; if one does not think about it as a competition which, apart from the World Cup, has strictly limited

PRUDENTIAL TROPHY 1978
ENGLAND v NEW ZEALAND—1st Match
Played at Scarborough, 15 July
Toss: New Zealand   Result: **England** won by 19 runs
Man of the Match: G. A. Gooch

*captain
†wicket-keeper

ENGLAND			FALL OF WICKETS	
J. M. Brearley*	c Burgess b Boock	31	1st	67
G. A. Gooch	c Parker b Cairns	94	2nd	178
C. T. Radley	c Parker b Cairns	41	3rd	181
D. I. Gower	c Burgess b Cairns	4	4th	185
I. T. Botham	c Anderson b Cairns	3	5th	185
G. R. J. Roope	b Cairns	11	6th	198
G. Miller	c Edwards b Hadlee	2	7th	198
R. W. Taylor†	*lbw* b Hadlee	0	8th	198
J. K. Lever	*not out*	5		
M. Hendrick	*not out*	2		
R. G. D. Willis	*did not bat*			
Extras	(*b* 2, *lb* 10, *w* 1)	13		
TOTAL	(8 wickets – 55 overs)	**206**		

NEW ZEALAND			FALL OF WICKETS	
J. G. Wright	*run out (Botham/Lever)*	18	1st	28
R. W. Anderson	c Taylor b Hendrick	12	2nd	43
G. P. Howarth	c Taylor b Hendrick	42	3rd	51
M. G. Burgess*	b Botham	1	4th	62
J. M. Parker	b Willis	7	5th	91
G. N. Edwards†	c Gower b Gooch	12	6th	97
R. J. Hadlee	st Taylor b Gooch	1	7th	105
B. E. Congdon	*not out*	52	8th	173
B. L. Cairns	*run out (Botham)*	23		
R. O. Collinge	*not out*	5		
S. L. Boock	*did not bat*			
Extras	(*lb* 13, *w* 1)	14		
TOTAL	(8 wickets – 55 overs)	**187**		

NEW ZEALAND	O	M	R	W	ENGLAND	O	M	R	W
Hadlee	11	3	22	2	Willis	11	1	35	1
Collinge	11	0	46	0	Hendrick	11	1	35	2
Cairns	11	3	28	5	Lever	11	2	25	0
Congdon	11	2	25	0	Botham	11	1	43	1
Boock	9	1	57	1	Miller	1	0	6	0
Howarth	2	0	15	0	Gooch	10	1	29	2

Umpires: D. J. Constant and J. G. Langridge
Attendance: 7,565. Receipts: £20,679.

appeal and means little to anybody, apart from the extra cash for players and organisers.

After Gooch had been brilliantly run out for 0, Radley joined his captain, who was again put down early in his innings and eventually caught behind for 27. Radley then found a succession of positive and exciting partners; Gower, Randall, and Botham. They systematically ravished the New Zealand attack, 278 runs coming in 55 overs for the loss of five wickets, and were especially severe on the unfortunate Cairns, whose 11 overs cost no fewer than 84 runs. Radley ran fast and improvised splendidly, Gower flowed, Randall glittered, and Botham hammered – including 22 in Hadlee's final over.

There was no way the New Zealanders were going to score 279 runs against the England attack, and to make matters worse, Parker was unable to bat because of an injured back. Wright gave his team a promising start, and the first fifty came up faster than England's. But the needless running out of Edgar and a fine leg-side stumping of Howarth ignited a disastrous collapse: five wickets tumbled in 12 balls. Only a late, and spectacular, flourish from Cairns enabled his side to reach the comparative respectability of 152. On this occasion Brearley, with a massive total behind him, could afford his spinners, and Edmonds and Miller picked up some wickets.

PRUDENTIAL TROPHY 1978
ENGLAND v NEW ZEALAND—2nd Match
Played at Old Trafford, Manchester, 17 July
Toss: England   Result: **England** won by 126 runs
Man of the Match: C. T. Radley   *captain
Men of the Series: C. T. Radley (E) and B. L. Cairns (NZ)   †wicket-keeper

ENGLAND			FALL OF WICKETS	
J. M. Brearley*	c Edwards b Bracewell	27	1st	0
G. A. Gooch	run out (Collinge/Edwards)	0	2nd	44
C. T. Radley	not out	117	3rd	149
D. I. Gower	run out (Edwards)	50	4th	238
D. W. Randall	run out (Anderson/Edwards)	41	5th	278
I. T. Botham	c Edgar b Hadlee	34		
G. Miller				
R. W. Taylor†				
P. H. Edmonds	did not bat			
J. K. Lever				
R. G. D. Willis				
Extras	(lb 6, w 1, nb 2)	9		
TOTAL	(5 wickets – 55 overs)	**278**		

NEW ZEALAND			FALL OF WICKETS	
J. G. Wright	b Botham	30	1st	44
B. A. Edgar	run out (Gooch)	31	2nd	80
G. P. Howarth	st Taylor b Edmonds	12	3rd	80
G. N. Edwards†	c Randall b Miller	0	4th	84
M. G. Burgess*	c Taylor b Willis	0	5th	84
B. E. Congdon	c Randall b Edmonds	2	6th	85
R. J. Hadlee	c Gower b Miller	1	7th	88
B. L. Cairns	c Botham b Edmonds	60	8th	133
R. O. Collinge	c Gooch b Lever	3	9th	152
B. P. Bracewell	not out	0		
J. M. Parker	absent hurt			
Extras	(b 7, lb 6)	13		
TOTAL	(41.2 overs)	**152**		

NEW ZEALAND	O	M	R	W
Hadlee	11	1	70	1
Collinge	11	0	48	0
Bracewell	11	0	41	1
Congdon	11	2	26	0
Cairns	11	0	84	0

ENGLAND	O	M	R	W
Willis	9	5	21	1
Lever	7	0	28	1
Miller	11	4	27	2
Botham	7	0	24	1
Edmonds	7.2	1	39	3

Umpires: H. D. Bird and B. J. Meyer
Attendance: 15,718 (9,718 paid). Receipts: £23,759.

PRUDENTIAL TROPHY RECORDS 1972–78

*Not out/unbroken

Highest Total	278—5	England v New Zealand	Manchester	1978
Lowest Total	70	Australia v England	Birmingham	1977
Highest Aggregate	531	India (265) v England (266—6)	Leeds	1974
Biggest Victories	8 wkts	West Indies beat England	The Oval	1973
	8 wkts	Pakistan beat England	Birmingham	1974
	132 runs	England beat Pakistan	Manchester	1978
Narrowest Victory	1 wkt	England beat West Indies	Leeds	1973
Highest Score	125*	G. S. Chappell: Australia v England	The Oval	1977
Fastest Hundred	88 balls	M. J. Khan: Pakistan v England	Nottingham	1974
Highest Partnership for each Wicket				
1st 161		D. L. Amiss and J. M. Brearley: England v Australia	The Oval	1977
2nd 148		R. D. Robinson and G. S. Chappell: Australia v England	The Oval	1977
3rd 105		C. T. Radley and D. I. Gower: England v New Zealand	Manchester	1978
4th 105		D. I. Gower and G. R. J. Roope: England v Pakistan	The Oval	1978
5th 64		G. D. Barlow and G. A. Gooch: England v West Indies	Scarborough	1976
6th 42		A. W. Greig and A. P. E. Knott: England v India	Leeds	1974
7th 77		A. W. Greig and A. P. E. Knott: England v Australia	Lord's	1972
8th 68		B. E. Congdon and B. L. Cairns: New Zealand v England	Scarborough	1978
9th 40		R. W. Taylor and D. L. Underwood: England v Pakistan	Birmingham	1974
10th 24		Sikander Bakht and Liaquat Ali: Pakistan v England	Manchester	1978
Best Bowling	5–18	G. J. Cosier: A v E	Birmingham	1977
Most Economical Bowling	11–4–12–1	L. R. Gibbs: W I v E	The Oval	1973
Most Expensive Bowling	11–0–84–0	B. L. Cairns: N Z v E	Manchester	1978
Wicket- Keeping – Most Dismissals				
4 (all ct)		R. W. Marsh: Australia v England	Birmingham	1972
4 (all ct)		A. P. E. Knott: England v New Zealand	Swansea	1973
4 (all ct)		R. W. Marsh: Australia v England	Birmingham	1977
4 (3ct, 1st)		R. D. Robinson: Australia v England	The Oval	1977
Fielding – Most Catches				
3		A. W. Greig: England v West Indies	Leeds	1973
3		B. S. Bedi: India v England	Leeds	1974

TOURISTS' FIRST-CLASS MATCHES AND AVERAGES

RESULTS
Played 16   Won 5   Drew 7   Lost 4

D. H. ROBINS' XI at Eastbourne, 21, 22, 23 (no play) June. Match drawn. New Zealanders 269 (B. A. Edgar 56, M. G. Burgess 50) and 32—1. D. H. Robins' XI 184—6d (G. A. Gooch 57).

SUSSEX at Hove, 24, 26, 27 June. New Zealanders won by 68 runs. New Zealanders 266 (G. N. Edwards 83, G. P. Howarth 78) and 236—5d (B. A. Edgar 74, J. G. Wright 63, M. G. Burgess 51). Sussex 167 (C. P. Phillipson 60, B. E. Congdon 5—40) and 267 (C. P. Phillipson 62).

GLOUCESTERSHIRE at Bristol, 28, 29, 30 June. Match drawn. Gloucestershire 227 (Zaheer Abbas 83) and 207—3d (Zaheer Abbas 121*, D. R. Shepherd 53*). New Zealanders 179—6d (G. P. Howarth 69, M. G. Burgess 56, B. M. Brain 5—48) and 253—6 (R. W. Anderson 122, B. A. Edgar 50).
On 30 June Zaheer Abbas became the first batsman to score 1,000 runs in first-class matches in the 1978 season. He scored a hundred before lunch on the third day (15* to 121*).

SOMERSET at Taunton, 1, 2, 3 July. Match drawn. Somerset 349—5d (P. M. Roebuck 131*, D. Breakwell 100*) and 144—6d. New Zealanders 218—8d (B. A. Edgar 81) and 93—0 (B. A. Edgar 54*).

GLAMORGAN at Swansea, 5, 6, 7 July. Match drawn. Glamorgan 198 (J. A. Hopkins 82, B. L. Cairns 5—51) and 263—8d (J. A. Hopkins 85, M. J. Llewellyn 80, B. L. Cairns 5—87). New Zealanders 235—8d (B. A. Edgar 61) and 98—7.

MIDDLESEX at Lord's, 8, 10, 11 July. New Zealanders won by an innings and 10 runs. Middlesex 133 and 82 (S. L. Boock 5—9, G. N. Edwards held five catches). New Zealanders 225 (J. M. Parker 50).

WARWICKSHIRE at Birmingham, 12, 13, 14 July. New Zealanders won by an innings and 52 runs. Warwickshire 177 (G. W. Humpage 55) and 185 (R. N. Abberley 56, R. J. Hadlee 7—77). New Zealanders 414—4d (B. E. Congdon 110*, J. M. Parker 100*, G. P. Howarth 83, J. G. Wright 61).

SCOTLAND at Broughty Ferry, 19, 20, 21 July. New Zealanders won by an innings and 157 runs. Scotland 190 (J. E. Ker 50) and 125. New Zealanders 472—8d (R. W. Anderson 155, B. A. Edgar 113, R. O. Collinge 63*).

YORKSHIRE at Leeds, 22, 24, 25 July. Match drawn. New Zealanders 263—4d (B. A. Edgar 92, G. P. Howarth 67) and 249—9d (J. G. Wright 111). Yorkshire 281—5d (G. Boycott 103*, J. H. Hampshire 90) and 75—2.

ENGLAND (1st Test) at The Oval, 27, 28, 29, 31 (no play) July, 1 August. England won by 7 wickets. (See match report for full scorecard.)

LANCASHIRE at Manchester, 5, 7, 8 (no play) August. Match drawn. New Zealanders 241—5d (J. M. Parker 104*, R. W. Anderson 59). Lancashire 95—1 (A. Kennedy 53*).

ENGLAND (2nd Test) at Nottingham, 10, 11, 12, 14 August. England won by an innings and 119 runs. (See match report for full scorecard.)

New Zealand opener John Wright in distress after being struck in the throat by a ball from Willis in the tourists' match against Warwickshire. Recovering, he went on to score 61.

YOUNG ENGLAND at Leicester, 16, 17, 18 August. Match drawn. Young England 272—8d (D. I. Gower 108, M. W. Gatting 88) and 235—6d (C. J. Tavaré 83). New Zealanders 240 (B. E. Congdon 58) and 132—1 (R. W. Anderson 58*).

WORCESTERSHIRE at Worcester, 19, 20, 21 August. New Zealanders won by 7 wickets. Worcestershire 193 and 252 (C. N. Boyns 71). New Zealanders 319 (J. G. Wright 65, G. N. Edwards 57, N. Gifford 6—68) and 127—3 (M. G. Burgess 55*).

ENGLAND (3rd Test) at Lord's, 24, 25, 26, 28 August. England won by 7 wickets. (See match report for full scorecard.)

T. N. PEARCE'S XI at Scarborough, 2, 4, 5 September. T. N. Pearce's XI won by 38 runs. T. N. Pearce's XI 274—5d (C. E. B. Rice 90*, B. Dudleston 90, D. W. Randall 61) and 238—6d (B. Dudleston 64, C. E. B. Rice 54*). New Zealanders 246—9d (G. N. Edwards 50, P. Willey 5—65) and 228 (P. Willey 7—73).

D. B. Close, currently professional for Todmorden (Lancashire League), made his only first-class appearance of the season, captained the winning side, scored 8 and 1, and took 1—31 in 8 overs.

The tour also included five non-first-class matches: a two-day match against Minor Counties, a one-day match against Lavinia, Duchess of Norfolk's XI, and three limited-overs games. Losses (4): England (2 Prudential Trophy matches); Minor Counties (by 3 wickets with two balls to spare); and Lavinia, Duchess of Norfolk's XI (by 1 run). Abandoned—rain (1): T. N. Pearce's XI (40 overs).

BATTING AND FIELDING   *Not out

	M	I	NO	HS	Runs	Av	100	50	Ct	St
G. P. Howarth	12	20	2	123	816	45.33	1	5	11	—
B. A. Edgar	15	24	2	113	823	37.40	1	8	20	—
J. M. Parker	12	17	2	104*	549	36.60	2	—	7	1
R. W. Anderson	14	24	3	155	739	35.19	2	2	6	—
B. E. Congdon	13	21	5	110*	556	34.75	1	1	10	—
J. G. Wright	14	24	3	111	675	32.14	1	4	6	—
M. G. Burgess	15	24	1	68	552	24.00	—	5	8	—
R. O. Collinge	6	5	1	63*	91	22.75	—	1	—	—
G. N. Edwards	14	21	3	83	401	22.27	—	3	22	1
G. B. Troup	1	1	0	19	19	19.00	—	—	1	—
B. L. Cairns	11	16	2	41	239	17.07	—	—	7	—
J. M. McIntyre	9	9	4	24*	85	17.00	—	—	3	—
S. L. Boock	13	14	10	14*	57	14.25	—	—	5	—
G. B. Thomson	7	3	2	9	13	13.00	—	—	2	—
R. J. Hadlee	10	13	0	40	149	11.46	—	—	9	—
D. R. Hadlee	1	1	0	8	8	8.00	—	—	—	—
B. P. Bracewell	9	10	3	10*	18	2.57	—	—	4	—
TOTALS	176	247	43	(155)	5,790	28.38	8	29	121	2

BOWLING

	O	M	R	W	Av	BB	5wI	10wM	Balls/ wkt	Runs/ 100b
R. J. Hadlee	280.4	72	714	41	17.41	7–77	2	1	41	42
S. L. Boock	386.3	156	865	39	22.17	5–9	1	—	59	37
B. L. Cairns	370	101	882	35	25.20	5–51	2	1	63	40
B. E. Congdon	288.2	85	650	23	28.26	5–40	1	—	75	38
B. P. Bracewell	221.2	38	694	24	28.91	3–38	—	—	55	52
G. B. Thomson	188	50	521	15	34.73	4–42	—	—	75	46
R. O. Collinge	158	35	455	13	35.00	3–43	—	—	73	48
J. M. McIntyre	204.4	71	546	14	49.00	3–40	—	—	88	44
D. R. Hadlee	16	0	70	1	—	1–70	—	—	96	73
G. P. Howarth	12	2	47	3	—	2–12	—	—	24	65
J. M. Parker	5	1	30	1	—	1–30	—	—	30	100
G. B. Troup	37	6	108	2	—	1–37	—	—	111	49
TOTALS	2,167.3	617	5,582	211	26.45	(7–77)	6	2	62	43

FIVE MONTHS

21 November 1977 – 21 April 1978

Henry Blofeld

In seven and a half weeks between 23 January 1978 and 17 March, I watched all six Test match countries playing Test cricket – something which I doubt has ever before been possible. Furthermore, during this period I also watched two days of Packer 'super-test' cricket in Perth. The international fixture list becomes increasingly congested.

If, in the end, nothing more than a personal record, these seven and a half weeks formed part of as remarkable a winter's cricket as any cricket correspondent or fanatical enthusiast can ever have undertaken. The mass of established Test cricket was unique, but it was, of course, a winter completely dominated by the advent of Kerry Packer's World Series Cricket. The entire cricket world had been thrown into disarray in a manner which had never happened before. The game had been split down the middle; no one who had the faintest notion of the issues involved remained indifferent, and already lifelong friends had become enemies. This is still one of the saddest aspects of World Series Cricket.

I left Heathrow on 21 November, three days before Packer's crowded programme of television matches was due to start at the VFL Park, the Australian (Rules) Football ground at Waverley on the outskirts of Melbourne. In an attempt to adapt cricket for television, the game had been submerged by the razzamatazz of show business in a way which had never happened before.

The arguments for and against the setting-up of World Series Cricket are well enough known not to be repeated here. Maybe there had been some overreaction by the leading protagonists of both sides. WSC was not going to solve the financial problems of cricket overnight or maybe at any time; nor was the presence of WSC going to bring about the immediate or even eventual disintegration of traditional Test cricket. It was certainly a threat to the traditional game, but maybe it would also have beneficial effects.

I was initially hostile to the concept of WSC, for it was undoubtedly a massive asset-stripping operation. Sixty of the game's best players, or greatest assets, had been bought by Packer's organisation in order to set up and make successful a form of cricket which, if it succeeded, could only be to the lasting harm of established Test and first-class cricket. Nonetheless, I arrived in Melbourne at the start of a five-month period in which I was going to write a book about the Packer intrusion, prepared to give both the man and his cricket a chance.

From the moment I stepped out of a car at the VFL Park on 23 November, Packer and his organisation were to be my closest travelling companions; throughout the following months in Australia, in Pakistan, in

Australia again, in New Zealand, and finally in the West Indies. In Australia there was the battle between WSC and the official series between Australia and India; in Pakistan there was the attempt by Packer and certain people who were committed opponents of the Pakistan Board of Control to infiltrate three of Pakistan's WSC players back into the Pakistan side. This almost led to the refusal by the England players to take part in the third Test match in Karachi.

New Zealand was mercifully free from the Packer influence, none of their players having been signed by WSC, although we had our share of dramas there when New Zealand beat England for the first time in a Test match. Finally, the situation in the West Indies was more confused than anywhere else, and in Georgetown the old West Indies side, staffed mainly by Packer players, disintegrated. Lloyd, the captain, resigned and the other Packer players pulled out in sympathy. Packer himself flew to Georgetown, Barbados, and Jamaica and in general terms gained approval from most territories to take his Australian and West Indies sides to the Caribbean in 1979. He drummed up great support for himself from the West Indian public; and by the same token a deep suspicion of the West Indies Board of Control and their motives developed in the same area.

I watched nine days of World Series Cricket in Melbourne and came away certain that, although traditional cricket might suffer because of the opposition, it would not ultimately lose. My first impression of Packer cricket was its complete unreality. Gold, red, and light blue caps made players who were household names seem almost anonymous. Was that really Dennis Lillee in that glittering gold cap? The WSC T-shirts, the sun hats, the huge WSC insignia painted on to the grass behind the stumps at each end for the benefit of the television viewers, the constant assurances by the television commentators that this was the greatest in a way that Muhammad Ali could not have bettered, and the game itself with crash helmets and bouncers and batsmen being interviewed for television as they came out; all this to crowds of less than 3,000. Somehow it was not cricket.

Any venture aimed at defeating established tradition is bound to take time to get off the ground. I may have been guilty of trying to judge too hastily. By the time these words are read, Packer's second season will have run its course in direct opposition to an Ashes series that must be the centrepiece of established cricket. The World Series players are going to be dressed in coloured clothes, and I daresay other gimmicks will have appeared. At the time of writing one can only guess at the outcome, but at the end of it, perhaps we will have a better idea of the ability of WSC to survive. I do not believe that any amount of gimmicks will ever overcome the one permanent defect of this type of cricket; one that was made abundantly clear to me just before lunch on that first day of World Series Cricket on 24 November. Tony Greig, captaining a Rest of the World side, had put an Australian Eleven into bat. Half an hour before lunch he brought on Derek Underwood, and when he had been bowling for twenty minutes Greg Chappell played no stroke at a ball which went on with the bowler's arm and was bowled. As I saw Greg Chappell walk to the pavilion I never thought that, as an Englishman, I could ever have watched that moment with such total and supreme indifference. It simply did not matter; and to my mind no amount of prizemoney was going to make it matter. If the final result was of no importance, its component parts were equally irrelevant.

While the first super-test was in progress in Melbourne, the first Test between Australia and India was taking place at Brisbane. It was a magnificent game of cricket which Australia won by 16 runs on the last day. Bobby Simpson's young Australian side seemed to have captured the imagination of the public and the game had been watched by good crowds.

I heard the final result of this match while flying from Melbourne to Singapore on the way to join the England side in Peshawar on the North-West frontier of Pakistan. The new England side, under Mike Brearley's captaincy, had made a satisfactory start to the tour. They won their provincial match on the charming old army ground in Peshawar, and this was only the second first-class match an England side had won in Pakistan on three tours. Utterly lifeless pitches are a reason for so many drawn matches; so, too, is an attitude of mind in Pakistan which regards defeat by a visiting cricket side as national humiliation and therefore prevents their players from taking even the smallest risk in the hope of winning. Then, there are constant crowd interruptions. The umpires often restart a game as much as seven or eight minutes late after an interval and are not prepared to take action over abysmally slow over-rates. Cricket matches are constantly reaching a stalemate situation.

By the time the England side arrived in Lahore for the first Test match, rumours were flying around that Pakistan were trying to bring their Packer players back from Australia for the three Tests. When the England side went to the Gaddafi Stadium on the first morning of the match, no one could be sure who their opponents would be.

Pakistan's leading players had shown dissent the previous year when they threatened not to play against New Zealand in the second Test in Hyderabad unless they were paid more money. Their anger was aimed at what they considered to be the autocratic way in which Abdul Hafeez Kardar, then president of the Board of Control for Cricket in Pakistan, ran the game. Kardar had seen the players early on the morning the match began, had promised them more money, and went back on his word in Karachi, where the third Test was played. The Board then chose a side to tour Australia and the West Indies, but the government stepped in and the Board was suspended. A new group of selectors was appointed, Mushtaq was reinstated as captain, and a new touring party was chosen.

Although Kardar had given up the presidency of the Board, there was little doubt that he was still the *éminence grise* behind the present Board during the England tour. The enemies of Kardar, who included Hanif Mohammad and Omar Kureishi, were anxious to discredit Kardar and his cronies and to bring back the Packer players from Australia. Packer himself was only too happy to fall in with their plans, for he was desperately anxious that his players should be accepted back into traditional Test cricket. All through his battle with the establishment Packer did his best to split the opposition, and if he could gain recognition by the Pakistan Board – in direct contravention of the agreement of the International Cricket

Conference which had stated that no member country could deal unilaterally with Packer – he would have done just that.

The Packer players did not appear for the first Test, in which England had rather the worst of a drawn match. Haroon Rashid made the first of his two hundreds in the series and looked a wonderfully exciting player, while Mudassar Nazar made the slowest hundred in the history of Test cricket, taking nine hours and seventeen minutes to reach three figures. England were indebted to a painstakingly slow innings by Boycott and then a fine innings of 98 not out by Miller, who failed by two runs to make his first first-class hundred.

Throughout this series the cricket was often incidental to other issues and incidents, and for two days running this first match was interrupted by rioting spectators. On the first occasion the civil police, who seem to be roundly disliked by the public, started it off. Mudassar Nazar was 98 when he played a ball to fine leg and many of the younger members of the crowd came running on to the ground to congratulate him. In fact, the batsmen were only able to run a single, but the spectators were reluctant to leave the field. One policeman, wielding his *lathi* with great hostility, struck a boy as he ran off the field and this incensed the crowd on the popular side of the ground. They poured on to the field and chased the policemen off. Order was restored only when the military police – Pakistan was in a state of Martial Law – arrived on the scene. At no time were the players in any danger.

The riot on the second day was an altogether more sinister affair. Under the terms of Martial Law, public gatherings were forbidden, and therefore a crowd of 30,000 at a Test match was irresistible for the supporters of ex-President Bhutto, in prison being tried for the political murder of an opponent. Mrs Bhutto and her daughter, who had been President of the Union at Oxford University in 1977, arrived at the ground and walked round the back of the stands, and it was no time before the supporters of the two main political parties, the PPP (Bhutto's party) and the PNA were fighting. The disturbance began when rioters burst into the ladies' enclosure and threw their chairs over the fence on to the field of play; soon the battle was being conducted on the playing area. The Test match was abandoned for the day, and for the remaining days of the match the terracing was filled with as many plain-clothed policemen as spectators. It was not an altogether happy atmosphere.

By the time the two sides reassembled in Hyderabad for the second Test, the Chief Martial Law Administrator, General Zia-Ul-Haq, had been made aware of the warring elements in Pakistan's cricket administration, and on the rest day of this match he called a meeting at Rawalpindi, where the state of cricket in the country was discussed. The details of the meeting were not readily available and there were sharply conflicting stories.

After the meeting Omar Kureishi and his group made contact with the Packer organisation, the result being that Mushtaq, Zaheer, and Imran arrived in Karachi to play in the third Test. However, this is getting ahead of the story, for England were hard-pressed to avoid defeat in Hyderabad. Haroon Rashid made another hundred, by some distance the best innings I

saw in Pakistan and one which showed that players of the highest class can
overcome the conditions. Indeed, it was an innings which made his
subsequent failures in England in 1978 appear all the more staggering.
England were then dismissed by the leg-breaks of Abdul Qadir, who bowled
quite beautifully, and if Wasim Bari had not delayed his declaration for so
long in Pakistan's second innings I think Qadir would have won the match
for Pakistan. As it was Boycott and Brearley batted England to safety on the
last day, but Pakistan were nearer to victory than the scores suggest.

From Hyderabad, England went to Bahawalpur and then to Lahore for
the last of the one-day internationals before going on to Karachi for the
third Test. By the time they reached Lahore, Mushtaq, Imran, and Zaheer
were in Karachi. Omar Kureishi had flown to Singapore where he had met
Kerry Packer and had given him an assurance that these three would play in
the Test match.

Four of the England side – Boycott, Willis, Old, and Randall – had been
approached by Packer and had turned him down. Now they and the rest of
the England party felt strongly that these three should not play in the third
Test. After consultations by telephone with Lord's they issued a statement
expressing their views in strong terms, saying that they were not only
concerned about the present series but also about Australia's in the West
Indies the coming March. (The West Indies Board had already said they
would play their Packer signings.)

The England side played a one-day game in Karachi before the third Test,
and while batting Brearley had his arm broken by Sikander Bakht. He
returned immediately to England for medical attention, but before leaving –

*The moment that ended Mike Brearley's tour of Pakistan. His arm was broken after being struck
by a rising ball from Sikander Bakht in a one-day match at Karachi.*

Zaheer Abbas, one of three WSC players flown to Karachi for the third Pakistan-England Test, participated only as a spectator, though the role had attractions.

that same night – he read out the players' statement at a press conference and announced that Boycott would take on the captaincy. He also disclosed that Radley was flying as a replacement to Karachi from Sydney where, ironically, he was coaching in a scheme set up by none other than Kerry Packer.

The situation simmered on for two days. It was also ironical that Boycott, whose oft-stated ambition had been to captain England, now found that in all probability he might not have a team to captain in his first Test as such. There were constant calls to Lord's, and the tour selectors refused to announce the England side until the morning of the match. I believe that if the Packer players had been in the Pakistan side, the England players would not have taken part. However, the situation was averted when, at 10.15 the night before the match, the president of the Pakistan Board called a press conference in his room at the Intercontinental Hotel and a statement was read in which it was stated categorically that Pakistan would not choose their Packer players, then or at any time in the future.

The Chief Martial Law Administrator was in Karachi and had been fully briefed, and he was no doubt responsible for this statement. Kardar was thought to have the ear of the general and he would have been extremely hostile to the Packer players. He was, in fact, in the next room while this statement was being read.

The Test match, therefore, went on, and it turned out to be one of the dullest games of cricket possible to imagine. No more than 170 runs were scored on any of the five days and perhaps the issues that immediately preceded the match swamped the actual cricket. After these dramatic events Pakistan's position seemed clear enough; but after their defeat in England during 1978, the Board was again disbanded, new selectors were chosen, and the Packer players were back in the Pakistan side for the series against India late in 1978.

Perth, at the end of January, made a strong contrast as I prepared to watch two more days of super-test cricket. The World Series players were beside themselves with anger at the way in which the England players had threatened not to play in Karachi if the Packer players were selected by Pakistan. There was particular hostility towards Boycott, who had written a contentious article in a Sydney newspaper; and who had, of course, himself withdrawn his services from the England side for three years.

This super-test came immediately after the two 'days' of night cricket in Melbourne which had been WSC's most successful outing so far and had, in the eyes of Australians, established their credibility. It had made exciting television and had been a success. On one night they had attracted a crowd of more than 24,000, their best of the season. The white ball against the black sightscreen was also a success, and WSC were generally much more buoyant than when I had left them in Melbourne.

Nonetheless, the inherent weakness in their cricket remained. It was played between non-representative sides and therefore there was nothing with which spectators could identify. On the first day of this match the Rest of the World made more than 400 for the loss of one wicket: Barry Richards 207, Gordon Greenidge retired hurt with 114, and Viv Richards 70 not out at the end of the day. Viv Richards went on to 170 the next day, and the day after that Greg Chappell also made 170. Arguably the three greatest batsmen in the world had all passed 170, and yet the crowd did not exceed 4,000 on any day of the match. Because the authorities had prevented Packer from using the Western Australia Cricket Association ground, he had requisitioned Gloucester Park, the trotting track just across the road from the WACA. It had been turned into an extremely pleasant ground, but the citizens of Perth were unimpressed.

After two days in Perth I travelled to Adelaide to watch the last four days of the fifth, and deciding, Test match between Australia and India, the sides having won two matches each before the start. The game was played to a thrilling finish with Australia winning by 47 runs after India had been set to score 493 in the fourth innings and had come agonisingly close to an incredible victory. Moreover, it was watched by good crowds, and there was no doubt that established cricket had won the first round against its hybrid opponent.

A thrilling series against India may have been made possible by the very fact of Packer, for had Lillee, Greg Chappell, and company played for Australia, India's task would probably have been quite hopeless. As it was, the cricket may have been of a lower standard, but because of the closeness of the series this was of no importance. It gave the public more pleasure than Packer cricket, which may have had a higher standard of play but no meaning.

It was refreshing to arrive in New Zealand and to find oneself free from the pressures of Packer cricket for the first time since leaving England. In Pakistan, England had not really answered the problems thrown up by the defection of Greig, Knott, Underwood, and Woolmer. Bob Taylor was undoubtedly the finest wicket-keeper in the world, but Edmonds had still not found the consistency a left-arm spinner needs, although he had bowled beautifully in the last Test in Karachi. Randall had had a poor tour, Rose did not seem to be quite a Test cricketer, and Roope had been in desperate trouble against the spin in Pakistan. Botham had not had a good winter either. He had been ill at the wrong time in Pakistan, and then was unlikely to win back a place in the Test side in conditions that suited spin rather than seam. By the time they reached New Zealand England were still an extremely vulnerable side.

The first Test was played in Wellington, and on a damp green pitch England were beaten by New Zealand for the first time; and deservedly so. It was a fast bowler's pitch and Richard Hadlee bowled decisively for New Zealand. In a low-scoring match Wright batted with great concentration for New Zealand and Boycott spent seven and a half hours over 77 in England's first innings. For all that, this innings may have been counter-productive to England's cause. Being so much the best batsman in the match, Boycott should have been prepared to think rather more in terms of attack, especially with a weak batting side behind him. As it was, his colleagues, seeing him make it look so difficult, may understandably have felt, when their turns came, that they had little or no chance before leaving the pavilion.

Yet England had to score only 137 in the final innings to win, Boycott having won the toss and put New Zealand into bat. Once again Hadlee, some of whose antics suggested he had been watching too much of Lillee, was too much for the batsmen after Boycott had driven over the top of a half-volley from Collinge.

The match was not without a strong element of controversy, for the umpiring seemed at times to be questionable. The New Zealand umpires are remarkably reluctant to give a batsman out leg before wicket, and after the first day's play Boycott sought a meeting with the umpires and voiced his objections. The result appeared to be that they panicked and erred in the opposite direction for the rest of the match. They were wrong to allow Boycott to talk to them in this way.

There was also trouble with the fast bowlers' follow-throughs. Collinge was guilty when New Zealand were bowling and Botham was at fault for England. They were both allowed to follow-through on the pitch without being warned, and this undoubtedly affected its condition. Weak umpiring often causes friction between sides and the legacy of this match was unfortunately felt for most of the series.

The second Test was played in Christchurch, where England won by 174 runs and Botham really announced himself as a genuine Test all-rounder. There was no doubt about his bowling, but now he made a magnificent hundred in the first innings and went on to hold some remarkable catches close to the wicket in addition to taking eight wickets. Edmonds also played a splendid innings, of 50, and showed that if he paid more attention to his ·

batting he should score more runs for England and Middlesex. His bowling, too, was good and he began to show the control that had sometimes been missing in Pakistan.

One unfortunate incident in this match came when, in England's innings, Euan Chatfield ran out Derek Randall for backing up too far. It was a shabby gesture on Chatfield's part; and as the television film showed later, at the moment Chatfield's arm came over Randall's bat was still in the crease. Chatfield then checked himself to take off the bails while Randall continued the momentum of his walk and was narrowly run out. There was no question of Randall trying to steal an unfair advantage.

The third Test was played at Auckland and there, in his second Test match, Radley made 158, an innings which was to establish him in the England side. It was not his best innings by any means and he made a bad start, but he had compiled a large score when, for most of the past four months, one had continually been complaining that England's batsmen were getting themselves out for scores of between 20 and 30. Radley may not be an ideal answer to England's problems, but there are no ideal answers about and at least he sells his wicket dearly; which is more than can be said for some.

Geoff Howarth made a hundred in each innings for New Zealand, batting extremely well and in so doing showed how disappointing his results had been for such a talented cricketer. When England left New Zealand, one felt that real progress had been made in their search for replacements for their Packer players and that there was every reason for England to face the future with optimism.

I left Auckland for London via Sydney, Singapore, and Bahrain, and after two days at home I flew to Barbados to watch the second Test between West Indies and Australia. I also saw the third in Guyana and the fourth in Trinidad. The non-Packer Australians had already had a desperately unlucky start to their tour. In the first Test, in Trinidad, they had been put in to bat on a wet pitch and found West Indies' fast bowlers altogether too much for them. They lost easily. It had not been an entirely happy match. Douglas Sang Hue, for a long time the West Indies' leading umpire and who had stood for Packer's WSC in Australia in the preceding months, had angered the Australians with his decisions, and they asked the West Indian authorities that he should not stand again in the series.

The Australians moved to Barbados for the second Test, and it was during this match that the trouble – which eventually led to Clive Lloyd's resignation and the refusal of the other Packer players to take part in the third Test in Georgetown – began to build up.

The Test ended in three days with a win for West Indies by nine wickets, but it contained some of the best cricket I saw all winter. Before the match, Jeff Thomson had said that if Australia were to make any headway, he would have to do it for them. Thomson could not have given Simpson more support as vice-captain than he did in the West Indies, and in conversation he made several interesting comparisons between the cricket he played under Ian Chappell and under Bobby Simpson. They made his eventual decision to defect to Packer in October 1978 all the more surprising.

Australia, put in to bat, started well, Graeme Wood showing that he would get into just about any Test side in the world at any time as an opening batsman. But they were without Toohey, who broke his jaw in the first Test, and after a reasonable start they collapsed against the pace of Roberts and Daniel. West Indies began their first innings soon after tea on the first day, and for the last 75 minutes of play Thomson produced the most inspiring piece of fast bowling I have ever seen. In this time he took three wickets for 40 in 6.5 overs, and if luck – even justice – had been on his side he might have had six or seven wickets. He panicked the strong West Indies batting line-up, and this was more true of Viv Richards than anyone else.

Thomson finished with six wickets for 77, but West Indies built a lead of 38 and Australia, bowled out for 178 in their second innings, again found the pace too much for them. Wood made his second fifty of the match and confirmed all the impressions made on the first day. On the third afternoon West Indies had to score 141, and with Greenidge batting beautifully they lost only one wicket in the process.

A week before this match began, the West Indian Packer players had, through their spokesman Deryck Murray, been asked by Jeff Stollmeyer, chairman of the West Indies Board of Control, if they were available for West Indies' tour of India and Sri Lanka which began on 11 November 1978. They were given two weeks to reply and were told that if no answer was forthcoming it would be assumed they were unavailable. Murray immediately contacted the Packer organisation in Australia, with the result that, during the second Test match, two of Packer's colleagues, Austin Robertson – who along with John Cornell had helped develop the original idea – and a solicitor named Turnbull, arrived in Bridgetown for talks with various of the players already signed for Packer.

The West Indies Board had been the only one prepared to continue playing their Packer players, but their sympathy for Packer was tested just before the first Test when, led by the Packer element, the West Indies players said they would not play unless they received a massive increase in pay. They received most of what they asked for. Sensing the new danger, the Board summoned the five players in the side who were not contracted to Packer – Kallicharran, Parry, Croft, Haynes, and Austin – to a meeting and received a verbal assurance from all five that they would not consider signing for Packer if approached before the start of the third Test in Georgetown. By this time, it was thought, the West Indies Board would have come forward with greatly improved terms.

It seemed that they were safe. But the day after the Bridgetown Test ended it was revealed that Croft, Haynes, and Austin had signed for Packer in spite of the undertaking they had given the Board. Packer now controlled 18 of the West Indies' best players. Not surprisingly, the Board were shaken; and perhaps for the first time realised the true nature of their opponent, whom they had tried hard to accommodate.

Packer's thoughts seemed clear enough. With 18 players he must have felt certain that the West Indies Board would feel obliged to do a deal with him over the release of their players if they were going to carry out their tour to India. They would, therefore, have dealt with him unilaterally and the opposition would again have been split. If, on the other hand, he alienated all the support he had in the West Indies he himself would fly to the Caribbean – as he eventually did – and go over the heads of the cricket authorities to the politicians to obtain agreement in principle to bring his World Series Cricket to the Caribbean. (A tour was later planned for early 1979.)

During the Australians' game against Guyana, some of the anti-Packer, pro-Packer feeling crept on to the field when Croft broke Yallop's jaw and then laid out Yardley with a vicious bouncer that hit him on the head. The West Indies selectors came to Georgetown during that match to pick their side for the third Test. At their meeting, to which Clive Lloyd as captain was co-opted, it was agreed in principle that, with the Indian tour coming up and the availability of the Packer players still uncertain, although the deadline had passed, they would use the last three Tests to give young, untried players Test match experience.

Lloyd agreed to this, but when the meeting broke up in the early hours of the morning he found that he was being asked to agree to the dropping of Deryck Murray, his vice-captain and confidante, Haynes and Austin. He objected strongly and then announced that he would resign from the captaincy. He confirmed this to the press the next day, without telling his own Board, and a phoney war existed for a day or two until, 36 hours before the match, it was announced that the other Packer players would pull out in support.

The West Indies selectors had then to pick a largely untried side which they had already brought to Georgetown lest this should happen. The following day, the day before the match, Packer himself flew into Georgetown in a private jet and endless meetings and press conferences spelled out the dramas.

It was feared that the public in Guyana, who have been restless at other Test matches, might protest; but in fact this was a marvellous game of cricket, played out peacefully before one of the fairest crowds I have ever seen. It was a tremendous credit to Guyana. Australia won by three wickets, Wood and Serjeant making splendid hundreds after Australia, requiring 359 to win, had lost three wickets for 22 in the final innings. Alvin Greenidge (no relation to Gordon although from Barbados), Basil Williams (Jamaica), Larry Gomes (Trinidad and formerly of Middlesex), and Norbert Phillip (Windward Island and now of Essex) were the outstanding players in the new West Indies side. There was no doubt to my mind that in two or three years, with experience, these players would develop into another formidable West Indies side.

All through these days of turmoil, the Australian management of Fred Bennett and captain Bobby Simpson kept wonderfully calm. They viewed the arrival of Packer with suspicion, feeling I am sure that he would tell his players what to do and therefore dictate to the West Indies Board which side to pick. The Australian Board had taken an uncompromising attitude to Packer and felt that if this happened the West Indies would be letting them down.

While Packer went on to Barbados, where he collected all his players and principal supporters to the Sandy Lane Hotel for a two-day reunion, the teams moved on from Guyana and gathered again in the middle of April for the fourth Test in Trinidad. Here, public opinion was deeply opposed to the West Indies Board and an action group had been formed to boycott the Test. As a result, the beautiful Queen's Park Oval was almost completely empty.

The home authority lost a great deal of money, for Queen's Park Oval is their only big ground and they desperately need big gates for the two Tests traditionally played there. Furthermore, there was an unreal atmosphere to this match, which ended in victory for West Indies after the Australian batsmen had panicked against the none-too-frightening off-spin of Parry on a pitch which, as always happens at Port-of-Spain, was taking a good deal of spin. West Indies thus won the rubber, which in terms of appeasing public opinion was probably the best result. But I could not help feeling sorry for the Australians. They had been under tremendous pressure throughout the tour and had come through it splendidly. I felt they deserved at least to draw the series.

I flew back to London from Trinidad to finish my book about the Packer Affair and to collect my thoughts on an astonishing five months of cricket. The Australians went on to Kingston, Jamaica, where, after more umpiring controversy over Sang Hue, the Test ended with a riot on the fifth day when Australia seemed the likely winners. The two umpires refused to make up the time lost on an unscheduled sixth day – as happened in the Test against Cowdrey's side in 1967–68 – and so the game ended in a draw. It was a sad end to a sad series.

When I left England on 21 November, I did not have the smallest idea where Packer would lead; when I returned on 21 April I was not much the wiser. But I was sure of one thing; namely that Packer would fight to the end to beat the authorities and to make his cricket work. He is an opponent who must never be underestimated, and this is surely the one undeniable fact that the story of these five months makes clear.

A RIVALRY RENEWED

Pakistan v India 1978–79

Patrick Eagar

Last autumn Pakistan achieved revenge for their defeat by India in the first series between the two countries 25 years earlier. A long time to wait. The other two series had been shared with 10 draws in 10 matches. This time Pakistan ensured success by recalling their Packer players, by preparing an unusually grassy wicket at Lahore, and by achieving the first-ever Test result, other than on a matting surface, at Karachi.

The first Test was at Faisalabad, a small, dusty town some 60 miles from Lahore. Hyderabad, venue of the second Test against England earlier in the year, was not included. Perhaps the success of the Pakistani spinner Abdul Qadir during that Test had something to do with it. He took six for 44 in England's first innings and the Pakistanis were not going to risk letting the Indian spinners loose on a wicket that might take spin.

Pakistan had little trouble in amassing 503 for eight, thanks largely to an imperial innings by Zaheer and a dogged one by Miandad. Zaheer had, until this series, a dismal record in Pakistan and this was his first Test century on home soil. India, undaunted by the size of their target, made 462 for nine in reply, thanks largely to Gavaskar and Viswanath. However, by this stage the proceedings had taken the best part of four days and the two sides were heading for the thirteenth draw in the 16 matches they had ever played against each other.

At Lahore, two pitches awaited the tourists. One, a typical Pakistani wicket, looked dead a day before the Test began. The other was noticeably greener. The Maharaja of Baroda, the Indian manager, was still wondering the evening before the Test which of the two wickets would be used.

The Pakistanis, not surprisingly, opted for the greener of the two, and India lost the toss. At 49 for four things were going badly enough for the Indians, but then the luckless Mohinder Amarnath was laid out by a bouncer from Imran and carried motionless from the ground. He returned later, only to be dismissed by another bouncer, this time from Sarfraz, as he trod on his wicket attempting to hook. India struggled to 199. The Pakistani innings was notable for night-watchman Wasim Bari's highest score in Test cricket and another elegant display from Zaheer, whose 235 not out was his third Test double century. Pakistan eventually declared at 539 for six, equalling India's highest score at Madras in 1960–61. The rivalry between the two countries is so acute that Mushtaq came in for a degree of local criticism for his premature declaration.

India at one time looked as if they would again provide one of their famous rearguard actions to save the Test. Both Gavaskar (97) and Chauhan (93) were perhaps unlucky to be given out. Viswanath stayed and

Above: The luckless Mohinder Amarnath, hooking at Sarfraz, steps back on his wicket.

Below: India's Sunil Gavaskar moves Miandad; Wasim Bari and Sarfraz follow the ball.

contributed 83, which together with an entertaining 43 from Kapil Dev, India's 19-year-old new fast bowler, should have been enough. However, Viswanath lost concentration and was bowled by, of all people, Mudassar Nazar. The vulnerable Indian tail then collapsed, leaving Pakistan to get 126 to win. This they achieved against the clock despite much time-wasting gamesmanship from Bedi.

India should have felt safe enough at Karachi, for apart from one Test on a matting wicket there had never been a result there. Bedi won the toss and Gavaskar batted well for his century but obtained little support. Kapil Dev, coming in at number 9 made an exhilarating 59 and was rapidly assuming the title of all-rounder. Ghavri had also done his best to hold the Indian tail together, but eventually they were all out for 344. Pakistan put in a good team effort to make 481, only two of their players failing to get into the twenties but only Miandad making a century.

Crowd interruptions were a constant problem, as is often the case in Pakistan when the spectators get bored. The police had to lay on one *lathi* charge and it is reported that some tear-gas was used on the third day.

India's second innings' 300, which again relied heavily on Gavaskar (137), should have been enough to draw the match. On the last evening Pakistan were faced with 164 runs in 26 overs – nearly 6.5 per over – but in this age of one-day cricket, and with a Pakistan side packed with experts in this field, it was an interesting challenge. Majid Khan and Asif Iqbal opened, and it is to India's credit that such a formidable pair should have fallen behind the clock. However, where Kapil Dev and Ghavri had succeeded, Bedi blundered. He put himself on to bowl against Imran who, with eight wickets in hand, could afford to have a swing. Swing he did, taking 18 runs off one over. Miandad (63) and Imran (31) took Pakistan to victory with seven balls to spare.

As with most Test series over the past year, Kerry Packer's influence was felt. Two of his players, Imran and Mushtaq, seemed to take every possible opportunity to wear their WSC shirts with the Packer symbol clearly visible, and one of his men, Lynton Taylor, watched the whole Lahore match from the refuge of the Pakistani dressing-room. Throughout the series Sarfraz and Imran, in particular, tended to overdo the bouncer – another by-product of Packer cricket. This aspect was noticeable earlier in the year when Packer's West Indians outplayed Australia in the Caribbean. It is almost as if the bouncer has become the fast bowler's stock ball, with the good-length delivery reserved as a surprise weapon.

The series as a whole had an historic aspect. This was the first time the two countries had met for 17 years, and it was the encouragement needed for the governments to ease border restrictions. Normally it would take at least several months for an Indian to obtain a visa to visit Pakistan. For this series, and in particular at Lahore, a Test match ticket was all that was needed for a visa to be granted. The Indian border is a mere half-hour drive from the Gadaffi Stadium in Lahore – along a narrow road which spreads through the dusty city outskirts, past the famous Shalimar Gardens and numerous animal markets, then out into the countryside with brick kilns every few hundred yards. Finally, after a village on this main road, the

An historic moment for four Sikhs from Amritsar, returning to the land of their forebears on a one-day visa issued for the second Pakistan-India Test at Lahore.

kilometer posts to the border reach zero. There, on each day of the Test, a number of Indians, the Sikhs among them conspicuous in their turbans, would pass through the customs channels marked 'Test ticket holders only'. They had all come from the Indian town of Amritsar, half an hour on the far side of the border. For many this was their first visit to the town of their birth since Partition, and there were many young people clutching sketch maps drawn by their fathers from memory of 30 years before. All, Indians and Pakistanis, were surprised to rediscover that they had only a religion between them. The almost common languages of Urdu and Hindi were enough to ensure that new friendships were made as late-night conversations continued into the small hours.

Pakistan may have righted an old score, but at the individual level, at least, the two countries must surely have drawn together just a little.

Right: The hirsute Mike Selvey turned in a series of magnificent performances for Middlesex in 1978 and was rewarded with a total of 101 wickets for the first-class season.

THE COUNTY COMPETITIONS 1978

SCHWEPPES CHAMPIONSHIP 1978

The Schweppes Championship was won by Kent, despite a splendid fight by Essex, a late run by Middlesex, who lost too many key players to England, and the efforts of Somerset, who could claim to have been just about the unluckiest team of the year ever. Obviously Kent's success owed much to WSC, which was responsible for them having three internationals in their side for the entire summer, and it was significant that Underwood's remarkable 110 wickets cost only 14 runs apiece. This great left-arm spinner not surprisingly proved the decisive factor in the race for the title. In three-day cricket, bowlers who take wickets are vital, even if their importance has been reduced to some extent by the artificial first innings limitation. It is also interesting to note than another Kent Packer signing, Woolmer, finished second in the national bowling averages. However, his haul of wickets was only 20 and therefore was of no great significance.

Among the most encouraging features of the summer were the improved form shown by Yorkshire, whose rise from twelfth to fourth was obtained without the assistance of an overseas player, and the considerable number of promising young batsmen who substantiated their claims with runs in the middle. However, before going into raptures about the deeds of the likes of Tavaré, Roebuck, Sharp, Larkins, Bainbridge, Hopkins, K.D. Smith, Gatting and many more, it would be wise to examine some of the county attacks.

It would be necessary to go back to the years immediately following the last war to find quite so many anaemic bowling sides. Any batsman must have fancied his chances of scoring runs against Glamorgan, Hampshire, Northamptonshire, Warwickshire, or Worcestershire, and he should not have been too worried by the prospect, in fact ought to have relished the opportunity, of going to the crease against Somerset and Gloucestershire once the shine was off the ball. Derbyshire, without Hendrick and Miller, and Nottinghamshire, minus Rice and Hadlee, looked friendly enough, while it is hard to imagine any of the Yorkshire bowlers, other than Old, commanding a regular place in any of their strong sides. The Surrey bowling, apart from two members, lacked bite. There were only six counties with good, reasonably well-balanced attacks. It certainly cannot be a bad era in which to be a batsman, though it should be stressed that the fielding and catching have improved. This means that 'lives' are fewer, and the prevention of what in the past would have been certain runs is more frequent.

In addition to the high standard of the fielding throughout the clubs, the wicket-keeping is extremely good. Just as no team can afford an indifferent 'keeper at soccer, no team can afford a poor wicket-keeper. Although there appears to be no immediate successor to Taylor and Knott, there has been talk that he might come from Lancashire, Gloucestershire, Surrey, or Kent.

Although it was a most encouraging season for home-grown talent, at long last, some 10 years too late, the TCCB have woken to the obvious fact that a surfeit of overseas cricketers on the county circuit must automatically have an adverse effect on our own players. It would be most unwise to believe the renaissance of English cricket has taken place, but almost certainly it has started. However, if the future is bright, possibly even brilliant, the present is no more than utilitarian, as can be seen from the touring party for Australia. Only one of the six specialist batsmen, Boycott, had scored more than 1,000 runs in Test cricket.

The way the players from abroad continue to dominate the game at home is also very revealing. Of the 17 first-class counties, 16 at present have overseas cricketers under contract, although under the new ruling only two can be included at a time, except in special circumstances. In 10 clubs in 1978, the player with the highest aggregate was an import, and in 11 clubs overseas players topped the batting averages while another eight occupied second or third place.

It might be argued that the aggregate is unfair because the best native batsmen, apart from those under contract to WSC, were on Test duty and therefore could not have obtained so many runs for their county. The weakness of such an argument is that the figures of the current England players, apart from Boycott, are unremarkable, and that 11 counties have an overseas batsman who, if qualified, would walk into our national team on ability. Brearley and company have beaten Australia, New Zealand, and Pakistan, the latter without their best players. The really big question is how well would they fare, especially the batsmen, against West Indies, or even South Africa, whose players have recently been even more successful for their adopted counties than the Caribbean mercenaries?

Groome on the attack for Sussex at The Oval. Richards and Roope are Surrey's fielders.

SCHWEPPES COUNTY CHAMPIONSHIP 1978 FINAL TABLE

	P	W	L	D	Bonus Points Batting	Bonus Points Bowling	Total Points
1 **Kent** (1)	22	13	3	6	56	80	292
2 Essex (6)	22	12	1	9	55	74	273
3 Middlesex (1)	21	11	5	5	48	75	255
4 Yorkshire (12)	22	10	3	9	58	55	233
5 Somerset (4)	22	9	4	9	44	76	228
6 Leicestershire (5)	22	4	5	13	57	68	173
7 Nottinghamshire (17)	22	3	7	12	63	67	166
8 Hampshire (11)	21	4	6	11	53	60	161
9 Sussex (8)	22	4	7	11	43	66	151*
10 Gloucestershire (3)	21	4	8	9	42	55	145
11 Warwickshire (10)	22	4	5	13	39	56	143
12 Lancashire (16)	21	4	8	9	29	64	135*
13 Glamorgan (14)	22	3	8	11	43	54	133
14 Derbyshire (7)	22	3	7	12	33	63	132
15 Worcestershire (13)	22	2	5	15	56	51	131
16 Surrey (14)	22	3	7	12	36	58	130
17 Northamptonshire (9)	20	2	6	12	41	56	121

Figures in brackets show the 1977 positions.
*Total excludes six points deducted by TCCB for breach of regulations governing players' registration.
Three matches were abandoned without a ball being bowled and are excluded from the above table: Gloucestershire v Northamptonshire at Bristol and Middlesex v Hampshire at Lord's on May 3, 4, 5, and Lancashire v Northamptonshire at Manchester on September 6, 7, 8.

RESULTS
Figures in brackets after each county in the result line show the total number of points gained from that match, followed by a breakdown of bonus points, e.g. Surrey (19:3/4) shows that Surrey gained 19 points from the match: 12 for winning, plus 3 batting bonus points, plus 4 bowling bonus points. Bonus points are awarded as follows during the first 100 overs of each first innings:

BATTING	POINTS	BOWLING
150—199 runs	*1*	*3 or 4 wickets taken*
200—249 runs	*2*	*5 or 6 wickets taken*
250—299 runs	*3*	*7 or 8 wickets taken*
300 runs and over	*4*	*9 or 10 wickets taken*

*Denotes a not out innings or unbroken partnership.

3, 4, 5 May
DERBYSHIRE (4:1/3) drew with SOMERSET (4:0/4) at Burton upon Trent. No play possible on third day. Derbyshire 192. Somerset 84–8.

GLAMORGAN (0) drew with WORCESTERSHIRE (1:1/0) at Cardiff. No play possible on first and third days. Worcestershire 194–1 (G. M. Turner 97*, P. A. Neale 78*).

GLOUCESTERSHIRE (0) v NORTHAMPTONSHIRE (0) at Bristol. Match abandoned without a ball being bowled.

LANCASHIRE (6:2/4) drew with SUSSEX (6:2/4) at Manchester. No play possible on third day. Sussex 223 (Imran Khan 72, D. P. Hughes 5–46) and 25–0. Lancashire 213 (C. H. Lloyd 114*, F. C. Hayes 50, G. G. Arnold 7–44).

LEICESTERSHIRE (3:3/0) drew with ESSEX (1:0/1) at Leicester. No play possible on third day. Leicestershire 250–4d (B. Dudleston 75, B. F. Davison 60). Essex 51–1.

MIDDLESEX (0) v HAMPSHIRE (0) at Lord's. Match abandoned without a ball being bowled.

WARWICKSHIRE (0) drew with SURREY (0) at Birmingham. No play possible on first day. Single innings match begun with less than 8 hours remaining. Surrey 247–5d (G. R. J. Roope 59, G. P. Howarth 54, Younis Ahmed 54). Warwickshire 20–2.

YORKSHIRE (2:2/0) drew with KENT (3:0/3) at Leeds. No play possible on third day. Yorkshire 222–8 closed (100 overs) (G. Boycott 61).

Surrey's John Edrich, batting against Sussex early in the season. Though he took his tally of first-class hundreds to 103, he generally experienced a summer of mixed fortune.

10, 11, 12 May

ESSEX (18:2/4) beat MIDDLESEX (4:0/4) by 109 runs at Chelmsford. Essex 228 (K. S. McEwan 81, J. E. Emburey 5–76) and 182 (K. W. R. Fletcher 76). Middlesex 141 (R. E. East 6–66) and 160 (G. D. Barlow 62, C. T. Radley 61).

KENT (20:4/4) beat HAMPSHIRE (5:3/2) by 4 wickets at Canterbury. Hampshire 282–9 closed (100 overs) (C. G. Greenidge 76) and 135. Kent 307–5d (A. G. E. Ealham 102*, C. J. Tavaré 88, R. A. Woolmer 59) and 113–6 (J. W. Southern 5–61).

DERBYSHIRE (18:2/4) beat LANCASHIRE (2:0/2) by 9 wickets at Manchester. Lancashire 138 (G. Miller 5–43) and 168 (C. H. Lloyd 55). Derbyshire 257 (G. Miller 95) and 53–1.

SOMERSET (17:3/2) beat GLAMORGAN (7:3/4) by 9 wickets at Taunton. Glamorgan 263–6 closed (100 overs) (A. Jones 102, M. J. Llewellyn 73) and 165 (P. D. Swart 58, M. A. Nash 55, I. T. Botham 6–66). Somerset 287 (D. J. S. Taylor 78, D. Breakwell 50*, G. Richards 5–55) and 145–1 (B. C. Rose 51*) *M. A. Nash hit four successive balls from D. Breakwell for six in the second innings.*

SURREY (6:2/4) drew with SUSSEX (5:1/4) at The Oval. Surrey 201–9 closed (100 overs)

(R. D. V. Knight 55) and 195 (G. P. Howarth 97, J. R. T. Barclay 5–72). Sussex 186 (J. J. Groome 50, P. I. Pocock 5–74) and 206–8 (Imran Khan 69).

WARWICKSHIRE (18:4/2) beat YORKSHIRE (5:4/1) by 34 runs at Birmingham. Warwickshire 307–4 closed (100 overs) (D. L. Amiss 127) and 139 (G. B. Stevenson 5–60). Yorkshire 302–6 closed (100 overs) (G. Boycott 115, J. H. Hampshire 73) and 110 (D. J. Brown 5–53).

WORCESTERSHIRE (4:4/0) drew with NOTTING-HAMSHIRE (7:3/4) at Worcester. Nottinghamshire 272–1 closed (100 overs) (M. J. Harris 148*, P. A. Todd 58) and 262–7d (C. E. B. Rice 56, M. J. Harris 53, J. D. Birch 52*). Worcestershire 312–9 closed (100 overs) (P. A. Neale 68) and 45–1.

24, 25, 26 May

GLOUCESTERSHIRE (5:3/2) drew with WORCES-TERSHIRE (8:4/4) at Bristol. Worcestershire 306–5 closed (100 overs) (J. A. Ormrod 160*, G. M. Turner 76) and 221–4d (J. A. Ormrod 88*, P. A. Neale 79*). Gloucestershire 253 (D. R. Shepherd 64, Zaheer Abbas 60, M. D. Partridge 50) and 184–7 (A. W. Stovold 61, A. Tait 53, A. P. Pridgeon 5–48)

HAMPSHIRE (19:3/4) beat SURREY (7:3/4) by 3

wickets at Portsmouth. Surrey 265 (D. M. Smith 115, R. P. Baker 91, K. Stevenson 5–72) and 113 (J. W. Southern 5–45). Hampshire 278 (B. A. Richards 73, C. G. Greenidge 70, P. I. Pocock 5–79) and 103–7.

LEICESTERSHIRE (7:4/3) drew with WARWICK-SHIRE (4:3/1) at Leicester. Warwickshire 278–8d (A. I. Kallicharran 129, G. W. Humpage 110) and 163–1 (K. D. Smith 102*). Leicestershire 368–4 closed (104 overs) (J. C. Balderstone 101, J. F. Steele 99, B. Dudleston 56).

MIDDLESEX (19:3/4) beat LANCASHIRE (6:2/4) by 1 wicket at Lord's. Lancashire 242 (J. Simmons 90*) and 175 (M. W. W. Selvey 5–75). Middlesex 252 (G. D. Barlow 73*, M. J. Smith 55) and 169–9 (M. W. Gatting 88).

NORTHAMPTONSHIRE (7:3/4) drew with NOT-TINGHAMSHIRE (7:3/4) at Northampton. Northamptonshire 250–9 closed (100 overs) (W. Larkins 107, D. S. Steele 56) and 215–4d (A. J. Lamb 82*). Nottinghamshire 260–9d (P. A. Todd 89, D. W. Randall 66, M. J. Harris 62) and 204–5 (C. E. B. Rice 77, D. W. Randall 50).

KENT (20:4/4) beat SOMERSET (6:2/4) by 66 runs at Taunton. Kent 303–9 closed (100 overs) (C. J. Tavaré 105, G. W. Johnson 62, J. Garner 5–65) and 191 (R. A. Woolmer 54, C. H. Dredge 5–53). Somerset 214 (B. C. Rose 89*, I. V. A. Richards 60, J. N. Shepherd 5–70) and 214 (G. I. Burgess 55, D. L. Underwood 5–74).

YORKSHIRE (6:3/3) drew with DERBYSHIRE (7:4/3) at Sheffield. Derbyshire 336–7d (A. J. Borrington 137, E. J. Barlow 94) and 197–6d (A. J. Borrington 61, E. J. Barlow 56*). Yorkshire 272 (J. H. Hampshire 72, D. L. Bairstow 60, P. Carrick 50) and 187–5 (J. D. Love 53*).

27, 29, 30 May

GLAMORGAN (8:4/4) drew with HAMPSHIRE (6:4/2) at Swansea. Glamorgan 307–5 closed (100 overs) (A. Jones 147, J. A. Hopkins 80, M. J. Llewellyn 57*) and 270–7d (A. Jones 100, P. D. Swart 51). Hampshire 300–9d (C. G. Greenidge 95, D. R. Turner 92) and 166–5 (M. N. S. Taylor 54*).

A. Jones scored two hundreds in a match for the third time; it was the first instance in any first-class match at Swansea.

MIDDLESEX (7:4/3) drew with SUSSEX (5:2/3) at Lord's. Middlesex 351–8d (C. T. Radley 105, G. D. Barlow 76, M. J. Smith 61) and 140–6d. Sussex 230–8 closed (100 overs) and 184–6 (M. A. Buss 79*).

NORTHAMPTONSHIRE (3:2/1) drew with LEICES-TERSHIRE (7:4/3) at Northampton. Northamptonshire 230–8 closed (100 overs) (G. Cook 96)

and 321–7d (T. J. Yardley 93, P. Willey 77, W. Larkins 60). Leicestershire 317–4 closed (100 overs) (B. F. Davison 180* and R. W. Tolchard 77* added 212* for the fifth wicket) and 175–5.

NOTTINGHAMSHIRE (20:4/4) beat DERBYSHIRE (2:0/2) by 8 wickets at Nottingham. Nottinghamshire 320–6 closed (100 overs) (R. J. Hadlee 101*, C. E. B. Rice 85) and 145–2. Derbyshire 129 (R. J. Hadlee 5–25) and 335 (E. J. Barlow 127, G. Miller 71, K. Cooper 5–40).

SOMERSET (20:4/4) beat GLOUCESTERSHIRE (3:1/2) by 10 wickets at Taunton. Somerset 387–5 closed (100 overs) (P. A. Slocombe 108, I. T. Botham 86, P. M. Roebuck 80*, I. V. A. Richards 67) and 14–0. Gloucestershire 150 (I. T. Botham 5–35) and 248 (Zaheer Abbas 140, H. R. Moseley 6–35).

In Gloucestershire's first innings, A. Tait was run out by I. T. Botham after leaving his crease under the erroneous impression that he had been caught at slip.

SURREY (19:3/4) beat ESSEX (4:2/2) by 8 wickets at The Oval. Essex 222 and 214 (K. S. McEwan 73, R. E. East 57). Surrey 290–6 closed (103 overs) (G. R. J. Roope 113*, G. P. Howarth 56) and 147–2 (R. D. V. Knight 63*).

WORCESTERSHIRE (8:4/4) drew with WARWICK-SHIRE (5:2/3) at Worcester. Worcestershire 304–7 closed (100 overs) (D. J. Humphries 111*, J. A. Ormrod 86) and 207–3d (P. A. Neale 80*, E. J. O. Hemsley 57). Warwickshire 216 (D. L. Amiss 53, D. J. Humphries held five catches) and 234–6 (D. L. Amiss 88, K. D. Smith 80).

27, 28 May

YORKSHIRE (19:3/4) beat LANCASHIRE (4:0/4) by an innings and 32 runs in two days at Leeds. Lancashire 123 (C. H. Lloyd 58, G. B. Stevenson 8–65) and 105 (H. P. Cooper 6–26). Yorkshire 260 (P. Carrick 105, J. H. Hampshire 54).

D. L. Bairstow held five catches in Lancashire's first innings and eight in the match.

---

31 May, 1, 2 June

LEICESTERSHIRE (18:2/4) beat DERBYSHIRE (4:0/4) by an innings and 10 runs in two days at Derby. Leicestershire 225 (J. F. Steele 118). Derbyshire 75 and 140.

ESSEX (20:4/4) beat KENT (1:0/1) by an innings and 41 runs at Ilford. Essex 337–3 closed (100 overs) (G. A. Gooch 108, M. H. Denness 76, K. W. R. Fletcher 69*). Kent 120 (J. K. Lever 5–38) and 176 (N. Phillip 5–38).

LANCASHIRE (17:1/4) beat WORCESTERSHIRE (4:0/4) by 233 runs at Manchester. Lancashire

163 (C. H. Lloyd 54) and 306–2 (D. Lloyd 121*, F. C. Hayes 113). Worcestershire 131 and 105 (W. Hogg 5–32).

MIDDLESEX (19:3/4) beat NORTHAMPTONSHIRE (3:0/3) by 10 wickets in two days at Lord's. Middlesex 280–8 closed (100 overs) (G. D. Barlow 102*) and 16–0. Northamptonshire 130 (M. W. W. Selvey 6–57) and 163 (T. J. Yardley 97).

NOTTINGHAMSHIRE (20:4/4) beat YORKSHIRE (1:0/1) by 8 wickets at Worksop. Yorkshire 93 (R. J. Hadlee 6–39) and 398 (J. H. Hampshire 124, P. Carrick 67, C. Johnson 61, R. J. Hadlee 5–102). Nottinghamshire 426–8d (M. J. Harris 143, C. E. B. Rice 87) and 67–2.

SURREY (6:2/4) drew with SOMERSET (5:2/3) at The Oval. Somerset 225 (D. Breakwell 92, R. D. Jackman 5–63) and 217–9d. Surrey 246 and 71–2.

SUSSEX (8:4/4) drew with GLOUCESTERSHIRE (1:0/1) at Hove. Gloucestershire 129 and 381 (Zaheer Abbas 213). Sussex 424–7d (Imran Khan 167, G. D. Mendis 108) and 84–8.

3, 5, 6 June

SURREY (17:1/4) beat DERBYSHIRE (4:0/4) by 48 runs in two days at Ilkeston. Surrey 177 and 77 (A. J. Harvey-Walker 7–35). Derbyshire 112 (E. J. Barlow 50) and 94 (P. I. Pocock 5–58). *The Ilkeston pitch, on which 26 wickets fell on the second day, was reported to the TCCB and subsequently banned for the remainder of the season.*

ESSEX (20:4/4) beat NORTHAMPTONSHIRE (2:1/1) by an innings and 39 runs at Ilford. Northamptonshire 195 (P. Willey 112, J. K. Lever 7–56) and 223 (G. Cook 55, J. K. Lever 6–89). Essex 457–5d (K. S. McEwan 186, G. A. Gooch 129, B. R. Hardie 73*).
G. A. Gooch (129) and K. S. McEwan (186) shared a partnership of 321, beating the Essex second-wicket record in all first-class matches (294 by A. V. Avery and P. A. Gibb v Northamptonshire at Northampton in 1952).

GLAMORGAN (7:4/3) drew with LEICESTERSHIRE (8:4/4) at Swansea. Leicestershire 303–7 closed (100 overs) B. F. Davison 90, N. E. Briers 69) and 197–4d (J. F. Steele 109*). Glamorgan 302–9d (M. A. Nash 124* and G. Richards 74 added 166 for the eighth wicket, P. Booth 6–93) and 130–4.
Eleven batsmen were dismissed 'lbw' in the match, including five in Glamorgan's first innings.

LANCASHIRE (19:3/4) beat HAMPSHIRE (6:2/4) by 10 runs at Bournemouth. Lancashire 254 (F. C. Hayes 136*) and 130 (T. E. Jesty 6–50). Hampshire 228 (R. M. Ratcliffe 7–58) and 146 (W. Hogg 5–45).

KENT (17:1/4) beat MIDDLESEX (4:0/4) by 6 wickets at Lord's. Middlesex 98 and 193 (G. R. Dilley 5–32). Kent 196 (J. N. Shepherd 58, A. A. Jones 5–52) and 96–4.

NOTTINGHAMSHIRE (19:4/3) beat WARWICKSHIRE (3:0/3) by an innings and 169 runs in two days at Nottingham. Nottinghamshire 306–7 closed (100 overs) B. Hassan 81, D. W. Randall 66, M. J. Smedley 58). Warwickshire 56 and 81 (R. J. Hadlee 5–29).

SOMERSET (17:3/2) beat SUSSEX (8:4/4) by 4 wickets at Hove. Sussex 306–6 closed (100 overs) (Imran Khan 105*, J. R. T. Barclay 58, S. J. Storey 57) and 151 (K. F. Jennings 5–18). Somerset 259 (I. V. A. Richards 118, P. W. Denning 64, D. J. S. Taylor 52) and 199–6 (I. V. A. Richards 82).

YORKSHIRE (19:3/4) beat WORCESTERSHIRE (5:2/3) by 8 wickets at Middlesbrough. Worcestershire 200 and 185 (D. N. Patel 57). Yorkshire 314 (K. Sharp 89, R. G. Lumb 66) and 74–2.

10, 12, 13 June

DERBYSHIRE (20:4/4) beat GLAMORGAN (2:0/2) by an innings and 20 runs in two days at Chesterfield. Derbyshire 341–6 closed (100 overs) (P. N. Kirsten 206*). Glamorgan 140 and 181.

ESSEX (18:4/2) beat GLOUCESTERSHIRE (5:4/1) by 2 wickets at Gloucester. Gloucestershire 350–6 closed (100 overs) (M. J. Procter 203 and J. C. Foat 56 added 219 for the fifth wicket) and 267–6d (J. C. Foat 53*). Essex 305–3 closed (100 overs) (M. H. Denness 81, K. W. R. Fletcher 73*, K. S. McEwan 73, B. R. Hardie 52*) and 313–8 (N. Phillip 134, G. A. Gooch 50).
N. Phillip's first hundred in first-class cricket included seven sixes.

KENT (18:3/3) beat SUSSEX (7:3/4) by 9 wickets at Tunbridge Wells. Sussex 253–7 closed (100 overs) (C. P. Phillipson 67) and 149. Kent 261 (C. J. Tavaré 73, A. G. E. Ealham 57, J. Spencer 5–53) and 142–1 (C. J. C. Rowe 79*).

YORKSHIRE (19:4/3) beat LEICESTERSHIRE (8:4/4) by 4 wickets at Leicester. Leicestershire 327–8 closed (100 overs) (B. F. Davison 87, P. B. Clift 59*) and 265–7d (N. E. Briers 102). Yorkshire 322–9 closed (100 overs) (R. G. Lumb 50) and 271–6 (R. G. Lumb 103, C. W. J. Athey 87).
Yorkshire, set to score 271 runs in a minimum of 175 minutes, won with eight balls to spare.

NORTHAMPTONSHIRE (5:4/1) drew with WORCESTERSHIRE (5:4/1) at Northampton. Northamptonshire 312–4 closed (100 overs) (W. Larkins 170*) and 265–7d (D. S. Steele 117). Worcestershire 308–3 closed (100 overs)

With a maiden first-class hundred in June, West Indian fast bowler Norbert Phillip established himself among Essex supporters as a worthy successor to Keith Boyce.

(G. M. Turner 127, P. A. Neale 74, J. A. Ormrod 65) and 77–6.

SOMERSET (18:2/4) beat LANCASHIRE (4:0/4) by 4 wickets at Bath. Lancashire 136 and 304–9d (J. Abrahams 61). Somerset 210 (P. A. Slocombe 93* carried his bat through the innings) and 234–6 (I. V. A. Richards 71, P. M. Roebuck 50*).

SURREY (6:3/3) drew with NOTTINGHAMSHIRE (7:3/4) at The Oval. Nottinghamshire 262–8 closed (100 overs) (P. A. Todd 83) and 230–6d (C. E. B. Rice 82*). Surrey 266 (G. R. J. Roope 66, R. D. V. Knight 51, C. J. Richards 50) and 106–5 (J. H. Edrich 61*).

WARWICKSHIRE (16:0/4) beat MIDDLESEX (5:1/4) by 6 wickets at Birmingham. Middlesex 155 (R. G. D. Willis 6–44) and 169 (R. G. D. Willis 5–39). Warwickshire 146 (R. N. Abberley 61, W. W. Daniel 5–62) and 181–4 (D. L. Amiss 72).

14, 15, 16 June

GLAMORGAN (7:4/3) drew with ESSEX (8:4/4) at Cardiff. Essex 372–7 closed (100 overs) (K. S. McEwan 115, K. R. Pont 101, S. Turner 71*, A. H. Wilkins 5–96) and 103–1d (B. R. Hardie 61*). Glamorgan 301–9d (R. C. Ontong 116*, M. A. Nash 52) and 75–7.

GLOUCESTERSHIRE (20:4/4) beat DERBYSHIRE (2:0/2) by an innings and 19 runs at Gloucester. Gloucestershire 373–6 closed (100 overs) (M. J. Procter 122, Zaheer Abbas 104, D. R. Shepherd 72). Derbyshire 95 (J. H. Childs 5–24) and 139 (J. H. Childs 6–44).

KENT (20:4/4) beat SURREY (2:0/2) by an innings and 108 runs at Tunbridge Wells. Kent 311–6d (J. N. Shepherd 101, A. G. E. Ealham 61, R. A. Woolmer 52). Surrey 105 and 98 (G. W. Johnson 6–32).
F. J. Titmus, the Surrey coach, made his only appearance for the 1st XI of his adopted county, scoring 0* and 4*, and taking 1–35 in 14 overs.

NORTHAMPTONSHIRE (7:3/4) drew with WARWICKSHIRE (2:1/1) at Northampton. No play possible on third day. Northamptonshire 256–4 closed (100 overs) (D. S. Steele 68, P. Willey 50*). Warwickshire 156 (D. L. Amiss 55, T. M. Lamb 6–71).

SOMERSET (18:2/4) beat SUSSEX (2:1/1) by an innings and 38 runs at Bath. Sussex 155 (J. Garner 5–50) and 120. Somerset 313–6d (B. C. Rose 112, P. M. Roebuck 77).

WORCESTERSHIRE (6:4/2) drew with LEICESTERSHIRE (5:4/1) at Worcester. No play possible third day. Worcestershire 349–3 closed (100 overs) (E. J. O. Hemsley 141* and J. A. Ormrod 138 added 211 for the third wicket)

and 39–0. Leicestershire 302–6d (J. F. Steele 133, B. F. Davison 52).

YORKSHIRE (8:4/4) drew with MIDDLESEX (7:3/4) at Bradford. Yorkshire 307 (K. Sharp 91, J. H. Hampshire 61, M. W. W. Selvey 5–109) and 194–9. Middlesex 277.

17, 19, 20 June

GLAMORGAN (8:4/4) drew with GLOUCESTERSHIRE (7:3/4) at Cardiff. Gloucestershire 279 (M. J. Procter 99, J. C. Foat 50, M. A. Nash 5–78) and 359–2d (A. W. Stovold 139, J. C. Foat 102*, Zaheer Abbas 53). Glamorgan 345 (M. A. Nash 92, P. D. Swart 67, E. W. Jones 58) and 81–1.

KENT (19:3/4) beat MIDDLESEX (7:3/4) by 39 runs at Canterbury. Kent 297 (R. A. Woolmer 92, C. J. C. Rowe 84, A. A. Jones 6–89) and 183 (R. A. Woolmer 50, W. W. Daniel 5–49). Middlesex 278 (I. J. Gould 83, G. D. Barlow 72, K. B. S. Jarvis 5–56, P. R. Downton held five catches) and 163.

WARWICKSHIRE (19:3/4) beat LANCASHIRE (4:0/4) by 85 runs at Manchester. Warwickshire 250 (K. D. Smith 110) and 160 (D. L. Amiss 50, W. Hogg 7–84). Lancashire 140 (S. P. Perryman 6–42) and 185 (F. C. Hayes 68, S. P. Perryman 6–69).

NOTTINGHAMSHIRE (8:4/4) drew with SOMERSET (3:2/1) at Nottingham. Somerset 247 (M. J. Kitchen 50) and 259–3d (P. A. Slocombe 128*). Nottinghamshire 303–3d (C. E. B. Rice 117*, D. W. Randall 94) and 52–3.

HAMPSHIRE (20:4/4) beat SUSSEX (1:0/1) by an innings and 141 runs in two days at Hove. Sussex 77 (A. M. E. Roberts 5–20) and 204 (K. Stevenson 6–73). Hampshire 422–3d (C. G. Greenidge 211 and T. E. Jesty 125* added 242 for the third wicket, B. A. Richards 60).

YORKSHIRE (17:4/1) beat NORTHAMPTONSHIRE (8:4/4) by 5 wickets at Harrogate. Northamptonshire 320–3 closed (100 overs) (W. Larkins 118, D. S. Steele 102*, G. Cook 57) and 146 (P. Carrick 5–39). Yorkshire 310 (J. H. Hampshire 109, C. Johnson 53, D. L. Bairstow 50) and 157–5 (J. H. Hampshire 76).

24, 26, 27 June

ESSEX (20:4/4) beat HAMPSHIRE (3:0/3) by an innings and 73 runs at Chelmsford. Essex 310–8 closed (100 overs) (S. Turner 89*, K. S. McEwan 80, G. R. Stephenson held five catches). Hampshire 115 (N. Phillip 5–38) and 122 (J. K. Lever 6–51).

KENT (7:4/3) drew with NORTHAMPTONSHIRE (5:3/2) at Dartford. Northamptonshire 250–7 closed (100 overs) (W. Larkins 64, R. G.

Williams 60*) and 279-7 (G. Cook 88, D. S. Steele 67). Kent 377-5 closed (100 overs) (R. A. Woolmer 109, C. J. Tavaré 72).

LANCASHIRE (8:4/4) drew with GLAMORGAN (2:1/1) at Liverpool. No play possible first day. Lancashire 401-4 closed (100 overs) (C. H. Lloyd 110*, A. Kennedy 100, J. Abrahams 66, D. Lloyd 51). Glamorgan 195 (C. E. H. Croft 5-58).

LEICESTERSHIRE (6:2/4) drew with DERBYSHIRE (5:1/4) at Leicester. Leicestershire 206 (B. F. Davison 80) and 196-7d (D. I. Gower 61). Derbyshire 167 (G. Miller 77) and 119-2 (A. J. Borrington 59).

MIDDLESEX (19:3/4) beat NOTTINGHAMSHIRE (3:0/3) by an innings and 106 runs at Lord's. Nottinghamshire 137 (D. W. Randall 66) and 128 (P. H. Edmonds 6-36). Middlesex 371 (C. T. Radley 102, G. D. Barlow 75).

SOMERSET (6:3/3) drew with YORKSHIRE (8:4/4) at Taunton. Yorkshire 345-7 closed (100 overs) (C. W. J. Athey 131, D. L. Bairstow 56, R. G. Lumb 51) and 217-3d (J. H. Hampshire 65*, C. W. J. Athey 54). Somerset 253 (I. V. A. Richards 61) and 157-8.

WARWICKSHIRE (3:1/2) drew with GLOUCESTER-SHIRE (8:4/4) at Birmingham. Warwickshire 177 and 408-4 (D. L. Amiss 109, J. Whitehouse 102*, G. W. Humpage 68, R. N. Abberley 55). Gloucestershire 323 (J. C. Foat 100, D. A. Graveney 92, R. G. D. Willis 7-63).

28, 29, 30 June

LEICESTERSHIRE (20:4/4) beat HAMPSHIRE (3:0/3) by an innings and 101 runs at Southampton. No play possible on second day. Hampshire 106 and 93 (J. C. Balderstone 6-25). Leicestershire 300-7d (B. F. Davison 144, R. W. Tolchard 50*).

NORTHAMPTONSHIRE (20:4/4) beat DERBYSHIRE (2:1/1) by an innings and 40 runs at Northampton. Northamptonshire 344-4 closed (100 overs) (G. Cook 155, D. S. Steele 130). Derbyshire 151 (D. S. Steele 6-36) and 153 (D. S. Steele 5-39).

D. S. Steele achieved the first match double of 100 runs and 10 wickets for Northamptonshire since 1928 (V. W. C. Jupp). He added 279 for the second wicket with G. Cook.

KENT (19:3/4) beat SURREY (3:0/3) by an innings and 102 runs at The Oval. Kent 272-8 closed (100 overs) (C. J. Tavaré 64, A. G. E. Ealham 58). Surrey 95 and 75 (D. L. Underwood 9-32 – the best first-class innings analysis of the 1978 season).

SUSSEX (4:2/2) drew with NOTTINGHAMSHIRE (7:4/3) at Hove. Nottinghamshire 307-5 closed (100 overs) (D. W. Randall 157*, P. A. Todd

David Steele, in his last season for Northamptonshire, achieved the county's first match double since 1928, scoring 130 and capturing 11 Derbyshire wickets at Northampton.

Gloucestershire's left-arm spinner John Childs enjoyed a purple patch in June and July when he took 11 wickets v Derbyshire, 9 v Surrey, 12 v Hampshire and 9 v Leicestershire.

74) and 155–1d (P. A. Todd 69, M. J. Harris 53*). Sussex 200–8d (Imran Khan 113*) and 129–4 (Imran Khan 54).

SOMERSET (18:2/4) beat WARWICKSHIRE (7:3/4) by 7 wickets at Nuneaton. Warwickshire 250 (R. N. Abberley 77, D. L. Amiss 52) and 194–8d (D. L. Amiss 67). Somerset 230 (I. V. A. Richards 87, D. Breakwell 52*) and 216–3 (P. W. Denning 78*, I. V. A. Richards 55).

GLAMORGAN (17:1/4) beat WORCESTERSHIRE (4:0/4) by 175 runs at Worcester. Glamorgan 193 (J. A. Hopkins 63) and 200–7d (G. Richards 63*). Worcestershire 123 and 95.

1, 3, 4 July
DERBYSHIRE (0) drew with SUSSEX (0) at Chesterfield. No play possible on first and second days. Single innings match begun with less than eight hours remaining. Derbyshire 186–3d (A. Hill 50). Sussex 50–0.

ESSEX (8:4/4) drew with YORKSHIRE (6:3/3) at Chelmsford. Yorkshire 260–9 closed (100 overs) (D. L. Bairstow 56*) and 186–3 (G. Boycott 59, C. W. J. Athey 56). Essex 382–8 closed (100 overs) (K. S. McEwan 149 and K. W. R. Fletcher 75, added 206 for the third wicket, K. R. Pont 60).

LEICESTERSHIRE (2:0/2) drew with GLAMORGAN (0) at Leicester. No play possible on second day. Glamorgan 116–5d and 122–3d (J. A. Hopkins 55*). Leicestershire 0–0d and 9–3.

NOTTINGHAMSHIRE (4:3/1) drew with HAMPSHIRE (8:4/4) at Nottingham. Hampshire 309–4 closed (100 overs) (D. R. Turner 148*, T. E. Jesty 101) and 21–2. Nottinghamshire 272 (C. E. B. Rice 130, J. W. Southern 5–102).

GLOUCESTERSHIRE (18:4/2) beat SURREY (7:3/4) by 2 wickets at Guildford. Surrey 268–6 closed (100 overs) (J. H. Edrich 114 and R. D. V. Knight 90 added 205 for the third wicket) and 221 (M. A. Lynch 68, A. R. Butcher 54, J. H. Childs 5–90). Gloucestershire 334 (M. J. Procter 154, A. W. Stovold 77, P. I. Pocock 6–92) and 158–8.
M. J. Procter reached his hundred in 92 minutes. His 154 included eight sixes and 18 fours, cost an estimated £90 in lost balls, and included a hundred before lunch on the second day (11 to 154).*

WARWICKSHIRE (2:2/0) drew with NORTHAMPTONSHIRE (4:0/4) at Birmingham. No play possible on third day. Warwickshire 216 (T. A. Lloyd 54). Northamptonshire 47–0.

WORCESTERSHIRE (6:2/4) drew with MIDDLESEX

(8:4/4) at Worcester. Worcestershire 234 and 58–0. Middlesex 314 (I. J. Gould 128 and K. P. Tomlins 94 added 209 for the sixth wicket).

5, 6, 7 July

GLOUCESTERSHIRE (19:3/4) beat HAMPSHIRE (3:0/3) by 164 runs at Basingstoke. Gloucestershire 264–8d (Zaheer Abbas 132) and 207–4d (Sadiq Mohammad 85, A. W. Stovold 84). Hampshire 128 (T. M. Tremlett 50) and 179 (J. W. Southern 51, J. H. Childs 8–34).

LANCASHIRE (5:1/4) drew with KENT (5:1/4) at Manchester. Kent 179 and 164–0d (R. A. Woolmer 92*, C. J. C. Rowe 67*). Lancashire 162–9d (R. A. Woolmer 6–27) and 54–1.

MIDDLESEX (3:2/1) drew with ESSEX (4:0/4) at Lord's. Middlesex 218 (M. W. Gatting 50) and 134–5d (J. M. Brearley 70*). Essex 109–4d and 155–6 (K. S. McEwan 64).

8, 10, 11 July

GLAMORGAN (3:0/3) drew with SOMERSET (6:2/4) at Cardiff. No play possible on second day. Glamorgan 126 (I. T. Botham 7–61) and 65–2. Somerset 201–8d.

HAMPSHIRE (2:2/0) drew with WORCESTERSHIRE (6:3/3) at Portsmouth. Worcestershire 250–2d (G. M. Turner 155* and 193–9d (J. A. Ormrod 74). Hampshire 238–8d (M. N. S. Taylor 67, N. G. Cowley 64) and 104–4.

KENT (16:0/4) beat DERBYSHIRE (4:1/3) by 8 wickets at Maidstone. Derbyshire 176 (G. Miller 62, D. L. Underwood 5–41) and 99 (D. L. Underwood 6–38). Kent 127–8d (A. J. Mellor 5–52) and 149–2 (C. J. C. Rowe 73*, Asif Iqbal 57*).

LANCASHIRE (19:4/3) beat NOTTINGHAMSHIRE (7:4/3) by 138 runs at Manchester. Lancashire 353–7d (J. Simmons 106, J. Lyon 74*, C. H. Lloyd 66) and 218–5d (D. Lloyd 72, C. H. Lloyd 50). Nottinghamshire 300–7d (C. E. B. Rice 122, P. A. Todd 85) and 133.

LEICESTERSHIRE (17:1/4) beat GLOUCESTERSHIRE (7:3/4) by 4 wickets at Leicester. Gloucestershire 267–9d (M. J. Procter 89, Sadiq Mohammad 60, D. A. Graveney 60, J. F. Steele 5–54) and 187–8d (Sadiq Mohammad 50). Leicestershire 187 (J. F. Steele 79, J. H. Childs 6–64) and 268–6 (J. C. Balderstone 70, J. F. Steele 68).

NORTHAMPTONSHIRE (5:1/4) drew with SURREY (4:3/1) at Northampton. Surrey 250–9 closed (100 overs) (B. J. Griffiths 5–66) and 181–7d (A. R. Butcher 51). Northamptonshire 163–4d (D. S. Steele 51) and 189–4 (W. Larkins 84).

ESSEX (17:2/3) beat SUSSEX (6:3/3) by 4 wickets at Hove. Sussex 252–7d (G. D. Mendis 128, J. R. T. Barclay 55*) and 115 (J. K. Lever 7–32). Essex 210–7d (K. W. R. Fletcher 69) and 158–6 (G. A. Gooch 50).

Middlesex 'keeper Gould and Gatting applaud a magnificent catch by Featherstone to dismiss Lancashire's John Abrahams off the bowling of Emburey at Lord's.

All-rounder John Shepherd played a leading role in Kent's successful campaign for the Schweppes Championship in 1978 and takes a much-deserved benefit in 1979.

YORKSHIRE (18:2/4) beat WARWICKSHIRE (4:0/4) by 63 runs at Bradford. Yorkshire 227 (J. H. Hampshire 132) and 185-3d (R. G. Lumb 73, G. Boycott 55). Warwickshire 85 (C. M. Old 6-34) and 264 (R. N. Abberley 81, D. L. Bairstow held six catches).

12, 13, 14 July
DERBYSHIRE (7:3/4) drew with NORTHAMPTON-SHIRE (4:2/2) at Derby. Northamptonshire 241 (D. S. Steele 71, M. Hendrick 5-42) and 277-2d (D. S. Steele 82*, G. Cook 68, A. J. Lamb 63*, W. Larkins 60). Derbyshire 279-6d (G. Miller 91, P. N. Kirsten 87, H. Cartwright 66) and 61-3.

ESSEX (19:3/4) beat SOMERSET (3:0/3) by 200 runs at Colchester. Essex 270-8d (M. H. Denness 78, N. Phillip 59, B. R. Hardie 52) and 196-7d. Somerset 138 and 128 (J. K. Lever 6-33).

LANCASHIRE (16:0/4) beat GLOUCESTERSHIRE (5:1/4) by 7 wickets at Bristol. Gloucestershire 164 (R. M. Ratcliffe 5-54) and 133. Lancashire 127 (J. Simmons 81, M. J. Procter 7-45) and 171-3 (A. Kennedy 76, D. Lloyd 63).

HAMPSHIRE (5:1/4) drew with SUSSEX (5:1/4) at Portsmouth. Sussex 190 (J. W. Southern 5-32) and 214-4d (Imran Khan 62*, P. W. G. Parker 60). Hampshire 163 (Imran Khan 6-41) and 125-4 (J. M. Rice 63).

KENT (18:2/4) beat GLAMORGAN (7:3/4) by 6 wickets at Maidstone. Glamorgan 284-9 closed (100 overs) (J. A. Hopkins 97, R. C. Ontong 75, D. L. Underwood 5-64) and 140 (G. W. Johnson 6-64). Kent 202-9d (Asif Iqbal 51) and 226-4 (C. J. Tavaré 89*, J. N. Shepherd 65*).

MIDDLESEX (16:0/4) beat LEICESTERSHIRE (5:1/4) by 1 wicket at Lord's. Leicestershire 169 (J. C. Balderstone 52*, M. W. Gatting 5-59) and 98 (P. H. Edmonds 7-34). Middlesex 148 (M. W. Gatting 53, K. Higgs 7-44) and 120-9 (J. C. Balderstone 5-35).

WORCESTERSHIRE (18:2/4) beat NOTTINGHAM-SHIRE (5:1/4) by 152 runs at Newark. Worcestershire 231 (B. L. D'Oliveira 73, P. A. Neale 64, D. R. Doshi 6-67) and 203-7d (E. J. O. Hemsley 68*, D. J. Humphries 57). Nottinghamshire 152 and 130 (N. Gifford 5-42).

YORKSHIRE (17:1/4) beat SURREY (5:1/4) by 5 wickets at The Oval. Surrey 164 (R. D. V. Knight 60, S. Oldham 5-40) and 155 (R. D. V. Knight 56). Yorkshire 165 (R. D. Jackman 5-43) and 155-5 (R. G. Lumb 71).

15, 17, 18 July
ESSEX (19:3/4) beat WARWICKSHIRE (6:2/4) by 45 runs at Colchester. Essex 271 (M. H. Denness 71, B. R. Hardie 61) and 258-4d (M. H. Denness 126, M. S. A. McEvoy 51). Warwickshire 211 (A. I. Kallicharran 51, D. L. Amiss 50, R. E. East 5-54) and 273 (D. L. Amiss 122* carried his bat through the innings, E. E. Hemmings 51).

MIDDLESEX (18:2/4) beat GLAMORGAN (5:1/4) by 176 runs at Swansea. Middlesex 200 and 264 (I. J. Gould 77, R. O. Butcher 65, A. E. Cordle 5-33). Glamorgan 162 (M. W. W. Selvey 5-52) and 126 (G. Richards 58*, J. E. Emburey 6-29).

SUSSEX (18:2/4) beat GLOUCESTERSHIRE (4:0/4) by 127 runs at Bristol. Sussex 207 (A. Long 56*, B. M. Brain 5-51) and 231 (G. D. Mendis 85). Gloucestershire 107 (Imran Khan 7-52) and 204 (M. J. Procter 89).

NORTHAMPTONSHIRE (4:3/1) drew with YORK-SHIRE (6:3/3) at Northampton. Northamptonshire 280-7 closed (100 overs) (A. J. Lamb 72, P. Willey 58) and 287-5d (P. Willey 96* W. Larkins 60, T. J. Yardley 52*). Yorkshire 278-3 closed (100 overs) (C. W. J. Athey 114 and G. Boycott 113 added 202 for the second wicket) and 108-2.

NOTTINGHAMSHIRE (8:4/4) drew with LANCA-SHIRE (2:1/1) at Nottingham. Nottinghamshire 370-4 closed (100 overs) (C. E. B. Rice 213* – highest individual score of 1978 season – M. J. Smedley 87) and 85-1. Lancashire 160 and 483-7d (D. Lloyd 185, A. Kennedy 73, C. H. Lloyd 60, J. Abrahams 53). *C. E. B. Rice (213*) and M. J. Smedley (83*) added 229* in 167 minutes.*

SOMERSET (18:2/4) beat LEICESTERSHIRE (6:2/4) by 216 runs at Taunton. Somerset 219 (I. V. A. Richards 99, D. Breakwell 56) and 320-8d (I. V. A. Richards 110, P. M. Roebuck 50). Leicestershire 201 (P. B. Clift 61, R. W. Tolchard 50, C. H. Dredge 5-68) and 122.

SURREY (6:3/3) drew with HAMPSHIRE (6:4/2) at The Oval. Hampshire 315-8d (M. N. S. Taylor 62*, C. G. Greenidge 56, R. M. C. Gilliat 54) and 255-5d (J. M. Rice 61). Surrey 289-8 closed (104 overs) (R. D. V. Knight 78, Younis Ahmed 69*, M. A. Lynch 69) and 70-4.

WORCESTERSHIRE (2:2/0) drew with DERBYSHIRE (8:4/4) at Worcester. Derbyshire 320-2 closed (100 overs) (A. Hill 153*, I. S. Anderson 75, P. N. Kirsten 66) and 213-7d (A. J. Harvey-Walker 61). Worcestershire 227 (B. L. D'Oliveira 90) and 188-6.

26, 27, 28 July
DERBYSHIRE (5:2/3) drew with HAMPSHIRE (8:4/4) at Derby. Derbyshire 226 (P. N. Kirsten 63) and 147-5. Hampshire 356 (M. N. S. Taylor 93, N. G. Cowley 54).

KENT (18:2/4) beat LEICESTERSHIRE (4:3/1) by 5 wickets at Leicester. Leicestershire 256-9 closed (100 overs) (R. W. Tolchard 58) and 229-4d (J. F. Steele 88). Kent 200-4d (C. J. Tavaré 100*) and 286-5 (C. S. Cowdrey 69*, A. G. E. Ealham 61, C. J. C. Rowe 60).

ESSEX (15:3/0) beat NORTHAMPTONSHIRE (7:4/3) by 46 runs at Northampton. Essex 251-8d (K. W. R. Fletcher 82, N. Phillip 62) and 208. Northamptonshire 302-2d (A. J. Lamb 106*, D. S. Steele 60*, W. Larkins 60) and 111 (R. E. East 8-41).

MIDDLESEX (19:3/4) beat NOTTINGHAMSHIRE (4:1/3) by 111 runs at Nottingham. Middlesex 250-7d (M. J. Smith 63) and 181-3d (M. W. Gatting 57*). Nottinghamshire 181 (M. J. Harris 78, M. J. Smedley 60) and 139 (N. G. Featherstone 5-32).

SOMERSET (20:4/4) beat WORCESTERSHIRE (6:3/3) by 56 runs at Taunton. Somerset 364-8 closed (100 overs) (B. C. Rose 122, I. V. A. Richards 80, P. M. Roebuck 55) and 109. Worcestershire 299 (D. J. Humphries 80, P. A. Neale 75, E. J. O. Hemsley 53, J. Garner 5-77) and 118 (D. Breakwell 6-45).

SUSSEX (7:4/3) drew with SURREY (5:4/1) at Hove. Sussex 301-4d (G. D. Mendis 126, P. W. G. Parker 67) and 276-5d (P. W. G. Parker 99, Imran Khan 65). Surrey 328-7d

(A. R. Butcher 188, Younis Ahmed 72) and 115-9 (G. G. Arnold 5-33, A. C. S. Pigott 3-15 including the hat-trick).
A. C. S. Pigott's hat-trick represented the first wickets of his first-class career

WARWICKSHIRE (4:3/1) drew with LANCASHIRE (5:4/1) at Birmingham. Warwickshire 252-3d (D. L. Amiss 104, A. I. Kallicharran 85*) and 290-9d (K. D. Smith 74, D. L. Amiss 69). Lancashire 305-4d (C. H. Lloyd 118*, F. C. Hayes 80) and 161-5.

YORKSHIRE (20:4/4) beat GLAMORGAN (2:0/2) by an innings and 99 runs at Sheffield. No play possible on first day. Yorkshire 318-6 closed (100 overs) (G. Boycott 118 and R. G. Lumb 87 scored 206 for the first wicket). Glamorgan 122 (R. C. Ontong 50) and 97 (P. Carrick 7-35).

29, 31 July, 1 August
DERBYSHIRE (4:3/1) drew with YORKSHIRE (5:1/4) at Chesterfield. No play possible third day. Derbyshire 261-9 closed (100 overs) (J. Walters 90, A. Morris 55). Yorkshire 183-4 (J. H. Hampshire 56).

HAMPSHIRE (4:4/0) drew with SOMERSET (4:1/3) at Bournemouth. No play possible second day. Hampshire 318-7 closed (100 overs) (T. E. Jesty 117, C. G. Greenidge 57) and 70-2d. Somerset 169-2d (B. C. Rose 101*) and 65-4.

Mike Gatting of Middlesex scored his maiden first-class hundred in a single innings match against Yorkshire and took his second off Derbyshire in the following game.

ESSEX (20:4/4) beat LANCASHIRE (4:0/4) by an innings and 115 runs in two days at Southport. Essex 379 (K. S. McEwan 128, K. W. R. Fletcher 68). Lancashire 70 (J. K. Lever 5–23) and 194.
K. S. McEwan (128) scored 112* before lunch on the first day.

NORTHAMPTONSHIRE (4:0/4) drew with GLOUCES- TERSHIRE (3:2/1) at Northampton. No play possible third day. Gloucestershire 228. Northamptonshire 96–4 (W. Larkins 61*).

NOTTINGHAMSHIRE (6:2/4) drew with KENT (6:2/4) at Nottingham. Nottinghamshire 216 (C. E. B. Rice 57, P. A. Todd 51, K. B. S. Jarvis 5–74). Kent 201–9d (W. K. Watson 6–102).

SUSSEX (6:4/2) drew with LEICESTERSHIRE (4:0/4) at Hove. No play possible second day. Sussex 351–9d (J. R. T. Barclay 94, Javed Miandad 60, C. P. Phillipson 57). Leicestershire 124–6.

WARWICKSHIRE (3:1/2) drew with GLAMORGAN (3:3/0) at Birmingham. Glamorgan 292–6 closed (100 overs) (J. A. Hopkins 113 and A. Jones 92 scored 204 for the first wicket). Warwickshire 186–2 (D. L. Amiss 64, K. D. Smith 56).

WORCESTERSHIRE (4:4/0) drew with SURREY (3:0/3) at Worcester. No play possible on second day. Worcestershire 438–7 closed (100 overs) (J. A. Ormrod 173, G. M. Turner 150). Surrey 30–2.
G. M. Turner (150) scored 109* before lunch on the first day and shared a first-wicket partner- ship of 254 with J. A. Ormrod (173).

5, 7, 8 August
GLAMORGAN (19:3/4) beat NORTHAMPTONSHIRE (2:0/2) by an innings and 16 runs in two days at Cardiff. Glamorgan 283–5 closed (100 overs) (P. D. Swart 102*, M. J. Llewellyn 82). Northamptonshire 103 and 164 (A. J. Lamb 100, M. A. Nash 6–74).

GLOUCESTERSHIRE (3:0/3) drew with NOTTING- HAMSHIRE (2:2/0) at Cheltenham. No play possible second and third days. Nottingham- shire 221–8 closed (100 overs) (D. W. Randall 54). Gloucestershire 7–0.

HAMPSHIRE (6:3/3) drew with YORKSHIRE (7:3/4) at Southampton. Hampshire 269 (C. G. Greenidge 84, M. N. S. Taylor 52) and 115 (P. Carrick 5–43). Yorkshire 253–8d (B. Leadbeater 61) and 98–7.

KENT (18:4/2) beat LEICESTERSHIRE (6:3/3) by 120 runs at Canterbury. Kent 338–8 closed (100 overs) (R. A. Woolmer 137, Asif Iqbal 104*) and 157–5d (R. A. Woolmer 50).

Leicestershire 255–6 closed (100 overs) (B. F. Davison 106, J. C. Balderstone 90) and 120.

MIDDLESEX (3:0/3) drew with SURREY (0) at Lord's. No play possible second and third days. Surrey 138–7 (J. H. Edrich 72).

SOMERSET (18:2/4) beat WARWICKSHIRE (4:0/4) by 9 wickets at Weston-super-Mare. Warwick- shire 125 (I. T. Botham 6–43) and 165 (A. I. Kallicharran 53). Somerset 231 (P. W. Denning 56, C. C. Clifford 6–89) and 62–1.

WORCESTERSHIRE (18:2/4) beat SUSSEX (4:1/3) by 10 wickets at Eastbourne. Sussex 169 (G. G. Watson 6–45) and 100 (D. N. Patel 5–22). Worcestershire 255–9 closed (111 overs) (D. N. Patel 104, E. J. O. Hemsley 51, C. E. Waller 5–56) and 17–0.

9, 10, 11 August
DERBYSHIRE (0) drew with LANCASHIRE (0) at Chesterfield. No play possible first and second days. Single innings match begun with less than eight hours remaining. Derbyshire 201–8d (P. N. Kirsten 95). Lancashire 170–9.

ESSEX (7:3/4) drew with WORCESTERSHIRE (4:0/4) at Chelmsford. Essex 265 (S. Turner 55) and 128. Worcestershire 118 (R. E. East 6–34) and 199–8 (G. M. Turner 101).

GLOUCESTERSHIRE (12:0/0) beat GLAMORGAN (0) by 7 wickets at Cheltenham. No play possible first and second days. Single innings match begun with less than eight hours re- maining. Glamorgan 144. Gloucestershire 146–3. (A. W. Stovold 59).

KENT (5:1/4) drew with WARWICKSHIRE (4:0/4) at Canterbury. Kent 195 and 122–3d. Warwick- shire 130 (D. L. Underwood 7–38) and 64–4.

LEICESTERSHIRE (0) drew with SURREY (0) at Leicester. No play possible first and second days. Single innings match begun with less than eight hours remaining. Leicestershire 221–3d (B. F. Davison 80*, J. C. Balderstone 57). Surrey 172–4 (G. R. J. Roope 61*, Younis Ahmed 53).

MIDDLESEX (12:0/0) beat YORKSHIRE (0) by 167 runs at Lord's. No play possible first day. Single innings match begun with less than eight hours remaining. Middlesex 263–7d (M. W. Gatting 103*, N. G. Featherstone 92). Yorkshire 96 (J. E. Emburey 6–25).

SOMERSET (4:0/4) drew with HAMPSHIRE (4:2/2) at Weston-super-Mare. Hampshire 205 and 135–5d. Somerset 100–6d and 191–7 (P. W. Denning 60, P. M. Roebuck 54*).

SUSSEX (17:1/4) beat NORTHAMPTONSHIRE (4:0/4) by 9 wickets at Eastbourne. Northamptonshire 104 (C. E. Waller 5–30) and 143. Sussex 153 and 96–1.

12, 14, 15 August

ESSEX (6:2/4) drew with LEICESTERSHIRE (6:2/4) at Chelmsford. Essex 200 (K. W. R. Fletcher 68*) and 182–5d (B. R. Hardie 68*, K. W. R. Fletcher 55). Leicestershire 222 and 46–5.

GLAMORGAN (7:4/3) drew with NOTTINGHAMSHIRE (5:4/1) at Swansea. Glamorgan 302–3 closed (100 overs) (J. A. Hopkins 116, P. D. Swart 56*, G. Richards 55*) and 67–2. Nottinghamshire 379–8 closed (100 overs) (C. E. B. Rice 213 and H. T. Tunnicliffe 69* added 208 for the sixth wicket).

GLOUCESTERSHIRE (5:1/4) drew with HAMPSHIRE (5:1/4) at Cheltenham. No play possible first day. Gloucestershire 151 (Zaheer Abbas 58) and 219 (M. J. Procter 59). Hampshire 189 (C. G. Greenidge 95).

LANCASHIRE (2:0/2) drew with SURREY (0) at Blackpool. No play possible second and third days. Surrey 112–6.

MIDDLESEX (19:3/4) beat DERBYSHIRE (3:0/3) by an innings and 77 runs at Lord's. Derbyshire 139 (W. W. Daniel 5–42, M. W. W. Selvey 5–74) and 62 (M. W. W. Selvey 6–26). Middlesex 278–7d (M. W. Gatting 128, K. P. Tomlins 55*).

NORTHAMPTONSHIRE (15:1/2) beat SOMERSET (6:2/4) by 2 wickets with 2 balls to spare at Wellingborough. No play possible first day. Somerset 200–6d (V. J. Marks 51) and 158–2d (P. A. Slocombe 56, I. V. A. Richards 50*). Northamptonshire 172–9d (D. S. Steele 56) and 189–8 (A. J. Lamb 62*).

KENT (20:4/4) beat WORCESTERSHIRE (4:1/3) by 10 wickets at Worcester. Worcestershire 173 (G. M. Turner 53, K. B. S. Jarvis 8–97) and 165 (E. J. O. Hemsley 52). Kent 329–7d (J. N. Shepherd 100*, C. J. Tavaré 89, R. A. Woolmer 61) and 10–0.

YORKSHIRE (3:3/0) drew with SUSSEX (2:0/2) at Leeds. No play possible second day. Yorkshire 252–6d (J. H. Hampshire 85, R. G. Lumb 82).

19, 21, 22 August

DERBYSHIRE (5:1/4) drew with ESSEX (5:1/4) at Derby. No play possible third day. Essex 171 and 122–4. Derbyshire 173.

KENT (20:4/4) beat GLOUCESTERSHIRE (2:1/1) by 10 wickets in two days at Folkestone. Kent 347–4 closed (100 overs) (Asif Iqbal 171, C. J. Tavaré 72) and 6–0. Gloucestershire 152 and 200 (D. A. Graveney 64, R. W. Hills 6–64).

LEICESTERSHIRE (20:4/4) beat LANCASHIRE (2:0/2) by an innings and 29 runs in two days at Leicester. Leicestershire 328–6 closed (100 overs) (R. W. Tolchard 77*, J. Birkenshaw 70*, P. B. Clift 52). Lancashire 147 (R. Illingworth 5–44) and 152 (P. B. Clift 6–29).

NORTHAMPTONSHIRE (7:4/3) drew with HAMPSHIRE (7:4/3) at Northampton. Hampshire 302–8 closed (100 overs) (M. N. S. Taylor 86*, C. G. Greenidge 71) and 194 (D. S. Steele 76, P. Willey 63*, A. J. Lamb 54) and 14–1.

MIDDLESEX (20:4/4) beat SOMERSET (4:0/4) by 8 wickets at Taunton. Middlesex 328 (N. G. Featherstone 89, C. T. Radley 80) and 58–2. Somerset 118 (P. A. Slocombe 35* carried his bat through the innings) and 266 (B. C. Rose 99, M. W. W. Selvey 5–59).

SURREY (20:4/4) beat GLAMORGAN (4:2/2) by 7 wickets at The Oval. Surrey 403–5 closed (100 overs) (A. R. Butcher 176 and R. D. V. Knight 119 added 211 for the third wicket) and 148–3 (A. R. Butcher 78*, G. R. J. Roope 55*). Glamorgan 205 (M. J. Llewellyn 61, P. I. Pocock 6–73) and 343 (R. C. Ontong 116, M. A. Nash 63, Intikhab Alam 6–126).

WARWICKSHIRE (6:2/4) drew with SUSSEX (3:1/2) at Birmingham. No play possible third day. Sussex 199 (Javed Miandad 60) and 120–3 (Javed Miandad 53*). Warwickshire 296 (K. D. Smith 132* carried his bat through the innings).

YORKSHIRE (16:4/0) beat NOTTINGHAMSHIRE (6:3/3) by 8 wickets at Scarborough. Nottinghamshire 294–2 closed (100 overs) (M. J. Harris 98, P. A. Todd 76, D. W. Randall 66*) and 176 (M. J. Harris 51, D. L. Bairstow made five dismissals). Yorkshire 325–8 closed (100 overs) (G. Boycott 129, J. D. Love 99) and 147–2 (R. G. Lumb 57*).

23, 24, 25 August

GLAMORGAN (16:3/1) beat SUSSEX (7:3/4) by 6 wickets at Swansea. Sussex 274–3 closed (100 overs) (S. P. Hoadley 112, Javed Miandad 110*) and 270–7d (P. W. G. Parker 112). Glamorgan 260 (P. D. Swart 103, M. A. Nash 54) and 285–4 (J. A. Hopkins 102, M. J. Llewellyn 78*, R. C. Ontong 54).

MIDDLESEX (20:4/4) beat GLOUCESTERSHIRE (5:1/4) by an innings and 14 runs in two days at Bristol. Gloucestershire 187 (M. J. Procter 71, D. A. Graveney 59*) and 128 (M. W. W. Selvey 5–76). Middlesex 329 (R. O. Butcher 142, N. G. Featherstone 78, M. J. Procter 5–89).

WARWICKSHIRE (19:3/4) beat HAMPSHIRE (6:2/4) by 37 runs at Bournemouth. Warwickshire 286–9 closed (100 overs) (A. I. Kallicharran

129) and 222–9d (K. D. Smith 70, N. G. Cowley 5–93). Hampshire 207 (C. C. Clifford 5–43) and 264 (C. G. Greenidge 112, D. R. Turner 85, S. P. Perryman 7–49).

KENT (7:3/4) drew with ESSEX (5:2/3) at Folkestone. Essex 226 (N. Phillip 60, K. S. McEwan 58) and 228 (K. S. McEwan 57, D. L. Underwood 6–73). Kent 270 (C. J. Tavare 87, R. E. East 6–117) and 111–5.
On 25 August D. L. Underwood became the first bowler to take 100 wickets in first-class matches in the 1978 season.

NOTTINGHAMSHIRE (7:3/4) drew with LEICESTERSHIRE (6:2/4) at Nottingham. Nottinghamshire 261–9 closed (100 overs) (C. E. B. Rice 73, P. A. Todd 65) and 203–5d (M. J. Harris 113). Leicestershire 227 (R. W. Tolchard 103*) and 199–7 (N. E. Briers 79, B. F. Davison 50, D. R. Doshi 6–73).

WORCESTERSHIRE (6:4/2) drew with LANCASHIRE (5:4/1) at Worcester. Worcestershire 395–3 closed (100 overs) (B. L. D'Oliveira 146* and E. J. O. Hemsley 105* added 233* for the fourth wicket, G. M. Turner 96) and 261–9d (P. A. Neale 67). Lancashire 390–6 closed (100 overs) (C. H. Lloyd 120, B. W. Reidy 88, A. Kennedy 70) and 139–4 (J. Abrahams 62).

26, 28, 29 August
DERBYSHIRE (20:4/4) beat NOTTINGHAMSHIRE (6:4/2) by 16 runs at Derby. Derbyshire 306–6 closed (100 overs) (H. Cartwright 77*, P. N. Kirsten 69) and 120 (K. Cooper 6–32). Nottinghamshire 303–9 closed (100 overs) (D. W. Randall 72, M. J. Smedley 59, J. D. Birch 51) and 107 (G. Miller 5–46).

ESSEX (20:4/4) beat SURREY (4:0/4) by an innings and 107 runs in two days at Southend. Surrey 96 and 108 (J. H. Edrich 61* carried his bat through the innings, N. Phillip 5–47, J. K. Lever 5–50). Essex 311 (B. R. Hardie 109, K. S. McEwan 69, K. R. Pont 52, Intikhab Alam 5–45).

GLOUCESTERSHIRE (7:3/4) drew with SOMERSET (6:3/3) at Bristol. Somerset 264–9 closed (100 overs) (P. A. Slocombe 87, P. W. Denning 68) and 216 (P. A. Slocombe 75). Gloucestershire 275–7 closed (100 overs) (P. Bainbridge 72*) and 191–7 (M. J. Procter 90).

HAMPSHIRE (15:2/1) beat KENT (8:4/4) by 7 wickets at Bournemouth. Kent 329–4 closed (100 overs) (Asif Iqbal 115*, G. W. Johnson 95, C. J. Tavaré) and 218–4d (G. W. Johnson 65). Hampshire 236 (C. G. Greenidge 136, D. L. Underwood 5–52) and 313–3 (C. G. Greenidge 120, T. E. Jesty 106*).
C. G. Greenidge's second hundred of the match was his third in successive first-class innings, and was scored before lunch on the third day.

YORKSHIRE (19:3/4) beat LANCASHIRE (4:0/4) by 10 wickets at Manchester. Lancashire 128 (G. B. Stevenson 5–61) and 155 (F. C. Hayes 73*, C. M. Old 5–47). Yorkshire 251 (C. M. Old 100*, J. D. Love 55) and 36–0.

LEICESTERSHIRE (7:4/3) drew with NORTHAMPTONSHIRE (5:2/3) at Leicester. Leicestershire 322–7 closed (100 overs) (B. F. Davison 70, J. C. Balderstone 51) and 186–8d (B. F. Davison 54). Northamptonshire 205–7 closed (100 overs) (P. Willey 61, P. J. Watts 57*) and 136–3 (G. Cook 61).

SUSSEX (19:3/4) beat MIDDLESEX (7:3/4) by 107 runs at Hove. Sussex 279 (J. R. T. Barclay 96) and 346–5d (Javed Miandad 127, S. P. Hoadley 60, Imran Khan 53). Middlesex 287 (N. G. Featherstone 108, R. O. Butcher 63) and 231 (G. D. Barlow 77).

WARWICKSHIRE (4:4/0) drew with WORCESTERSHIRE (4:4/0) at Birmingham. Warwickshire 303–2 closed (100 overs) (D. L. Amiss 155* and T. A. Lloyd 93 added 228 for the second wicket) and 390–4d (D. L. Amiss 112, A. I. Kallicharran 101*, K. D. Smith 59). Worcestershire 395–2 closed (100 overs) (G. M. Turner 202*, E. J. O. Hemsley 106*, P. A. Neale 70) and 84–0.

30, 31 August, 1 September
ESSEX (4:0/4) drew with DERBYSHIRE (4:0/4) at Southend. Essex 141 (G. A. Gooch 60, M. Hendrick 5–32) and 190–5d (G. A. Gooch 84). Derbyshire 146 (J. K. Lever 6–55) and 184–9 (R. E. East 5–70).
Kent became County Champions on 1 September when Essex failed to beat Derbyshire.

GLAMORGAN (5:2/3) drew with WARWICKSHIRE (7:4/3) at Cardiff. Warwickshire 326–7 closed (100 overs) (D. L. Amiss 162) and 199–7d. Glamorgan 240–7 closed (100 overs) (R. C. Ontong 64, A. L. Jones 54) and 254–8 (P. D. Swart 66, J. A. Hopkins 62).
D. L. Amiss scored his third hundred in successive first-class innings.

LEICESTERSHIRE (8:4/4) drew with NOTTINGHAMSHIRE (3:1/2) at Leicester. No play possible second day. Leicestershire 326–6 closed (100 overs) (B. F. Davison 142, J. F. Steele 77). Nottinghamshire 172 (D. W. Randall 52, R. Illingworth 6–38) and 46–4.
Playing in his final first-class match, R. Illingworth took five wickets in an innings for the 103rd time.

SURREY (6:4/2) drew with LANCASHIRE (7:3/4) at The Oval. Surrey 351 (R. D. V. Knight 128, G. R. J. Roope 105, P. J. W. Allott 5–98) and 145–2d (J. H. Edrich 53*). Lancashire 274–5d (D. Lloyd 136*) and 95–4.

WORCESTERSHIRE (5:3/2) drew with GLOUCES-TERSHIRE (6:4/2) at Worcester. Gloucestershire 367–5d (Sadiq Mohammad 176, P. Bainbridge 66) and 184–7d (P. Bainbridge 76*). Worcestershire 256–6d (G. M. Turner 115) and 49–1.

6, 7, 8 September
HAMPSHIRE (20:4/4) beat GLAMORGAN (4:1/3) by 59 runs at Southampton. Hampshire 318–8d (M. N. S. Taylor 103*, G. R. Stephenson 66, D. J. Rock 53) and 234–4d (C. G. Greenidge 133 including the fastest first-class hundred of 1978 in 82 minutes to win the Lawrence Trophy). Glamorgan 191 (A. Jones 66) and 302 (A. Jones 75, R. C. Ontong 74).

LANCASHIRE (0) v NORTHAMPTONSHIRE (0) at Manchester. Match abandoned without a ball being bowled.

ESSEX (15:0/3) beat NOTTINGHAMSHIRE (5:2/3) by 9 wickets at Nottingham. Nottinghamshire 200–8d (D. W. Randall 86, P. A. Todd 59) and 143–5d. Essex 122–7d and 222–1 (A. W. Lilley 100*, G. A. Gooch 97).
Alan William Lilley, aged 19, scored 22 and 100* on his debut in first-class cricket. His hundred included four sixes and nine fours.

MIDDLESEX (19:3/4) beat SURREY (4:0/4) by 10 wickets in two days at The Oval. Surrey 122 and 224 (A. R. Butcher 79). Middlesex 279 (R. O. Butcher 81, J. M. Brearley 65, Intikhab Alam 5–81) and 69–0.

SUSSEX (17:1/4) beat KENT (7:3/4) by 45 runs at Hove. Sussex 181 and 263 (Javed Miandad 76). Kent 267 (J. N. Shepherd 61, C. J. C. Rowe 59, R. A. Woolmer 56) and 132 (C. E. Waller 5–69).

WARWICKSHIRE (3:1/2) drew with DERBYSHIRE (4:2/2) at Birmingham. Derbyshire 201–5d (P. N. Kirsten 63) and 236–9d (J. Walters 84). Warwickshire 181–5d (A. I. Kallicharran 63*, T. A. Lloyd 59) and 227–8 (D. L. Amiss 75, A. I. Kallicharran 67).
On 8 September D. L. Amiss became the first (and only) batsman to score 2,000 runs in first-class matches in the 1978 season.

WORCESTERSHIRE (3:3/0) drew with SOMERSET (7:3/4) at Worcester. Worcestershire 259–9d (J. A. Ormrod 116, E. J. O. Hemsley 81, I. T. Botham 6–86) and 254–3d (P. A. Neale 103*, D. J. Humphries 80). Somerset 251–2d (B. C. Rose 111, P. A. Slocombe 106*) and 251–6 (P. A. Slocombe 98).

YORKSHIRE (12:0/0) beat GLOUCESTERSHIRE (0) by 2 wickets at Scarborough. No play possible first day. Single innings match begun with less than eight hours remaining. Gloucestershire 161 (A. W. Stovold 59* carried his bat through the innings, M. J. Procter 50, S. Oldham 4–6). Yorkshire 162–8 (C. W. J. Athey 56).

COUNTY CHAMPIONS 1864–1978

1864	Surrey	1896	Yorkshire	1938	Yorkshire
1865	Nottinghamshire	1897	Lancashire	1939	Yorkshire
1866	Middlesex	1898	Yorkshire	1946	Yorkshire
1867	Yorkshire	1899	Surrey	1947	Middlesex
1868	Nottinghamshire	1900	Yorkshire	1948	Glamorgan
1869	{ Nottinghamshire / Yorkshire }	1901	Yorkshire	1949	{ Middlesex / Yorkshire }
		1902	Yorkshire		
1870	Yorkshire	1903	Middlesex	1950	{ Lancashire / Surrey }
1871	Nottinghamshire	1904	Lancashire		
1872	Nottinghamshire	1905	Yorkshire	1951	Warwickshire
1873	{ Gloucestershire / Nottinghamshire }	1906	Kent	1952	Surrey
		1907	Nottinghamshire	1953	Surrey
1874	Gloucestershire	1908	Yorkshire	1954	Surrey
1875	Nottinghamshire	1909	Kent	1955	Surrey
1876	Gloucestershire	1910	Kent	1956	Surrey
1877	Gloucestershire	1911	Warwickshire	1957	Surrey
1878	Undecided	1912	Yorkshire	1958	Surrey
1879	{ Nottinghamshire / Lancashire }	1913	Kent	1959	Yorkshire
		1914	Surrey	1960	Yorkshire
1880	Nottinghamshire	1919	Yorkshire	1961	Hampshire
1881	Lancashire	1920	Middlesex	1962	Yorkshire
1882	{ Nottinghamshire / Lancashire }	1921	Middlesex	1963	Yorkshire
		1922	Yorkshire	1964	Worcestershire
1883	Nottinghamshire	1923	Yorkshire	1965	Worcestershire
1884	Nottinghamshire	1924	Yorkshire	1966	Yorkshire
1885	Nottinghamshire	1925	Yorkshire	1967	Yorkshire
1886	Nottinghamshire	1926	Lancashire	1968	Yorkshire
1887	Surrey	1927	Lancashire	1969	Glamorgan
1888	Surrey	1928	Lancashire	1970	Kent
1889	{ Nottinghamshire / Lancashire / Surrey }	1929	Nottinghamshire	1971	Surrey
		1930	Lancashire	1972	Warwickshire
		1931	Yorkshire	1973	Hampshire
1890	Surrey	1932	Yorkshire	1974	Worcestershire
1891	Surrey	1933	Yorkshire	1975	Leicestershire
1892	Surrey	1934	Lancashire	1976	Middlesex
1893	Yorkshire	1935	Yorkshire	1977	{ Middlesex / Kent }
1894	Surrey	1936	Derbyshire		
1895	Surrey	1937	Yorkshire	1978	Kent

COUNTY CAPS AWARDED 1978

Derbyshire	H. Cartwright, P. N. Kirsten
Essex	N. Phillip
Gloucestershire	A. J. Brassington
Hampshire	N. G. Cowley, J. W. Southern
Kent	C. J. Tavaré
Northamptonshire	B. J. Griffiths, A. J. Lamb, T. M. Lamb, T. J. Yardley
Nottinghamshire	R. J. Hadlee
Somerset	P. A. Slocombe
Surrey	R. D. V. Knight, C. J. Richards
Sussex	Imran Khan
Warwickshire	K. D. Smith
Worcestershire	J. Cumbes, D. J. Humphries, P. A. Neale
Yorkshire	G. B. Stevenson

Glamorgan, Lancashire, Leicestershire and Middlesex did not award any new caps

Far left: Come in, number one. In Warwickshire's last Championship match of the season, Dennis Amiss became the first and only batsman to score 2,000 runs in the 1978 first-class season.

THE FIRST-CLASS COUNTIES

DERBYSHIRE

President: The Duke of Devonshire
Chairman: F. Burton
Secretary: D. A. Harrison
Captain: 1978 E. J. Barlow
1979 D. S. Steele
Colours: Chocolate, amber and pale blue
Headquarters:
County Cricket Ground, Nottingham Road, Derby DE2 6DA.

Honours: County Champions (1) 1936
Gillette Cup Finalists (1) 1969
Benson and Hedges Cup Finalists (1) 1978
1st XI Home Grounds 1979:
Chesterfield (Queen's Park); Burton upon Trent (Allied Breweries Ground); Derby; Long Eaton (Trent College).

The Derbyshire revival that began when that splendid, competitive all-rounder, Barlow, took over the helm faded somewhat in 1978, at least in terms of results. In the Schweppes Championship they slipped from a very respectable seventh to a disappointing fourteenth, although they began the season in a style that suggested this was going to be their year. Possibly it might have been had they not lost three key players, Taylor, Miller, and Hendrick, to the national team for much of the season, but there was no way that a side of their somewhat restricted ability could withstand such losses.

To add to these problems, Wright, their New Zealand opener who had done so well for them the previous summer, was on duty for his country and Barlow missed a few games through injury. Although there was no shortage of quantity when it came to reserves – 21 players represented the county in the Championship – the quality was lacking.

Nevertheless, Derbyshire did have the satisfaction of reaching the final of the Benson and Hedges Cup. It would have been both pleasing and appropriate if the drive and zest that Barlow brought to Derbyshire had been tangibly rewarded with an honour, but unfortunately Lord's simply underlined the fundamental weakness of his side; a shortage of authoritative batting necessary to produce a close contest.

As one would expect from a county whose bowlers have always been mean, Derbyshire's attack, when Hendrick and Miller were both available, was well above average. The main seam support for Hendrick came from Tunnicliffe, Barlow, and Russell, and even when their internationals were on England duty the bowling continued to be adequate. A large number of replacements were tried with varying degrees of success, and of course the brilliance of Taylor behind the stumps was greatly missed.

Derbyshire all-rounder Geoff Miller, playing for MCC against Middlesex at Lord's, makes a spectacular but unsuccessful attempt to dismiss his England captain, Brearley.

The big weakness was a lack of runs. It was significant that the South African, Kirsten, alone made more than 1,000 runs and there were only four individual centuries in the Championship. Barlow played some splendid innings, but neither Borrington nor Hill was as consistent as in the previous summer, and the promising Cartwright must consider himself lucky to retain a permanent place in the side with a Championship average of 17, indicative perhaps of the lack of good batsmen available.

Miller enjoyed a successful all-round season at county level, but he will need to improve both his batting and his bowling if he is to become an international class all-rounder. At the moment he does not appear to be beating the outside of the bat enough on a good wicket, and he should be scoring the occasional century.

Although the return of Wright will bring more stability to the batting, the retirement of Barlow will leave a gap that will be hard to fill. Not only was he a fine all-round cricketer, but he gave his side a new confidence in themselves. Unless they sign another outstanding international cricketer, it is difficult to see how Derbyshire in 1979 can be seriously challenging for honours. If they are not careful they could easily find themselves back where they were before Barlow came to their rescue, unless the England selectors should decide to ignore Taylor, Hendrick, and Miller.

Schweppes County Championship: 14th	Won 3	Lost 7	Drawn 12
All First-Class Matches:	Won 3	Lost 7	Drawn 14
Gillette Cup:	Lost to Middlesex in 2nd round		
Benson and Hedges Cup:	Lost to Kent in final		
John Player League:	8th Won 6	Lost 7	No result 3

DERBYSHIRE 1978 FIRST-CLASS AVERAGES

BATTING and FIELDING

* Not out

	M	I	NO	HS	Runs	Av	100	50	Ct	St
G. Miller	12	20	4	95	604	37.75	—	5	13	—
P. N. Kirsten	20	35	4	206*	1133	36.54	1	7	11	—
E. J. Barlow	16	25	4	127	765	36.42	1	3	25	—
J. G. Wright	4	7	0	164	226	32.28	1	—	1	—
A. J. Borrington	17	27	3	137	669	27.87	1	2	3	—
J. Walters	14	22	4	90	482	26.77	—	2	2	—
F. W. Swarbrook	12	16	6	60*	240	24.00	—	1	5	—
A. Hill	24	41	1	153*	928	23.20	1	2	12	—
J. W. Lister	3	6	0	48	137	22.83	—	—	1	—
A. J. Harvey-Walker	9	13	2	80	230	20.90	—	2	4	—
H. Cartwright	24	37	4	77*	644	19.51	—	2	8	—
A. Morris	5	7	0	55	116	16.57	—	1	4	—
I. S. Anderson	6	10	1	75	140	15.55	—	1	3	—
M. Hendrick	14	13	6	33	108	15.42	—	—	6	—
J. M. H. Graham-Brown	11	17	2	43	209	13.93	—	—	1	—
R. W. Taylor	10	12	1	32	136	12.36	—	—	24	2
P. E. Russell	15	12	2	22	90	9.00	—	—	15	—
C. J. Tunnicliffe	19	23	4	45	146	7.68	—	—	7	—
R. C. Wincer	10	10	4	16*	43	7.16	—	—	5	—
A. J. Mellor	5	7	2	10*	19	3.80	—	—	—	—
A. J. McLellan	14	14	5	11*	27	3.00	—	—	17	—

BOWLING

	O	M	R	W	Av	BB	5wI	10wM
M. Hendrick	393.5	129	781	56	13.94	5–32	2	—
P. E. Russell	235.4	88	423	21	20.14	4–23	—	—
E. J. Barlow	214.5	58	528	24	22.00	4–34	—	—
A. J. Harvey-Walker	145	42	408	17	24.00	7–35	1	1
C. J. Tunnicliffe	456.4	127	1241	44	28.20	4–30	—	—
F. W. Swarbrook	134	43	344	12	28.66	4–22	—	—
G. Miller	371.2	121	869	30	28.96	5–43	2	—
J. Walters	166	31	497	16	31.06	3–70	—	—
P. N. Kirsten	207.4	55	581	18	32.27	4–51	—	—
R. C. Wincer	203.2	40	680	19	35.78	4–42	—	—

Also bowled: I. S. Anderson 43–10–150–2; H. Cartwright 1–0–1–0; J. M. H. Graham-Brown 114.2–28–338–7; A. Hill 2–0–14–0; A. J. Mellor 106–33–305–9; A. Morris 16–2–58–0.

ESSEX

President: T. N. Pearce
Chairman: A. G. Waterman
Secretary/Manager: P. Edwards
Captain: K. W. R. Fletcher
Colours: Blue, gold and red
Headquarters:
The County Ground, New Writtle Street, Chelmsford CM2 0RW.

Honours: Second in County Championship (1) 1978 John Player League Runners-up (3) 1971, 1976, 1977
1st XI Home Grounds 1979: Chelmsford; Colchester (Castle Park); Ilford (Valentine's Park); Southend-on-Sea (Southchurch Park).

The 1978 team were almost certainly the strongest that Essex have ever fielded. On all types of wicket, and in the four different forms of county cricket, they were probably the best equipped team in the country, yet they have still to win a major honour. They finished second in the Schweppes Championship, were one run away from a place in the Gillette Cup final, in which one would have expected them to beat Sussex, and were not quite able to maintain their usual tempo in the John Player League, having been runners-up for the two previous seasons.

Essex were astutely led by Fletcher, who also batted splendidly. Tactically shrewd, he is two years younger than Brearley and a superior batsman, with an average of over 40 in more than 50 Tests to support that claim. It was odd that Fletcher never appeared to be considered when nobody could think of an alternative to the runless Middlesex skipper.

The batting, spearheaded by the dashing McEwan, was extremely strong, with Gooch, Fletcher, a much improved Hardie, Denness, Pont and a volatile, forceful tail in which as good a batsman as Lever often came in last. Not only was it powerful, but it could gather runs quickly enough to allow the bowlers time to dismiss the opposition twice. Phillip, in his first season, proved the perfect replacement as a dashing all-rounder for Boyce, and Turner again showed his worth as a bits-and-pieces cricketer. Lever had a most distinguished season with the ball, while East, with his haul of over 90 wickets, was second only to Underwood as the most successful spinner in the land. Acfield, with fewer opportunities, provided the contrast with his nagging off-breaks.

All the ingredients for at last carrying off a title were there: plenty of batting, including three players of genuine quality, and a formidable, balanced attack well supported in the field and behind the stumps. What went wrong, apart from the psychological disadvantage of never having broken through that particular barrier? Essex supporters will point to the fact that if only the selectors had not included Lever in the England squad, Essex would surely have beaten Worcestershire, and perhaps Kent as well, which would have been sufficient to give them the Championship. Furthermore, the rain often fell unkindly when they were in a winning position. They defeated the previous season's co-champions, Middlesex, by over 100 runs and the other co-champions, Kent, three weeks later by an innings and 41 runs. Of their outright wins, 42 per cent were by an innings margin, and they lost only one game to Kent's three.

However, although the absence of Lever, as twelfth man for England, was irritating, and lessened the chances of Essex, it must be appreciated that these would have been far worse had he been a regular member of the Test team. The really ironic feature was that the person who played the biggest part in Essex not winning the Championship was Kerry Packer, whose actions meant that Kent had three WSC men permanently available. It was only their presence that prevented Essex from winning a title with a performance which in any normal summer would have been sufficient.

Despite the disappointment, the future for the county is bright; and they should break their duck in 1979. Not the least pleasing feature was that their new, young opening batsman, Lilley, celebrated his first-class début with a century against Nottinghamshire in the last game of the season; here, certainly, is a name to watch. If anyone should doubt the practical value of expert coaching at an early age, he would do well to look at the Essex team. Of the six who learned their cricket in the county, four were attending the Ilford Indoor School regularly before they were 12.

Schweppes County Championship:	2nd	Won 12 Lost 1 Drawn 9	
All First-Class Matches:		Won 12 Lost 1 Drawn 11	
Gillette Cup:	Lost to Somerset in semi-final		
Benson and Hedges Cup:	Failed to qualify for Q-F (4th in Group D)		
John Player League:	6th	Won 7 Lost 6 No result 3	

ESSEX 1978 FIRST-CLASS AVERAGES

BATTING and FIELDING * Not out

	M	I	NO	HS	Runs	Av	100	50	Ct	St
K. S. McEwan	24	37	3	186	1682	49.47	5	8	21	—
K. W. R. Fletcher	24	35	8	89	1127	41.74	—	10	28	—
B. R. Hardie	23	33	7	109	1044	40.15	1	6	27	—
G. A. Gooch	15	25	1	129	933	38.87	2	5	16	—
S. Turner	23	29	8	89*	636	30.28	—	3	13	—
N. Phillip	20	28	4	134	645	26.87	1	3	4	—
M. H. Denness	22	37	2	126	870	24.85	1	4	10	—
K. R. Pont	12	18	2	101	366	22.87	1	2	8	—
R. E. East	23	26	5	57	391	18.61	—	1	14	—
N. Smith	24	24	6	59*	323	17.94	—	1	51	8
D. R. Pringle	3	5	1	50*	60	15.00	—	1	1	—
M. S. A. McEvoy	4	6	0	51	87	14.50	—	1	2	—
J. K. Lever	21	14	7	8	55	7.85	—	—	8	—
D. L. Acfield	22	15	9	12*	44	7.33	—	—	8	—

Also batted: (2 matches) M. K. Fosh 10, 32, 3, 0 (1 ct); (1 match) A. W. Lilley 22, 100*. S. J. Malone played in one match without batting.

BOWLING

	O	M	R	W	Av	BB	5wI	10wM
J. K. Lever	645.5	147	1555	102	15.24	7–32	9	1
R. E. East	700.2	226	1506	92	16.36	8–41	6	1
N. Phillip	583.1	113	1591	71	22.40	6–33	4	—
S. Turner	531	149	1183	48	24.64	4–9	—	—
D. L. Acfield	454.1	125	1013	36	28.13	3–33	—	—

Also bowled: G. A. Gooch 16–3–37–2; S. J. Malone 15–6–28–1; K. R. Pont 65–17–193–3; D. R. Pringle 23–8–50–1.

Left: The South African Ken McEwan, with an average of just under 50, played a leading role in Essex's chase for the Schweppes Championship title.

GLAMORGAN

Patron: Sir Edward Lewis
President: Judge Rowe Harding
Chairman: O. S. Wheatley
Secretary: P. B. Clift
Captain: A. Jones
Colours: Blue and gold
Headquarters:
6 High Street, Cardiff CF1 1YU.

Honours: County Champions (2) 1948, 1969
Gillette Cup Finalists (1) 1977
1st XI Home Grounds 1979:
Cardiff (Sophia Gardens);
Ebbw Vale (Welfare Ground);
Swansea (St Helen's).

After all the excitement of 1977 when Glamorgan reached, somewhat fortuitously, the Gillette Cup final, it was back to the wrong half of the table in both the Schweppes Championship and the Sunday League, an exit from the Gillette in the second round, and elimination from the Benson and Hedges Cup in the quarter-finals. These performances could be said to represent a fairly accurate assessment of the strength of the team; indeed they probably did rather better than their actual ability warranted. Certainly, several more-accomplished clubs are to be found below them in both tables, because the Welshmen were never beaten without a hard fight.

The Glamorgan batting was adequate. Hopkins continued to improve, headed the averages, and with the ever-dependable Alan Jones gave the county an above-average opening partnership. Both topped 1,000 runs and they scored three centuries each. The former is clearly going to be an invaluable member of the side for years to come, but one wonders how they will replace the latter. This was the eighteenth consecutive season in which Alan has reached four figures, and he continued to captain the side neatly and efficiently; rather as he bats. Although Llewellyn played most attractively on occasions, this dashing lefthander did not quite come up to expectations. Richards scored runs and showed improved form with the bat in the middle order, but his bowling figures make rather painful reading. The hard-hitting Nash enjoyed one of his best-ever summers as a batsman, striking the second century of his career and moving into the all-rounder category.

Runs were also provided by the two South Africans, Swart and Ontong, both of whom are competent all-rounders. Swart was their one main-line bowler to secure his wickets, 36 in the Championship, for under 30 apiece. He averaged over 30 with the bat, including three centuries. Ontong also hit a couple of centuries, but his 22 wickets in the Championship cost 38 apiece. Such figures show that both players are most competent bits and pieces cricketers, who also field very well; and there are a great many English cricketers who fall into that category. But they are not, as yet anyway, the match-winners which one hopes all-rounders from abroad will prove to be. It must be said that the Glamorgan imports, including established Test players, have, for one reason or another, seldom been able to achieve the expected results.

With the occasional exception, the Welshmen did not suffer from lack of runs, their fielding was above average and frequently brilliant, and Eifion

With 1,000 runs and 43 wickets to his credit in 1978, Peter Swart was the more successful of the two South African imports at Glamorgan.

Jones kept wicket most efficiently. Their fundamental weakness lay in an attack that was totally inadequate. It lacked real pace, incisive spin and penetration, as is shown by the fact that most of their bowlers returned averages in the high thirties or forties. Admittedly the Glamorgan wickets were inclined to assist the batsmen, but no team can expect to win matches with bowling figures of that kind. In addition, their bowling was too medium-paced and friendly even for the lesser requirements of the one-day game.

Schweppes County Championship:	13th	Won 3 Lost 8 Drawn 11	
All First-Class Matches:		Won 4 Lost 8 Drawn 12	
Gillette Cup:		Lost to Somerset in 2nd round	
Benson and Hedges Cup:		Lost to Warwickshire in quarter-final	
John Player League:		10th Won 6 Lost 8 No result 2	

GLAMORGAN 1978 FIRST-CLASS AVERAGES

BATTING and FIELDING   * Not out

	M	I	NO	HS	Runs	Av	100	50	Ct	St
J. A. Hopkins	24	42	3	116	1358	34.82	3	7	18	—
M. J. Llewellyn	21	31	6	82	849	33.96	—	7	9	—
R. C. Ontong	21	34	4	116*	969	32.30	2	5	7	—
P. D. Swart	23	37	3	115	1078	31.70	3	5	19	—
A. Jones	24	39	1	147	1133	29.81	3	3	4	—
G. Richards	22	36	10	74	768	29.53	—	5	6	—
M. A. Nash	23	34	5	124*	794	27.37	1	5	10	—
D. A. Francis	7	10	1	56	154	17.11	—	2	5	—
A. L. Jones	9	16	2	54	213	15.21	—	1	5	—
A. E. Cordle	15	15	3	33*	161	13.41	—	—	8	—
B. J. Lloyd	24	28	8	27	245	12.25	—	—	10	—
E. W. Jones	22	25	5	58	232	11.60	—	1	40	1
P. G. Crowther	4	7	0	27	47	6.71	—	—	1	—
A. H. Wilkins	18	21	10	17	61	5.54	—	—	10	—
A. J. Mack	5	4	2	8*	8	4.00	—	—	2	—

Also batted: (2 matches) G. C. Holmes 17*, 1*, 8, 11 (1 ct).

BOWLING

	O	M	R	W	Av	BB	5wI	10wM
A. J. Mack	77.3	26	195	16	12.18	4–28	—	—
P. D. Swart	358	73	1112	43	25.86	4–24	—	—
A. H. Wilkins	369.3	74	1267	37	34.24	5–96	1	—
M. A. Nash	519.2	135	1631	42	38.83	6–74	2	—
R. C. Ontong	262.5	57	856	22	38.90	4–95	—	—
G. Richards	218.3	45	750	19	39.47	5–55	1	—
B. J. Lloyd	561.3	154	1590	40	39.75	4–82	—	—
A. E. Cordle	307.5	73	864	21	41.14	5–33	1	—

Also bowled: G. C. Holmes 4–0–41–0; J. A. Hopkins 2–0–10–0; A. Jones 2.3–0–10–0; A. L. Jones 0.2–0–4–0.

GLOUCESTERSHIRE

Patron: The Duke of Beaufort
President: B. O. Allen
Chairman: J. K. R. Graveney
Secretary: A. S. Brown
Captain: M. J. Procter
Colours: Blue, gold, brown, sky-blue, green and red
Headquarters:
County Ground, Nevil Road, Bristol BS7 9EJ.

Honours: County Champions (3) 1874, 1876, 1877
Joint Champions (1) 1873
Gillette Cup Winners (1) 1973
Benson and Hedges Cup Winners (1) 1977
1st XI Home Grounds 1979:
Bristol; Cheltenham (College Ground); Gloucester (Winget Sports Ground); Moreton-in-Marsh.

Gloucestershire continued to justify their reputation as the most unpredictable of all the counties. One season they are to be found challenging for a title, or have reached one of the finals; the next they are languishing near the bottom. Last season witnessed a down-swing, with the County dropping from a Championship-contending third to tenth in the Schweppes table, finishing an improbable, almost unbelievable, last in the John Player League, and achieving no major success in the knockout cups. These setbacks occurred despite Procter, who had another tremendous season with both bat and ball, as well as continuing to lead his team with skill and enthusiasm. It is easy to understand why Gloucestershire supporters were so keen to retain his services.

Procter averaged more than 50 with the bat, scored over 1,600 runs, which was considerably more than Zaheer, sent down more overs than anybody, often reverting from pace to off-breaks on very slow pitches, and was the leading wicket-taker. No club could ask for more. Zaheer, who was not called on by Pakistan because of his Packer connections, was easily the next most successful batsman, hitting six centuries, including a double hundred against Sussex. Sadiq Mohammad, when he returned after the tour, provided the consistency and class that Stovold and a much improved Foat were never quite able to achieve. With Shepherd out of form it could be said that one reason for the club's decline was that they were always at least one batsman light, although the considerable improvement shown by Graveney in this department camouflaged the weakness to some degree.

The other main cause for the poor showing was that their attack was at least one main bowler short. Procter and Brain made an excellent opening pair with the new ball, the former still a great bowler, while the latter has been consistently underrated. However, they needed a class third seamer, someone to pick up around 50 wickets in the season at 25 apiece. Childs, who has looked a slow left-armer of considerable promise for some time, but has had to contend with the presence of Graveney, also a left-arm spinner, in the same team, clearly established himself as the number one last summer. Graveney's advance with the bat coincided with a marked decline with the ball, and no team can really afford to have the wickets of any main bowler costing 53 runs each, as Graveney's did in the Championship.

Successive centuries against Glamorgan and Warwickshire by James Foat helped reward those Gloucestershire supporters who maintained faith in his potential during leaner times.

Behind the stumps Brassington continued to impress, and another pleasing feature was the batting of the youthful Bainbridge at the end of the season. Sadly Hignell, who had played so well in 1977 and also did well at Cambridge, was completely out of touch.

It is hopeless trying to predict the future for Gloucestershire. If Procter happens to be in peak all-round form they are always capable of winning any limited-overs match, but unless they find one, preferably two, additional batsmen and two bowlers, it is difficult to see them climbing the Championship ladder. Although the weather was cruel, especially during the Cheltenham Festival, Gloucestershire's only win throughout July and August was a one-day affair against Glamorgan. That type of performance does not bode well for this year, but they are a 'yo yo' team who, against all logic, could surprise everybody by once again being on the up and up.

Schweppes County Championship:	10th	Won 4	Lost 8	Drawn 9 (Abandoned 1)
All First-Class Matches:		Won 5	Lost 8	Drawn 11 (Abandoned 1)
Gillette Cup:	Lost to Lancashire in 2nd round			
Benson and Hedges Cup:	Failed to qualify for Q-F (4th in Group A)			
John Player League:	17th Won 3 Lost 11 No result 2			

GLOUCESTERSHIRE 1978 FIRST-CLASS AVERAGES

BATTING and FIELDING　　　　　　　　　　　　　　　　　　　* Not out

	M	I	NO	HS	Runs	Av	100	50	Ct	St
P. Bainbridge	3	5	2	76*	233	77.66	—	3	1	—
M. J. Procter	21	36	3	203	1655	50.15	3	7	11	—
Zaheer Abbas	22	35	1	213	1535	45.14	6	4	15	—
Sadiq Mohammad	13	22	2	176	774	38.70	1	3	4	—
A. W. Stovold	21	35	2	139	962	29.15	1	5	9	3
J. C. Foat	19	29	4	102*	722	28.88	2	3	7	—
D. A. Graveney	24	35	8	92	740	27.40	—	4	16	—
D. R. Shepherd	16	24	1	72	446	19.39	—	3	4	—
A. Tait	11	19	1	53	348	19.33	—	2	2	—
M. D. Partridge	7	10	3	50	133	19.00	—	1	2	—
N. H. C. Cooper	6	12	0	94	219	18.25	—	1	4	—
B. M. Brain	23	27	7	35	268	13.40	—	—	3	—
J. Davey	15	19	6	20*	135	10.38	—	—	4	—
J. H. Shackleton	7	9	4	22	49	9.80	—	—	5	—
A. J. Hignell	11	19	0	44	182	9.57	—	—	10	—
A. J. Brassington	21	30	3	22	192	7.11	—	—	42	3
J. H. Childs	19	16	11	4*	28	5.60	—	—	8	—

Also batted: (2 matches) I. C. Crawford 73, 2, 14; (1 match) S. Williams 0. B. K. Shantry played in one match without batting.

BOWLING

	O	M	R	W	Av	BB	5wI	10wM
B. M. Brain	573.2	138	1589	76	20.90	5–48	2	—
M. J. Procter	665.2	185	1649	69	23.89	7–45	2	—
J. H. Childs	520.2	154	1440	59	24.40	8–34	5	2
J. Davey	309.3	65	900	30	30.00	4–52	—	—
D. A. Graveney	517	156	1425	31	45.96	4–47	—	—

Also bowled: P. Bainbridge 25–8–59–0; N.H.C. Cooper 3–0–26–0; I. C. Crawford 17–8–37–0; J. C. Foat 1–0–7–0; M. D. Partridge 85–15–312–3; Sadiq Mohammad 4.3–3–8–0; J. H. Shackleton 96–22–275–4; B. K. Shantry 39–6–167–3; D. R. Shepherd 4.5–0–26–0; A. Tait 0.1–0–0–0; Zaheer Abbas 8–1–26–0.

HAMPSHIRE

President: R. Aird
Chairman: G. Ford
Secretary: A. K. James
Captain: 1978 R. M. C. Gilliat
1979 G. R. Stephenson
Colours: Blue, gold and white
Headquarters:
County Ground, Northlands
Road, Southampton SO9 2TY.

Honours: County Champions (2)
1961, 1973
John Player League Champions
(2) 1975, 1978
1st XI Home Grounds 1979:
Southampton; Basingstoke
(May's Bounty); Bournemouth
(Dean Park); Portsmouth
(United Services Officers'
Ground).

For Trevor Jesty, 1978 was a summer to savour. In addition to topping 1,000 runs comfortably, he won the John Player League bowling award by taking four or more wickets three times.

Any county with three players of the class of Richards and Greenidge, probably the best, certainly the most explosive, opening pair of batsmen in the world, and Roberts, a very fast and accurate bowler capable of running through a Test side, must fancy its chances of winning at least one of the four trophies. Unfortunately, neither Richards nor Roberts was totally committed to his adopted county and tended to bat or bowl to true ability only when in the mood. This attitude cannot have pleased the ordinary members of the Hampshire team who, though not in the same class as Richards or Roberts, at least never gave less than their best.

In his unhappy book, Richards explained, not very convincingly, why he had become disillusioned with county cricket, though he was willing to accept the wages and a tax-free benefit. It made one wonder whether he had ever really loved the game as distinct from batting. During the summer, both Richards and Roberts left the club and then, to the intense pleasure of everybody, Hampshire won the John Player League with what can only be described as a somewhat limited side. If this made their success all the more surprising, it also made it more delightful.

To win honours without that pair, having failed with them in the team, does show the importance of an undivided dressing-room, and it is a considerable tribute to the leadership of Gilliat, a far better skipper than was often realised outside his county. His retirement, announced after the season had finished, leaves the county weaker than the departure of his more illustrious team members during the season could ever have done.

However, the spur that made victory really possible was Hampshire's third overseas player, Greenidge, who has always loved playing for Hampshire and on the departure of his team-mates was able to pull out that considerable extra – sometimes on one leg – which was to win vital games in the last few weeks. This included a breathtaking century in the final Sunday game of the season which, with Somerset losing to Essex on the same day, gave Hampshire the title. Although Hampshire finished level on points with both Somerset and Leicestershire, they had a fractionally better run-rate.

The genius of Greenidge apart, the main runs were provided by Jesty, Turner, Gilliat, and Cowley, with competent support coming from those two typical county seam bowling all-rounders, Taylor and Rice. The invaluable Stephenson, who takes his benefit in 1979, kept wicket with considerable distinction and proved a capable deputy in Gilliat's absence.

The Hampshire attack, particularly without Roberts, was short of real penetration and, on a good wicket, most batsmen would fancy their chances against them. This was emphasised in the last Championship match of the season against one of the weaker teams, Glamorgan. Although they eventually won by 59 runs, it was the first Championship victory Hampshire had obtained at Southampton for more than four years. What they do have is the type of tidy bowling suitable for limited-overs cricket and the limitation of a Championship first innings to 100 overs. Such artificial restrictions mean they do not have to worry about bowling out the opposition, while in that number of overs their batting is certainly capable of scoring as many runs as the opposition; indeed, considerably more should Greenidge click.

Stevenson improved, Tremlett is still struggling to establish himself at county level, and Rice falls into the category of a third, or fourth, county seamer. Taylor moves the ball off the seam and Jesty, at around medium pace, does swerve the ball late away from the bat. Their two finger spinners, the left-arm Southern and the right-arm Cowley, are both steady, with the former able to exploit helpful conditions. Nonetheless, neither yet appears capable of turning in the figures normally needed to win two, perhaps three, matches per season.

Schweppes County Championship:	8th Won 4 Lost 6 Drawn 11 (Abandoned 1)
All First-Class Matches:	Won 5 Lost 6 Drawn 12 (Abandoned 1)
Gillette Cup:	Lost to Leicestershire in 2nd round
Benson and Hedges Cup:	Failed to qualify for Q-F (3rd in Group B)
John Player League:	1st Won 11 Lost 3 No result 2

HAMPSHIRE 1978 FIRST-CLASS AVERAGES

BATTING and FIELDING   * Not out

	M	I	NO	HS	Runs	Av	100	50	Ct	St
C. G. Greenidge	19	34	1	211	1771	53.66	5	9	34	—
M. N. S. Taylor	22	29	9	103*	770	38.50	1	6	8	—
D. R. Turner	23	42	3	148*	1255	32.17	3	2	9	—
T. E. Jesty	23	42	5	125*	1174	31.72	5	2	10	—
B. A. Richards	6	11	0	73	337	30.63	—	2	8	—
M. C. J. Nicholas	3	5	2	40*	77	25.66	—	—	2	—
R. M. C. Gilliat	16	27	9	54	453	25.16	—	1	13	—
R. B. Elms	3	2	0	48	48	24.00	—	—	—	—
A. M. E. Roberts	9	14	5	37*	209	23.22	—	—	—	—
T. M. Tremlett	6	10	2	50	183	22.87	—	1	1	—
J. M. Rice	19	31	2	63	630	21.72	—	3	15	—
N. G. Cowley	23	38	5	64	650	19.69	—	2	16	—
D. J. Rock	7	13	0	54	231	17.76	—	2	6	—
G. R. Stephenson	23	30	5	66	350	14.00	—	1	46	9
J. W. Southern	23	22	8	51	148	10.57	—	1	7	—
N. E. J. Pocock	5	8	1	18	71	10.14	—	—	8	—
K. Stevenson	21	21	4	19	111	6.52	—	—	8	—

Also batted: (2 matches) V. P. Terry 5, 8, 3.

BOWLING

	O	M	R	W	Av	BB	5wI	10wM
A. M. E. Roberts	254.1	74	617	27	22.85	5–20	1	—
J. W. Southern	762.3	247	1833	76	24.11	5–32	4	—
J. M. Rice	267.1	70	709	29	24.44	4–49	—	—
N. G. Cowley	672.3	192	1700	56	30.35	5–93	1	—
K. Stevenson	515.5	101	1706	56	30.46	6–73	2	—
M. N. S. Taylor	346.1	104	900	27	33.33	5–67	1	—
T. E. Jesty	257.5	71	660	19	34.73	6–50	1	—

Also bowled: R. B. Elms 27–6–89–1; C. G. Greenidge 4–2–8–1; N. E. J. Pocock 3–0–5–0; B. A. Richards 1–0–1–0; G. R. Stephenson 0.1–0–1–0; T. M. Tremlett 95–27–219–7.

KENT

Patron:	HRH The Duke of Kent
President:	T. A. Pearce
Chairman:	W. C. W. Brice
Secretary:	Gp. Capt. M. D. Fenner
Captain:	A. G. E. Ealham
Colours:	Red and white
Headquarters:	St Lawrence Ground, Old Dover Road, Canterbury CT1 3NZ.

Honours: County Champions (6) 1906, 1909, 1910, 1913, 1970, 1978
Joint Champions (1) 1977
Gillette Cup Winners (2) 1967, 1974
Benson and Hedges Cup Winners (3) 1973, 1976, 1978
John Player League Champions (3) 1972, 1973, 1976
1st XI Home Grounds 1979: Canterbury (St Lawrence Ground); Dartford (Hesketh Park); Folkestone (Cheriton Road); Maidstone (The Mote); Tunbridge Wells (Nevill Ground).

There can be no doubt that the best all-purpose team throughout the seventies has been Kent. In this period they have won the Schweppes Championship twice and shared it once, won the Gillette Cup once, won the Benson and Hedges Cup three times, and won the John Player League three times. If their side had not been so frequently depleted by international calls, this outstanding record would be even better. It was, therefore, inevitable that they would do extremely well last summer, having their three Packer men, Underwood, Woolmer and Asif, available throughout the season. Indeed, few counties would not fancy their chances of carrying off some title with three players of such calibre ever present, especially in a wet summer.

The outcome was that Kent won the Schweppes County Championship, carried off the Benson and Hedges Cup, and finished fifth in the John Player League. Underwood was the leading wicket-taker in the country, Woolmer had a fine season with both bat and ball, and Asif had the happy knack of contributing a match-winning knock when most needed. Yet it would be wrong to imagine that Kent were solely dependent on this talented trio for success. Theirs was essentially a team effort, and nobody played a more vital part than Alan Ealham, a big-hearted county cricketer who suddenly found himself appointed captain and did a very good job to weld together a side which could so easily have been split by the internal problems. Alan also batted well, and Kent were seldom short of runs because of a quality batting line-up. Tavaré impressed everyone and many believed he should have gone with the England party to Australia; Cowdrey, Rowe, and Johnson all played some very good innings. In addition, there were a number of highly promising apprentices from the second XI keen to push their way into the first team.

Kent had a number of useful bowlers but, particularly on good wickets, not enough class bowlers. Jarvis is an above-average county new-ball bowler who could well go higher, but one gains the impression that he does not always think enough about his chosen trade. Johnson bowled his off-breaks effectively, Rowe turned in one or two useful spells, Hills was steady, and the outstanding Underwood did all, and often more, that was asked of him.

If the Kent attack had certain limitations, runs were never easy to come by against them because of the fielding, which was quite brilliant and a joy to behold. Behind the stumps Downton did well, but he will be at university for part of next summer. As their three Packer players have been offered contracts, the way is obviously open for Kent to re-engage Knott for this period. Apart from being a world-class 'keeper, he would obviously strengthen still further a formidable batting side.

Although the highlight of the summer was the winning of the Championship, for many the abounding memory of Kent cricket in 1978 will be John Shepherd, who epitomises all that is best in the game. Throughout the season he was continually making that vital breakthrough, producing the runs just when the game appeared to be slipping away, or holding an improbable catch. It is John's benefit this year, and it is a most deserved one.

Schweppes County Championship:	1st	Won 13	Lost 3	Drawn 6
All First-Class Matches:		Won 13	Lost 3	Drawn 8
Gillette Cup:		Lost to Somerset in quarter-final		
Benson and Hedges Cup:		Winners		
John Player League:	10th	Won 6	Lost 8	No result 2

KENT 1978 FIRST-CLASS AVERAGES

BATTING and FIELDING   * Not out

	M	I	NO	HS	Runs	Av	100	50	Ct	St
Asif Iqbal	18	25	6	171	934	49.15	3	2	18	—
C. J. Tavaré	24	37	5	105	1432	44.75	2	10	48	—
R. A. Woolmer	21	34	3	137	1245	40.16	2	9	25	—
J. N. Shepherd	20	28	6	101	785	35.68	2	3	12	—
C. J. C. Rowe	20	35	5	85	1065	35.50	—	7	7	—
A. G. E. Ealham	23	32	4	102*	856	30.57	1	5	15	—
G. W. Johnson	24	31	6	95	685	27.40	—	3	19	—
C. S. Cowdrey	17	17	4	69*	291	22.38	—	1	11	—
G. S. Clinton	6	8	2	33	113	18.83	—	—	2	—
D. L. Underwood	22	17	6	25	145	13.18	—	—	7	—
R. W. Hills	14	13	2	31*	122	11.09	—	—	3	—
P. R. Downton	24	20	6	31	147	10.50	—	—	53	4
N. J. Kemp	3	2	1	8*	8	8.00	—	—	—	—
G. R. Dilley	4	4	2	8	11	5.50	—	—	3	—
K. B. S. Jarvis	24	14	7	12	22	3.14	—	—	5	—

BOWLING

	O	M	R	W	Av	BB	5wI	10wM
D. L. Underwood	815.1	359	1594	110	14.49	9.32	8	2
R. A. Woolmer	135.4	46	292	20	14.60	6–27	1	—
G. W. Johnson	510.4	173	1084	56	19.35	6–32	2	—
K. B. S. Jarvis	579.5	134	1790	80	22.37	8–97	3	1
R. W. Hills	263.2	63	803	24	33.45	6–64	1	—
J. N. Shepherd	601.2	166	1573	44	35.75	5–70	1	—

Also bowled: Asif Iqbal 73–15–228–8; G. S. Clinton 1–0–8–2; C. S. Cowdrey 12–5–20–0; G. R. Dilley 75–19–197–8; A. G. E. Ealham 0.2–0–4–0; N. J. Kemp 28–4–91–3; C. J. C. Rowe 84.3–30–211–3; C. J. Tavaré 5–1–20–1.

After an uncertain start, Asif Iqbal found international form in the second half of the summer to boost Kent in their Championship campaign and to head their averages.

LANCASHIRE

Patroness: Her Majesty The Queen
President: T. A. Higson
Chairman: C. S. Rhoades
Secretary: C. D. Hassell
Captain: F. C. Hayes
Colours: Red, green and blue
Headquarters:
Old Trafford Cricket Ground,
Manchester M16 0PX.

Honours: County Champions (8) 1881, 1897, 1904, 1926, 1927, 1928, 1930, 1934
Joint Champions (4) 1879, 1882, 1889, 1950
Gillette Cup Winners (4) 1970, 1971, 1972, 1975
John Player League Champions (2) 1969, 1970.
1st XI Home Grounds 1979:
Manchester (Old Trafford); Blackpool (Stanley Park); Liverpool (Aigburth); Southport.

In that they shuffled uncertainly from sixteenth to twelfth in the Schweppes Championship, and leapt forward from an absolutely nonsensical sixteenth to fifth in the John Player League, Lancashire could be said to have displayed a slight improvement. Moreover, in some respects they were unlucky. Lee, who has been their principal wicket-taker for several seasons, was out of action through injury; Hogg, a most promising recruit to the seam-bowling brigade, broke down during the summer; and the weather, though universally bad, hit Lancashire harder than most counties. In retrospect, it was not that Lancashire had a bad season, but merely that with their staff and resources they should have been capable of doing better.

Once again the county failed to play to potential, and the hoped-for transformation under the new captain, Hayes, who took over from David Lloyd – who had resigned the leadership and had in fact been an above-average county captain – did not occur. Hayes' problems as skipper were not assisted by the unpredictability of his own batting, with occasional innings of brilliance and charm being interspersed by barren spells. However, his major difficulty was the same as his predecessor had experienced; the lack of complete harmony in the dressing-room. That total involvement by every player, such an essential ingredient for success, was missing, which of course is why the club have recently failed to do themselves justice in terms of results.

In all departments, batting, bowling and fielding, Lancashire were stronger than the majority of the other counties, but again no honours came their way. Too many of their players returned figures that were less than might have been expected. As Clive Lloyd is rated as one of the best and most exciting batsmen in the world, his aggregate of just over 1,000 runs for 36 Championship innings must be considered disappointing. Croft is a genuinely quick bowler who appeared to be relatively more successful at hitting batsmen than the stumps, which did suggest he had failed to get his priorities right. In 17 Championship matches this highly paid international opening bowler captured only 55 wickets, even though he had support at the other end and was backed up by fine fielding, so it came as no surprise that he was not re-engaged. Ratcliffe, like the two other main seamers, Croft and

With Lancashire's bowling weakened by the injuries to Lee and Hogg, all-rounder Bernard Reidy was called on to bowl more than he might have expected at the beginning of the season. His batting average did more credit to his true ability.

Hogg, took his wickets economically, but the three spinners, Simmons, Hughes and Arrowsmith, were noticeably less successful in terms of aggregate and average, even though it was a wet summer. In addition, Arrowsmith never lived up to the promise he showed at the back end of 1977.

This to some extent explains why Lancashire did not win more Championship matches, but it does not explain why they were no more than competent in limited-overs cricket. After all, they have a splendid tradition in this form of the game, their attack was admirably suited to its requirements, their fielding was excellent, and their batting, at least on paper, bristled with strokemakers and possessed experience as well as considerable depth.

Although below his best, Clive Lloyd struck four sparkling centuries, while both David Lloyd and Frank Hayes made over 1,000 runs with averages of over 30, figures indicating competent county players rather than genuine international cricketers. Kennedy, putting the disasters of 1977 behind him, found some of the form that made him appear such a good prospect when he first came into the team, but Abrahams was rather fortunate to retain his place in a side with so much reserve strength, although he certainly saved many runs in the field. Presumably the diminutive Pilling must be nearing the end of his first-class career, for he made only a limited number of appearances. The big surprise was that Wood, who was quite illogically recalled to the England eleven for one Test, was soon afterwards dropped from his county team. He may lack the class required to be genuine international material, but in terms of playing ability alone there is no way he could not have been good enough for the present Lancashire team. There is every reason to suppose that in his benefit year he will re-establish himself as a regular fixture in the side.

What of the future? Although Lancashire clearly have sufficient ability and reserve cover to do well, especially in the one-day game, they need to find a new zest. Something is wrong when a club regularly fails to produce the results it is capable of achieving. Nevertheless, Lancashire are certainly worth a bet in the John Player League, and it would come as no surprise if they appeared at Lord's in one of the two finals.

Schweppes County Championship:	12th	Won 4	Lost 8	Drawn 9 (Abandoned 1)
All First-Class Matches:		Won 5	Lost 8	Drawn 10 (Abandoned 1)
Gillette Cup:	Lost to Sussex in semi-final			
Benson and Hedges Cup:	Failed to qualify for Q-F (3rd in Group A)			
John Player League:	5th	Won 9	Lost 6	No result 1

LANCASHIRE 1978 FIRST-CLASS AVERAGES

BATTING and FIELDING   * Not out

	M	I	NO	HS	Runs	Av	100	50	Ct	St
C. H. Lloyd	21	36	6	120	1116	37.20	4	6	21	—
F. C. Hayes	20	34	5	136*	1049	36.17	2	4	15	—
D. Lloyd	22	37	2	185	1113	31.80	3	3	18	—
B. W. Reidy	10	15	3	88	360	30.00	—	1	2	—
A. Kennedy	19	31	2	100	859	29.62	1	4	8	—
J. Simmons	22	30	7	106	663	28.82	1	2	22	—
J. Abrahams	19	30	2	126	654	23.35	1	4	12	—
B. Wood	8	12	1	103	214	19.45	1	—	5	—
R. M. Ratcliffe	20	23	5	48	318	17.66	—	—	8	—
H. Pilling	8	13	1	49	203	16.91	—	—	2	—
D. P. Hughes	13	17	2	72	243	16.20	—	1	13	—
R. Arrowsmith	13	10	4	24*	96	16.00	—	—	4	—
J. Lyon	21	25	3	74*	267	12.13	—	1	49	3
C. E. H. Croft	18	22	3	19*	124	6.52	—	—	1	—
W. Hogg	11	14	5	19	50	5.55	—	—	—	—
P. J. W. Allott	4	2	1	1	1	1.00	—	—	1	—

Also batted: (2 matches) C. J. Scott 1*, 8 (3 ct); (1 match) P. G. Lee 1; R. J. Sutcliffe 10*, 0*.

BOWLING

	O	M	R	W	Av	BB	5wI	10wM
W. Hogg	256.4	58	775	38	20.39	7–84	3	—
R. M. Ratcliffe	571.3	151	1532	70	21.88	7–58	3	—
C. E. H. Croft	431.3	101	1266	56	22.60	5–58	1	—
D. P. Hughes	191.1	54	517	22	23.50	5–46	1	—
P. J. W. Allott	129	12	456	14	32.57	5–98	1	—
R. Arrowsmith	320.1	106	889	27	32.92	4–49	—	—
J. Simmons	501	146	1203	35	34.37	3–33	—	—

Also bowled: J. Abrahams 1–1–0–0; A. Kennedy 26–10–59–2; P. G. Lee 8–2–26–2; D. Lloyd 3.5–1–11–0; B. W. Reidy 163–29–515–6; R. J. Sutcliffe 12–3–37–1; B. Wood 87–28–240–8.

LEICESTERSHIRE

President: W. Bentley
Chairman: C. H. Palmer
Secretary/Manager:
    F. M. Turner
Captain: 1978 R. Illingworth
    1979 K. Higgs
Colours: Scarlet and dark
    green
Headquarters:
County Ground, Grace Road,
Leicester LE2 8AD.

Honours: County Champions (1)
1975
Benson and Hedges Cup
Winners (2) 1972, 1975
John Player League Champions
(2) 1974, 1977
1st XI Home Ground 1979:
Leicester (Grace Road).

The 1978 season saw the end of Illingworth's highly successful reign as captain of Leicestershire. His astute leadership, combined with his considerable all-round ability, has done wonders for a county which, until his arrival, had never won anything and had seldom even suggested they might. Admittedly, honours are now much easier to acquire, with four titles (at least one too many?) available each year and only 17 competitors. Nevertheless, Illingworth moulded together a side largely composed of misfits and discards from other counties into a team that was always a serious threat in all competitions. Although Leicestershire have still to win the Gillette Cup, under Illingworth's captaincy they have been County champions, easily the most difficult feat, and have carried off both the John Player League and the Benson and Hedges Cup twice.

They were fortunate in one respect that, until last summer, they seldom provided any players for international duty. This makes a difference, and it is noticeable that their best days came after Illingworth had lost the England captaincy and could devote himself entirely to the affairs of his adopted county.

Although last summer Leicestershire always looked as if they might carry off something, they never quite succeeded. The nearest they came was to finish level on points with Hampshire, the winners, and Somerset in the John Player League. The truth was that too many of the team had reached the veteran or near-veteran stage, and this showed on occasions in the field. Furthermore, their new young hope, Gower, who emerged in a blaze of runs and headlines, was lost to his county on Test duty for more than half of the season. And in his nine Championship matches for his county, this exciting young lefthander proved conspicuously less successful than he was for England, scoring only 347 runs in 15 innings.

Once again Davison was the main provider of runs, hitting four centuries, making over 1,600 and averaging 51. With his agility in the field to support his dynamic batting, it is unfortunate that this very good player has been denied the opportunity of playing at the highest level. His main support came from the sound and reliable Steele and Balderstone and the more dashing Tolchard, whose selection as second 'keeper for Australia owed more to his ability with the bat than behind the stumps. There were also ample runs to be had from the lower order, where Clift struck to good effect

Rhodesian-born all-rounder Paddy Clift strikes to good effect for Leicestershire.

and Illingworth was always on hand to steady the boat. Although the usually dependable Dudleston had a disappointing summer, Birkenshaw enjoyed a good all-round season and Briers looked an exceptional prospect for the future.

In a seam dominated era in which teams often consider more than one spinner a luxury, it was refreshing to find a county with four; Balderstone, a flighty slow left-armer particularly effective against batsmen who want to play everything from the crease (and there are a number around), the flatter Steele, and those two contrasting off-spinners, Illingworth and Birkenshaw. This quartet of slow bowlers not only captured two-fifths of the wickets taken in three-day matches, but were used to good effect in limited-overs cricket.

That old warrior, 'hit-the-deck' Higgs, topped the bowling averages and Leicestershire's young fast bowler, Taylor, had an encouraging first season. Booth bowled well at times, and at medium pace Clift was invaluable, but the county have never really replaced McKenzie, a new ball bowler of genuine pace and penetration.

They are hoping that within a year or so the teenager Agnew, who came straight out of Public School cricket, will prove to be the man. Having spent the winter in Australia sharpening up his trade, he is one of the players one hopes will ensure a bright future for this very well administered Midlands county.

This summer Leicestershire are led by the experienced Higgs, presumably a stop-gap appointment. There is every reason to expect that he will do a sound job and that the club will finish near the top of the two Leagues and continue as serious candidates in one or other of the knockout competitions, especially if other members of their up-and-coming brigade should emulate Gower.

Schweppes County Championship:	6th Won 4	Lost 5	Drawn 13
All First-Class Matches:	Won 5	Lost 5	Drawn 14
Gillette Cup:	Lost to Essex in quarter-final		
Benson and Hedges Cup:	Failed to qualify for Q-F (3rd in Group C)		
John Player League:	3rd Won 11	Lost 3	No result 2

LEICESTERSHIRE 1978 FIRST-CLASS AVERAGES

BATTING and FIELDING   * Not out

	M	I	NO	HS	Runs	Av	100	50	Ct	St
B. F. Davison	23	35	3	180*	1644	51.37	4	9	8	—
R. W. Tolchard	24	35	16	103*	841	44.26	1	5	39	7
J. F. Steele	22	34	3	133	1182	38.12	3	6	28	—
J. Birkenshaw	22	26	9	70*	506	29.76	—	1	10	—
N. E. Briers	16	24	2	116*	601	27.31	2	2	6	—
D. I. Gower	11	17	2	61	405	27.00	—	1	5	—
J. C. Balderstone	24	36	1	101	931	26.60	1	5	9	—
M. Schepens	5	8	2	39	147	24.50	—	—	3	—
P. B. Clift	22	26	7	61	465	24.47	—	3	13	—
K. Shuttleworth	6	5	2	27*	70	23.33	—	—	11	—
B. Dudleston	15	22	1	75	454	21.61	—	2	4	—
R. Illingworth	17	15	5	39*	209	20.90	—	—	5	—
P. Booth	18	10	2	25*	99	12.37	—	—	2	—
K. Higgs	18	11	6	13*	51	10.20	—	—	13	—
L. B. Taylor	11	6	1	16	27	5.40	—	—	4	—
J. P. Agnew	4	1	0	1	1	1.00	—	—	—	—

Also batted: (2 matches) N. G. B. Cook 2*, 31 (1 ct); G. J. Parsons 7, 3. A. Ward played in one match without batting.

BOWLING

	O	M	R	W	Av	BB	5wI	10wM
K. Higgs	381	112	923	41	22.51	7–44	1	—
P. B. Clift	519.4	156	1209	51	23.70	6–29	1	—
J. C. Balderstone	368.5	104	914	38	24.05	6–25	2	—
R. Illingworth	261.4	86	635	25	25.40	6–38	2	—
J. F. Steele	229.5	62	566	22	25.72	5–54	1	—
L. B. Taylor	278.2	47	962	36	26.72	4–32	—	—
J. Birkenshaw	344.2	83	874	30	29.13	3–23	—	—
P. Booth	293.2	63	870	29	30.00	6–93	1	—
K. Shuttleworth	159.4	45	436	13	33.53	3–27	—	—

Also bowled: J. P. Agnew 67.4–13–215–6; N. E. Briers 16–2–40–1; N. G. B. Cook 38–16–83–3; B. F. Davison 5–0–29–0; B. Dudleston 2–0–11–0; G. J. Parsons 17–1–78–0; A. Ward 29–7–70–4.

MIDDLESEX

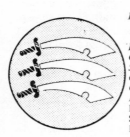

Patron: HRH The Prince Philip, Duke of Edinburgh
President: G. O. B. Allen
Chairman: F. G. Mann
Secretary: A. W. Flower
Captain: J. M. Brearley
Colours: Blue
Headquarters:
Lord's Cricket Ground, St John's Wood Road, London NW8 8QN.

Honours: County Champions (6) 1866, 1903, 1920, 1921, 1947, 1976
Joint Champions (2) 1949, 1977
Gillette Cup Winners (1) 1977
Benson and Hedges Cup Finalists (1) 1975
1st XI Home Ground 1979: Lord's.

Middlesex, county champions for the past two seasons, slipped to third place in the Schweppes final table, finished near the bottom of the John Player League, and failed to carry off either of the knockout cups. At first glance this might suggest the county was not as powerful as it had been and had begun to slip, but that was not the case. The full 1978 eleven was, in fact, stronger that either the 1977 or the 1976 teams. Edmonds and Emburey have never bowled better and were the finest pair of spinners in the country. Jones returned after injury, Gatting supported the description of an exciting prospect with fine all-round performances – including breaking that three-figure barrier with the bat for the first time – and Barlow rediscovered something approaching his true form. Featherstone enjoyed a successful summer, a most impressive 142 by Butcher suggested that he is just about ready to command a permanent place, and Gould, as well as improving considerably behind the stumps, contributed some valuable innings.

The simple reason why Middlesex failed to win an honour is that they supplied so many players for the six Tests and the one-day internationals. Brearley, Edmonds, and Radley were on permanent national duty, and Emburey was eventually called up. Even their not-inconsiderable reserve strength could cover the loss of their captain, their most dependable batsman, and their two main slow bowlers.

Few would dispute that at full strength Middlesex were the most accomplished side in the County Championship. Their attack had greater penetration and was much better balanced than Kent's, the eventual winners, and it was more menacing than that of Essex, who finished second. In Daniel they have a genuinely fast bowler, ideal for making the initial breakthrough, ending a stubborn stand, and destroying the tail. After Botham, Selvey, who finished the season with 101 wickets, was just about the most accomplished swing bowler in the country. Gatting showed himself to be a very useful third seamer and Jones was a more formidable pace bowler than many counties had as their first choice. As support spinner to the main pair, Featherstone was as good as many front-line slow bowlers elsewhere. Middlesex thus possessed an attack capable of bowling out opponents on all types of pitches and in all conditions.

The Londoners' batting was not as impressive as their bowling, especially as both regular openers, Brearley and Smith, had indifferent seasons. Nonetheless, it was usually good enough for the purpose, and Middlesex tended to score their runs briskly, thus giving their bowlers more time to dismiss the other side. Radley, always a reliable and proficient acquirer of runs at county level, continued to produce quantities of them for both England and Middlesex. The belligerent left-handed Barlow and Gatting were ideal for providing that extra impetus to press home an advantage, or to chase a total, while the elegant Featherstone continued to please without

Impressive performances by John Emburey for Middlesex won him an England cap against New Zealand at Lord's and a place in last winter's touring team to Australia.

again scoring quite as many runs as he promised. Tomlins, like Butcher, revealed considerable promise,

With batsmen of that calibre around, with distinctly useful performers like Edmonds in the lower order, and with the confident expectation that Brearley and Smith will regain their true form, the future for Middlesex is bright. They are sure to be up with the leaders in the County Championship and must stand an excellent chance of reaching one of the cup finals. They have the ability, the blend, the confidence, and the captain, and the major obstacle to their aspirations is again likely to be international calls.

The one slight question mark about the Middlesex team last season was in the John Player League, in which they made tactical blunders from time to time. Perhaps, having dropped out of the race comparatively early, they subconsciously lost some of their normal drive. When there is nothing much at stake, these forty or fewer overs' scrambles can become an anticlimax.

Schweppes County Championship: 3rd	Won 11	Lost 5	Drawn 5	(Abandoned 1)
All First-Class Matches:	Won 11	Lost 6	Drawn 7	(Abandoned 1)
Gillette Cup:	Lost to Lancashire in quarter-final			
Benson and Hedges Cup:	Lost to Derbyshire in quarter-final			
John Player League:	15th	Won 5	Lost 9	No result 2

MIDDLESEX 1978 FIRST-CLASS AVERAGES

BATTING and FIELDING
* Not out

	M	I	NO	HS	Runs	Av	100	50	Ct	St
C. T. Radley	12	18	1	105	615	36.17	2	3	13	—
R. O. Butcher	10	14	0	142	464	33.14	1	3	18	—
M. W. Gatting	24	36	4	128	1024	32.00	2	5	19	—
G. D. Barlow	24	35	2	102*	1016	30.78	1	6	15	—
N. G. Featherstone	19	27	1	108	740	28.46	1	3	15	—
J. M. Brearley	11	17	3	70*	394	28.14	—	3	6	—
I. J. Gould	22	31	4	128	706	26.14	1	2	50	5
M. J. Smith	23	34	1	63	726	22.00	—	3	3	—
K. P. Tomlins	11	16	2	94	295	21.07	—	2	8	—
P. H. Edmonds	11	14	2	43*	233	19.41	—	—	10	—
W. N. Slack	10	16	1	52	268	17.86	—	1	7	—
S. J. Poulter	3	3	0	36	47	15.66	—	—	—	—
J. E. Emburey	22	29	6	33	284	12.34	—	—	13	—
W. W. Daniel	21	24	12	30*	132	11.00	—	—	3	—
M. W. W. Selvey	24	28	8	19*	164	8.20	—	—	8	—
A. A. Jones	12	17	2	33	80	5.33	—	—	2	—

Also batted: (2 matches) A. S. Patel 25*, 22, 9 (1 ct); M. O. C. Sturt 2, 9 (6 ct, 1 st); (1 match) R. Herkes 0*

BOWLING

	O	M	R	W	Av	BB	5wI	10wM
M. W. Gatting	144.3	33	350	24	14.58	5–59	1	—
W. W. Daniel	453.3	113	1114	76	14.65	5–42	3	—
P. H. Edmonds	315	95	649	42	15.45	7–34	2	—
M. W. W. Selvey	743.5	199	1929	101	19.09	6–26	8	1
J. E. Emburey	684.2	201	1455	71	20.49	6–25	3	—
N. G. Featherstone	140.3	39	365	13	28.07	5–32	1	—
A. A. Jones	247.4	45	840	29	28.96	6–89	2	—

Also bowled: J. M. Brearley 1–1–0–0; R. Herkes 5–3–9–0; A. S. Patel 12–0–55–2; C. T. Radley 1–1–0–0; K. P. Tomlins 8–2–16–0.

NORTHAMPTONSHIRE

President: R. R. Garratt
Chairman: H. W. Wright
Secretary: K. C. Turner
Captain: P. J. Watts
Colours: Maroon
Headquarters:
County Ground,
Wantage Road,
Northampton NN1 4TJ.

Honours: County Championship
Runners-up (4) 1912, 1957, 1965,
1976
Gillette Cup Winners (1) 1976
1st XI Home Grounds 1979:
Northampton; Luton,
Bedfordshire; Milton Keynes,
Buckinghamshire; Tring,
Hertfordshire; Wellingborough
(School Ground).

Nobody should be remotely surprised that Northamptonshire finished bottom of the Schweppes Championship, close to the foot of the John Player League, and were unable to make any serious impression in either of the cup competitions. Their slide had really begun in 1977, when they were ninth in the county table and last in the Sunday League, though it must be admitted they have always been ill-suited to that particular form of the game.

For various reasons the Northamptonshire committee decided to dispense with their former captain, Mushtaq Mohammad, still an all-rounder of international calibre and in 1977 easily their most successful batsman. They also sacked their Indian slow left-arm spinner, Bedi, who had not proved as successful as expected. Nevertheless, he had still captured far more wickets for fewer runs in 1977 than any of Northamptonshire's bowlers were able to do in the wet summer of 1978, an irony Bedi must have enjoyed.

In addition to these two serious losses, Dye, who had bowled so well for them since leaving Kent, and the dependable and most experienced Virgin both decided to retire from first-class cricket. Furthermore, their main strike bowler, the excitable Sarfraz Nawaz, was on duty with Pakistan for the first half of the summer. This meant, in effect, that Northamptonshire had lost half their side, including a high proportion of their best players. Unless replacements of high quality, and in quantity, were forthcoming, failure was inevitable.

One of the main essentials for doing well in the Schweppes Championship is the ability to bowl out the opposition twice, something that was clearly beyond the capability of that fragile Northamptonshire attack. Its weakness is well illustrated by the fact that David Steele, who seldom got on with his left-arm spinners when Mushtaq and Bedi were in the side, was the only one of their main-line bowlers to return an average of under 30.

One could not but feel sorry for Jim Watts, who was summoned from retirement to lead a team which was already doomed. He was given an attack that lacked the penetration needed for the three-day game and the accuracy for the limited-overs one. He simply did not have a sporting chance.

Although in terms of collective results 1978 was a disaster, there were encouraging individual performances, the most exciting being the transformation of Larkins from a youngster of considerable potential into a handsome strokemaker with an England look about him. Many felt he should have been included in the Australian party, for he was surely as good as, and must in time become considerably better than, half of those chosen for their batsmanship. One good judge described his century against Surrey as just about the most exciting innings he had seen played by an Englishman for more than a decade.

Willey enjoyed a fine all-round season, and if his off-breaks were rather expensive, it cannot have helped to operate in an ultra-weak bowling side. How he must have wished that he was chosen as a batsman for England last summer, against Pakistan and New Zealand, when runs were so much easier to come by than against West Indies in 1976 when the flack was really flying.

In his first season of county cricket, the South African, Allan Lamb, did well to top the batting averages and should score heavily for his adopted county in the years ahead. Steele, in addition to his performances with the ball, once again provided that solidity to the batting which was especially valuable in times of stress, but the figures of the young all-rounder, Williams, were disappointing. Although Cook played well and sensibly on many occasions, he did not make any marked advance on his form of the previous summer. The two seamers, newcomer Tim Lamb, formerly of Middlesex, and Griffiths toiled away without really suggesting they would ever be more than run-of-the-mill practitioners.

The outlook for 1979 cannot be described as bright, especially as Steele has departed to Derbyshire. Larkins, Lamb, Willey, and Cook should provide sufficient runs, but even with Sarfraz available more often it is hard to see Northamptonshire winning many matches. Their immediate requirements are, quite simply, three or preferably four class players.

Schweppes County Championship:	17th	Won 2	Lost 6	Drawn 12 (Abandoned 2)
All First-Class Matches:		Won 2	Lost 6	Drawn 13 (Abandoned 2).
Gillette Cup:	Lost to Kent in 2nd round			
Benson and Hedges Cup:	Failed to qualify for Q-F (4th in Group C)			
John Player League:	13th	Won 5	Lost 8	No result 3

NORTHAMPTONSHIRE 1978 FIRST-CLASS AVERAGES

BATTING and FIELDING   * Not out

	M	I	NO	HS	Runs	Av	100	50	Ct	St
A. J. Lamb	17	27	8	106*	883	46.47	2	5	10	—
W. Larkins	21	37	3	170*	1343	39.50	3	7	12	—
D. S. Steele	21	36	5	130	1182	38.12	3	9	24	—
P. Willey	21	33	8	112	893	35.72	1	6	7	—
G. Cook	21	37	2	155	1177	33.62	1	7	20	—
T. J. Yardley	18	26	6	97	611	30.55	—	3	22	—
R. G. Williams	16	20	5	60*	399	26.60	—	1	8	—
I. M. Richards	7	4	1	23	54	18.00	—	—	—	—
P. J. Watts	13	15	1	57*	185	13.21	—	1	1	—
G. Sharp	19	20	4	27*	193	12.06	—	—	32	3
T. M. Lamb	21	18	4	33	139	9.92	—	—	6	—
B. J. Griffiths	19	12	8	11	31	7.75	—	—	5	—
Sarfraz Nawaz	9	11	3	20	61	7.62	—	—	2	—
A. Hodgson	4	6	3	10	22	7.33	—	—	—	—

Also batted: (2 matches) R. M. Carter 8*; V. A. Flynn 15, 6* (1 ct).

Wayne Larkins – reproduction of his 1978 form should bring international honours in 1979.

BOWLING

	O	M	R	W	Av	BB	5wI	10wM
D. S. Steele	378.3	109	976	37	26.37	6–36	3	1
T. M. Lamb	492.5	115	1370	46	29.78	6–71	1	—
B. J. Griffiths	554	103	1591	51	31.19	5–66	1	—
Sarfraz Nawaz	276.3	81	613	19	32.26	4–28	—	—
A. Hodgson	105.2	21	351	10	35.10	3–29	—	—
P. Willey	623.1	180	1438	39	36.87	4–61	—	—
R. G. Williams	160.1	35	461	10	46.10	4–48	—	—

Also bowled: R. M. Carter 15–3–43–0; G. Cook 2.2–0–18–0; A. J. Lamb 3.5–1–13–2; W. Larkins 44–9–142–3; I. M. Richards 53–10–154–7; P. J. Watts 73–18–182–8.

NOTTINGHAMSHIRE

President: H. T. Milnes
Chairman: J. R. Heatley
Chief Executive:
    P. G. Carling
Captain: M. J. Smedley
Colours: Green and gold
Headquarters:
Trent Bridge Cricket Ground,
Nottingham NG2 6AG.

Honours: County Champions
(12) 1865, 1868, 1871, 1872, 1875,
1880, 1883, 1884, 1885, 1886,
1907, 1929
Joint Champions (5) 1869, 1873,
1879, 1882, 1889
1st XI Home Grounds 1979:
Nottingham (Trent Bridge);
Worksop (Town Ground).

The 1978 season certainly gave Nottinghamshire supporters something to
smile about as their team rose from bottom place to seventh in the
Schweppes Championship. Yet although that improvement was overdue, it
had seemed completely impossible when, before the commencement of the
Championship season, near farce occurred with the committee deciding to
sack their captain and leading player, Rice, because he had signed for WSC.
Fortunately, after Rice had taken legal action for unfair dismissal, the
matter was settled out of court and he was re-engaged, though not as
captain. He proceeded to demonstrate eloquently his worth as a cricketer
with the best summer of his career.

Nottinghamshire's revival stemmed from three different factors, two of
which were connected with the Rice affair. First, Clive Rice showed
conclusively that he is an outstanding all-rounder of Test calibre, and one
must regret that he has never had the opportunity of taking part in the
highest form of the game. He comfortably topped the national batting
averages, produced a whole series of sparkling innings, fielded brilliantly,
and bowled very effectively until he damaged his back, at one stage forming
with Hadlee just about the most lethal double spearhead on the county
circuit. A Sobers or a Procter would have been pushed to contribute more to
his side than Rice, and one cannot help feeling he would also have made an
inspiring skipper.

Secondly, and in some respects even more vital, was the dramatic arrival
of Richard Hadlee, whose aggressive pace bowling plainly rattled the
opposing clubs. As a result, the rest of the team suddenly realised that
victories, for so long a rarity, were there for the taking. Even though it was a
different matter after Hadlee joined the New Zealand party, his
performances with the ball, and occasionally with the bat, had filled them
with fresh hope and a new spirit. The ironic feature was that Hadlee went to
Trent Bridge as an emergency replacement for the dismissed Rice.

The third factor was the form of Randall, who, after the disasters of 1977,
proved that he was still one of the finest, and certainly one of the most
entertaining, batsmen in the country. Moreover, as he was not called on by
the England selectors, apart from the one-day internationals,
Nottinghamshire could benefit from his talents for the whole of the season.
Randall's reward was a trip to Australia, where he found the faster
pitches much to his taste and established himself as something better
than an accomplished county batsman.

Harris and Todd frequently provided their side with that valuable substantial start to the innings, which Rice and Randall would capitalise on to the full. Smedley, who was re-appointed captain, gave stability to the middle order. He continued to lead his side quietly and efficiently, indeed as he had done in the poor season of 1977, which again illustrates that the right results will not come without the players.

With Hadlee and Rice available, Nottinghamshire had a formidable attack, but when the former departed to the Kiwis and the latter injured his back it became distinctly insipid. No county can afford a bowler whose reward for more than 500 overs is 26 Championship wickets costing well over 50 apiece. The leading wicket-taker in the Championship matches was Cooper, recovered from injury and a most promising prospect. However, at the moment he is better suited to supporting Hadlee and Rice than opening with the new ball.

The unluckiest of the bowlers was the Indian left-arm spinner, Doshi. Because of the ruling prohibiting more than two recently registered overseas players playing in one county team simultaneously, he never had the opportunity to operate after Hadlee and Rice had softened up the opposition. Nevertheless, in all first-class matches he was the county's leading wicket-taker, and one has the feeling that once he became fully

Bruce French continued to impress with his smart performances behind the stumps, and the improvement in his batting suggested he may be a strong contender for the England job.

acclimatised to English conditions he could be most effective. He has not been re-engaged by Nottinghamshire, because of the regulations concerning cricketers from abroad, and any county looking for a spinner could do far worse.

The dash of Hassan with the bat and in the field was restricted because of a broken finger, but French continued to impress behind the stumps. The decision to omit him from the Gillette Cup game against Kent, in order to strengthen the batting, could well have cost Nottinghamshire the match.

The county can afford to look more confidently to this summer than they have been able to for several years. The Championship is probably beyond their grasp, but they could meet with success in one of the limited-overs competitions, something which has so far eluded them.

Schweppes County Championship:	7th	Won 3 Lost 7	Drawn 12
All First-Class Matches:		Won 3 Lost 7	Drawn 14
Gillette Cup:	Lost to Yorkshire in 2nd round		
Benson and Hedges Cup:	Lost to Kent in quarter-finals		
John Player League:	13th	Won 4 Lost 7	No result 5

NOTTINGHAMSHIRE 1978 FIRST-CLASS AVERAGES

BATTING and FIELDING   * Not out

	M	*I*	*NO*	*HS*	*Runs*	*Av*	*100*	*50*	*Ct*	*St*
C. E. B. Rice	22	35	7	213*	1727	61.67	5	7	22	—
R. J. Hadlee	7	8	4	101*	193	48.25	1	—	1	—
D. W. Randall	23	38	7	157*	1461	47.12	2	10	11	—
M. J. Harris	23	36	4	148*	1315	41.09	3	6	13	—
P. A. Todd	24	40	0	89	1181	29.52	—	10	6	—
M. J. Smedley	23	31	4	83*	660	24.44	—	4	18	—
B. Hassan	8	9	0	81	220	24.44	—	1	5	—
J. D. Birch	13	16	2	52*	308	22.00	—	2	6	—
W. K. Watson	5	3	1	28*	44	22.00	—	—	—	—
B. N. French	21	25	8	66	300	17.64	—	1	36	7
R. A. White	17	16	3	44*	220	16.92	—	—	8	—
H. T. Tunnicliffe	9	12	3	69*	148	16.44	—	1	6	—
K. S. Mackintosh	14	14	5	23*	124	13.77	—	—	6	—
R. E. Dexter	4	7	2	22	65	13.00	—	—	2	—
D. R. Doshi	14	13	7	23	51	8.50	—	—	2	—
K. Cooper	23	18	3	19	102	6.80	—	—	10	—
C. C. Curzon	4	4	0	26	26	6.50	—	—	2	1
M. E. Allbrook	5	5	3	3*	8	4.00	—	—	—	—

Also batted: (2 matches) K. Saxelby 0, 3*, 0 (1 ct); (1 match) J. T. Curzon 1 (1 ct); P. J. Hacker 0; R. T. Robinson 9, 27* (1 ct).

BOWLING

	O	*M*	*R*	*W*	*Av*	*BB*	*5wI*	*10wM*
R. J. Hadlee	216.3	48	555	37	15.00	6–29	4	1
C. E. B. Rice	322.3	82	835	41	20.36	4–25	—	—
K. Cooper	473.5	92	1439	53	27.15	6–32	2	—
D. R. Doshi	628.5	159	1585	57	27.80	6–33	3	1
W. K. Watson	151.3	34	486	15	32.40	6–102	1	—
K. S. Mackintosh	239	47	693	16	43.31	4–49	—	—
R. A. White	541	145	1515	27	56.11	4–73	—	—

Also bowled: M. E. Allbrook 74–10–278–5; J. D. Birch 77–9–282–2; J. T. Curzon 5–1–22–0; P. J. Hacker 6–0–51–0; M. J. Harris 41–10–142–4; B. Hassan 14–4–52–0; D. W. Randall 1.4–0–8–0; K. Saxelby 28.2–1–123–1; H. T. Tunnicliffe 100–26–304–7.

SOMERSET

President: C. R. M. Atkinson
Chairman: L. G. Creed
Secretary: R. G. Stevens
Captain: B. C. Rose
Colours: Black, white and
   maroon
Headquarters:
County Cricket Ground,
St James's Street,
Taunton TA1 1JT.

Honours: Third in County
Championship (4) 1892, 1958,
1963, 1966
Gillette Cup Finalists (2) 1967,
1978
John Player League Runners-up
(3) 1974, 1976, 1978
1st XI Home Grounds 1979:
Taunton; Bath (Recreation
Ground); Bristol (Imperial
Athletic Ground); Glastonbury
(Morlands); Weston-s-Mare
(Clarence Park); Yeovil
(Westland).

The words from the song 'almost there' sum up the Somerset story of 1978. They were almost there in the Schweppes Championship, the Gillette Cup, and the John Player League. Under their new skipper, Rose, they enjoyed the best all-round summer in the history of the club, but ended up winning nothing. Like Essex, with whom they fought two epic battles at Taunton, they have yet to carry off a major honour. However, if they continue to display the same skill and enthusiasm as last year, they must surely break through the barrier soon.

In first-class cricket Somerset did not really possess the balance required to capture the Championship, and in the circumstances finishing fifth was highly satisfactory. It may even have been higher than their ability warranted, because their attack, so often minus Botham on Test duty and Garner, was not geared to bowling out opponents twice in three days.

On the other hand, Somerset were plainly a side to be feared in any limited-overs game. For a start, a major innings from Vivian Richards was usually sufficient to ensure victory, provided the bowlers performed adequately. On their march to the Gillette Cup final, the West Indian supplied a couple of centuries and a fifty. The trouble was that his colleagues were inclined to become over-dependent on his genius, which tended to camouflage what, apart from Garner and Botham, was no more than adequate bowling, short of variety and real penetration. In the Lord's final Somerset used five seamers, and it must be admitted that once Garner and Botham had been seen off, most counties would have fancied their chances of jogging along at four or more per over against them. This point had already been made in the previous rounds, in which Warwickshire rattled up 293, Glamorgan 260, and Essex 287.

It was only natural that Vivian Richards, currently the finest batsman in the world, should dwarf his team-mates, but they were certainly not a one-man team. Indeed, they possess possibly the most promising clutch of young batsmen in the country. Roebuck, despite an ugly stance, looked the most likely to establish himself in the Test team. Rose, besides leading the side most creditably, was a highly competent lefthander, but he might be happier batting at number 5, for he often appeared uncertain against the new ball

After being so close to a dream début as his county's captain, Brian Rose will be working hard for Somerset's elusive first title in 1979. A repeat of last season's form and approach would say much for the character of the side and its captain.

and very fast bowling. Denning, a dashing lefthander, proved particularly well suited to the demands of the limited-overs game, whereas the sounder, slower Slocombe was more at home in first-class cricket. The Oxford University batsman and handy off-spinner Marks was another outstanding prospect, possessing an excellent temperament, while that old warrior, Burgess, continued to give good service as a seamer and in the lower order as a batsman.

When Garner was not available, Moseley did a good job with the new ball, Dredge was a useful fast-medium bowler with a slingy action that made him a shade sharper than he looked, Jennings was a typical medium-paced seamer, and Breakwell bowled his slow left-arm spinners accurately without turning the ball enough to exploit fully a helpful pitch. He also played some useful, cheerful innings down the order.

Somerset and their supporters are hoping that 1979 will see them break their duck and carry off an honour. Their best chance should be in one of the knockout Cup competitions, for which they will be assured of the services of that marvellous international all-rounder Botham, an outstanding competitor and a genuine entertainer. His absence for part of the season on Test match duty weakens their Championship chances. The outlook in the West Country is obviously bright, and a spirit of adventure and excitement pervades all their home grounds. It is no longer sleepy, peaceful old Somerset, and in 1979 they should be there, not almost there.

Schweppes County Championship:	5th	Won 9	Lost 4	Drawn 9
All First-Class Matches:		Won 9	Lost 4	Drawn 11
Gillette Cup:	Lost to Sussex in final		
Benson and Hedges Cup:	Lost to Kent in semi-final		
John Player League:	2nd	Won 11	Lost 3	No result 2

SOMERSET 1978 FIRST-CLASS AVERAGES

BATTING and FIELDING   * Not out

	M	I	NO	HS	Runs	Av	100	50	Ct	St
I. V. A. Richards	21	38	4	118	1558	45.82	2	10	21	—
P. A. Slocombe	23	40	8	128*	1221	38.15	3	5	11	—
B. C. Rose	24	41	5	122	1263	35.08	4	3	11	—
P. M. Roebuck	23	37	8	131*	944	32.55	1	6	10	—
D. Breakwell	16	23	5	100*	579	32.16	1	4	5	—
P. W. Denning	22	39	3	78*	925	25.69	—	5	13	—
V. J. Marks	11	18	3	51	304	20.26	—	1	7	—
M. J. Kitchen	13	20	2	50	359	19.94	—	1	12	—
I. T. Botham	10	14	0	86	275	19.64	—	1	5	—
G. I. Burgess	16	23	5	55	336	18.66	—	1	12	—
D. J. S. Taylor	23	29	5	78	424	17.66	—	2	55	9
K. F. Jennings	17	19	10	31*	152	16.88	—	—	11	—
H. R. Moseley	14	9	3	30	62	10.33	—	—	7	—
C. H. Dredge	20	19	3	23	148	9.25	—	—	6	—
D. R. Gurr	4	5	3	4	12	6.00	—	—	1	—
J. Garner	4	5	2	6*	12	4.00	—	—	2	—

Also batted: (1 match) M. Olive 3, 1. T. Gard (2 ct) played in two matches without batting.

BOWLING

	O	M	R	W	Av	BB	5wI	10wM
J. Garner	170.1	61	351	22	15.95	5–50	3	—
I. T. Botham	369.5	77	1051	58	18.12	7–61	5	—
H. R. Moseley	348.1	103	813	41	19.82	6–35	1	—
D. Breakwell	445.1	135	1007	41	24.56	6–45	1	—
K. F. Jennings	442.3	147	1041	40	26.02	5–18	1	—
C. H. Dredge	573.1	137	1473	56	26.30	5–53	2	—
D. R. Gurr	104	25	296	11	26.90	4–65	—	—
V. J. Marks	349.4	99	945	31	30.48	4–48	—	—
G. I. Burgess	363	136	890	27	32.96	5–25	1	—

Also bowled: P. W. Denning 7–2–25–0; I. V. A. Richards 89.5–16–268–8; P. M. Roebuck 101–28–272–4; B. C. Rose 8.2–1–31–1; P. A. Slocombe 4–1–11–0.

SURREY

Patroness: Her Majesty The Queen
President: M. J. C. Allom
Chairman: R. Subba Row
Secretary: I. F. B. Scott-Browne
Captain: R. D. V. Knight
Colours: Chocolate
Headquarters: Kennington Oval, London SE11 5SS.

Honours: County Champions (18) 1864, 1887, 1888, 1890, 1891, 1892, 1894, 1895, !899, 1914, 1952, 1953, 1954, 1955, 1956, 1957, 1958, 1971
Joint Champions (2) 1889, 1950
Benson and Hedges Cup Winners (1) 1974
1st XI Home Grounds 1979: The Oval; Byfleet (BAC Ground); Guildford (Woodbridge Road).

The 1978 season was one that Surrey supporters will want to forget and put behind them. The club won nothing, nor indeed ever suggested that there was any likelihood of them doing so. They were always struggling, finishing an unacceptable sixteenth in the Schweppes Championship and near the bottom of the John Player League. It must have been most discouraging for Roger Knight in his first summer as captain, although on a personal level he batted competently and improved as a captain. Moreover, he can take some comfort from the knowledge that there are indications to suggest improved performances, both this summer and in the future.

First, Surrey have signed a distinctly sharp bowler from the West Indies, Sylvester Clarke, who should win the odd match for his adopted county and could cause a certain amount of havoc among opposing sides. Second, a further six pitches have been dug up and, judging from how the first experimental pitch played last summer, the six should provide some of the pace that has been missing for so long from The Oval square. These new wickets will not be available until 1980 but should then prove a considerable asset to a side with up-and-coming seamers and potentially plenty of good batting. It will also make it easier for the county to obtain a definite result in three days without depending on declarations and chases against the clock. The possibility of a result breeds excitement, which can so often breed success. Third, a high percentage of the county staff are young, have not reached their prime, and should, with increased confidence and encouragement – not always that much in evidence at The Oval in recent years – improve.

The setbacks of last season were largely the result of two basic weaknesses that the finest captaincy could not have cured: an attack that was short in penetration, and batting that was strangely and needlessly inconsistent.

Surrey's two teenaged seamers, Wilson and Thomas, naturally lacked the maturity to provide their admirable and hardworking all-rounder Jackman with the support he required, but both could turn out to be very useful performers. Not surprisingly, the dead Oval pitches, combined with an unusually high number of wet wickets, did not suit the leg-breaks of Intikhab, whereas Pocock had a splendid summer. There are many who still believe him to be the finest off-spinner in the country, and that he was unlucky not to have been recalled to the international scene.

Surrey's teenage fast bowler David Thomas began impressively by taking the first four Sussex wickets for one run in a Sunday League match, but later success was irregular.

When available, Edrich brought stability and technique to the batting; Knight, a good-looking front-foot county all-rounder, played to his form; Butcher, yet another left-hander, enjoyed a fair season with the occasional brilliant purple patch. In a side which might be termed top heavy with 'cack-handers', Smith's batting could be said to have stood still, while the more talented Younis again failed to produce the figures and was not re-engaged. Roope may be a shade short of class at international level, but in county cricket he is an attractive and considerable run-maker capable of scoring even more heavily. If he does this in 1979, if Howarth bats as well as he did for New Zealand, and if Lynch fulfils his obvious potential, the county should be able to provide their bowlers with worthwhile targets to bowl at.

One of the satisfactory features of 1978 was the form shown by Richards behind the stumps. At 20 he has already established himself as an accomplished county 'keeper, was capped, and may well possess that extra flair to take him into the big time and the big money.

Schweppes County Championship:	16th	Won 3	Lost 7	Drawn 12
All First-Class Matches:		Won 3	Lost 8	Drawn 13
Gillette Cup:	Lost to Essex in 2nd round			
Benson and Hedges Cup:	Failed to qualify for Q–F (3rd in Group D)			
John Player League:	10th	Won 6	Lost 8	No result 2

SURREY 1978 FIRST-CLASS AVERAGES

BATTING and FIELDING   * Not out

	M	I	NO	HS	Runs	Av	100	50	Ct	St
G. R. J. Roope	15	24	6	113*	752	41.77	2	5	22	—
R. D. V. Knight	22	38	6	128	1233	38.53	3	7	16	—
G. P. Howarth	9	17	1	179*	559	34.93	1	3	4	—
A. R. Butcher	19	33	2	188	994	32.06	2	4	4	—
J. H. Edrich	18	29	5	114	733	30.54	1	4	9	—
Younis Ahmed	15	23	4	72	514	27.05	—	4	9	—
D. M. Smith	17	27	6	115	463	22.04	1	—	6	—
M. A. Lynch	14	24	0	101	451	18.79	1	2	7	—
R. P. Baker	11	17	3	91	249	17.78	—	1	4	—
C. J. Richards	23	29	10	50	310	16.31	—	1	24	7
R. D. Jackman	23	30	7	42	319	13.86	—	—	13	—
P. H. L. Wilson	9	4	4	9*	9	—	—	—	1	—
Intikhab Alam	23	32	2	34	266	8.86	—	—	10	—
A. Needham	5	5	0	21	33	6.60	—	—	1	—
I. R. Payne	5	6	0	28	33	5.50	—	—	8	—
D. J. Thomas	13	16	3	12	70	5.38	—	—	5	—
P. I. Pocock	21	22	4	17*	91	5.05	—	—	7	—

Also batted: (1 match) S. S. Surridge 2* (1 ct); F. J. Titmus 0*, 4* (1 ct).

BOWLING

	O	M	R	W	Av	BB	5wI	10wM
P. I. Pocock	662.4	201	1615	67	24.10	6–73	5	—
R. D. Jackman	590.2	134	1707	70	24.38	5–26	3	—
Intikhab Alam	623.2	197	1570	59	26.61	6–126	3	—
R. D. V. Knight	161.2	41	432	14	30.85	3–22	—	—
P. H. L. Wilson	105.2	22	355	11	32.27	4–56	—	—
R. P. Baker	166.4	28	573	17	33.70	3–54	—	—
D. J. Thomas	272.1	60	844	16	52.75	4–47	—	—

Also bowled: A. R. Butcher 53–7–192–1; G. P. Howarth 9–3–22–1; M. A. Lynch 14.1–1–59–2; A. Needham 33.2–9–103–2; I. R. Payne 34–4–133–2; G. R. J. Roope 47–10–141–2; D. M. Smith 11–2–50–1; F. J. Titmus 14–1–35–1; Younis Ahmed 9–2–27–0.

SUSSEX

President: H. T. Bartlett
Chairman: A. Crole-Rees
Secretary: S. R. Allen
Captain: A. Long
Colours: Dark blue, light blue and gold
Headquarters: County Ground, Eaton Road, Hove BN3 3AN.

Honours: County Championship Runners-up (6) 1902, 1903, 1932, 1933, 1934, 1953
Gillette Cup Winners (3) 1963, 1964, 1978
John Player League Runners-up (1) 1976
1st XI Home Grounds 1979: Hove; Eastbourne (The Saffrons); Hastings (Central Ground); Horsham; Pagham.

In 1977 Sussex had enjoyed a reasonable, if unexceptional, playing season, and would clearly have finished bottom of any popularity poll held among the other 16 counties. The outlook for last summer was hardly propitious. The committee sacked their golden boy, Tony Greig, as captain for comments he had made about Boycott in a Sydney newspaper, and he was also suspended by the TCCB for the first half of the season for the same offence. Miandad was with the Pakistan tourists, and the most brilliant of their young players, Wessels, was doing his South African national service and would only be occasionally available. The captaincy was given to Long, their experienced wicket-keeper from Surrey, in the hope that he could introduce harmony to a side bound, in the circumstances, to have more problems than most. To make matters worse, when Greig did return briefly to the team, he failed to make any significant contribution with either bat or ball. As a result, he decided to sever his relationship with the county, where for many years he had been king. It was a sad finish, because, although he had not always done himself justice as a player, Tony did bring a considerable presence and personality to the game.

If at that juncture anybody, even the most ardent Sussex supporter, had said that Long would receive the Gillette Cup at Lord's in September, he would have been laughed at. After all, the county had managed to scrape home by only two runs against Staffordshire! Nevertheless, the players, under Long's sensible, practical, honest leadership, started to respond to the challenge and ended up by beating the county champions, Kent, by 45 runs, and capturing the Gillette Cup, results which would have been inconceivable only two months earlier.

Much of the credit for this remarkable transformation must go to the emergency captain, Long, although the regular availability of both Miandad and Parker did bring a much-needed stability to a very unpredictable batting line-up. The efforts of Long were recognised by the committee, and rewarded by his appointment for 1979, but a successor will eventually be needed. Parker looks to be the logical candidate.

Miandad, who had an unhappy time with Pakistan, recovered his form with Sussex, playing some brilliant innings and finishing top of the averages, while Parker displayed a maturity and a composure throughout the Gillette campaign to suggest he might well establish himself in the national team

within a couple of years. The most improved batsman in the side was
Phillipson, who developed from a somewhat erratic seamer and tailender
into a more than useful acquirer of runs in the middle order. Mendis and
Barclay were a promising opening pair, with the latter's off-breaks
suggesting he could be moving from the batsman who can bowl into the all-
rounder category.

Imran Khan is world class; an exciting, sometimes erratic all-rounder, a
natural match-winner both as a dashing batsman and as a fast bowler. With
his pronounced inswing he was the perfect partner for the former Surrey and
England opening bowler, Arnold, who was in his first season. Arnold still
makes the ball leave the bat, and remains one of the most feared bowlers in
the land. At Hove, this pair with the new ball were especially formidable.

Waller, one of the four ex-Surrey players on the staff, had an outstanding
season, heading the bowling averages with his slow left-arm spin whereas he

*Paul Phillipson's strokes might not all have been strictly textbook, but they were spectacularly
effective as he made the transition from bowler to all-rounder in 1978.*

had been bottom the previous year! Nevertheless, Sussex have something of a problem, because Cheatle, who is a better batsman and younger, is also an orthodox slow left-arm spin bowler of considerable promise. This is bound to prove something of an embarrassment, for it is difficult for a county to provide sufficient cricket to keep both contented. Once again Spencer did an admirable job as stock bowler, and the fielding was always good and frequently brilliant. Behind the stumps, Long was, as usual, neat and unobtrusive, missing very little.

With the new spirit and the confidence gained from the Gillette Cup success, Sussex can afford to look forward eagerly to 1979, although it must be admitted that it would come as no surprise if they fail to retain their title.

Schweppes County Championship: 9th	Won 4	Lost 7	Drawn 11
All First-Class Matches:	Won 4	Lost 8	Drawn 12
Gillette Cup:	Winners		
Benson and Hedges Cup:	Lost to Somerset in quarter-finals		
John Player League: 8th	Won 6	Lost 7	No result 3

SUSSEX 1978 FIRST-CLASS AVERAGES

BATTING and FIELDING   *Not out

	M	I	NO	HS	Runs	Av	100	50	Ct	St
Javed Miandad	8	12	2	127	586	58.60	2	4	5	—
Imran Khan	22	37	5	167	1339	41.84	3	6	8	—
P. W. G. Parker	14	25	2	112	781	33.95	1	3	3	—
T. J. Head	3	5	2	31	92	30.66	—	—	6	1
G. D. Mendis	20	36	4	128	979	30.59	3	1	14	—
J. R. T. Barclay	22	40	4	103	979	27.19	1	4	9	—
M. A. Buss	14	20	3	79*	398	23.41	—	2	9	—
C. P. Phillipson	22	36	4	70	749	23.40	—	5	11	—
A. Long	21	28	7	56*	410	19.52	—	1	47	3
S. P. Hoadley	7	12	0	112	232	19.33	1	1	4	—
R. G. L. Cheatle	15	14	4	49	182	18.20	—	—	19	—
A. W. Greig	5	8	1	32	122	17.42	—	—	4	—
S. J. Storey	16	23	3	57	331	16.55	—	1	7	—
K. C. Wessels	4	8	0	29	123	15.37	—	—	6	—
J. J. Groome	9	17	1	50	229	14.31	—	1	2	—
J. Spencer	17	22	8	30	189	13.50	—	—	8	—
K. B. Smith	4	8	1	43	90	12.85	—	—	1	—
G. G. Arnold	17	23	4	29	237	12.47	—	—	3	—
C. E. Waller	13	13	7	14*	55	9.16	—	—	11	—
A. C. S. Pigott	6	6	0	11	33	5.50	—	—	1	—

Also batted: (2 matches) P. J. Graves 31, 21, 5; R. P. T. Marshall 4*, 4*, 2*, 0*; (1 match) G. S. le Roux 17*, 0.

BOWLING

	O	M	R	W	Av	BB	5wI	10wM
G. G. Arnold	401	102	910	49	18.57	7–44	2	—
C. E. Waller	371	125	861	46	18.71	5–30	3	—
J. Spencer	496.5	143	1158	46	25.17	5–53	1	—
M. A. Buss	179.2	52	473	18	26.27	3–47	—	—
J. R. T. Barclay	200	48	532	19	28.00	5–72	1	—
Imran Khan	543	128	1391	49	28.38	7–52	2	—
R. G. L. Cheatle	314.2	85	968	24	40.33	4–89	—	—
C. P. Phillipson	193	37	702	16	43.87	3–72	—	—

Also bowled: A. W. Greig 111–21–321–6; Javed Miandad 25–2–101–3; G. S. le Roux 31–7–107–1; R. P. T. Marshall 48–6–216–2; G. D. Mendis 1–0–9–0; A. C. S. Pigott 69–8–306–9; S. J. Storey 97–27–235–6.

WARWICKSHIRE

President: Brig. Sir R. A. G.
Calthorpe
Chairman: C. C. Goodway
Secretary: A. C. Smith
Captain: J. Whitehouse
Colours: Blue, gold and silver
Headquarters:
County Ground, Edgbaston,
Birmingham B5 7QU.

Honours: County Champions (3)
1911, 1951, 1972
Gillette Cup Winners (2) 1966,
1968
1st XI Home Grounds 1979:
Birmingham (Edgbaston):
Nuneaton (Griff & Coton).

Warwickshire, a middle of the table team going nowhere in particular, experienced a mediocre summer and never really suggested they possessed the qualities to do anything else. Whitehouse's success as captain produced no noticeable difference in performance, except his own. Both his batting aggregate and average were more than cut in half, reflecting the unfortunate effect of the new responsibility.

It cannot have helped the team spirit having a Packer player, Amiss, in a side obviously hostile to WSC. Amiss, in addition to being an exceptionally pleasant person, had been marvellously consistent for the club and was the most prolific run-getter in the land last summer with more than 2,000 runs to his credit. Yet when the Warwickshire committee, at the end of the season, decided not to offer him another contract, his colleagues, unlike many Warwickshire supporters who want him reinstated, publicly approved this decision.

It was easy to understand why the county finished eleventh in the Schweppes Championship and why 60 per cent of their matches were drawn. Their attack, with Willis so often absent on international duty, struggled to bowl out opposing sides, and their batting, despite the presence of two world-class players, was too inconsistent. What was peculiar was their continued failure to make any impact in the John Player League. It just did not make sense for them to finish one off the bottom rung with the talent they have available. The time is long overdue for their players to come to terms with the particular requirements of this competition, which after all did start back in 1969.

The chief support for the run-happy Amiss, who completed no fewer than seven first-class centuries, came from Kallicharran and Smith. The latter could still prove to have that little extra which divides the good batsman from the outstanding one, and if the little lefthander, who is now captain of West Indies, was not always at his best, he still returned a first-class average of 43, which was higher than that of any batsman in the England Test team apart from Boycott.

The form shown by the rest of the recognised batsmen was disappointing, especially when taking into account that friendly Edgbaston pitch. Whitehouse, Humpage, and Abberley all returned figures that were inferior to those of the previous summer. However, the young lefthander, Lloyd, indicated that within a year or so he should fill with distinction one of the

David Smith, from whom Warwickshire will expect large innings in the absence of Amiss.

key places in the batting line-up, and the rather top-heavy tail could usually be relied on to hit out bravely or defend stubbornly.

When the fast and very hostile Willis was absent, the bulk of the bowling was done by Perryman, who found wickets harder to obtain and more expensive than in 1977, and the big-hearted and, to use a contradiction in colours, evergreen Brown. Hemmings, who should have revelled in the wet summer with his off-breaks, lost both his form and his place, while Rouse also slipped back. However, Clifford, an off-spinner from Yorkshire who came late into the side, turned in several encouraging performances, and it is hoped he will become the slow bowler the county have wanted since the retirement of Gibbs.

The Warwickshire fielding, like that of all the clubs, was competent, but it did not match the consistent brilliance of Kent, for example. Behind the stumps Humpage continued to improve, although there are still some reservations as to his ability when standing up to spinners.

At the time of writing it is difficult to be unduly optimistic about Warwickshire's chances in 1979. Unless they obtain at least one international-class batsman, and more support for Willis, it is difficult to imagine them challenging seriously for honours, apart perhaps from the Gillette Cup, in which luck and the right draw at the right time can help a middle-of-the-table team to the final.

Schweppes County Championship: 11th	Won 4	Lost 5	Drawn 13
All First-Class Matches:	Won 4	Lost 6	Drawn 14
Gillette Cup:	Lost to Somerset in 1st round		
Benson and Hedges Cup :	Lost to Derbyshire in semi-final		
John Player League:	16th Won 4	Lost 11	No result 1

WARWICKSHIRE 1978 FIRST-CLASS AVERAGES

BATTING and FIELDING   * Not out

	M	I	NO	HS	Runs	Av	100	50	Ct	St
D. L. Amiss	23	41	3	162	2030	53.42	7	11	14	—
A. I. Kallicharran	16	29	5	129	1041	43.37	3	5	10	—
K. D. Smith	23	39	4	132*	1187	33.91	3	5	6	—
R. N. Abberley	15	25	2	81	625	27.17	—	6	6	—
T. A. Lloyd	15	23	3	93	526	26.30	—	3	15	—
G. W. Humpage	21	31	3	110	663	23.67	1	2	29	3
J. Whitehouse	24	40	8	102*	740	23.12	1	—	9	—
E. E. Hemmings	14	18	4	51	275	19.64	—	1	8	—
P. R. Oliver	17	22	1	47	322	15.33	—	—	7	—
D. J. Brown	16	19	6	38	171	13.15	—	—	6	—
S. J. Rouse	10	12	1	40	137	12.45	—	—	1	—
C. C. Clifford	11	12	5	20	76	10.85	—	—	7	—
R. G. D. Willis	12	12	2	23*	88	8.80	—	—	9	—
C. Maynard	3	3	1	9	17	8.50	—	—	4	—
R. W. Flower	9	8	4	10*	23	5.75	—	—	—	—
S. P. Perryman	24	24	6	17*	97	5.38	—	—	10	—
D. C. Hopkins	9	9	0	11	33	3.66	—	—	4	—

Also batted: (1 match) R. LeQ. Savage 5*; G. P. Thomas 4, 1.

BOWLING

	O	M	R	W	Av	BB	5wI	10wM
R. G. D. Willis	286.2	67	735	40	18.37	7–63	3	1
D. J. Brown	405	80	1160	40	29.00	5–53	1	—
S. P. Perryman	591.3	172	1527	50	30.54	7–49	3	1
C. C. Clifford	431.3	115	1220	38	32.10	6–89	2	—
E. E. Hemmings	376.1	88	1142	28	40.78	4–51	—	—
S. J. Rouse	142.4	27	565	12	47.08	4–63	—	—
R. W. Flower	173	42	554	10	55.40	3–45	—	—

Also bowled: D. L. Amiss 3–0–20–0; D. C. Hopkins 123.3–31–361–4; A. I. Kallicharran 19–5–48–4; T. A. Lloyd 15–5–35–1; P. R. Oliver 222–41–657–7; R. LeQ. Savage 4–0–18–0; J. Whitehouse 1–1–0–0.

WORCESTERSHIRE

President: Rev. Prebendary W. R. Chignell
Chairman: J. G. E. Lampard
Secretary: M. D. Vockins
Captain: N. Gifford
Colours: Dark green and black
Headquarters: County Ground, New Road, Worcester WR2 4QQ.

Honours: County Champions (3) 1964, 1965, 1974
John Player League Champions (1) 1971
Gillette Cup Finalists (2) 1963, 1966
Benson and Hedges Cup Finalists (2) 1973, 1976
1st XI Home Ground 1979: Worcester.

Although Worcestershire finished a disappointing fifteenth in the Schweppes Championship, securing only two victories in the process, they were a hard side to beat, as the fact that 15 of their 22 matches were drawn illustrates. To some extent this may have resulted from the natural, native caution of their captain. But the main cause was that, although the county possessed several high-scoring batsmen, their attack, without their main strike bowler, Holder, was short on penetration, especially on those pitches at Worcester.

Turner, who is a true international opener and had the added incentive of a benefit, predictably climbed aboard the run waggon to finish second in the national averages after a lean start. Nonetheless, one cannot help feeling that his skill and concentration at the crease would have meant rather more if these had been employed on behalf of his country, rather than his adopted county. Special registration was certainly never intended to take players out of international circulation. Turner's chief associates in the run-getting business were Ormrod, who has seldom, if ever, batted quite so well, Hemsley, no longer restricted by footballing commitments, Neale, and, when fit, the evergreen D'Oliveira.

Once Richards resigned from Hampshire, Turner and Ormrod became the most prolific opening pair on the county circuit, consistently churning out runs. However, when they eventually departed, or occasionally failed, too much depended on the much improved Neale and Hemsley, especially when D'Oliveira was missing. In the middle order Humphries, who also did well behind the stumps, was invaluable. He received good support on occasions from that promising all-rounder Patel and from his captain Gifford, who, as he has done so frequently over the years, provided the impetus with a charge, or resisted stubbornly according to the demands of the situation.

The problem which faced Gifford, and indeed a large number of county skippers, was how to remove the opposition with a bowling line-up that was seldom more than tidy and lacked the teeth required for first-class cricket. Such limitations are less important in the John Player League, in which Worcestershire managed to rise from thirteenth to fourth place.

Gifford himself remained a very efficient left-arm spinner, but he lacked adequate seam and spin support. Pridgeon, the Australian Watson, and Cumbes formed a rather insipid pace trio at county level; reasonable third

and fourth seamers but hardly the spearhead, as is borne out by the high cost of the 130-odd Championship wickets they captured between them. Good batsmen should fancy their chances of making runs against Worcestershire these days, and it was no surprise that D'Oliveira, in the winter of his cricketing life, finished second in their bowling averages to their West Indian Holder, who was absent for the majority of the summer.

It would appear that the county's best chance of success for 1979 will again lie in one of the limited-overs competitions, where the tactical deployment of the fielders by Gifford is quite masterly. Furthermore, there is probably no better pacer of a match-winning innings in this form of cricket than Turner who, having opened the batting, will still be there at the victory with the one over remaining.

Schweppes County Championship: 15th	Won 2	Lost 5	Drawn 15
All First-Class Matches:	Won 3	Lost 6	Drawn 16
Gillette Cup:	Lost to Derbyshire in 1st round		
Benson and Hedges Cup:	Failed to qualify for Q-F (4th in Group B)		
John Player League:	4th Won 10 Lost 5 No result 1		

WORCESTERSHIRE 1978 FIRST-CLASS AVERAGES

BATTING and FIELDING   * Not out

	M	I	NO	HS	Runs	Av	100	50	Ct	St
G. M. Turner	22	38	7	202*	1711	55.19	6	4	20	—
J. D. Inchmore	4	2	1	34	48	48.00	—	—	—	—
J. A. Ormrod	24	41	7	173	1535	45.14	5	4	21	—
B. L. D'Oliveira	17	22	5	146*	728	42.82	1	2	4	—
E. J. O. Hemsley	24	37	7	141*	1168	38.93	3	6	17	—
P. A. Neale	24	40	6	103*	1182	34.76	1	9	10	—
D. J. Humphries	24	32	5	111*	743	27.51	1	3	44	8
C. N. Boyns	10	13	2	71	255	23.18	—	1	8	—
N. Gifford	22	24	12	37*	278	23.16	—	—	10	—
D. N. Patel	23	29	0	104	544	18.75	1	1	8	—
G. G. Watson	21	24	5	38	266	14.00	—	—	7	—
S. P. Henderson	4	6	1	32*	65	13.00	—	—	5	—
B. J. R. Jones	10	16	0	61	182	11.37	—	1	8	—
A. P. Pridgeon	21	22	7	32	93	6.20	—	—	7	—
V. A. Holder	5	5	0	23	30	6.00	—	—	1	—
J. Cumbes	19	16	8	11	46	5.75	—	—	5	—

Also batted: (1 match) H. G. Wilcock 0 (4 ct).

BOWLING

	O	M	R	W	Av	BB	5wI	10wM
B. L. D'Oliveira	193.2	48	483	17	28.41	5–48	1	—
N. Gifford	667.3	210	1557	54	28.83	6–68	2	—
A. P. Pridgeon	587.2	115	1771	59	30.01	4–38	—	—
V. A. Holder	179	31	468	15	31.20	4–52	—	—
G. G. Watson	503	83	1535	48	31.97	6–45	1	—
D. N. Patel	398.1	94	1126	35	32.17	5–22	1	—
J. Cumbes	435	95	1207	31	38.93	4–52	—	—
C. N. Boyns	152.2	21	566	12	47.16	3–92	—	—

Also bowled: E. J. O. Hemsley 21.5–3–81–0; S. P. Henderson 5–0–21–0; J. D. Inchmore 86–23–223–4; P. A. Neale 9–0–46–0.

Left: One of county cricket's more travelled practitioners, Jim Cumbes was awarded his first-ever county cap by Worcestershire in 1978.

YORKSHIRE

Patroness:	HRH The Duchess of Kent
President:	Sir Kenneth Parkinson
Chairman:	A. H. Connell
Secretary:	J. Lister
Captain:	1978 G. Boycott
	1979 J. H. Hampshire
Colours:	Oxford blue, Cambridge blue and gold

Headquarters:
Headingley Cricket Ground, Leeds LS6 3BU.

Honours: County Champions (31) 1867, 1870, 1893, 1896, 1898, 1900, 1901, 1902, 1905, 1908, 1912, 1919, 1922, 1923, 1924, 1925, 1931, 1932, 1933, 1935, 1937, 1938, 1939, 1946, 1959, 1960, 1962, 1963, 1966, 1967, 1968
Joint Champions (2) 1869, 1949
Gillette Cup Winners (2) 1965, 1969
Benson and Hedges Cup Finalists (1) 1972
John Player League Runners-up (1) 1973

1st XI Home Grounds 1979:
Leeds (Headingley); Bradford (Park Avenue); Harrogate (St George's Road); Huddersfield (Fartown); Hull (The Circle, Anlaby Road); Middlesbrough (Acklam Park); Scarborough; Sheffield (Abbeydale Park).

The sacking of Geoff Boycott as captain of Yorkshire at the end of the season caused such a furore and so much unpleasantness that it tended to obscure the many good and happy features of the summer. The bitter battle by Geoff and his supporters to be reinstated was fought in the press and on the television, and it culminated in a Special General Meeting at which the decision of the committee was upheld by a very large majority of the members. A cynic might suggest that the real sin of the Yorkshire committee was not in dismissing Boycott, but in taking eight years to reach that conclusion.

Geoff has been the most accomplished batsman in the country for more than a decade, has an exceptional knowledge of the game, is an astute tactician, and is absolutely dedicated to Yorkshire cricket. These qualities would have been more than sufficient for him to have secured the England captaincy on a permanent basis, had he not possessed some basic weaknesses as a leader, not the least being his inability to recognise them himself.

In 1978 Yorkshire were far more impressive in all forms of the game than they had been the previous year. Nowhere was this more apparent than in the Schweppes Championship, in which they moved up from an undistinguished twelfth to an impressive fourth. Boycott and Hampshire, the new captain, stood head and shoulders above all the other batsmen. Both averaged over fifty, and if this was no more than one would have expected from Boycott, it was a real vintage performance by Hampshire, who succeeded in ousting his colleague from top spot in the averages.

Not surprisingly the rest of the batting tended to suffer by comparison, although the left-handed Sharp, still only in his teens, excited everybody with his enormous potential. One can only pray that he will not join that depressingly long list of young Yorkshire batsmen who, in recent years, have been hailed as England prospects, only to become no more than

Yorkshire's David Bairstow, considered unlucky not to be selected for the tour of Australia, later joined the England team as a replacement for the injured Tolchard.

competent county performers. After the disasters of 1977 Athey experienced a much better season with the bat, and also put in some useful spells of medium-paced seam bowling, but in complete contrast Love suffered a horrid summer, while Lumb might be said to have stood still.

There was plenty of middle- and indeed lower-order support for the main batsmen. Carrick and Old both fall into the all-rounder category, Stevenson produced several lively innings, and Bairstow backed up his unsuccessful claims for the deputy wicket-keeper spot in Australia with his ability to make runs when they were most wanted in both three- and one-day cricket.

Whenever Old was missing on Test duty, or injured, the Yorkshire attack was tidy and efficient, but it contained nobody challenging seriously for an international place. Stevenson, Oldham, and Cooper, all honest, accurate seamers, lacked that extra snap which makes batsmen apprehensive on an easy pitch. In a wet summer Carrick's wickets were too few and too costly to be in keeping with the very high traditions of Yorkshire left-armers. Sadly their off-spinner, Cope, was banned for the second time in his career, but Whiteley, in his first season, took full advantage of the situation. His Championship victims cost him under 20 apiece, figures one used to expect automatically from a front-line Yorkshire bowler, though this is no longer the case.

Is there any reason why this northern county has produced few very high quality bowlers in the last decade? Brian Close lays much of the blame on limited-overs cricket in the county's main nursery, the Leagues. This has led to the accent being put on containment, rather than on the taking of wickets. Brian is convinced, and he could well be right, that if the Leagues abandoned restricted overs, except for cup games, the whole standard of Yorkshire cricket would be raised. It would obviously encourage the young, usually erratic fast bowler, and also the slow bowler who relies on spin and flight. These are, of course, the type of bowlers who win Championship and Test matches.

What will happen this summer under the leadership of Hampshire, for at the moment of writing Boycott is undecided about his future? If, as expected, he leaves Yorkshire, his runs will be much missed, but the extra responsibility thrust on the younger players could well prove beneficial. Although the attack does not appear to be quite strong enough to carry off the Championship, Yorkshire should maintain a place in the top seven, and they must stand an excellent chance of winning one of the limited-overs competitions. After all, they are weaned on this type of cricket. They field extremely well, their bowling is mean, and the batting should be good enough if their young batsmen are prepared to shed some of their inhibitions. The time for Yorkshire to capture a title is long overdue, and success would go a long way to healing the rifts that occurred among their supporters during the winter.

Schweppes County Championship: 4th	Won 10	Lost 3	Drawn 9
All First-Class Matches:	Won 10	Lost 3	Drawn 11 (Abandoned 1)
Gillette Cup:	Lost to Sussex in quarter-finals		
Benson and Hedges Cup:	Failed to qualify for Q-F (4th in Group D)		
John Player League:	7th Won 7 Lost 7	No result 2	

YORKSHIRE 1978 FIRST-CLASS AVERAGES

BATTING and FIELDING

* Not out

	M	I	NO	HS	Runs	Av	100	50	Ct	St
J. H. Hampshire	22	36	6	132	1596	53.20	3	9	12	—
G. Boycott	14	22	1	129	1074	51.14	5	3	3	—
C. M. Old	9	10	5	100*	197	39.40	1	—	4	—
P. Carrick	24	30	11	105	670	35.26	1	3	10	—
K. Sharp	16	24	4	91	656	32.80	—	3	2	—
R. G. Lumb	23	37	3	107	1070	31.47	2	8	19	—
G. B. Stevenson	15	18	4	70*	416	29.71	—	1	5	—
J. D. Love	14	19	2	107	461	27.11	1	3	8	—
B. Leadbeater	4	7	1	61	155	25.83	—	1	3	—
C. W. J. Athey	21	35	2	131	846	25.63	2	4	21	—
C. Johnson	7	14	3	61	276	25.09	—	2	4	—
D. L. Bairstow	24	36	7	60	725	25.00	—	4	61	10
H. P. Cooper	19	16	5	40	186	16.90	—	—	11	—
A. Sidebottom	6	4	2	16	27	13.50	—	—	1	—
G. A. Cope	15	17	6	44	133	12.09	—	—	7	—
J. P. Whiteley	9	5	3	8	14	7.00	—	—	6	—
S. Oldham	20	11	7	7	22	5.50	—	—	3	—

Also batted: (1 match) S. N. Hartley 11, 20. S. Stuchbury played in one match without batting.

BOWLING

	O	M	R	W	Av	BB	5wI	10wM
C. M. Old	353.5	101	807	44	18.34	6-34	2	—
J. P. Whiteley	172.5	46	475	22	21.59	4-14	—	—
C. W. J. Athey	93	26	268	11	24.36	3-38	—	—
G. A. Cope	342.3	114	784	32	24.50	4-34	—	—
G. B. Stevenson	331.3	69	1034	42	24.61	8-65	3	—
S. Oldham	485	115	1326	53	25.01	5-40	1	—
P. Carrick	648.2	226	1449	52	27.86	7-35	4	1
H. P. Cooper	447	113	1191	37	32.18	6-26	1	—

Also bowled: D. L. Bairstow 9-2-15-1; G. Boycott 12-6-13-0; J. H. Hampshire 9-0-45-2; S. N. Hartley 2-0-6-0; C. Johnson 2-0-5-0; J. D. Love 6-2-16-0; A. Sidebottom 84-11-309-7; S. Stuchbury 15.5-1-60-2.

THE EQUIPMENT REVOLUTION

Trevor Bailey

Between 1860 and 1960 many changes occurred in the world of cricket. W. G. Grace reorganised the whole technique of batting. Overarm gradually replaced round-arm and lob bowling as the main form of attack. The googly was discovered, swerve was harnessed and, in the eternal battle between bat and ball, new tactics were introduced.

The lbw law was altered on several occasions, with results often different from those intended. Bodyline was invented to reduce the effectiveness of Sir Donald Bradman, which underlines that there is nothing new about the increase in physical intimidation which has crept into the game in recent years. Two world wars and a social revolution killed off the amateur and the patron. Five days became the acceptable duration for Test matches; and with the great improvement made by West Indies and the other major cricket-playing countries, plus the fast travel available, the number of Tests increased to such a degree that international cricket statistics have lost much of their point. In recent years, sponsorship, limited-overs cricket, and television arrived to rescue a game that has never really been financially viable as a professional sport.

All these numerous changes were, however, circumstantial rather than fundamental. The basic equipment – willow bat, hand-stitched leather ball, stumps, pads – has not altered much in the 100 years following the second half of the last century. The stumps have grown a little higher and wider, the pads no longer have vents at the front and, like the gloves, provide greater protection. If a player of the sixties were to be transported back to the end of the Victorian era, he would be more surprised by the field placings than by the bat and ball. The bat would probably be long-handled and a shade more rigid, while the ball would quickly lose its shine. Longevity of shine is the result of modern treatment by the manufacturers, and of artificial fertilisers that produce the lush green grass which protects and polishes the gloss.

However, in the past decade something close to a revolution has occurred in the shape and composition of cricket equipment. In the market of today are to be found some very odd-looking bats, lightweight moulded pads with only two straps and which are a third of the weight of a conventional pair, mitten-shaped batting gloves, slipper boots, elbow protectors, and crash helmets.

The second stage of the equipment revolution will surely take place in clothing, and follow tennis, with those ultra-conservative whites giving way to something more trendy. These need not be tasteless, and certainly few would quibble at what was worn by any of the 1978 Wimbledon finalists. Colourful gear was due to be sported during the Packer World Series in the winter of 1978–79, and it should be remembered that gaily coloured shirts were regularly worn in the early days of the game.

One sensible change in cricket equipment would surely be white tracksuit-style trousers, rather than old – frequently ancient – 'batters'. In first-class cricket, batting trousers which are used entirely for batting, or wicket-keeping, become creased, dirty, and sweaty. The right type of tracksuit trouser, which could absorb the sweat, would be much more suitable and could be washed, rather than dry-cleaned.

The principal manufacturers have recently introduced a number of bats that are shaped differently from those used so effectively by Grace, Trumper, Hobbs, Hammond, Bradman, Hutton, and Sobers. These design changes were unquestionably influenced by television. When cricketers first appeared in front of the cameras, it was difficult, frequently impossible, to pick out the make of bat. But the manufacturers quickly realised the opportunity of advertising their name and product without going to the considerable expense of buying space. The inevitable outcome was that the markings on bats increased enormously in size and colour, with the result that they are now easy to identify.

The next logical development was to produce a bat with a different colour, or different shape. The former was simple, tried and then outlawed by the game's administrators who, not surprisingly, did not favour a blue bat. However, there was nothing objectionable about a differently shaped bat, provided it had the same width of blade. This new innovation also fitted the trend of county players towards heavier bats. An ever-increasing number were moving from one weighing about 2lb 3oz to one weighing about 2lb 8oz. But while they wanted the extra weight, they still demanded the same feel in the 'pick-up'.

The manufacturers solved this problem by giving their newly designed, shaped bats a larger striking area. With the traditional bat, with which the likes of Bradman and Hobbs had managed to put together a few runs from time to time, to obtain maximum power it was necessary to hit the ball in the middle of the drive. This presented comparatively few problems to great players who would never have worried about larger striking areas. However, the larger striking area does assist the less accomplished, while the thicker edges also increase the life-span of the bat.

Such a variety of bats is available today that one cannot but admire the ingenuity of the manufacturers, not only in the different ways in which they have reshaped and redistributed the weight of their bats, but also in their use of colourful designs guaranteed to make their products instantly recognisable both at long range and, even more vital, on the television screen. Gray Nicholls, for example, have several versions of their 'scoop' bats with wood scooped out of the back and the cavity, or cavities, painted red to facilitate recognition. St Peters have introduced a bat with what might be termed a flat plateau covering much of the back, while Slazengers also have a flattened bat with a rounded rather than the more traditional finish.

Among the heavy artillery is to be found the appropriately named Jumbo from Surridges. Considering the large amount of wood at the back, this bat does pick up remarkably well. Another heavyweight is the Maxi

The batsman as an advertising billboard: St Peter's are the beneficiary as the camera picks up the bat and gloves of former Hampshire opener Barry Richards.

from Gunn and Moore, though with its extra-thick handle and edges it could just as easily be called the 'chunky'. It is certainly easy to push the ball to the boundary with this fearsome weapon, but it has hardly been designed for the delicate late cut.

Although a bat with holes in the blade has been tried, the prize for originality must surely go to W & S, who have brought out a completely reversible bat. Definitely one to confuse wicket-keepers, this bat has provided Ray East, who used one in county cricket, with runs as well as comedy.

In addition to altering the shape of many of their bats and redistributing the weight with the intention, not always fulfilled, of increasing driving potential, the manufacturers have experimented successfully with various protective treatments designed to give longer life. In the case of Slazengers, the bat treated in this fashion is termed 'poly-armoured' and has a slightly glossy look. It, and similar brethren from other manufacturers, has the advantage of not needing to be oiled, sandpapered, or 'knocked in' before use in the middle. A damp rag will clean off dirt. Moreover, the protective covering is especially useful against some of those imported cannon balls found masquerading as cricket balls.

On similar protective lines, Surridge have brought out a bat which is encased in a tough, transparent skin. At the end of the season it can be returned to the factory, cleaned up, and re-sheathed to look like new. This, of course, is a more sophisticated and attractive version of those old velum-covered bats which, over the years, have provided so much service in minor club and village cricket.

The lasting qualities of bats are also affected by pressing, as well as by the age and quality of the willow. In general, the initial drive from a softly pressed bat will be sweeter than from one pressed harder, but the bat will not last as long.

The manufacturers have also improved the facial appearance of bats by bleaching, which gives them a white appearance whereas the natural colour of willow is yellow. This has the added advantage of camouflaging blemishes that could be seen on the blades of the cheaper bats. These did not affect performance, but were unsightly.

The revolution in the design and the composition of cricket equipment has been accompanied by an escalation in prices, which has even managed to outstrip the galloping inflation of the period. In the case of a bat this is somewhat surprising, even though the price of a top-grade cleft, which the manufacturer would purchase for around £1 only five years ago, now costs him about £4.50, while the price of cane for the handle has also risen sharply. However, one of the main reasons why bats have become so expensive is a dramatic increase in marketing costs. In the past a manufacturer would put the name of an outstanding batsman on some of his bats – a Hutton, a Bradman, or a Weekes. The player would normally be paid a commission and a percentage for every one sold with his name on it. For obvious reasons, bats with the autograph of a great player had a special appeal for children. Now the manufacturers are finding it necessary to pay first-class cricketers considerable sums for simply agreeing to use their bats, whereas formerly they simply received them free of charge.

Cricket is becoming a distinctly expensive game, as can be seen from the following, approximate, 1977 retail prices for equipment for a county and a normal club cricketer. A leading manufacturer expected his top-grade bat to be costing more than £40 in 1978.

Top grade bat £35–£39; Club bat £25–£30.

Pads, buckskin or super-lightweight £25–£30; Club pads, PVC £13–£15.

Gloves, top-grade £13; Club gloves £7–£9.

Trousers £16 and upwards, but some adequate for club cricket obtainable for £9–£11.

Shirts, top-grade £9 and upwards; Club standard £7–£8.

Sweaters, sleeveless, depending on whether with club colours or plain, £8–£16; long sleeved £14–£20.

Thick socks £1.75–£2; the trend is towards tennis socks with padded soles at around £1.35.

Boots, leather £19 and upwards; PVC £14–£16.

Abdominal protector £4; Thigh pad £2.25–£4.50.

Wicket-keeping gloves, top grade £22–£24; Club standard £16–£18.

Top-quality cricket ball £14.95; Club standard £5.50–£8; the cheapest English quartered ball £6.50.

Individual cricket bag, plastic £16–£20. Players are tending to turn more to a suitcase type with bat compartment, £12.50–£16.

This is an extension of an article by Trevor Bailey which first appeared in the Financial Times *on 15 June 1978.*

Test Match, Prudential Trophy, and Cup Final Attendances and Receipts 1978

Match		Venue	Paying Attendance	Total Attendance including Members	Gross Receipts
England v Pakistan	1st Test	Birmingham	17,059	28,500	£38,438
	2nd Test	Lord's	44,955	48,055	£124,652
	3rd Test	Leeds	16,546	26,250	£58,263
England v New Zealand	1st Test	The Oval	27,842	36,900	£71,719
	2nd Test	Nottingham	28,761	38,500	£80,975
	3rd Test	Lord's	55,334	65,334	£142,549
	TEST MATCH TOTALS		190,497	243,539	£516,596
Prudential Trophy –					
England v Pakistan		Manchester	4,133	8,133	£11,375
		The Oval	5,035	7,535	£16,100
England v New Zealand		Scarborough	7,565	7,565	£20,679
		Manchester	9,718	15,718	£23,759
Benson and Hedges Cup Final		Lord's	21,767	25,267	£93,710
Gillette Cup Final		Lord's	21,792	25,292	£99,204
TOTALS			260,507	333,049	£781,423

OTHER FIRST-CLASS MATCHES 1978

MCC

MIDDLESEX at Lord's, 19, 20 (no play), 21 (no play) April. Match drawn. Middlesex 167 (J. M. Brearley 51, I. T. Botham 5–43 including the hat-trick). MCC 45–3.

I. T. Botham achieved the hat-trick on the first afternoon of the season by bowling C. T. Radley, G. D. Barlow and N. G. Featherstone. Earlier T. E. Jesty had taken a wicket with his first ball of the season.

PAKISTANIS at Lord's, 17, 18, 19 May. Match drawn. (*See Pakistan Tour section for scores.*)

Scotland v Ireland

Played at Shawholm, Glasgow, 12 (no play), 13, 14 (no play) August. Match drawn. Scotland 74–7.

Cambridge University

Played 9   Won 0   Drawn 7   Lost 2
ESSEX at Cambridge, 19, 20, 21 April. Match drawn. Essex 351–4d (K. S. McEwan 109* retired hurt, K. W. R. Fletcher 89, D. R. Pringle 50*) and 99–4 (N. Smith 59*). Cambridge U. 190 (P. W. G. Parker 60).

MIDDLESEX at Cambridge, 26 (no play), 27, 28 April. Match drawn. Middlesex 275–7d (M. W. Gatting 61, C. T. Radley 53, W. N. Slack 52). Cambridge U. 118–6 (P. W. G. Parker 59*).

GLOUCESTERSHIRE at Cambridge, 29 April, 1 (no play), 2 (no play) May. Match drawn. Gloucestershire 337 (Zaheer Abbas 100).

LEICESTERSHIRE at Cambridge, 10, 11, 12 May. Leicestershire won by 8 wickets. Cambridge U. 228 (P. W. G. Parker 66, A. J. Hignell 61) and 95. Leicestershire 230–2d (N. E. Briers 116*) and 94–2.

SURREY at Cambridge, 17, 18, 19 May. Match drawn. Cambridge U. 213 (A. J. Hignell 108, R. D. Jackman 5–26) and 298 (A. J. Hignell 145). Surrey 319–1d (G. P. Howarth 179* and R. D. V. Knight 103* added 256* for the second wicket) and 148–7.

A. J. Hignell was the first to score a hundred in each innings of a first-class match for Cambridge University since 1960 when R. M. Prideaux achieved the feat v Somerset at Taunton.

LANCASHIRE at Cambridge, 7, 8, 9 June. Lancashire won by an innings and 57 runs. Cambridge U. 135 (R. M. Ratcliffe 6–45) and 204. Lancashire 396–6d (J. Abrahams 126, B. Wood 103, D. P. Hughes 72).

NOTTINGHAMSHIRE at Cambridge, 14, 15, 16 (no play) June. Match drawn. Nottinghamshire 314–9d (D. W. Randall 120, B. N. French 66, M. E. Allbrook 7–79). Cambridge U. 203–6 (A. M. Mubarak 77, M. K. Fosh 71, D. R. Doshi 6–33).

DERBYSHIRE at Cambridge, 17, 19, 20 June. Match drawn. Cambridge U. 178 and 244–5 (M. K. Fosh 109, D. J. Littlewood 51). Derbyshire 358–7d (A. J. Harvey-Walker 80, F. W. Swarbrook 60*).

OXFORD UNIVERSITY at Lord's, 28, 29 (no play), 30 June. Match drawn. (See p. 171 for full scorecard.)

Oxford University

Played 10   Won 0   Drawn 6   Lost 4
SOMERSET at Oxford, 19, 20, 21 April. Match drawn. Oxford U. 157 (G. I. Burgess 5–25) and 144. Somerset 197.

WARWICKSHIRE at Oxford, 26 (no play), 27 (no play), 28 April. Match drawn. Warwickshire 109–1 (R. N. Abberley 51*).

KENT at Oxford, 29 April, 1 (no play), 2 (no play) May. Match drawn. Kent 100–1.

GLOUCESTERSHIRE at Oxford, 10, 11, 12 May. Gloucestershire won by 127 runs. Gloucestershire 313–6d (N. H. C. Cooper 94, I. C. Crawford 73) and 164–6d (A. Tait 53). Oxford U. 216 (R. P. Moulding 63, J. O. D. Orders 51) and 134.

YORKSHIRE at Oxford, 17, 18, 19 May. Match drawn. Yorkshire 468–6d (R. G. Lumb 107 and J. D. Love 107 added 217 for the second wicket, K. Sharp 86, G. B. Stevenson 70*) and 205–5d (P. Carrick 57). Oxford U. 125 (D. A. Kayum 57, P. Carrick 6–33) and 156–3 (J. A. Claughton 87).

SUSSEX at Oxford, 24, 25, 26 May. Match drawn. Sussex 300–9d (J. R. T. Barclay 103, M. A. Buss 51) and 168–7d (C. P. Phillipson 70). Oxford U. 241 (J. A. Claughton 130) and 162–6 (R. P. Moulding 68).

GLAMORGAN at Oxford, 31 May, 1, 2 June. Glamorgan won by 238 runs. Glamorgan 357–8d (P. D. Swart 115, M. J. Llewellyn 58, D. A. Francis 56) and 141–3d (D. A. Francis, 54, G. Richards 51*). Oxford U. 141 and 119.

HAMPSHIRE at Oxford, 14, 15, 16 June. Hampshire won by an innings and 99 runs. Oxford U. 149 (G. Pathmanathan 55) and 125. Hampshire 373–5d (D. R. Turner 134 and T. E. Jesty 98 added 211 for the third wicket, D. J. Rock 54).

Somerset's Ian Botham started 1978 in style with an all-bowled hat-trick for MCC against Middlesex at Lord's and ended the season with exactly 100 first-class wickets.

WORCESTERSHIRE at Worcester, 24, 26, 27 June. Worcestershire won by 7 wickets. Oxford U. 255 (R. P. Moulding 77*, D. A. Kayum 51) and 180 (J. O. D. Orders 79). Worcestershire 265 (J. A. Ormrod 117) and 171–3 (B. J. R. Jones 61).

CAMBRIDGE UNIVERSITY at Lord's, 28, 29 (no play), 30 June. Match drawn. (See p. 171 for full scorecard.)

CAMBRIDGE UNIVERSITY

BATTING and FIELDING   *Not out   †Blue 1978

	M	I	NO	HS	Runs	Av	100	50	Ct	St
†P. W. G. Parker	8	11	2	66	411	45.66	—	4	8	—
†A. J. Hignell	9	13	1	145	479	39.91	2	1	7	—
†M. K. Fosh	8	11	1	109	296	29.60	1	1	1	—
†A. M. Mubarak	6	11	0	77	205	18.63	—	1	3	—
†D. J. Beaumont	4	6	1	31	90	18.00	—	—	2	—
†N. F. M. Popplewell	9	11	2	46	157	17.44	—	—	1	—
M. G. Howat	7	8	1	31	118	16.85	—	—	2	—
†D. J. Littlewood	9	10	3	51	95	13.57	—	1	10	5
†A. R. Dewes	5	8	0	32	99	12.37	—	—	1	—
N. C. Crawford	5	6	0	30	71	11.83	—	—	1	—
†S. J. Gardiner	8	9	3	14	59	9.83	—	—	3	—
†M. E. Allbrook	9	9	2	18	68	9.71	—	—	—	—
†I. A. Greig	5	5	0	10	26	5.20	—	—	1	—
I. G. Peck	5	6	0	11	22	3.66	—	—	1	—

Played in two matches: M. M. Bishop 0. 0* (1ct).

BOWLING

	O	M	R	W	Av	BB	5wI	10wM
†M. E. Allbrook	250.2	66	713	24	29.70	7–79	2	—
†P. W. G. Parker	49.2	10	183	6	30.50	2–23	—	—
†I. A. Greig	87	17	283	8	35.37	3–73	—	—
M. G. Howat	140	33	370	9	41.11	2–31	—	—
†S. J. Gardiner	161.1	53	459	11	41.72	4–52	—	—
†N. F. M. Popplewell	166.1	38	540	5	108.00	2–118	—	—

Also bowled: M. M. Bishop 40—10—119—2; N. C. Crawford 8—1—33—0; †A. R. Dewes 33—3—146—1; †A. J. Hignell 30.5—5—118—0.

OXFORD UNIVERSITY

BATTING and FIELDING   *Not out   †Blue 1978

	M	I	NO	HS	Runs	Av	100	50	Ct	St
†R. P. Moulding	8	11	2	77*	276	30.66	—	3	5	—
†J. O. D. Orders	8	13	1	79	335	27.91	—	2	2	—
†D. A. Kayum	5	7	0	57	194	27.71	—	2	6	—
†J. A. Claughton	10	15	0	130	366	24.40	1	1	5	—
†V. J. Marks	4	7	0	60	152	21.71	—	1	1	—
P. J. Dean	2	4	0	39	75	18.75	—	—	1	—
†G. Pathmanathan	7	9	0	55	166	18.44	—	1	7	—
N. D. Morrill	5	7	1	20*	83	13.83	—	—	3	—
J. J. Hamilton-Dalrymple	3	4	2	15	27	13.50	—	—	1	—
D. N. Brettell	3	4	0	30	49	12.25	—	—	1	—
D. H. Price	4	8	0	27	93	11.62	—	—	3	—
†R. LeQ. Savage	4	7	4	12	34	11.33	—	—	2	—
†P. B. Fisher	10	14	1	35	138	10.61	—	—	8	3
R. R. C. Wells	4	6	0	29	54	9.00	—	—	1	—
J. M. Knight	6	8	1	19	61	8.71	—	—	1	—
†G. V. Marie	9	11	0	27	87	7.90	—	—	1	—
†S. M. Wookey	7	8	1	15*	44	6.28	—	—	2	—
†C. J. Ross	6	7	1	4	7	1.16	—	—	1	—

Played in two matches: M. G. L'Estrange 16, 16 (2ct); J. P. Pearce 5*, 0*, 1*. *Played in one match:* P. C. G. Donald 1.

BOWLING

	O	M	R	W	Av	BB	5wI	10wM
†V. J. Marks	109.3	34	272	14	19.42	3–4	—	—
†C. J. Ross	86.1	24	224	8	28.00	4–34	—	—
†R. LeQ. Savage	113.1	28	366	11	33.27	4–97	—	—
J. J. Hamilton-Dalrymple	81	12	260	7	37.14	3–34	—	—
†S. M. Wookey	144.1	32	427	11	38.81	3–61	—	—
J. M. Knight	93.3	22	237	6	39.50	3–36	—	—
†G. V. Marie	234	66	620	15	41.33	3–48	—	—
†J. O. D. Orders	73.1	12	244	5	48.80	2–16	—	—

Also bowled: D. N. Brettell 28—14—39—3; N. D. Morrill 76—18—251—4; J. P. Pearce 61.1—22—157—4; D. H. Price 55—15—174—2.

THE UNIVERSITY MATCH 1978
Played at Lord's, London, 28, 29 (*no play*), 30 June
Toss: Cambridge   Result: Match drawn

*captain
†wicket-keeper

CAMBRIDGE UNIVERSITY

M. K. Fosh	c Pathmanathan b Ross	5	*not out*		27
A. M. Mubarak	c Savage b Ross	16	*lbw b* Marks		9
P. W. G. Parker	c Kayum b Savage	24	c Pathmanathan b Marks		61
A. J. Hignell*	c Savage b Ross	8	*not out*		20
I. A. Greig	st Fisher b Marie	10			
D. J. Beaumont	*lbw b* Savage	0			
A. R. Dewes	c Moulding b Savage	5			
N. F. M. Popplewell	*lbw b* Marks	2			
S. J. Gardiner	st Fisher b Marks	2			
D. J. Littlewood†	c Kayum b Marks	0			
M. E. Allbrook	*not out*	1			
Extras	(*lb* 18, *nb* 1)	19	(*nb* 1)		1
TOTAL		92	(2 wickets)		118

OXFORD UNIVERSITY

G. Pathmanathan	b Allbrook	14
J. A. Claughton*	c Hignell b Gardiner	10
V. J. Marks	c Fosh b Allbrook	60
D. A. Kayum	c Parker b Allbrook	27
J. O. D. Orders	c Littlewood b Gardiner	32
R. P. Moulding	*lbw b* Allbrook	6
P. B. Fisher†	c Gardiner b Allbrook	0
S. M. Wookey	*lbw b* Gardiner	1
G. V. Marie	b Allbrook	18
R. LeQ. Savage	c Parker b Gardiner	8
C. J. Ross	*not out*	0
Extras	(*b* 10, *lb* 4, *nb* 2)	16
TOTAL		192

OXFORD UNIVERSITY

	O	M	R	W	O	M	R	W
Wookey	8	1	12	0				
Ross	11	3	26	3	2	2	0	0
Savage	13	7	21	3	13	4	56	0
Marie	4	1	10	1	2	0	8	0
Marks	5.3	3	4	3	13	4	53	2

CAMBRIDGE UNIVERSITY

	O	M	R	W
Greig	3	0	10	0
Popplewell	3	0	9	0
Allbrook	22	3	81	6
Gardiner	17.1	4	52	4
Dewes	4	0	24	0

Umpires: W. E. Alley and R. T. Wilson

FALL OF WICKETS

	Cambridge		Oxford	
Wkt	1st	2nd	1st	2nd
1st	15	10	27	
2nd	35	89	27	
3rd	43		119	
4th	65		120	
5th	66		131	
6th	77		133	
7th	82		134	
8th	91		171	
9th	91		189	
10th	92		192	

Nottinghamshire's dashing all-rounder Clive Rice began the summer at odds with his county but ended triumphantly at the head of the first-class batting averages.

FIRST-CLASS AVERAGES 1978

BATTING (Qualification: 8 innings average 10.00)   * Not out

	M	I	NO	HS	Runs	Av	100	50
C. E. B. Rice	23	37	9	213*	1,871	66.82	5	9
G. M. Turner	22	38	7	202*	1,711	55.19	6	4
C. G. Greenidge	19	34	1	211	1,771	53.66	5	9
D. L. Amiss	23	41	3	162	2,030	53.42	7	11
J. H. Hampshire	22	36	6	132	1,596	53.20	3	9
B. F. Davison	23	35	3	180*	1,644	51.37	4	9
G. Boycott	16	25	1	131	1,233	51.37	6	3
M. J. Procter	21	36	3	203	1,655	50.15	3	7
K. S. McEwan	24	37	3	186	1,682	49.47	5	8
Asif Iqbal	18	25	6	171	934	49.15	3	2
A. J. Lamb	17	27	8	106*	883	46.47	2	5
D. W. Randall	24	40	7	157*	1,525	46.21	2	11
I. V. A. Richards	21	38	4	118	1,558	45.82	2	10
J. A. Ormrod	24	41	7	173	1,535	45.14	5	4
Zaheer Abbas	22	35	1	213	1,535	45.14	6	4
C. J. Tavaré	25	39	5	105	1,534	45.11	2	11
R. W. Tolchard	24	35	16	103*	841	44.26	1	5
A. I. Kallicharran	16	29	5	129	1,041	43.37	3	5
B. L. D'Oliveira	17	22	5	146*	728	42.82	1	2
Imran Khan	22	37	5	167	1,339	41.84	3	6
G. A. Gooch	21	33	3	129	1,254	41.80	2	9
K. W. R. Fletcher	24	35	8	89	1,127	41.74	—	10
M. J. Harris	23	36	4	148*	1,315	41.09	3	6
G. P. Howarth	21	37	3	179*	1,375	40.44	2	8
G. R. J. Roope	19	29	7	113*	888	40.36	2	6
R. A. Woolmer	21	34	3	137	1,245	40.16	2	9
B. R. Hardie	23	33	7	109	1,044	40.15	1	6
E. J. O. Hemsley	24	37	7	141*	1,168	38.93	3	6
R. D. V. Knight	22	38	6	128	1,233	38.53	3	7
M. N. S. Taylor	22	29	9	103*	770	38.50	1	6
P. A. Slocombe	23	40	8	128*	1,221	38.15	3	5
D. S. Steele	21	36	5	130	1,182	38.12	3	9
J. F. Steele	22	34	3	133	1,182	38.12	3	6
D. I. Gower	21	31	2	111	1,098	37.86	2	5
Javed Miandad	21	32	6	127	983	37.80	2	6
P. W. G. Parker	22	36	4	112	1,192	37.25	1	7
C. H. Lloyd	21	36	6	120	1,116	37.20	4	6
Sadiq Mohammad	26	42	3	176	1,449	37.15	2	6
W. Larkins	25	44	5	170*	1,448	37.12	3	7
C. T. Radley	18	26	1	106	923	36.92	3	5
P. N. Kirsten	20	35	4	206*	1,133	36.54	1	7
E. J. Barlow	16	25	4	127	765	36.42	1	3
J. N. Shepherd	20	28	6	101	785	35.68	2	3
C. J. C. Rowe	20	35	5	85	1,065	35.50	—	7
P. Willey	22	35	9	112	921	35.42	1	6
F. C. Hayes	21	35	5	136*	1,055	35.16	2	4
B. C. Rose	24	41	5	122	1,263	35.08	4	3
P. A. Neale	24	40	6	103*	1,182	34.76	1	9
M. J. Llewellyn	21	31	6	82	849	33.96	—	7

	M	I	NO	HS	Runs	Av	100	50
K. D. Smith	23	39	4	132*	1,187	33.91	3	5
G. Miller	18	25	5	95	674	33.70	—	5
J. A. Hopkins	25	44	3	116	1,371	33.43	3	7
M. W. Gatting	26	39	4	128	1,166	33.31	2	6
R. O. Butcher	10	14	0	142	464	33.14	1	3
P. M. Roebuck	23	37	8	131*	944	32.55	1	6
P. Carrick	25	32	11	105	679	32.33	1	3
R. C. Ontong	21	34	4	116*	969	32.30	2	5
G. Cook	23	40	2	155	1,226	32.26	1	7
D. R. Turner	23	42	3	148*	1,255	32.17	3	2
J. G. Wright	18	31	3	164	901	32.17	2	4
D. Breakwell	16	23	5	100*	579	32.16	1	4
A. R. Butcher	19	33	2	188	994	32.06	2	4
D. Lloyd	22	37	2	185	1,113	31.80	3	3
T. E. Jesty	24	43	6	125*	1,174	31.72	5	2
P. D. Swart	23	37	3	115	1,078	31.70	3	5
K. Sharp	18	27	5	91	695	31.59	—	3
R. G. Lumb	23	37	3	107	1,070	31.47	2	8
G. D. Barlow	24	35	2	102*	1,016	30.78	1	6
R. P. Moulding	8	11	2	77*	276	30.66	—	3
B. A. Richards	6	11	0	73	337	30.63	—	2
G. D. Mendis	20	36	4	128	979	30.59	3	1
A. G. E. Ealham	23	32	4	102*	856	30.57	1	5
T. J. Yardley	18	26	6	97	611	30.55	—	3
J. H. Edrich	18	29	5	114	733	30.54	1	4
S. Turner	23	29	8	89*	636	30.28	—	3
B. W. Reidy	10	15	3	88	360	30.00	—	1
A. Jones	24	39	1	147	1,133	29.81	3	3
J. Birkenshaw	22	26	9	70*	506	29.76	—	1
A. Kennedy	19	31	2	100	859	29.62	1	4
G. Richards	22	36	10	74	768	29.53	—	5
P. A. Todd	24	40	0	89	1,181	29.52	—	10
A. W. Stovold	21	35	2	139	962	29.15	1	5
J. C. Foat	19	29	4	102*	722	28.88	2	3
J. Simmons	22	30	7	106	663	28.82	1	2
N. G. Featherstone	19	27	1	108	740	28.46	1	3
J. D. Love	15	20	3	107	483	28.41	1	3
G. B. Stevenson	17	19	4	70*	426	28.40	—	1
J. O. D. Orders	8	13	1	79	335	27.91	—	2
A. J. Borrington	17	27	3	137	669	27.87	1	2
D. J. Humphries	24	32	5	111*	743	27.51	1	3
D. A. Graveney	26	35	8	92	740	27.40	—	4
G. W. Johnson	24	31	6	95	685	27.40	—	3
M. A. Nash	23	34	5	124*	794	27.37	1	5
N. E. Briers	16	24	2	116*	601	27.31	2	2
J. R. T. Barclay	23	41	4	103	1,006	27.18	1	4
R. N. Abberley	15	25	2	81	625	27.17	—	6
Younis Ahmed	15	23	4	72	514	27.05	—	4
I. T. Botham	17	20	0	108	538	26.90	2	1
N. Phillip	20	28	4	134	645	26.87	1	3
J. Walters	14	22	4	90	482	26.77	—	2
J. C. Balderstone	24	36	1	101	931	26.60	1	5
R. G. Williams	16	20	5	60*	399	26.60	—	1
B. Dudleston	16	24	1	90	608	26.43	—	4
T. A. Lloyd	15	23	3	93	526	26.30	—	3
I. J. Gould	22	31	4	128	706	26.14	1	2
P. W. Denning	22	39	3	78*	925	25.69	—	5
C. W. J. Athey	23	38	2	131	906	25.16	2	4
R. M. C. Gilliat	16	27	9	54	453	25.16	—	1
C. Johnson	7	14	3	61	276	25.09	—	2
D. L. Bairstow	24	36	7	60	725	25.00	—	4
M. H. Denness	22	37	2	126	870	24.85	1	4
M. Schepens	5	8	2	39	147	24.50	—	—
P. B. Clift	22	26	7	61	465	24.47	—	3

	M	I	NO	HS	Runs	Av	100	50
M. J. Smedley	23	31	4	83*	660	24.44	—	4
B. Hassan	8	9	0	81	220	24.44	—	1
J. A. Claughton	10	15	0	130	366	24.40	—	1
M. K. Fosh	10	15	1	109	341	24.35	1	1
J. M. Brearley	19	27	4	70*	558	24.26	—	4
F. W. Swarbrook	12	16	6	60*	240	24.00	—	1
P. H. Edmonds	18	21	6	46*	359	23.93	—	—
G. W. Humpage	21	31	3	110	663	23.67	1	2
C. M. Old	14	15	5	100*	236	23.60	1	—
M. A. Buss	14	20	3	79*	398	23.41	—	2
C. P. Phillipson	22	36	4	70	749	23.40	—	5
J. Abrahams	19	30	2	126	654	23.35	1	4
A. M. E. Roberts	9	14	5	37*	209	23.22	—	—
A. Hill	24	41	1	153*	928	23.20	1	2
C. N. Boyns	10	13	2	71	255	23.18	—	1
N. Gifford	22	24	12	37*	278	23.16	—	—
K. R. Pont	12	18	2	101	366	22.87	1	2
T. M. Tremlett	6	10	2	50	183	22.87	—	1
C. S. Cowdrey	17	17	4	69*	291	22.38	—	1
D. M. Smith	17	27	6	115	463	22.04	1	—
M. J. Smith	23	34	1	63	726	22.00	—	3
J. D. Birch	13	16	2	52*	308	22.00	—	2
J. Whitehouse	25	42	8	102*	744	21.88	1	—
J. M. Rice	19	31	2	63	630	21.72	—	3
A. J. Hignell	20	32	1	145	661	21.32	2	1
K. P. Tomlins	11	16	2	94	295	21.07	—	2
R. Illingworth	17	15	5	39*	209	20.90	—	2
A. J. Harvey-Walker	9	13	2	80	230	20.90	—	—
V. J. Marks	15	25	3	60	456	20.72	—	2
R. J. Hadlee	17	21	4	101*	342	20.11	1	—
M. J. Kitchen	13	20	2	50	359	19.94	—	1
N. G. Cowley	23	38	5	64	650	19.69	—	2
E. E. Hemmings	14	18	4	51	275	19.64	—	1
A. Long	21	28	7	56*	410	19.52	—	1
H. Cartwright	24	37	4	77*	644	19.51	—	2
D. R. Shepherd	16	24	1	72	446	19.39	—	3
A. Tait	11	19	1	53	348	19.33	—	2
S. P. Hoadley	7	12	0	112	232	19.33	1	1
B. Wood	9	13	1	103	228	19.00	1	—
M. D. Partridge	7	10	3	50	133	19.00	—	1
G. S. Clinton	6	8	2	33	113	18.83	—	—
M. A. Lynch	14	24	0	101	451	18.79	1	2
D. N. Patel	23	29	0	104	544	18.75	1	1
G. I. Burgess	16	23	5	55	336	18.66	—	1
A. M. Mubarak	6	11	0	77	205	18.63	—	1
R. E. East	23	26	5	57	391	18.61	—	1
G. Pathmanathan	7	9	0	55	166	18.44	—	1
N. H. C. Cooper	6	12	0	94	219	18.25	—	1
R. G. L. Cheatle	15	14	4	49	182	18.20	—	—
N. Smith	24	24	6	59*	323	17.94	—	1
W. N. Slack	10	16	1	52	268	17.86	—	1
R. P. Baker	11	17	3	91	249	17.78	—	1
D. J. Rock	7	13	0	54	231	17.76	—	2
D. J. S. Taylor	23	29	5	78	424	17.66	—	2
R. M. Ratcliffe	20	23	5	48	318	17.66	—	—
N. F. M. Popplewell	9	11	2	46	157	17.44	—	—
A. W. Greig	5	8	1	32	122	17.42	—	—
B. N. French	22	26	8	66	308	17.11	—	1
D. A. Francis	7	10	1	56	154	17.11	—	2
R. A. White	17	16	3	44*	220	16.92	—	—
H. Pilling	8	13	1	49	203	16.91	—	—
H. P. Cooper	19	16	5	40	186	16.90	—	—
K. F. Jennings	17	19	10	31*	152	16.88	—	—
M. G. Howat	7	8	1	31	118	16.85	—	—

	M	I	NO	HS	Runs	Av	100	50
S. J. Storey	16	23	3	57	331	16.55	—	1
H. T. Tunnicliffe	9	12	3	69*	148	16.44	—	1
C. J. Richards	23	29	10	50	310	16.31	—	1
D. P. Hughes	13	17	2	72	243	16.20	—	1
R. Arrowsmith	13	10	4	24*	96	16.00	—	—
I. S. Anderson	6	10	1	75	140	15.55	—	1
K. C. Wessels	4	8	0	29	123	15.37	—	—
P. R. Oliver	17	22	1	47	322	15.33	—	—
A. L. Jones	9	16	2	54	213	15.21	—	1
J. J. Groome	9	17	1	50	229	14.31	—	1
M. Hendrick	17	15	6	33	127	14.11	—	—
G. R. Stephenson	23	30	5	66	350	14.00	—	1
G. G. Watson	21	24	5	38	266	14.00	—	—
J. M. H. Graham-Brown	11	17	2	43	209	13.93	—	—
R. D. Jackman	23	30	7	42	319	13.86	—	—
K. S. Mackintosh	14	14	5	23*	124	13.77	—	—
D. J. Littlewood	9	10	3	51	95	13.57	—	1
J. Spencer	17	22	8	30	189	13.50	—	—
A. E. Cordle	15	15	3	33*	161	13.41	—	—
B. M. Brain	23	27	7	35	268	13.40	—	—
P. J. Watts	13	15	1	57*	185	13.21	—	1
D. L. Underwood	22	17	6	25	145	13.18	—	—
D. J. Brown	16	19	6	38	171	13.15	—	—
J. E. Emburey	25	33	7	42	338	13.00	—	—
R. LeQ. Savage	5	8	5	12	39	13.00	—	—
K. B. Smith	4	8	1	43	90	12.85	—	—
G. Sharp	20	21	5	27*	204	12.75	—	—
Sarfraz Nawaz	18	19	7	32*	151	12.58	—	—
G. G. Arnold	17	23	4	29	237	12.47	—	—
S. J. Rouse	10	12	1	40	137	12.45	—	—
P. Booth	18	10	2	25*	99	12.37	—	—
A. R. Dewes	5	8	0	32	99	12.37	—	—
B. J. Lloyd	24	28	8	27	245	12.25	—	—
J. Lyon	21	25	3	74*	267	12.13	—	1
G. A. Cope	15	17	6	44	133	12.09	—	—
D. H. Price	4	8	0	27	93	11.62	—	—
E. W. Jones	22	25	5	58	232	11.60	—	1
B. J. R. Jones	10	16	0	61	182	11.37	—	1
R. W. Taylor	16	17	1	32	179	11.18	—	—
R. W. Hills	14	13	2	31*	122	11.09	—	—
W. W. Daniel	21	24	12	30*	132	11.00	—	—
C. C. Clifford	11	12	5	20	76	10.85	—	—
R. G. D. Willis	18	16	5	23*	117	10.63	—	—
J. K. Lever	22	15	7	30	85	10.62	—	—
P. B. Fisher	10	14	1	35	138	10.61	—	—
J. W. Southern	23	22	8	51	148	10.57	—	1
J. Davey	15	19	6	20*	135	10.38	—	—
H. R. Moseley	14	9	3	30	62	10.33	—	—
K. Higgs	18	11	6	13*	51	10.20	—	—
N. E. J. Pocock	5	8	1	18	71	10.14	—	—

BOWLING (Qualification: 10 wickets in 10 innings)

	O	M	R	W	Av	BB	5wI	10wM
D. L. Underwood	815.1	359	1,594	110	14.49	9–32	8	2
R. A. Woolmer	135.4	46	292	20	14.60	6–27	1	—
W. W. Daniel	453.3	113	1,114	76	14.65	5–42	3	—
M. Hendrick	473.5	167	895	59	15.16	5–32	2	—
J. K. Lever	681.1	160	1,610	106	15.18	7–32	9	1
P. H. Edmonds	503	172	912	60	15.20	7–34	2	—
M. W. Gatting	168.3	36	411	26	15.80	5–59	1	—
R. J. Hadlee	497.1	120	1,269	78	16.26	7–77	6	2

	O	M	R	W	Av	BB	5wI	10wM
R. E. East	700.2	226	1,506	92	16.36	8–41	6	1
I. T. Botham	605.2	141	1,640	100	16.40	8–34	10	1
C. M. Old	520.1	166	1,108	64	17.31	7–50	4	—
R. G. D. Willis	474.2	116	1,197	65	18.41	7–63	5	1
G. G. Arnold	401	102	910	49	18.57	7–44	2	—
C. E. Waller	371	125	861	46	18.71	5–30	3	—
M. W. W. Selvey	743.5	199	1,929	101	19.09	6–26	8	1
G. W. Johnson	510.4	173	1,084	56	19.35	6–32	2	—
H. R. Moseley	348.1	103	813	41	19.82	6–35	1	—
P. E. Russell	235.4	88	423	21	20.14	4–23	—	—
C. E. B. Rice	322.3	82	835	41	20.36	4–25	—	—
W. Hogg	256.4	58	775	38	20.39	7–84	3	—
J. E. Emburey	799.3	243	1,641	79	20.77	6–25	3	—
B. M. Brain	573.2	138	1,589	76	20.90	5–48	2	—
J. P. Whiteley	172.5	46	475	22	21.59	4–14	—	—
R. M. Ratcliffe	571.3	151	1,532	70	21.88	7–58	3	—
E. J. Barlow	214.5	58	528	24	22.00	4–34	—	—
N. Phillip	583.1	113	1,591	71	22.40	6–33	4	—
K. Higgs	381	112	923	41	22.51	7–44	1	—
C. E. H. Croft	431.3	101	1,266	56	22.60	5–58	1	—
A. M. E. Roberts	254.1	74	617	27	22.85	5–20	1	—
K. B. S. Jarvis	598.5	139	1,863	80	23.28	8–97	3	1
D. P. Hughes	191.1	54	517	22	23.50	5–46	1	—

John Lever of Essex, one of four bowlers to capture 100 wickets in first-class matches in 1978.

	O	M	R	W	Av	BB	5wI	10wM
P. B. Clift	519.4	156	1,209	51	23.70	6–29	1	—
M. J. Procter	665.2	185	1,649	69	23.89	7–45	2	—
A. J. Harvey-Walker	145	42	408	17	24.00	7–35	1	1
J. C. Balderstone	368.5	104	914	38	24.05	6–25	2	—
P. I. Pocock	662.4	201	1,615	67	24.10	6–73	5	—
J. W. Southern	762.3	247	1,833	76	24.11	5–32	4	—
C. W. J. Athey	93	26	268	11	24.36	3–38	—	—
R. D. Jackman	590.2	134	1,707	70	24.38	5–26	3	—
J. H. Childs	520.2	154	1,440	59	24.40	8–34	5	2
J. M. Rice	267.1	70	709	29	24.44	4–49	—	—
G. A. Cope	342.3	114	784	32	24.50	4–34	—	—
D. Breakwell	445.1	135	1,007	41	24.56	6–45	1	—
S. Turner	531	149	1,183	48	24.64	4–9	—	—
Sarfraz Nawaz	445	116	998	40	24.95	5–39	1	—
S. Oldham	485	115	1,326	53	25.01	5–40	1	—
J. Spencer	496.5	143	1,158	46	25.17	5–53	1	—
R. Illingworth	261.4	86	635	25	25.40	6–38	2	—
J. F. Steele	229.5	62	566	22	25.72	5–54	1	—
P. D. Swart	358	73	1,112	43	25.86	4–24	—	—
G. B. Stevenson	375.3	79	1,144	44	26.00	8–65	3	—
L. B. Taylor	300.2	50	1,040	40	26.00	4–32	—	—
K. F. Jennings	442.3	147	1,041	40	26.02	5–18	1	—
M. A. Buss	179.2	52	473	18	26.27	3–47	—	—
C. H. Dredge	573.1	137	1,473	56	26.30	5–53	2	—
D. S. Steele	378.3	110	976	37	26.37	6–36	3	1
Intikhab Alam	623.2	197	1,570	59	26.61	6–126	3	—
V. J. Marks	459.1	133	1,217	45	27.04	4–48	—	—
P. Carrick	682	232	1,529	56	27.30	7–35	4	1
G. Miller	484.2	170	1,020	37	27.56	5–43	2	—
K. Cooper	481.5	93	1,467	53	27.67	6–32	2	—
J. R. T. Barclay	207	49	554	20	27.70	5–72	1	—
N. G. Featherstone	140.3	39	365	13	28.07	5–32	1	—
D. L. Acfield	454.1	125	1,013	36	28.13	3–33	—	—
C. J. Tunnicliffe	456.4	126	1,241	44	28.20	4–30	—	—
Imran Khan	543	128	1,391	49	28.38	7–52	2	—
B. L. D'Oliveira	193.2	48	483	17	28.41	5–48	1	—
F. W. Swarbrook	134	43	344	12	28.66	4–22	—	—
N. Gifford	667.3	210	1,557	54	28.83	6–68	2	—
A. A. Jones	247.4	45	840	29	28.96	6–89	2	—
D. J. Brown	405	80	1,160	40	29.00	5–53	1	—
J. Birkenshaw	344.2	83	874	30	29.13	3–23	—	—
D. R. Doshi	675.1	170	1,763	60	29.38	6–33	3	1
T. M. Lamb	492.5	115	1,370	46	29.78	6–71	1	—
J. Davey	309.3	65	900	30	30.00	4–52	—	—
P. Booth	293.2	63	870	29	30.00	6–93	1	—
A. P. Pridgeon	587.2	115	1,771	59	30.01	4–38	—	—
N. G. Cowley	672.3	192	1,700	56	30.35	5–93	1	—
K. Stevenson	515.5	101	1,706	56	30.46	6–73	2	—
S. P. Perryman	591.3	172	1,527	50	30.54	7–49	3	1
R. D. V. Knight	161.2	41	432	14	30.85	3–22	—	—
P. Willey	679.1	196	1,576	51	30.90	7–73	2	1
J. Walters	166	31	497	16	31.06	3–70	—	—
B. J. Griffiths	554	103	1,591	51	31.19	5–66	1	—
G. G. Watson	503	83	1,535	48	31.97	6–45	1	—
C. C. Clifford	431.3	115	1,220	38	32.10	6–89	2	—
D. N. Patel	398.1	94	1,126	35	32.17	5–22	1	—
H. P. Cooper	447	113	1,191	37	32.18	6–26	1	—
P. N. Kirsten	207.4	55	581	18	32.27	4–51	—	—
P. H. L. Wilson	105.2	22	355	11	32.27	4–56	—	—
R. Arrowsmith	320.1	106	889	27	32.92	4–49	—	—
G. I. Burgess	363	135	890	27	32.96	5–25	1	—
T. E. Jesty	260.5	73	663	20	33.15	6–50	1	—
M. N. S. Taylor	346.1	104	900	27	33.33	5–67	1	—
R. W. Hills	263.2	63	803	24	33.45	6–64	1	—

	O	M	R	W	Av	BB	5wI	10wM
K. Shuttleworth	159.4	45	436	13	33.53	3–27	—	—
R. P. Baker	166.4	28	573	17	33.70	3–54	—	—
M. E. Allbrook	324.2	76	991	29	34.17	7–79	2	—
A. H. Wilkins	369.3	74	1,267	37	34.24	5–96	1	—
J. Simmons	501	146	1,203	35	34.37	3–33	—	—
J. N. Shepherd	601.2	166	1,573	44	35.75	5–70	1	—
R. C. Wincer	203.2	40	680	19	35.78	4–42	—	—
S. M. Wookey	144.1	32	427	11	38.81	3–61	—	—
M. A. Nash	519.2	133	1,631	42	38.83	6–74	2	—
R. C. Ontong	262.5	57	856	22	38.90	4–95	—	—
J. Cumbes	435	95	1,207	31	38.93	4–52	—	—
G. Richards	218.3	45	750	19	39.47	5–55	1	—
B. J. Lloyd	561.3	154	1,590	40	39.75	4–82	—	—
R. G. L. Cheatle	314.2	85	968	24	40.33	4–89	—	—
E. E. Hemmings	376.1	88	1,142	28	40.78	4–51	—	—
A. E. Cordle	307.5	73	864	21	41.14	5–33	1	—
G. V. Marie	234	66	620	15	41.33	3–48	—	—
S. J. Gardiner	161.1	53	459	11	41.72	4–52	—	—
D. A. Graveney	558	175	1,492	35	42.62	4–47	—	—
K. S. Mackintosh	239	46	693	16	43.31	4–49	—	—
C. P. Phillipson	193	37	702	16	43.87	3–72	—	—
R. G. Williams	160.1	35	461	10	46.10	4–48	—	—
D. J. Thomas	296	66	923	20	46.15	4–47	—	—
S. J. Rouse	142.4	27	565	12	47.08	4–63	—	—
C. N. Boyns	152.2	21	566	12	47.16	3–92	—	—
R. W. Flower	173	42	554	10	55.40	3–45	—	—
R. A. White	541	145	1,515	27	56.11	4–73	—	—

The following bowlers took 10 wickets but bowled in fewer than 10 innings:

	O	M	R	W	Av	BB	5wI	10wM
A. J. Mack	77.3	26	195	16	12.18	4–28	—	—
J. Garner	170.1	61	351	22	15.95	5–50	3	—
D. R. Gurr	104	25	296	11	26.90	4–65	—	—
V. A. Holder	179	31	468	15	31.20	4–52	—	—
W. K. Watson	151.3	34	486	15	32.40	6–102	1	—
P. J. W. Allott	129	12	456	14	32.57	5–98	1	—
R. LeQ. Savage	117.1	28	384	11	34.90	4–97	—	—
A. Hodgson	105.2	21	351	10	35.10	3–29	—	—

FIELDING STATISTICS

71	D. L. Bairstow (61 ct, 10 st)		28	K. W. R. Fletcher
64	D. J. S. Taylor (55 ct, 9 st)		28	G. R. J. Roope
63	P. R. Downton (59 ct, 4 st)		28	J. F. Steele
59	N. Smith (51 ct, 8 st)		27	B. R. Hardie
55	I. J. Gould (50 ct, 5 st)		25	E. J. Barlow
55	G. R. Stephenson (46 ct, 9 st)		25	R. A. Woolmer
52	D. J. Humphries (44 ct, 8 st)		24	C. E. B. Rice
52	J. Lyon (49 ct, 3 st)		24	D. S. Steele
50	A. Long (47 ct, 3 st)		23	G. Cook
49	C. J. Tavaré		23	G. A. Gooch
47	R. W. Taylor (44 ct, 3 st)		22	C. W. J. Athey
46	R. W. Tolchard (39 ct, 7 st)		22	J. Simmons
45	A. J. Brassington (42 ct, 3 st)		22	T. J. Yardley
44	B. N. French (37 ct, 7 st)		21	C. H. Lloyd
41	E. W. Jones (40 ct, 1 st)		21	K. S. McEwan
36	G. Sharp (33 ct, 3 st)		21	J. A. Ormrod
34	C. G. Greenidge		21	I. V. A. Richards
32	G. W. Humpage (29 ct, 3 st)		20	G. M. Turner
31	C. J. Richards (24 ct, 7 st)			

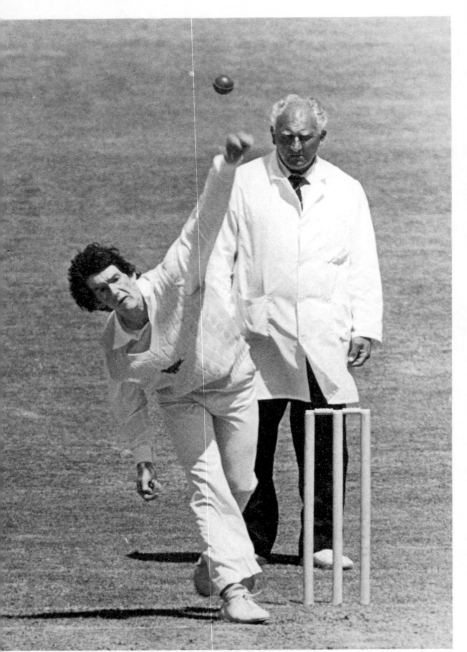

*Lovers of spin bowling rejoiced in the employment of Giles Cheatle in the Gillette Cup final.
Sussex captain Long was rewarded for his enterprise with two vital wickets.*

GILLETTE CUP 1978

1ST ROUND 5, 6, 7 July	2ND ROUND 19, 20 July	QUARTER-FINALS 2, 3, 4 August	SEMI-FINALS 16 August	FINAL 2 September
SOMERSET				
Warwickshire	SOMERSET			
GLAMORGAN (Bye)	Glamorgan†	SOMERSET		
NORTHAMPTONSHIRE (Bye)	Northamptonshire†		SOMERSET†	
KENT (Bye)	KENT	Kent†		
Shropshire†	Surrey			Somerset
SURREY				
ESSEX (Bye)	ESSEX†	ESSEX		
LEICESTERSHIRE (Bye)	LEICESTERSHIRE†		Essex	
HAMPSHIRE (Bye)	Hampshire	Leicestershire†		
LANCASHIRE (Bye)	LANCASHIRE†			SUSSEX
GLOUCESTERSHIRE (Bye)	Gloucestershire	LANCASHIRE†		
MIDDLESEX (Bye)	MIDDLESEX		Lancashire	
Worcestershire†	Derbyshire†	Middlesex		
DERBYSHIRE				
YORKSHIRE†	YORKSHIRE†	Yorkshire†		SUSSEX
Durham	Nottinghamshire		SUSSEX†	
NOTTINGHAMSHIRE (Bye)				
Devon†	Staffordshire†	SUSSEX		
STAFFORDSHIRE				
SUSSEX†	SUSSEX			
Suffolk				

† Home team.   Winning team in small capitals.

SEMI-FINAL

Sussex v Lancashire

Although Lancashire repeatedly failed to play to their potential during 1978, they started firm favourites to beat Sussex in the semi-final at Hove. What surprised was not that Sussex won, for nothing is ever certain in limited-overs cricket, but the extent and the decisiveness of their victory. There was scarcely a moment throughout this very one-sided contest when Lancashire suggested they might even make a game of it. And when one considers how close Sussex came to being eliminated by Staffordshire in an earlier round, this was rather odd.

Sussex, put in to bat on a well-grassed, yet amiable, pitch, made the most

Man of the Match Javed Miandad in a somewhat undignified pose after adding four to his total in the semi-final against Lancashire at Hove. Sussex were comfortable winners.

of the opportunity to amass 277 for eight in the 60 overs. Barclay and Mendis gave them a brisk start, and Miandad contributed a dashing 75, including 50 out of 62 in only 55 minutes. Parker, sensibly and correctly, supported him until Miandad departed, and then accelerated himself with several different but enterprising partners to make sure the scoreboard kept turning over quickly. The Northerners' bowling, apart from the steady Simmons, was inclined to be too short and lacked penetration.

Lancashire, with a plethora of lefthanders (five in the first six of their order), were soon in trouble against Imran and Arnold, both of whom swung the ball, and lost two wickets for only 11 runs. It now required a Clive Lloyd miracle to win the match but it was not forthcoming; even though Sussex were strangely generous and managed to drop him twice off successive balls. After tea, tight spells by Barclay and Spencer made certain that Lancashire would not reach their formidable objective, and they were dismissed in 51.4 overs, still needing 136 runs. In contrast to their opponents, Sussex bowled exceptionally well and so were able to contain such a formidable batting line-up.

SEMI-FINAL
SUSSEX v LANCASHIRE at Hove on 16 August
Sussex won by 136 runs
Toss: Lancashire
Man of the Match: Javed Miandad

* *captain*
† *wicket-keeper*

SUSSEX				LANCASHIRE	O	M	R	W
J. R. T. Barclay	c Lyon b Croft	19		Croft	12	1	53	3
G. D. Mendis	c Croft b Simmons	29		Ratcliffe	12	1	50	1
P. W. G. Parker	lbw b Croft	69		Reidy	12	1	65	0
Javed Miandad	b Croft	75		Simmons	12	4	34	1
Imran Khan	c Kennedy b Ratcliffe	26		Hughes	12	0	62	2
C. P. Phillipson	c and b Hughes	34		SUSSEX				
A. Long*†	c Reidy b Hughes	6		Imran	8	1	25	0
R. G. L. Cheatle	run out	2		Arnold	6	2	10	2
S. J. Storey	not out	4		Spencer	12	3	21	2
G. G. Arnold ⎱	did not bat			Storey	3	0	22	0
J. Spencer ⎰				Barclay	12	2	27	3
Extras	(b 1, lb 9, nb 1, w 2)	13		Phillipson	6	0	14	2
TOTAL	(8 wickets – 60 overs)	277		Cheatle	4.4	0	7	0

LANCASHIRE			FALL OF WICKETS		
A. Kennedy	c Spencer b Arnold	8	Wkt	Sx	La
D. Lloyd	lbw b Arnold	0	1st	30	10
J. Abrahams	c and b Spencer	25	2nd	59	11
C. H. Lloyd	c Storey b Barclay	40	3rd	182	71
F. C. Hayes*	c Imran b Spencer	6	4th	207	79
B. W. Reidy	b Barclay	11	5th	247	94
J. Simmons	c Miandad b Barclay	11	6th	259	101
D. P. Hughes	c Long b Phillipson	6	7th	271	115
J. Lyon†	run out	11	8th	277	118
R. M. Ratcliffe	c Imran b Phillipson	3	9th		126
C. E. H. Croft	not out	5	10th		141
Extras	(b 1, lb 6, nb 4, w 4)	15			
TOTAL	(51.4 overs)	141	Umpires: C. G. Pepper and		
			P. B. Wight		

Note: For the report and scorecard of the semi-final between Somerset and Essex at Taunton, please see the Match of the Season on p. 21.

*Left: Imran Khan,
whose first over of the
Gillette Cup final cost
Sussex 14 runs, and
whose brief innings was a
cricketing vignette with
Botham walking away
with the applause.
Below: Paul Parker's
unbeaten 62 saw
Sussex home against
Somerset and deservedly
brought him the Man
of the Match award.*

GILLETTE CUP FINAL 1978

Three middle-aged – in the cricketing sense – former Surrey players, two Pakistanis, an inexperienced slow left-armer who learned his cricket at Stowe, an opener born in Ceylon, a bowler turned batsman, a former and a present Cambridge Blue, and an Old Etonian: such was the somewhat improbable combination which carried off the Gillette Cup at Lord's by beating the favourites, Somerset. Sussex thoroughly deserved their five wickets victory because they bowled and fielded better than their opponents, who were unable to lift their game at the vital moment.

Probably the most encouraging feature of 1978 was the increase in the quality, and the quantity, of young home-produced players found in the county teams. This welcome trend was certainly reflected by individual performances in the Gillette final which, over the years, has tended to be the setting for some great overseas cricketer to demonstrate his skill. On this occasion all the serious candidates for the Man of the Match award were representatives of this new breed; Ian Botham, John Barclay, and Paul Parker.

Having won the toss, Arnold Long inserted Somerset because there appeared to be some moisture in the pitch that might assist his seamers. It did not work out that way, although Imran did take the first wicket; it was the slow left-armer, Cheatle, who removed Rose for 30 and had Roebuck caught off a most inviting full toss. Richards, too, found himself contained by Cheatle, and later by the more accurate off-spin of Barclay, who was to trap the great man sweeping and to dismiss Marks. The West Indian seemed weighed down with responsibility, and there were only occasional reminders of his genius. He was also frustrated by Long's astutely placed defensive fields and bowlers who remembered to bowl to them.

It was left to Botham to provide the innings with the necessary impetus with a fierce assault on Cheatle, but he received insufficient assistance at the other end. Burgess ran himself out and Taylor, misreading the situation, failed to provide Botham with enough of the strike, seemingly content with the occasional single. Botham's splendid innings of 80 included an improbable pick-up for six to mid-wicket off a respectable delivery from Arnold when the overs were running out and he had resorted to the slog.

Although 207 was not as large as the total should have been, only twice before in the final had teams batting second made more than 200 to win. Barclay and Mendis, after moments of uncertainty in the early overs, gave their team both the impetus and the start required against bowling that was inclined to be too short. Barclay, provided with the opportunity to cut, did so to good effect, assisted by the fact that Rose did not employ a deep cover.

When the total was 93 Mendis was caught, but at tea everything suggested that Sussex were well placed to cruise home with wickets and overs to spare. In a desperate effort to regain the initiative, Rose recalled his main strike bowlers, Botham and Garner, and for a few overs it looked as if his strategy might have worked. Botham, as usual, responded to the challenge. First he had Barclay caught, mis-hooking a bouncer, and then, after Garner had Miandad brilliantly caught by Taylor, he produced that little extra to hit Imran with a distinctly lively bouncer and followed this up with a ball that lifted from just short of a length to provide a spooned return catch.

Fortunately for Sussex, Parker, as well as being a most accomplished player, possesses an excellent temperament, well reflected by the consistency he displayed throughout the competition. He found an equally determined partner in the much-improved Phillipson. Surviving the threat of Botham and Garner, they took firm and sensible control against some distinctly ordinary bowling. Garner and Botham were brought back for the final fling, but with the fire now departed and unable to be rekindled, the batsmen punished them painfully. Parker completed a splendid half-century and Phillipson did not depart until the scores were level. He was trying to finish off the game a shade too quickly!

FINAL
SOMERSET v SUSSEX at Lord's, London on Saturday 2 September
Sussex won by 5 wickets
Toss: Sussex   * *captain*
Man of the Match: P. W. G. Parker   † *wicket-keeper*

SOMERSET			SUSSEX	O	M	R	W
B. C. Rose*	c Long b Cheatle	30	Imran	12	1	50	2
P. W. Denning	b Imran	0	Arnold	12	2	43	0
I. V. A. Richards	c Arnold b Barclay	44	Spencer	12	3	27	0
P. M. Roebuck	c Mendis b Cheatle	9	Cheatle	12	1	50	2
I. T. Botham	b Imran	80	Barclay	12	3	21	2
V. J. Marks	c Arnold b Barclay	4					
G. I. Burgess	run out	3	SOMERSET				
D. J. S. Taylor†	not out	13	Garner	12	3	34	1
J. Garner	not out	8	Dredge	10	2	26	1
K. F. Jennings ⎤			Botham	12	1	65	2
C. H. Dredge ⎦	did not bat		Jennings	9	1	29	0
Extras	(lb 10, nb 6)	16	Burgess	10	2	27	1
TOTAL	(7 wickets – 60 overs)	207	Denning	0.1	0	4	0

SUSSEX			FALL OF WICKETS			
J. R. T. Barclay	c Roebuck b Botham	44	Wkt	Sm	Sx	
G. D. Mendis	c Marks b Burgess	44	1st	22	93	
P. W. G. Parker	not out	62	2nd	53	106	
Javed Miandad	c Taylor b Garner	0	3rd	73	106	
Imran Khan	c and b Botham	3	4th	115	109	
C. P. Phillipson	c Taylor b Dredge	32	5th	151	207	
S. J. Storey	not out	0	6th	157		
A. Long*† ⎤			7th	194		
J. Spencer ⎥			8th			
G. G. Arnold ⎥	did not bat		9th			
R. G. L. Cheatle ⎦			10th			
Extras	(b 1, lb 9, nb 9, w 7)	26	Umpires: H. D. Bird and			
TOTAL	(5 wickets – 53.1 overs)	211	B. J. Meyer			

GILLETTE CUP RECORDS

Highest Total	371–4	Hampshire v Glamorgan at Southampton	1975
Highest Total Batting Second	297–4	Somerset v Warwickshire at Taunton	1978
Lowest Total	41	Cambridgeshire v Buckinghamshire at Cambridge	1972
	41	Middlesex v Essex at Westcliff-on-Sea	1972
	41	Shropshire v Essex at Wellington	1974
Biggest Victories	10 wkts	Northamptonshire beat Leicestershire at Leicester	1964
	10 wkts	Warwickshire beat Cambridgeshire at Birmingham	1965
	10 wkts	Sussex beat Derbyshire at Hove	1968
	10 wkts	Hampshire beat Nottinghamshire at Southampton	1977
	214 runs	Leicestershire beat Staffordshire at Stoke	1975
Highest Individual Score	177	C. G. Greenidge: Hampshire v Glamorgan at Southampton	1975

(80 hundreds have been scored in these matches)

Fastest Hundred	77 minutes R. E. Marshall (140): Hampshire v Bedfordshire at Goldington	1968

Highest Partnerships for Each Wicket

1st	227	R. E. Marshall and B. L. Reed: Hampshire v Bedfordshire, Goldington	1968
2nd	223	M. J. Smith and C. T. Radley: Middlesex v Hampshire, Lord's	1977
3rd	160	B. Wood and F. C. Hayes: Lancashire v Warwickshire, Birmingham	1976
4th	234*	D. Lloyd and C. H. Lloyd: Lancashire v Gloucestershire, Manchester	1978
5th	135	J. F. Harvey and I. R. Buxton: Derbyshire v Worcestershire, Derby	1972
6th	105	G. St A. Sobers and R. A. White: Nottinghamshire v Worcestershire, Worcester	1974
7th	107	D. R. Shepherd and D. A. Graveney: Gloucestershire v Surrey, Bristol	1973
8th	69	S. J. Rouse and D. J. Brown: Warwickshire v Middlesex, Lord's	1977
9th	87	M. A. Nash and A. E. Cordle: Glamorgan v Lincolnshire, Swansea	1974
10th	45	A. T. Castell and D. W. White: Hampshire v Lancashire, Manchester	1970
Best Bowling	7–15	A. L. Dixon: Kent v Surrey at The Oval	1967

Hat-tricks

J. D. F. Larter	Northamptonshire v Sussex	Northampton	1963
D. A. D. Sydenham	Surrey v Cheshire	Hoylake	1964
	(Sydenham took four wickets in five balls)		
R. N. S. Hobbs	Essex v Middlesex	Lord's	1968
N. M. McVicker	Warwickshire v Lincolnshire	Birmingham	1971

Wicket-keeping – Most Dismissals

5 Seven instances: R. Booth (Worcestershire); F. E. Collyer (Hertfordshire); A. P. E. Knott (Kent); D. L. Murray, twice (Nottinghamshire); J. T. Murray (Middlesex); S. C. Owen (Staffordshire)

Fielding – Most Catches

4		A. S. Brown	Gloucestershire v Middlesex	Bristol	1963
4		G. Cook	Northamptonshire v Glamorgan	Northampton	1972

GILLETTE CUP FINALISTS

1963 SUSSEX beat Worcestershire by 14 runs
1964 SUSSEX beat Warwickshire by 8 wickets
1965 YORKSHIRE beat Surrey by 175 runs
1966 WARWICKSHIRE beat Worcestershire by 5 wickets
1967 KENT beat Somerset by 32 runs
1968 WARWICKSHIRE beat Sussex by 4 wickets
1969 YORKSHIRE beat Derbyshire by 69 runs
1970 LANCASHIRE beat Sussex by 6 wickets
1971 LANCASHIRE beat Kent by 24 runs

1972 LANCASHIRE beat Warwickshire by 4 wickets
1973 GLOUCESTERSHIRE beat Sussex by 40 runs
1974 KENT beat Lancashire by 4 wickets
1975 LANCASHIRE beat Middlesex by 7 wickets
1976 NORTHAMPTONSHIRE beat Lancashire by 4 wickets
1977 MIDDLESEX beat Glamorgan by 5 wickets
1978 SUSSEX beat Somerset by 5 wickets

Chris Tavaré's half-century at Taunton in the Benson and Hedges Cup semi-final against Somerset won him the Gold Award and Kent a place in the final at Lord's.

BENSON AND HEDGES CUP 1978

Zonal Results

GROUP A	P	W	L	No Result	Pts
DERBYSHIRE	4	4	0	0	12
WARWICKSHIRE	4	3	1	0	9
Lancashire	4	2	2	0	6
Gloucestershire	4	1	3	0	6
Minor Counties (West)	4	0	4	0	0

GROUP B					
SOMERSET	4	3	0	1	10
GLAMORGAN	4	3	1	0	9
Hampshire	4	2	1	1	7
Worcestershire	4	1	3	0	3
Combined Universities	4	0	4	0	0

GROUP C					
SUSSEX	4	3	1	0	9*
MIDDLESEX	4	3	1	0	9*
Leicestershire	4	3	1	0	9
Northamptonshire	4	1	3	0	3
Minor Counties (East)	4	0	4	0	0

GROUP D					
KENT	4	3	1	0	9
NOTTINGHAMSHIRE	4	2	1	1	7*
Surrey	4	2	1	1	7
Essex	4	1	3	0	3
Yorkshire	4	1	3	0	3

* Qualified for the quarter-finals on higher wicket-taking rate.

Final Rounds

QUARTER-FINALS 7, 8 June	SEMI-FINALS 21, 22, 23 June	FINAL 22 July	†Home team. Winning team in small capitals.

```
KENT†            ⎫
                 ⎬ KENT      ⎫
Nottinghamshire  ⎭           ⎬ KENT      ⎫
Sussex†          ⎫           ⎪           ⎪
                 ⎬ Somerset† ⎭           ⎪
SOMERSET         ⎭                       ⎬ KENT
DERBYSHIRE†      ⎫                       ⎪
                 ⎬ DERBYSHIRE†           ⎪
Middlesex        ⎭           ⎫           ⎪
                            ⎬ Derbyshire ⎭
WARWICKSHIRE†    ⎫           ⎪
                 ⎬ Warwickshire ⎭
Glamorgan        ⎭
```

SEMI-FINAL
DERBYSHIRE v WARWICKSHIRE at Derby on 21, 22 June
Derbyshire won by 41 runs
Toss: Derbyshire
Gold Award Winner: A. J. Borrington

* *captain*
† *wicket-keeper*

DERBYSHIRE				WARWICKSHIRE	O	M	R	W
A. Hill	c Humpage b Perryman	21		Willis	11	3	30	3
A. J. Borrington	b Perryman	77		Brown	11	1	32	3
P. N. Kirsten	c Humpage b Willis	29		Perryman	11	1	33	2
E. J. Barlow*	b Willis	32		Lloyd	3	0	23	0
G. Miller	c Humpage b Brown	21		Hemmings	9	0	33	0
H. Cartwright	b Brown	2		Oliver	10	1	45	0
J. M. H. Graham-Brown	c and b Brown	1						
R. W. Taylor†	not out	10		DERBYSHIRE				
C. J. Tunnicliffe	b Willis	2		Hendrick	11	6	14	2
P. E. Russell	run out	1		Tunnicliffe	9	2	30	0
M. Hendrick	did not bat			Russell	9	0	46	2
Extras	(lb 7)	7		Miller	11	3	18	1
TOTAL	(9 wickets – 55 overs)	203		Barlow	6.4	0	26	3
				Kirsten	4	1	16	1

WARWICKSHIRE			FALL OF WICKETS		
D. L. Amiss	c Miller b Hendrick	1	*Wkt*	*D*	*Wa*
K. D. Smith	b Miller	34	1st	48	6
R. N. Abberley	c Russell b Hendrick	1	2nd	116	10
J. Whitehouse*	c Barlow b Russell	12	3rd	135	39
G. W. Humpage†	c Taylor b Barlow	78	4th	186	86
T. A. Lloyd	b Kirsten	4	5th	188	97
P. R. Oliver	c Miller b Russell	10	6th	188	121
E. E. Hemmings	run out	4	7th	197	141
D. J. Brown	b Barlow	2	8th	202	152
R. G. D. Willis	c Miller b Barlow	4	9th	203	162
S. P. Perryman	not out	0	10th		162
Extras	(b 5, lb 7)	12			
TOTAL	(50.4 overs)	162	Umpires: W. E. Alley and K. E. Palmer		

Mike Hendrick – economy personified in the semi-final against Warwickshire.

SEMI-FINAL
SOMERSET v KENT at Taunton on 21, 22, 23 June
Kent won by 41 runs
Toss: Somerset
Gold Award Winner: C. J. Tavaré

* *captain*
† *wicket-keeper*

KENT		
R. A. Woolmer	c Taylor b Jennings	23
G. W. Johnson	c Taylor b Moseley	5
C. J. Tavaré	c Burgess b Jennings	56
Asif Iqbal	c Richards b Botham	28
A. G. E. Ealham*	b Dredge	12
J. N. Shepherd	c Taylor b Botham	10
C. J. C. Rowe	c Botham b Moseley	17
C. S. Cowdrey	not out	12
P. R. Downton†	lbw b Botham	9
D. L. Underwood	not out	9
K. B. S. Jarvis	did not bat	
Extras	(b 5, lb 13, nb 1, w 4)	23
TOTAL	(8 wickets – 55 overs)	**204**

SOMERSET	O	M	R	W
Botham	11	1	39	3
Moseley	11	3	23	2
Burgess	11	4	32	0
Jennings	11	0	44	2
Dredge	11	2	43	1

KENT	O	M	R	W
Jarvis	9	2	29	1
Shepherd	9.2	2	16	2
Woolmer	11	4	25	2
Underwood	11	2	27	1
Asif	9	0	49	3
Johnson	2	0	4	0

SOMERSET		
P. W. Denning	c Ealham b Asif	44
P. A. Slocombe	lbw b Jarvis	7
I. V. A. Richards	c Ealham b Woolmer	9
M. J. Kitchen	c Downton b Woolmer	7
I. T. Botham	c Downton b Asif	15
B. C. Rose*	b Shepherd	48
G. I. Burgess	st Downton b Underwood	3
D. J. S. Taylor†	b Asif	10
C. H. Dredge	run out	5
K. F. Jennings	not out	2
H. R. Moseley	b Shepherd	0
Extras	(b 2, lb 9, w 2)	13
TOTAL	(51.2 overs)	**163**

FALL OF WICKETS

Wkt	K	Sm
1st	10	21
2nd	41	33
3rd	118	43
4th	121	59
5th	135	100
6th	154	117
7th	172	132
8th	186	156
9th		163
10th		163

Umpires: W. L. Budd and T. W. Spencer

Kent's opening bowler Kevin Jarvis – an early wicket-taker at Taunton.

Peter Kirsten was one of the few Derbyshire batsmen to come to terms with the Kent bowling in the Benson and Hedges Cup final but failed to provide the essential big innings.

BENSON AND HEDGES CUP FINAL 1978

Kent won their third Benson and Hedges Cup final without being seriously extended by a disappointing Derbyshire in an undistinguished match. They cruised home with six wickets and 13 overs to spare, their opponents being able to muster only the inadequate total of 147 on a reasonable pitch against a keen, but not especially devastating, attack that was splendidly backed up in the field. Like its six predecessors, this Benson and Hedges final failed to provide either the cricket or the excitement the occasion deserved, and it proved to be the flattest of all.

Without a miracle, alas rare at this stage of the competition, the outcome was a near certainty by halfway through the morning session. Borrington, Hill, and Barlow were all back in the pavilion, three body blows the fragile Derbyshire batting could not afford, Kirsten and Miller had become becalmed, and Underwood had sent down seven maiden overs, as well as claiming the vital wicket of Barlow.

Kirsten increased the tempo before lunch with some powerful strokes before holing out to a medium-paced bouncer from Asif. Miller continued to bat pleasantly and correctly in the afternoon session without ever suggesting that he could supply the impetus or the quantity of runs the situation demanded. The Derbyshire innings quietly subsided against the bowling of Shepherd, who picked up four wickets, and the pace of Jarvis in the 55th over for fewer than 150. Par for the course on that particular day must have been between 175 to 200 runs. This meant that Barlow had to gamble on his main bowlers achieving a major breakthrough, for without it there was no way he would contain the Kent batsmen to 148 runs. His bowling line-up, Hendrick apart, was not especially lethal with Wincer coming in for the experienced, but injured, Tunnicliffe.

Woolmer and Johnson batted sensibly yet avoided the obvious blunder of going too slowly and so putting unnecessary pressure on the later batsmen. Woolmer provided the one memorable innings of the afternoon; indeed, apart from the fielding and accurate, negative bowling, it was the only feature really worth remembering. His 79 was punctuated with fluent strokes, a reminder that he is among the best five English batsmen in county cricket.

Tavaré and Asif went cheaply, and when Woolmer was dismissed any Kent worries were quickly dispersed by a jolly stand between Ealham and Shepherd. It just was not Derbyshire's day; even their fielding was below its usual high standard, with Woolmer being put down on two occasions behind the stumps, though by that stage Kent supporters had already started opening the champagne.

FINAL
DERBYSHIRE v KENT at Lord's, London on Saturday 22 July
Kent won by 6 wickets
Toss: Derbyshire   ** captain*
Gold Award Winner: R. A. Woolmer   *† wicket-keeper*

DERBYSHIRE		
A. Hill	c Tavaré b Jarvis	17
A. J. Borrington	c Downton b Shepherd	0
P. N. Kirsten	c Shepherd b Asif	41
E. J. Barlow*	b Underwood	1
G. Miller	b Shepherd	38
H. Cartwright	c Ealham b Woolmer	12
A. J. Harvey-Walker	b Shepherd	6
R. W. Taylor†	c Downton b Shepherd	0
P. E. Russell	c Downton b Jarvis	4
R. C. Wincer	not out	6
M. Hendrick	run out	7
Extras	(lb 10, nb 1, w 4)	15
TOTAL	(54.4 overs)	**147**

KENT	O	M	R	W
Jarvis	9.4	3	19	2
Shepherd	11	2	25	4
Underwood	11	3	22	1
Woolmer	10	2	15	1
Asif	8	1	26	1
Johnson	5	0	25	0

DERBYSHIRE	O	M	R	W
Hendrick	11	2	23	0
Wincer	7	0	29	0
Russell	11	2	28	3
Barlow	8.4	0	44	1
Miller	2	0	8	0
Kirsten	2	0	14	0

KENT		
R. A. Woolmer	c Hendrick b Barlow	79
G. W. Johnson	c Barlow b Russell	16
C. J. Tavaré	b Russell	0
Asif Iqbal	c Taylor b Russell	9
A. G. E. Ealham*	not out	23
J. N. Shepherd	not out	19
C. J. C. Rowe		
C. S. Cowdrey		
P. R. Downton	did not bat	
D. L. Underwood		
K. B. S. Jarvis		
Extras	(lb 3, nb 1, w 1)	5
TOTAL	(4 wickets – 41.4 overs)	**151**

FALL OF WICKETS		
Wkt	D	K
1st	11	32
2nd	32	34
3rd	33	70
4th	88	117
5th	121	
6th	127	
7th	127	
8th	132	
9th	134	
10th	147	

Umpires: D. J. Constant and J. G. Langridge

Kent captain Alan Ealham in control in the closing stages of Kent's victory at Lord's.

BENSON AND HEDGES CUP RECORDS

Highest Total	327–4	Leicestershire v Warwickshire at Coventry	1972
Highest Total Batting Second	282	Gloucestershire v Hampshire at Bristol	1974
Lowest Total	61	Sussex v Middlesex at Hove	1978
Highest Match Aggregate	593	Hampshire (311–4) v Gloucestershire (282) at Bristol	1974
Lowest Match Aggregate (*55-overs match*)	123	Sussex (61) v Middlesex (62–2) at Hove	1978
Biggest Victories		10 wkts Essex beat Middlesex at Harlow	1973
		10 wkts Kent beat Minor Counties (S) at Canterbury	1975
		10 wkts Leicestershire beat Minor Counties (W) at Leicester	1976
		10 wkts Northamptonshire beat Minor Counties (E) at Horton	1977
		10 wkts Warwickshire beat Minor Counties (W) at Coventry	1977
		10 wkts Somerset beat Combined Universities at Taunton	1978
		186 runs Sussex beat Cambridge University at Hove	1974
Highest Individual Score	173*	C. G. Greenidge: Hampshire v Minor Counties (S) at Amersham	1973
		54 hundreds have been scored in these matches.	
Fastest Hundred		62 minutes: M. A. Nash (103*) Glamorgan v Hampshire, Swansea	1976

Highest Partnerships for Each Wicket

1st	199	M. J. Harris and B. Hassan: Nottinghamshire v Yorkshire, Hull	1973
2nd	285*	C. G. Greenidge and D. R. Turner: Hampshire v Minor Counties (S), Amersham	1973
3rd	227	M. E. J. C. Norman and B. F. Davison: Leicestershire v Warwickshire, Coventry	1972
		D. Lloyd and F. C. Hayes: Lancashire v Minor Counties (N), Manchester	1973
4th	165*	Mushtaq Mohammad and W. Larkins: Northants v Essex, Chelmsford	1977
5th	134	M. Maslin and D. N. F. Slade: Minor Counties (E) v Notts, Nottingham	1976
6th	114	M. J. Khan and G. P. Ellis, Glamorgan v Gloucestershire, Bristol	1975
7th	102	E. W. Jones and M. A. Nash, Glamorgan v Hampshire, Swansea	1976
8th	109	R. E. East and N. Smith: Essex v Northamptonshire, Chelmsford	1977
9th	81	J. N. Shepherd and D. L. Underwood: Kent v Middlesex, Lord's	1975
10th	61	J. M. Rice and A. M. E. Roberts: Hampshire v Gloucestershire, Bristol	1975
Best Bowling	7–12	W. W. Daniel: Middlesex v Minor Counties (E), Ipswich	1978

Most Economical Bowling

11–8–5–2	L. R. Gibbs: Warwickshire v Glamorgan, Cardiff	1972
11–7–5–4	M. Hendrick: Derbyshire v Minor Counties (N), Derby	1974
11–6–5–2	Intikhab Alam: Surrey v Glamorgan, Cardiff	1975

Most Expensive Bowling

11–0–80–0	J. Smith: Minor Counties (S) v Hampshire, Amersham	1973

Hat-tricks

G. D. McKenzie: Leicestershire v Worcestershire, Worcester	1972
K. Higgs: Leicestershire v Surrey, Lord's	1974
A. A. Jones: Middlesex v Essex, Lord's	1977
M. J. Procter: Gloucestershire v Hampshire, Southampton	1977

Fifty Runs and Five Wickets in a Match

M. J. Procter	154*	5–26	Gloucestershire v Somerset, Taunton	1972
B. E. A. Edmeades	50	5–22	Essex v Leicestershire, Ilford	1973
Imran Khan	65*	5–8	Sussex v Northamptonshire, Northampton	1978

Wicket-keeping – Most Dismissals

5 (all ct)	G. Sharp: Northamptonshire v Middlesex, Lord's	1974
5 (all ct)	D. L. Bairstow: Yorkshire v Derbyshire, Bradford	1975

Fielding – Most Catches

5	V. J. Marks: Combined Universities v Kent, Oxford	1976

PREVIOUS WINNERS 1972 Leicestershire 1973 Kent 1974 Surrey 1975 Leicestershire 1976 Kent 1977 Gloucestershire

Stephenson and Jesty acclaim the catch that won Hampshire's match against Middlesex and resulted, later in the evening, in Gilliat claiming the John Player League trophy.

JOHN PLAYER LEAGUE 1978

FINAL TABLE		P	W	L	NR	Pts	Run-rate	6s	4w
1	HAMPSHIRE (4)	16	11	3	2	48	**5.36**	42	5
2	Somerset (9)	16	11	3	2	48	4.58	24	2
3	Leicestershire (1)	16	11	3	2	48	4.26	17	3
4	Worcestershire (13)	16	10	5	1	42		22	6
5	Lancashire (16)	16	9	6	1	38		27	4
6	Essex (2)	16	7	6	3	34		16	3
7	Yorkshire (13)	16	7	7	2	32		19	2
8 {	Derbyshire (9)	16	6	7	3	30		20	3
	Sussex (4)	16	6	7	3	30		12	1
10 {	Glamorgan (8)	16	6	8	2	28		16	4
	Kent (6)	16	6	8	2	28		13	3
	Surrey (13)	16	6	8	2	28		19	3
13 {	Northamptonshire (17)	16	5	8	3	26		25	1
	Nottinghamshire (12)	16	4	7	5	26		19	1
15	Middlesex (3)	16	5	9	2	24		13	6
16	Warwickshire (9)	16	4	11	1	18		15	1
17	Gloucestershire (6)	16	3	11	2	16		24	1

Figures in brackets show the 1977 positions

PREVIOUS CHAMPIONS

1969 Lancashire	1972 Kent		1975 Hampshire
1970 Lancashire	1973 Kent		1976 Kent
1971 Worcestershire	1974 Leicestershire		1977 Leicestershire

Hampshire became the John Player League champions for the second time when they beat Middlesex by 26 runs in the final game of the season before an understandably ecstatic crowd at Bournemouth. In another thrilling climax to the tenth season of the competition they finished ahead on run-rate of unlucky Somerset and Leicestershire, who had both obtained the same number of points, 48. The differences were Hampshire 5.355, Somerset 4.580, and Leicestershire 4.265. Considering they achieved this success despite losing the services of Barry Richards and Andy Roberts during the season, nobody could possibly begrudge Hampshire their triumph.

The gap between the teams in the John Player League has narrowed since the competition began, as is seen from the fact that in 1977 both winner and runners-up, Leicestershire and Essex, acquired more points and victories than the 1978 champions. Even more rewarding evidence is to be found at the wrong end of the table, where Gloucestershire occupied bottom place although they were a highly respectable sixth in the previous year and are capable of beating most teams in a limited-overs match. Warwickshire dropped from ninth to sixteenth, but even more remarkable was the fall of

Middlesex from third to fifteenth. Although they were often without their Test stars, Middlesex have the reserves to attain a higher position, and nobody should be at all surprised if they finish ahead of the reigning champions, Hampshire, in 1979.

One of the dangers for a side in the Sunday League comes when it starts badly and the players realise early on that they have no chance of finishing among the front-runners. They are inclined to lose interest in a form of cricket which is not invariably enjoyable and entertaining. No county can have found this competition more frustrating than Northamptonshire, who, although they clawed their way off the bottom to finish thirteenth, have finished in the last four in no fewer than eight of the past ten seasons. They have always been ill-equipped for 40-over frolics, even when they were a much stronger side, and it is difficult to see how they are going to show a big improvement in the immediate future, despite the attacking batsmanship of the very exciting Wayne Larkins.

Although it is possible to pick some faults in the present formula for John Player League matches, especially on how results are obtained after the number of overs has been reduced by inclement weather, it remains an exciting, popular, and well-supported competition. Richard Gilliat, after capturing the title, suggested three interesting changes which he felt would improve the competition.

First, he would prefer to see the matches staged on the large county grounds rather than at 'out of town' venues; this because of the difficulty of using spinners on small grounds. He felt that field placings and the fielding itself were more exciting on the bigger grounds. Against this can be argued the enormous benefit to the game of taking the matches around the county, and the fact that the large crowds at smaller grounds make economic sense. Moreover, the size of the official county grounds themselves varies considerably: given the same basic conditions, runs are much easier to obtain at Taunton than at the much larger Oval, and the number of sixes would be reduced. Sixes appeal greatly to spectators, and also to the sponsor, who gave Greenidge £200 for hitting the most and rewarded all the six-hitters from their special £1,000 pool.

Secondly, Gilliat advocates that bowlers' run-ups should not be restricted to 15 paces, because this adversely affects fast bowlers like Daniel, Imran Khan, and Bob Willis. This is true, but the outcome would be that the medium-fast brigade with their marathon run-ups would be inflicted on spectators and viewers, and this in turn must considerably extend the playing time. It would certainly not appeal to television, for which this particular form of cricket has been tailor-made, and without television the sponsor would certainly not be prepared to provide so much money.

Thirdly, he would like to see lines drawn to prevent captains from employing ultra-negative tactics. Anything that prevents seven players being stationed around the leg-side boundary, or ends that depressing sight of numbers 10 and 11 (neither with any pretensions at batting) at the crease, needing 60 runs to win with five overs remaining and every fielder back on the boundary, must have much in its favour. There are problems, and it might well be worth some serious experiments.

Two Gordon Greenidge centuries, against Yorkshire in August and Middlesex in the final match, provided the impetus needed to push Hampshire to the top of the John Player League.

1978 AWARDS AND DISTRIBUTION OF PRIZE-MONEY

The total prize-money was £24,250.
£5,000 and Trophy to League Champions: HAMPSHIRE
£2,000 to runners-up: Somerset
£1,000 to third placing: Leicestershire
£100 each match to winners (shared in event of a 'no result')

£1,000 batsmen's pool. One share for every six hit. 343 sixes (fewer than in any other season of the competition) were hit by 122 players – each six being worth £2.92.
Six-hitters:
21 – C. G. Greenidge (**£200** award for most sixes)
14 – W. Larkins, I. V. A. Richards.
12 – B. F. Davison, Zaheer Abbas.
11 – C. H. Lloyd.
9 – F. C. Hayes.
7 – G. Cook, Intikhab Alam, A. M. E. Roberts, J. N. Shepherd.
6 – A. J. Hignell, M. J. Llewellyn, C. E. B. Rice.
5 – G. D. Barlow, I. T. Botham, J. H. Hampshire, D. J. Humphries, S. J. Rouse.
4 – A. R. Butcher, H. Cartwright, M. W. Gatting, G. A. Gooch, C. P. Phillipson, M. N. S. Taylor, D. R. Turner, G. M. Turner.
3 – D. L. Bairstow, J. D. Birch, B. L. D'Oliveira, E. J. O. Hemsley, G. W. Humpage, T. E. Jesty, P. N. Kirsten, M. J. Kitchen, K. S. McEwan, P. R. Oliver, K. R. Pont, M. J. Smedley, D. M. Smith, P. D. Swart, J. Walters, J. G. Wright.
2 – C. W. J. Athey, J. Birkenshaw, A. J. Borrington, M. H. Denness, R. W. Hills, V. A. Holder, Javed Miandad, A. Jones, A. J. Lamb, P. A. Neale, C. M. Old, R. C. Ontong, P. W. G. Parker, D. W. Randall, R. M. Ratcliffe, B. R. Reidy, D. R. Shepherd, G. R. Stephenson, P. A. Todd, C. J. Tunnicliffe.
1 – R. N. Abberley, G. G. Arnold, E. J. Barlow, G. Boycott, C. N. Boyns, B. M. Brain, G. I. Burgess, M. A. Buss, P. Carrick, H. P. Cooper, K. E. Cooper, A. E. Cordle, C. S. Cowdrey, A. G. E. Ealham, P. H. Edmonds, J. E. Emburey, K. W. R. Fletcher, D. I. Gower, A. J. Harvey-Walker, B. Hassan, E. E. Hemmings, R. Illingworth, Imran Khan, C. Johnson, E. W. Jones, A. I. Kallicharran, A. Kennedy, R. D. V. Knight, D. Lloyd, J. D. Love, R. G. Lumb, M. A. Lynch, G. Miller, J. A. Ormrod, A. S. Patel, D. N. Patel, N. Phillip, P. I. Pocock, M. J. Procter, D. J. Rock, P. M. Roebuck, G. R. J. Roope, Sadiq Mohammad, M. W. W. Selvey, G. Sharp, K. D. Smith, N. Smith, D. S. Steele, G. B. Stevenson, A. Tait, C. J. Tavaré, R. W. Tolchard, S. Turner, K. C. Wessels, R. A. White, R. A. Woolmer, A. Worsick, Younis Ahmed.

£1,000 bowlers' pool. One share for taking four or more wickets in a match. 49 instances (fewer than in any other season of the competition) by 42 bowlers – each share being worth £20.41.
Shareholders:
3 – T. E. Jesty (**£200** award for most instances).
2 – R. D. Jackman, J. K. Lever, A. P. Pridgeon, L. B. Taylor, A. H. Wilkins.
1 – C. N. Boyns, B. M. Brain, D. J. Brown, G. I. Burgess, P. B. Clift, H. P. Cooper, K. Cooper, C. E. H. Croft, W. W. Daniel, N. G. Featherstone, M. W. Gatting, N. Gifford, V. A. Holder, D. P. Hughes, Imran Khan, G. W. Johnson, A. A. Jones, P. N. Kirsten, W. Larkins, G. Miller, H. R. Moseley, M. A. Nash, C. M. Old, J. M. Rice, P. E. Russell, M. W. W. Selvey, J. N. Shepherd, J. Simmons, P. D. Swart, M. N. S. Taylor, D. J. Thomas, K. P. Tomlins, S. Turner, G. G. Watson, R. A. Woolmer, A. Worsick.

£250 for the fastest fifty in a match televised on BBC2:
C. H. Lloyd (Lancashire) who scored 50 off 33 balls against Hampshire at Portsmouth on 4 June.

JOHN PLAYER LEAGUE RECORDS

Highest Total	307-4	Worcestershire v Derbyshire at Worcester	1975
Highest Total Batting Second	261-8	Warwickshire v Nottinghamshire at Birmingham	1976
Lowest Total	23	Middlesex v Yorkshire at Leeds	1974
Highest Match Aggregate	525	Somerset (270-4) v Glos. (255) at Bristol (Imperial)	1975
Lowest Match Aggregate	117	Middlesex (76) v Northamptonshire (41) at	
(40 overs matches)		Northampton	1972

Biggest Victories

10 wkts	Sixteen instances by Derbyshire, Essex, Glamorgan, Hampshire, Leicestershire (2), Middlesex, Somerset, Surrey (3), Warwickshire (2), Worcestershire and Yorkshire (2).	
190 runs	Kent beat Northamptonshire at Brackley	1973
Highest Individual Score 155*	B. A. Richards: Hampshire v Yorkshire at Hull	1970

124 hundreds have been scored in the League, including nine by B. A. Richards and six by J. H. Hampshire.

Fastest Hundred	50 minutes	C. H. Lloyd (100*) Lancashire v Nottinghamshire at Nottingham	1974

Highest Partnerships for Each Wicket   *unbroken

1st	218	A. R. Butcher and G. P. Howarth: Surrey v Gloucestershire, The Oval	1976
2nd	179	B. W. Luckhurst and M. H. Denness: Kent v Somerset, Canterbury	1973
3rd	182	H. Pilling and C. H. Lloyd: Lancashire v Somerset, Manchester	1970
4th	175*	M. J. K. Smith and D. L. Amiss: Warwickshire v Yorkshire, Birmingham	1970
5th	163	A. G. E. Ealham and B. D. Julien: Kent v Leicestershire, Leicester	1977
6th	121	C. P. Wilkins and A. J. Borrington: Derbyshire v Warwickshire, Chesterfield	1972
7th	96*	R. Illingworth and J. Birkenshaw: Leicestershire v Somerset, Leicester	1971
8th	95*	D. Breakwell and K. F. Jennings: Somerset v Nottinghamshire, Nottingham	1976
9th	86	D. P. Hughes and P. Lever: Lancashire v Essex, Leyton	1973
10th	57	D. A. Graveney and J. B. Mortimore: Gloucestershire v Lancashire, Tewkesbury	1973

Best Bowling	8-26	K. D. Boyce: Essex v Lancashire at Manchester	1971
Most Economical Bowling	8-8-0-0	B. A. Langford: Somerset v Essex at Yeovil	1969
Most Expensive Bowling	8-0-79-1	R. E. East: Essex v Glamorgan at Swansea	1969

Hat-tricks (10)

A. Ward	Derbyshire v Sussex at Derby (*Ward took four wickets with successive balls*)	1970
R. Palmer	Somerset v Gloucestershire at Bristol	1970
K. D. Boyce	Essex v Somerset at Westcliff-on-Sea	1971
G. D. McKenzie	Leicestershire v Essex at Leicester	1972
R. G. D. Willis	Warwickshire v Yorkshire at Birmingham	1973
W. Blenkiron	Warwickshire v Derbyshire at Buxton	1974
A. Buss	Sussex v Worcestershire at Hastings	1974
J. M. Rice	Hampshire v Northamptonshire at Southampton	1975
M. A. Nash	Glamorgan v Worcestershire at Worcester	1975
A. Hodgson	Northamptonshire v Somerset at Northampton	1976

Fifty Runs and Five Wickets in a Match

C. J. R. Black	72*	6-25	Middlesex v Surrey at The Oval	1971
M. A. Buss	69	5-36	Sussex v Derbyshire at Eastbourne	1973
R. D. V. Knight	75	5-42	Sussex v Nottinghamshire at Nottingham	1977
G. W. Johnson	50	5-26	Kent v Surrey at The Oval	1974

Wicket-keeping – Most Dismissals

7 (6ct, 1st)	R. W. Taylor: Derbyshire v Lancashire at Manchester	1975

Fielding – Most Catches

5	J. M. Rice: Hampshire v Warwickshire at Southampton	1978

MISCELLANY
Minor Counties and Other Cricket 1978

Minor Counties Championship 1978

			P	W	L	D	NR	Pts	Av
1	DEVONSHIRE (4)	G	10	6	0	3	1	69	6.90
2	Durham (2)	G	10	5	0	3	2	61	6.10
3	Suffolk (1)	G	10	5	2	3	0	60	6.00
4	Buckinghamshire (6)	G	12	4	1	6	1	61	5.08
5	Berkshire (15)	G	10	3	2	4	1	46	4.60
6	Dorset (9)		10	3	1	5	1	45	4.50
7	Lancashire II (17)		8	2	0	3	3	35	4.37
8	Bedfordshire (10)		10	3	0	7	0	39	3.90
9	Shropshire (3)		10	2	1	6	1	38	3.80
10	Cheshire (13)		10	2	1	5	2	35	3.50
11	Wiltshire (16)		10	2	2	5	1	33	3.30
12	Norfolk (12)		12	2	4	5	1	36	3.00
13	Hertfordshire (7)		10	1	4	5	0	29	2.90
14	Lincolnshire (14)		10	1	1	7	1	28	2.80
	Somerset II (8)		10	2	3	5	0	28	2.80
	Staffordshire (5)		10	1	2	4	3	28	2.80
17	Cambridgeshire (21)		10	2	4	3	1	27	2.70
18	Northumberland (11)		12	0	4	6	2	18	1.50
19	Oxfordshire (20)		10	0	4	4	2	14	1.40
20	Cornwall (17)		10	0	8	2	0	11	1.10
21	Cumberland (19)		8	0	2	5	1	7	0.87

Figures in brackets show the 1977 positions.
G Qualified for Gillette Cup 1979.
A challenge match between Devonshire and Durham ended in a draw and Devonshire became Minor Counties champions under Rule 16 of the competition.

Tilcon Trophy

Played at Harrogate on 21, 22, 23 June

SURREY beat NOTTINGHAMSHIRE by 9 wickets.
Nottinghamshire 58 in 25.5 overs (R. D. Jackman 5–22, P. H. L. Wilson 4–11). Surrey 59–1 in 14.5 overs.
Man of the Match: P. H. L. Wilson.
Hugh Wilson (Surrey) made his county début in this match.

YORKSHIRE beat GLOUCESTERSHIRE by 5 wickets.
Gloucestershire 211–4 in 51 overs (A. Tait 123*, Zaheer Abbas 64). Yorkshire 214–5 in 42.1 overs (J. D. Love 70, C. Johnson 67).
Man of the Match: A. Tait.

FINAL
YORKSHIRE beat SURREY by 13 runs (match reduced to 10 overs).
Yorkshire 76–0 in 10 overs (D. L. Bairstow 39*, J. H. Hampshire 36*). Surrey 63–5 in 10 overs.
Man of the Match: C. M. Old (3–30).

PREVIOUS WINNERS	1976 Hampshire	1977 Nottinghamshire

RECORDS

Highest Total	254–8	Nottinghamshire v Middlesex	1977
Lowest Total	58	Nottinghamshire v Surrey	1978
Highest Individual Score	123*	A. Tait: Gloucestershire v Yorkshire	1978
Best Bowling Analysis	5–22	R. D. Jackman: Surrey v Nottinghamshire	1978

Fenner Trophy

Played at Scarborough on 30, 31 August, 1 September

NORTHAMPTONSHIRE beat SOMERSET by 5 wickets (match reduced to 40 overs).
Somerset 176–7 in 40 overs. Northamptonshire 179–5 in 33.3 overs (W. Larkins 50).
Man of the Match: W. Larkins.
Neil Russom (Somerset) made his county début in this match.

YORKSHIRE beat MIDDLESEX by 43 runs (match reduced to 10 overs).
Yorkshire 115–3 in 10 overs (K. Sharp 51* off 27 balls, C. W. J. Athey 46 off 20 balls). Middlesex 72–9 in 10 overs (C. M. Old 5–36).
Man of the Match: K. Sharp.

FINAL
NORTHAMPTONSHIRE beat YORKSHIRE by 8 wickets.
Yorkshire 133 in 44.5 overs. Northamptonshire 136–2 in 37.5 overs (G. Cook 55*).
Man of the Match: T. M. Lamb (3–25).

PREVIOUS WINNERS	1971 Kent	1974 Yorkshire	1977 Hampshire
	1972 Yorkshire	1975 Hampshire	
	1973 Kent	1976 Hampshire	

RECORDS

Highest Total	290–8	Hampshire v Gloucestershire	1975
Lowest Total	59	Warwickshire v Yorkshire	1974
Highest Individual Score	141*	B. W. Luckhurst: Kent v Lancashire	1973

(Six hundreds have been scored in these matches – B. W. Luckhurst is alone in scoring two.)

Best Bowling Analysis	5–23	A. G. Nicholson: Yorkshire v Warwickshire	1974

Second Eleven Championship 1978

					Bonus Points			
	P	W	L	D	Bt	Bw	Pts	Av
1 SUSSEX (5)	11	5	1	5	25	39	124	11.27
2 Essex (15)	12	4	2	6	49	34	125	10.41
3 Lancashire (4)	13	5	—	8	42	38	130	10.00
4 Warwickshire (7)	21	7	3	11	48	63	192	9.14
5 Yorkshire (1)	15	5	2	8	32	44	132	8.80
6 Hampshire (3)	16	3	1	12	45	51	132	8.25
7 Leicestershire (10)	16	4	2	10	39	42	125	7.81
8 Nottinghamshire (12)	17	3	3	11	44	51	127	7.47
9 Worcestershire (11)	19	2	8	9	49	57	128	6.73
10 Somerset (16)	9	1	3	5	18	32	60	6.66
11 Surrey (17)	10	1	2	7	22	32	66	6.60
12 Glamorgan (14)	15	3	6	6	27	38	95	6.33
13 Kent (2)	11	1	4	6	21	36	69	6.27
14 Middlesex (8)	14	1	5	8	35	39	84	6.00
15 Northamptonshire (13)	18	3	4	11	22	52	104	5.77
16 Derbyshire (6)	12	1	2	9	25	34	69	5.75
17 Gloucestershire (9)	11	2	3	6	14	25	63	5.72

Figures in brackets show the 1977 positions.

LIMITED-OVERS AVERAGES 1978

These combined one-day cricket averages include performances in Prudential Trophy, Gillette Cup, Benson and Hedges Cup and John Player League matches.

Batting (Qualification: 10 innings, average 23.00)   *Not out

	M	I	NO	HS	Runs	Av	100	50
C. H. Lloyd	21	21	6	119*	793	52.86	1	7
I. V. A. Richards	24	22	2	139*	988	49.40	2	7
C. G. Greenidge	17	17	0	122	765	45.00	2	5
D. R. Turner	18	18	3	96	669	44.60	—	7
A. I. Kallicharran	11	11	2	109	399	44.33	1	2
C. T. Radley	19	19	4	117*	661	44.06	1	5
D. I. Gower	19	19	3	114*	685	42.81	1	5
Zaheer Abbas	17	17	1	90	666	41.62	—	8
J. H. Hampshire	18	18	1	114*	693	40.76	2	3
A. J. Hignell	16	15	5	63	402	40.20	—	2
W. Larkins	19	18	3	107*	583	38.86	1	2
G. Cook	18	18	2	96	599	37.43	—	6
D. Lloyd	22	22	2	121*	728	36.40	1	4
K. S. McEwan	20	20	3	133	608	35.76	1	3
A. Hill	23	21	2	102*	658	34.63	1	5
Younis Ahmed	17	15	4	81*	381	34.63	—	2
G. A. Gooch	17	17	1	94	540	33.75	—	5
G. M. Turner	20	20	1	89	635	33.42	—	4
M. J. Procter	19	19	1	115	600	33.33	1	2
B. C. Rose	23	21	4	61	564	33.17	—	2
B. F. Davison	19	18	3	76	493	32.86	—	4
D. L. Amiss	22	22	1	99	689	32.80	—	4
C. E. B. Rice	16	16	1	120*	492	32.80	1	2
A. Kennedy	17	17	0	131	557	32.76	1	5
P. D. Swart	19	19	4	85*	490	32.66	—	4
P. A. Neale	20	20	3	58*	549	32.29	—	5
Asif Iqbal	17	17	2	71	484	32.26	—	5
P. W. Denning	23	23	2	145	674	32.09	1	4
P. W. G. Parker	17	16	3	69	414	31.84	—	4
T. E. Jesty	18	18	3	52	472	31.46	—	2
A. Jones	20	20	5	110*	465	31.00	1	2
J. Whitehouse	22	19	3	94	483	30.18	—	3
H. T. Tunnicliffe	15	12	5	53*	211	30.14	—	2
P. Willey	18	17	0	77	509	29.94	—	4
M. J. Kitchen	12	12	4	64*	239	29.87	—	1
B. A. Richards	13	12	0	65	358	29.83	—	2
D. W. Randall	17	17	2	53*	437	29.13	—	3
G. R. J. Roope	19	18	2	60*	463	28.93	—	2
M. J. Harris	13	12	3	59*	260	28.88	—	2
S. J. Rouse	15	13	5	36	231	28.87	—	—
T. A. Lloyd	16	14	6	54*	230	28.75	—	2
M. W. Gatting	21	21	5	71*	449	28.06	—	3
J. D. Birch	12	11	2	71	251	27.88	—	2
J. N. Shepherd	21	18	4	94	380	27.14	—	2
K. W. R. Fletcher	20	18	1	76*	461	27.11	—	3
J. M. Brearley	16	16	3	61*	350	26.92	—	1
I. T. Botham	23	19	2	80	453	26.64	—	3

	M	I	NO	HS	Runs	Av	100	50
M. H. Denness	19	17	0	102	448	26.35	1	2
R. W. Hills	16	11	5	27	157	26.16	—	—
A. R. Butcher	18	16	2	113*	364	26.00	1	1
D. L. Bairstow	21	20	5	48*	389	25.93	—	—
G. D. Barlow	21	18	2	58*	409	25.56	—	2
F. C. Hayes	20	20	4	70	409	25.56	—	2
C. S. Cowdrey	24	18	4	74	354	25.28	—	1
G. D. Mendis	20	19	1	56	455	25.27	—	3
G. W. Johnson	24	24	1	76	581	25.26	—	2
C. Johnson	11	11	2	67*	227	25.22	—	1
P. M. Roebuck	20	16	4	57	299	24.91	—	1
G. W. Humpage	21	21	3	78	444	24.66	—	4
B. R. Hardie	17	16	2	74	345	24.64	—	1
C. W. J. Athey	19	18	0	118	443	24.61	1	2
J. A. Ormrod	18	18	0	55	442	24.55	—	3
C. P. Phillipson	20	18	5	37*	318	24.46	—	—
P. A. Todd	17	17	0	79	406	23.88	—	4
C. J. Tavaré	24	24	2	136*	520	23.63	1	3
J. C. Balderstone	19	16	2	73	323	23.07	—	1
K. R. Pont	19	18	2	44*	369	23.06	—	—
M. N. S. Taylor	17	12	6	57*	138	23.00	—	1

BOWLING (Qualification: 20 wickets, average 25.00)

	O	M	R	W	Av	5w	BB
W. W. Daniel	151	37	401	35	11.45	2	7—12
E. J. Barlow	143.1	19	547	44	12.43	2	6—33
L. B. Taylor	107.5	10	415	31	13.38	1	5—23
K. Higgs	140.4	28	389	28	13.89	—	4—22
J. N. Shepherd	157.3	25	473	34	13.91	—	4—17
Imran Khan	187.5	31	539	37	14.56	1	5—8
C. M. Old	132	23	428	29	14.75	—	4—9
G. G. Arnold	116.3	22	384	26	14.76	—	4—37
R. G. D. Willis	187.2	47	544	35	15.54	—	4—4
V. A. Holder	100.3	8	360	23	15.65	—	4—26
S. Turner	152.2	19	523	33	15.84	1	5—35
H. R. Moseley	137.4	19	432	27	16.00	1	5—47
J. F. Steele	125.3	20	376	23	16.34	—	3—19
J. Spencer	146.2	26	436	26	16.76	—	3—11
P. Booth	113	7	430	25	17.20	—	3—23
A. P. Pridgeon	105	7	399	23	17.34	1	6—26
G. B. Stevenson	111	7	492	27	18.22	1	5—28
P. B. Clift	155.2	19	498	27	18.44	—	4—13
R. M. Ratcliffe	164.3	23	597	32	18.65	—	3—24
K. F. Jennings	138	21	449	24	18.70	—	3—37
I. T. Botham	213.4	24	733	39	18.79	—	4—16
C. H. Dredge	194.1	22	688	35	19.65	—	4—23
R. A. Woolmer	168.2	20	531	27	19.66	—	4—31
J. K. Lever	185.1	18	704	35	20.11	1	5—36
G. Miller	149.1	30	446	22	20.27	—	4—22
J. Cumbes	141.2	15	469	23	20.39	—	3—13
A. H. Wilkins	157.5	21	659	32	20.59	2	5—17
B. J. Griffiths	151.3	19	496	24	20.66	—	3—15
T. E. Jesty	113.2	6	512	24	21.33	1	5—32
J. M. Rice	114.1	7	473	22	21.50	—	4—39
P. H. Edmonds	135.2	29	437	20	21.85	—	3—35
K. B. S. Jarvis	178.4	26	615	28	21.96	—	3—20
G. I. Burgess	176	23	580	26	22.30	—	4—21
M. N. S. Taylor	133.5	12	492	22	22.36	—	4—36
R. D. Jackman	160.3	23	649	29	22.37	1	5—22
M. J. Procter	154	23	546	24	22.75	1	5—38

	O	M	R	W	Av	5w	BB
D. P. Hughes	97.3	5	515	22	23.40	2	5—23
J. Simmons	163	21	638	27	23.62	—	4—7
B. M. Brain	145.1	27	549	23	23.86	—	4—29
K. Cooper	129	14	554	23	24.08	—	4—35
P. I. Pocock	167	28	485	20	24.25	—	4—11
P. E. Russell	175	23	559	23	24.30	—	4—11

MOST ECONOMICAL BOWLING (Qualification: 100 overs, 3.30 runs/over)

	O	M	R	W	Runs/over
M. Hendrick	153	32	358	19	2.33
W. W. Daniel	151	37	401	35	2.65
K. Higgs	140.4	28	389	28	2.76
Imran Khan	187.5	31	539	37	2.86
M. A. Nash	131.5	32	378	27	2.86
R. G. D. Willis	187.2	47	544	35	2.90
P. I. Pocock	167	28	485	20	2.90
J. Spencer	146.2	26	436	26	2.97
G. Miller	149.1	30	446	22	2.98
J. F. Steele	125.3	20	376	23	2.99
J. N. Shepherd	157.3	25	473	34	3.00
A. J. Harvey-Walker	126.1	23	389	18	3.08
H. R. Moseley	137.4	19	432	27	3.13
R. A. Woolmer	168.2	20	531	27	3.15
P. E. Russell	175	23	559	23	3.19
C. J. Tunnicliffe	128.3	21	411	15	3.19
P. B. Clift	155.2	19	498	27	3.20
M. W. W. Selvey	151.2	17	487	19	3.21
P. H. Edmonds	135.2	29	437	20	3.22
P. Willey	130	16	419	13	3.22
C. M. Old	132	23	428	29	3.24
K. F. Jennings	138	21	449	24	3.25
B. J. Griffiths	151.3	19	496	24	3.27
D. L. Underwood	197.2	32	651	25	3.29
G. I. Burgess	176	23	580	26	3.29
G. G. Arnold	116.3	22	384	26	3.29

WICKET-KEEPING (Most dismissals)   FIELDING (Most catches)

Dismissals		Ct	St		Ct				Ct	
35	D. J. Humphries	31	4		18	C. J. Tavaré			11	M. J. Procter
34	R. W. Taylor	27	7		16	K. Higgs			11	G. R. J. Roope
31	R. W. Tolchard	29	2		16	J. M. Rice			10	J. M. Brearley
28	P. R. Downton	21	7		14	I. T. Botham			10	D. I. Gower
24	N. Smith	22	2		14	I. V. A. Richards			10	C. H. Lloyd
23	D. J. S. Taylor	21	2		12	E. J. Barlow			10	J. N. Shepherd
21	E. W. Jones	19	2		11	C. H. Dredge			10	J. Whitehouse
20	A. Long	16	4							

CAPTAINCY IN THE MODERN GAME

Trevor Bailey

Perhaps the nearest sporting equivalent to a county captain is the player-manager of a professional football club. Both decide and direct tactics. Both try to keep their players contented, especially when they have been dropped or are out of form, and both are directly responsible for their players' behaviour on and off the field. Both have a complete or at the very least a considerable say in the selection of the team. In the case of the cricket captain, he may choose his side with assistance – not always the right word – from a selection committee.

The ideal skipper, in addition to justifying his place as player, should also be guide, philosopher and friend to his team; a tactical genius, a diplomat, a psychologist, an inspirer. The slight snag is that anyone containing all these qualities would be unwilling to devote himself to cricket.

It also helps if a captain has a strong, well-balanced side, for without these two vital ingredients it is impossible to be really successful at cricket, or soccer. A good captain, or manager, will make the most of the talent at his disposal, but if this is sub-standard he cannot expect to win many matches, for all that his committee or board of directors and supporters will expect him to. On the other hand a mundane leader can achieve results if he has sufficient top-class batsmen and bowlers. This does not mean that a captain is not important, but given the right ingredients, like West Indies against England in 1976 or like England in 1978, few captains could hardly fail.

The football manager knows that if his club does not produce the required results within a comparatively, often ridiculously, short period of time he will be sacked, regardless of his own ability, and to a lesser degree this also applies in cricket. In these circumstances, therefore, it is difficult to understand why there should have been such a fuss when the Yorkshire committee decided to replace Geoff Boycott as captain. In eight years under his command the county had won nothing, although there are now four honours to be picked up each summer. With their great tradition, Yorkshiremen expect their team to succeed, and this barren spell must have worried them more than most. Manchester United, or Liverpool, would never have retained their manager after eight fruitless years, and unlike Boycott he would not have been surprised.

It is true that throughout his reign Geoff has never commanded an outstanding team. His committee have deliberately avoided the obvious practical advantages of signing on stars from abroad and have continued to engage only home-born Yorkshire talent, which in the long term must benefit both county and country. Nevertheless, one feels that a Brian Close, in a period of eight years, would have conjured up at least one honour.

One of 1978's happiest captains. Arnold Long, taking over in unhappy circumstances, gave Sussex a sense of unity and purpose that resulted in their winning the Gillette Cup.

As captain, Geoff has shown himself to be very sound, if occasionally over-cautious, for like any true Yorkshireman he prefers to bet on certainties. Had he led England against Pakistan and New Zealand in England last summer, his team would have won convincingly, and he is probably better suited to skippering a high quality eleven than a limited county. As a world-class batsman himself and a perfectionist he, like so many of the same ilk, finds it hard to tolerate, let alone understand, the second best.

However, he clearly has never been a natural leader or a motivator. If he had possessed one of these characteristics he would inevitably have established himself as captain of England long ago for he had great ability plus a very deep knowledge of the game. That this never occurred speaks for itself, as does the fact that the present England players were pleased when Bob Willis was appointed their vice-captain for the Australian tour. They had not been completely happy in the way Boycott handled the team after Mike Brearley was injured in Pakistan in 1977–78. They respected his ability, but he failed to inspire.

Since the abolition of the amateur, the task of appointing a county captain has become more difficult. The committee seldom had any problems dispensing with the services of an amateur captain should they have made a mistake in their original choice, or for some other reason. Moreover they could afford to appoint a young talented cricketer who might be lacking in tactical finesse, but who often brought a fresh enthusiasm and life to the job, and they would know that this would be accepted by the senior professionals.

Another great advantage enjoyed by an amateur captain was that, because of his independence, he could afford to tell his committee exactly what to do if they were interfering too much or failing to provide him with the proper support. It has to be admitted that there have been, and still are, some well-meaning but very limited administrators and committeemen among the counties. All too often, men with the best possible intentions and sincerity have been lacking both in foresight and in understanding of the players, who can be extremely difficult. This, of course, is one of the reasons why Kerry Packer was able to turn the cricket world upside down.

These days a county appreciates that if the captaincy is given to a young international cricketer, there is a good chance of losing his services as a player if the committee decide to replace him. Therefore the tendency is to play absolutely safe and appoint the most senior member, or one of the most senior members, of the staff. Somebody they know will do a competent, thoroughly professional job and will retire while still in harness, thus avoiding any unpleasantness that can so easily occur.

Some captains, having lost the job, are prepared to serve under another captain; David Lloyd under Frank Hayes at Lancashire for example. But it can create a tricky situation, not only for the deposed skipper but also for his successor. Unless, of course, the former has given up the role voluntarily because he does not want the responsibility or – and there are not many of these about – he realises his own limitations.

There can be no doubt that the top-class player who has lost the captaincy will tend to gravitate to another county, as exampled by Tom Graveney to Worcestershire, Peter Richardson to Kent, Brian Close to Somerset, and Mike Denness to Essex. Understandably, many clubs prefer to avoid the risk of losing one of their best cricketers and settle for the senior professional, even if some of the zest and enthusiasm may have departed.

This policy makes life difficult for the England selectors, who by tradition are inclined to pick one of the county captains to lead England. The senior professional may be well past his international prime, or he may never have reached that standard. Even less helpful, from the selectors' viewpoint, is the club, like Gloucestershire or Derbyshire, which has an overseas import at the helm. It must be admitted that last summer there were not many serious rivals for Brearley's crown, but he must surely have forfeited it if England had been playing stronger opposition and he had experienced the same horrid patch.

Although it is clearly an asset to have had the experience of captaining a county before leading England, it is not absolutely essential. Two of England's most successful skippers, Sir Len Hutton and Ray Illingworth, both of whom came back with the Ashes, relied on their lengthy apprenticeship in Yorkshire, their considerable knowledge of Test cricket as players, and on their own ability as cricketers. There can be no doubt that these attributes are considerably more valuable than having led a county team to victory in the John Player League.

In Illingworth's case, Ray had already been made captain of Leicestershire when he took command of England, but it was only for a mere handful of matches and his real credentials were Yorkshire. On the other hand it is unlikely that he would have been considered for the post he filled with such distinction, let alone been given the opportunity, had he not left his native county to lead Leicestershire.

It is beginning to look as if, in the future, selectors will have to look beyond the county skippers for their captain of England. This would, in fact, benefit the clubs, because they must be better off under a leader who is with them throughout the summer and can devote his efforts entirely to their cause. It is significant that Leicestershire were far more successful after Ray Illingworth had lost the captaincy of the national team.

Apart from the obvious prestige, a county skipper who is also captain of England, or for that matter is a permanent member of the England eleven, must be something of a handicap. What football club would tolerate a player-manager who was missing on other activities for much of the season? Would Kent have sacked Mike Denness if he had been able to concentrate entirely on domestic matters? Tony Greig would surely have been more successful with Sussex had he been able to spend more time with them.

Right: Yorkshire's new captain John Hampshire, whose performances will be the subject of much discussion in 1979.

LOOKING AHEAD TO 1979

REGISTER OF COUNTY PLAYERS

All first-class and Test match career statistics are complete to the end of the 1978 season.

The forename by which a player is known is shown in bold type.

The county in which a player is born is given only when this differs from the one he now represents. For registration purposes a cricketer's 'county of birth' is determined in accordance with boundaries existing at the time of his birth and the County of London is divided between Essex, Kent, Middlesex, and Surrey. Similarly, for overseas players, names of countries given are those in being at the time of their birth.

Abbreviations

*	Not out
av	Average
b	Born
BB	Best innings bowling analysis
cap	Awarded county 1st XI cap
ct	Catches
F-c	First-class
HS	Highest score
LB	Bowls leg-breaks
LF	Bowls left-arm fast
LFM	Bowls left-arm fast-medium
LHB	Bats left-handed
LM	Bowls left-arm medium
OB	Bowls off-breaks
occ	Occasional
RF	Bowls right-arm fast
RFM	Bowls right-arm fast-medium
RHB	Bats right-handed
RM	Bowls right-arm medium
SLA	Bowls orthodox slow-left-arm
SLC	Bowls slow left-arm 'chinamen'
st	Stumpings
WK	Wicket-keeper

ABBERLEY, Robert Neal, b Birmingham 22 Apr 44, RHB, occ RM. WARWICKSHIRE cap 1966. F-c career: 255 matches; 10,003 runs (av 24.69); 3 hundreds; 4 wkts (av 71.25); 168 ct. HS 117* v Essex (Birmingham) 1966. BB 2–19 v Oxford U. (Oxford) 1972.

Experienced, neat, rather on-side conscious batsman.

ABRAHAMS, John, b Cape Town, South Africa 21 Jul 52. LHB, occ OB. LANCASHIRE – uncapped. F-c career: 83 matches; 2,541 runs (av 23.97), 2 hundreds; 50 ct. HS 126 v Cambridge U. (Cambridge) 1978.

Promising left-hand batsman and brilliant fielder.

ACFIELD, David Laurence, b Chelmsford 24 Jul 47. RHB, OB. ESSEX cap 1970. F-c career: 248 matches; 1,229 runs (av 9.10); 578 wkts (av 28.22); 87 ct. HS 42 Cambridge U. v Leicester (Leicester) 1967. BB 7–36 v Sussex (Ilford) 1973.

Extremely accurate off-break bowler who is also effective in limited-overs cricket. He is not a big finger spinner, but is capable of winning a match on a pitch giving assistance.

AGNEW, Jonathan Philip, b Macclesfield, Cheshire, 4 Apr 60. RHB, RF. LEICESTERSHIRE – uncapped. F-c career: 4 matches; 1 run (av 1.00): 6 wkts (av 35.83); 0 ct. HS 1. BB 3–51 v Northants (Leicester) 1978.

A young fast bowler who came from public school cricket into the Leicestershire side. Won Whitbread Award and went to Australia. In the next few years could prove to be England's outstanding pace bowler.

ALLBROOK, Mark Edward, b Frimley, Surrey 15 Nov 54. RHB, OB. NOTTINGHAMSHIRE – uncapped. F-c career: 44 matches; 320 runs (av 8.64); 75 wkts (av 44.97); 14 ct. HS 39 Cambridge U. v Yorks (Cambridge) 1976. BB 7–79 Cambridge U. v Notts (Cambridge) 1978.

Accurate off-break bowler who, at present, does not spin the ball sufficiently.

ALLOTT, Paul John Walter, b Altrincham, Cheshire. 14 Sep 56. RHB, RFM. LANCASHIRE – uncapped. F-c career: 4 matches; 1 run (av 1.00); 14 wkts (av 32.57); 1 ct. HS 1. BB

5–98 v Surrey (Oval) 1978.
Promising seamer.

AMISS, Dennis Leslie, b Birmingham 7 Apr 43.
RHB, occ SLA/LM. WARWICKSHIRE cap 1965.
50 England caps 1966–77, scoring 3,612 runs
(av 46.30) with 11 hundreds, HS 262*. F-c
career: 437 matches; 28,366 runs (av 43.24),
68 hundreds; 18 wkts (av 38.88); 284 ct. HS
262* England v West Indies (Kingston) 1973–
74. BB 3–21 v Middlesex (Lord's) 1970.
Took longer than most to establish himself as
an England regular. Originally chosen as a
middle-order batsman, but following a rewarding spell with Warwickshire as an opener, he
took over this role with enormous success at
international level. Has become one of the
really great accumulators of runs, with a wide
range of strokes, a fine defence, and endless
patience. There is now an air of inevitability
about his batting, so that, once he has settled in,
a century seems probable. It is also noticeable
how his concentration never wavers; like all
outstanding players, can accelerate when needs
dictate. Celebrated his recall to Test cricket
after a lean spell against Australian pace with
hundreds against both West Indies and India,
but lost his place in 1977. Signed for WSC, and
in 1978 was the only batsman to score 2,000
runs.

ANDERSON, Iain Stuart, b Derby 24 Apr 60.
RHB, occ OB. DERBYSHIRE – uncapped. F-c
career: 6 matches; 140 runs (av 15.55); 2 wkts
(av 75.00); 3 ct. HS 75 v Worcs (Worcester)
1978. BB 1–24 v Northants (Derby) 1978 – on
debut.
A good, teenage batsman who represented
Young England.

ARNOLD, Geoffrey Graham, b Earlsfield 3
Sep 44. RHB, RFM. SUSSEX uncapped. Played
for Surrey 1963–77 (cap 1967). 34 England caps
1967–75, scoring 421 runs (av 12.02), HS 59, and
taking 115 wkts (av 28.29), BB 6–45. F-c career:
305 matches; 3,443 runs (av 13.99); 985 wkts
(av 21.70), 1 hat-trick; 104 ct. HS 73 MCC
under-25 v Central Zone (Sahiwal) 1966–67.
BB 8–41 Surrey v Glos (Oval) 1967.
Still one of the best new ball bowlers in
England. Has excellent control, a late away
swing, and a vicious 'nip-backer'. Although
not truly fast, he has the ability to produce a
respectable bouncer. Can be used as either a
shock or stock bowler. A competent bat in the
later order, especially when he remembers to
play and hit straight.

ARROWSMITH, Robert, b Denton 21 May 52.
RHB, SLA. LANCASHIRE – uncapped. F-c
career: 35 matches; 213 runs (av 8.52); 89 wkts
(av 27.86); 10 ct. HS 30* v Australians (Manchester) 1977. BB 6–29 v Oxford U. (Oxford)
1977. Took 5–57 on debut.
Tall left-arm spinner with a teasing flight.

He did not make the expected advance in
1978, but remains an interesting prospect.

ASIF IQBAL RAZVI, b Hyderabad, India 6
Jun 43. RHB, RM KENT cap 1968. Captain
1977. 45 Pakistan caps 1964–77, scoring 2,748
runs (av 37.64) with 8 hundreds, HS 175, and
taking 50 wkts (av 28.02), BB 5–48. F-c career:
369 matches; 19,541 runs (av 37.22), 36
hundreds; 286 wkts (av 29.57); 279 ct. HS 196
National Bank v PIA (Lahore) 1976–77. BB
6–45 Pakistan Eaglets v Cambridge U. (Cambridge) 1963.
An exciting strokemaker, capable of changing the course of any game by the virtuosity of
his batting. A graceful and exciting batsman,
very quick on his feet, he is at his most effective
when attacking. A useful second-line seamer
and brilliant all-purpose fieldsman. Signed for
WSC.

ATHEY, Charles **William** Jeffrey, b Middlesbrough 27 Sep 57. RHB, occ OB. YORKSHIRE –
uncapped. F-c career: 49 matches; 1,658 runs
(av 23.35); 50 ct, 1 st. HS 131* v Sussex (Leeds) 1976.
BB 3–38 v Surrey (Oval) 1978.
A young batsman in the true Yorkshire
tradition, with a sound technique and plenty
of strokes.

Bill Athey of Yorkshire.

BAINBRIDGE, Philip, b Stoke-on-Trent, Staffs 16 Apr 58. RHB, RM. GLOUCESTERSHIRE – uncapped, F-c career: 11 matches; 444 runs (av 31.71); 7 ct. HS 76* v Worcs (Worcester) 1978.

Young batsman who showed high promise at the end of the season, scoring 233 runs and topping the batting averages in his five innings for the 1st XI.

BAIRSTOW, David Leslie, b Bradford 1 Sep 51. RHB, WK. YORKSHIRE cap 1973. F-c career: 213 matches; 5,307 runs (av 20.56), 2 hundreds; 4 wkts (av 37.75); 478 ct, 76 st. HS 106 v Glam (Middlesbrough) 1976 and 106 Griqualand West v Natal B (Pietermaritzburg) 1976–77. BB 3–82 Griqualand West v Transvaal B (Johannesburg) 1976–77.

Has become one of the better wicket-keepers on the circuit; also a useful batsman. Was thought unlucky not to have been selected for the winter tour of Australia.

BALDERSTONE, John Christopher, b Huddersfield, Yorks 16 Nov 40. RHB, SLA. LEICESTERSHIRE cap 1973. Played for Yorks 1961–69. 2 England caps 1976, scoring 39 runs (av 9.75), HS 35, and taking 1 wkt (av 80.00). F-c career: 209 matches; 8,800 runs (av 31.20); 13 hundreds; 245 wkts (av 24.51), 1 hat-trick; 101 ct. HS 178* v Notts (Nottingham) 1977. BB 6–25 v Hants (Southampton) 1978.

A sound, consistent county batsman and also a useful, extremely slow left-arm spinner.

BARCLAY, John Robert Troutbeck, b Bonn, West Germany 22 Jan 54. RHB, OB. SUSSEX cap 1976. F-c career: 113 matches; 4,146 runs (av 22.41), 3 hundreds; 102 wkts (av 31.13); 84 ct. HS 112 v Warwicks (Hove) 1977. BB 6–94 v Lancs (Manchester) 1976.

Determined young player who established himself as the regular opening bat. Also a useful off-spinner.

BARLOW, Graham Derek, b Folkestone, Kent 26 Mar 50. LHB, occ RM. MIDDLESEX cap 1976. 3 England caps 1976–77, scoring 17 runs (av 4.25), HS 7*. F-c career: 111 matches; 4,888 runs (av 31.33), 7 hundreds; 1 wkt (av 13.00); 62 ct. HS 160* v Derbys (Lord's) 1976. BB 1–6.

Exciting left-hand strokemaker. Effective and entertaining, he hits the ball hard and is a superb fieldsman in the covers or in the deep.

BIRCH, John Dennis, b Nottingham 18 Jun 55. RHB, RM. NOTTINGHAMSHIRE – uncapped. F-c career: 49 matches; 1,025 runs (av 16.53); 35 wkts (av 49.02); 28 ct. HS 86 v Glam (Worksop) 1977. BB 6–64 v Hants (Bournemouth) 1975.

A promising all-rounder who batted well on occasions but was less successful with the ball.

BIRKENSHAW, Jack, b Rothwell, Yorks 13 Nov 40. LHB, OB. LEICESTERSHIRE cap 1965. Played for Yorks 1958–60. 5 England caps 1973–74, scoring 148 runs (av 21.14), HS 64 – on debut, and taking 13 wkts (av 36.07), BB 5–57. F-c career: 457 matches; 12,084 runs (av 23.55), 4 hundreds; 1,038 wkts (av 26.85), 2 hat-tricks; 293 ct. HS 131 v Surrey (Guildford) 1969. BB 8–94 v Somerset (Taunton) 1972.

A fine all-rounder who is inclined to be underrated and is unlucky not to have had more opportunities for England. Spins his off-breaks considerably and has a deceptive, dipping flight. Relatively more dangerous on a dry, than a wet, turner. Steady, stubborn batsman, always difficult to remove and a good fighter; especially sound against spin bowling.

BOOTH, Peter, b Shipley, Yorks 2 Nov 52. RHB, RFM. LEICESTERSHIRE cap 1976. F-c career: 69 matches; 512 runs (av 11.63); 133 wkts (av 27.27); 21 ct. HS 58* v Lancs (Leicester) 1976. BB 6–93 v Glam (Swansea) 1978.

Lively young seamer with a good high action.

BORE, Michael Kenneth, b Hull 2 Jun 47. RHB, LM/SLA. YORKSHIRE – uncapped. F-c career: 74 matches; 481 runs (av 8.43); 162 wkts (av 30.03); 27 ct. HS 37* v Notts (Bradford) 1973. BB 7–63 v Derbys (Scarborough) 1977.

Originally a left-arm seamer, he was converted into a quickish spinner.

BORRINGTON, Anthony John, b Derby 8 Dec 48. RHB, occ LB. DERBYSHIRE cap 1977. F-c career: 97 matches; 3,574 runs (av 24.47), 3 hundreds; 48 ct. HS 137 v Yorks (Sheffield) 1978.

Rather limited, but dependable, batsman and fine field.

BOTHAM, Ian Terrence, b Heswall, Cheshire 24 Nov 55. RHB, RM SOMERSET cap 1976. 11 England caps 1977–78, scoring 500 runs (av 41.66) with 3 hundreds, HS 108, and taking 64 wkts (av 16.54). BB 8–34. F-c career: 103 matches; 3,720 runs (av 26.57), 6 hundreds; 381 wkts (av 22.66), 1 hat-trick; 82 ct. HS 167* v Notts (Nottingham) 1976. BB 8–34 England v Pakistan (Lord's) 1978.

Has developed into a world-class all-rounder and an outstanding entertainer. A fine attacking bowler, he can swing the ball either way and keeps a full length, but also possesses a useful bouncer. A hard-hitting batsman with all the shots; especially impressive against pace. A natural competitor and an outstanding fielder, he should be a key member of the England XI for the next decade. His powerful physique enables him to bowl for long spells and play large innings.

Leicestershire's Peter Booth illustrates strict adherence to side-on principles.

BOYCOTT, Geoffrey, b Fitzwilliam 21 Oct 40. RHB, occ RM. YORKSHIRE cap 1963. Captain 1971–78. 74 England caps 1964–78, 4 as captain, scoring 5,675 runs (av 51.12) with 16 hundreds, HS 246*, and taking 7 wkts (av 50.00), BB 3–47. F-c career, 422 matches; 33,690 runs (av 56.81), 109 hundreds; 23 wkts (av 43.95); 172 ct. Only English batsman to average 100 in a home season: 100.12 in 1971. HS 261* MCC v WIBC President's XI (Bridgetown) 1973–74. BB 3–47 England v South Africa (Cape Town) 1964–65.

A great opening bat with a magnificent technique. Is especially adept at hitting boundaries through the covers off the back foot and is the best acquirer of runs in the country. He made a dramatic and effective return to international cricket in 1977 against the Australians after his self-imposed exile. Sacked as captain of Yorkshire after eight years and, at the time of writing, his future is uncertain.

BOYNS, Cedric Nigel, b Harrogate, Yorks 14 Aug 54. RHB, RM. WORCESTERSHIRE – uncapped. F-c career: 36 matches; 844 runs (av 17.95); 35 wkts (av 45.82); 37 ct. HS 95 v Yorks (Scarborough) 1976. BB 3–24 v Oxford U. (Oxford) 1977.

Cedric Boyns of Worcestershire.

Useful all-rounder who has yet to establish himself in county cricket. Brilliant field.

BRAIN, Brian Maurice, b Worcester 13 Sep 40. RHB, RFM. GLOUCESTERSHIRE cap 1977. Played for Worcestershire 1966–75 (cap 1966). F-c career: 205 matches; 1,337 runs (av 8.35); 702 wkts (av 23.67); 41 ct. HS 57 v Essex (Cheltenham) 1976. BB 8–55 Worcs v Essex (Worcester) 1975.

This tall, fast-medium bowler has, like good wine, improved with the years. Has always been capable of producing a very good delivery, but used to send down too many loose ones.

BRASSINGTON, Andrew James, b Bagnall, Staffs 9 Aug 54. RHB, WK. GLOUCESTERSHIRE cap 1978. F-c career: 55 matches; 518 runs (av 9.41); 105 ct, 20 st. HS 28 v Glam (Cardiff) 1975.

Considered by many to be the best young 'keeper in the country but it is a pity that he is not more proficient with the bat.

BREAKWELL, Dennis, b Brierley Hill, Staffs 2 Jul 48. LHB, SLA. SOMERSET cap 1976. Played for Northants 1969–72. F-c career: 181 matches; 3,650 runs (av 18.62), 1 hundred; 334 wkts (av 29.78); 68 ct. HS 100* v New Zealanders (Taunton) 1978. BB 8–39 Northants v Kent (Dover) 1970.

Steady left-arm bowler, but not a matchwinner. Useful batsman and fine field.

BREARLEY, John **Michael,** b Harrow 28 Apr 42, RHB, occ WK. MIDDLESEX cap 1964. Captain since 1971. 21 England caps 1976–78, 13 as captain, scoring 845 runs (av 25.60), HS 91. F-c career: 358 matches; 19,776 runs (av 36.96), 29 hundreds; 1 wkt (av 103.00); 330 ct, 12 st. HS 312* MCC under-25 v N. Zone (Peshawar) 1966–67. BB 1–21.

Has become an accomplished opener with plenty of determination, but is rather short of shots. Strong off his legs. Despite suffering a horrid patch in 1978, he retained the England captaincy, where he has such a fine record, even though fortunate in the lack of quality of the opposition. A quiet, unspectacular leader, with considerable charm and very good tactical knowledge. Middlesex, like England, have prospered under his captaincy.

BRIERS, Nigel Edwin, b Leicester 15 Jan 55. RHB. LEICESTERSHIRE – uncapped. F-c career: 32 matches; 1,254 runs (av 25.59), 2 hundreds; 1 wkt (av 40.00); 10 ct. HS 116* v Cambridge U. (Cambridge) 1978. BB 1–22.

Exceptionally promising young batsman with a graceful style.

BROWN, David John, b Walsall, Staffs 30 Jan 42. RHB, RFM. WARWICKSHIRE cap 1964. Captain 1975–77. 26 England caps 1965–69, scoring 342 runs (av 11.79), HS 44* and taking

79 wkts (av 28.31), BB 5–42. F-c career: 378 matches; 4,000 runs (av 12.15); 1,140 wkts (av 24.65); 154 ct. HS 79 v Derbys (Birmingham) 1972. BB 8–60 v Middx (Lord's) 1975.
His height and action enable him to extract bounce and he has refused to be dismayed by the setbacks he has experienced through injury. Stubborn tailender who plays straight.

BURGESS, Graham Iefvion, b Glastonbury 5 May 43. RHB, RM. SOMERSET cap 1968. F-c career: 251 matches; 7,109 runs (av 18.95), 2 hundreds; 474 wkts (av 28.55); 119 ct. HS 129 v Glos (Taunton) 1973. BB 7–43 v Oxford U. (Oxford) 1975.
Handy all-rounder; hard-hitting bat and useful medium-paced seamer.

BUTCHER, Alan Raymond, b Croydon 7 Jan 54, LHB, LM. SURREY cap 1975. F-c career: 107 matches; 3,839 runs (av 24.76), 4 hundreds; 77 wkts (av 37.05); 27 ct. HS 188 v Sussex (Hove) 1978. BB 6–48 v Hants (Guildford) 1972.
Talented left-hand opener who might become Edrich's successor. Marked his return to the county side with a run of big scores. Useful medium-pace, rather negative seam bowler; at his best in limited-overs cricket.

BUTCHER, Roland Orlando, b East Point, St Philip, Barbados 14 Oct 53. RHB, occ RM. MIDDLESEX – uncapped. F-c career: 41 matches; 1,699 runs (av 25.74), 1 hundred; 46 ct. HS 142 v Glos (Bristol) 1978.
Capable young batsman whose opportunities are limited owing to the strength of the Middlesex batting. Magnificent fielder.

CARRICK, Phillip ('Fergus'), b Armley 16 July 52 RHB, SLA. YORKSHIRE cap 1976. F-c career: 125 matches; 2,539 runs (av 19.99), 1 hundred; 355 wkts (av 26.31); 69 ct. HS 105 v Lancs (Leeds) 1978. BB 8–33 v Cambridge U. (Cambridge) 1973.
Orthodox, dependable slow left-arm spinner who has developed into an all-rounder. Does not yet win enough matches with the ball for a true Yorkshire left-arm slow bowler.

CARTER, Robert Michael, b King's Lynn, Norfolk, 25 May 60. RHB, RM. NORTHAMPTONSHIRE-uncapped. F-c career: 2 matches; 8 runs; 0 wkts; 0 ct. HS 8*.
Apprentice all-rounder.

CARTWRIGHT, Harold, b Halfway 12 May 1951. RHB. DERBYSHIRE cap 1978. F-c career: 80 matches; 2,312 runs (av 21.01), 1 hundred; 31 ct. HS 141* v Warwicks (Chesterfield) 1977.
Hard-hitting batsman and excellent fieldsman in the covers.

CHEATLE, Robert Giles Lenthall, b Paddington, Middx 31 Jul 53. LHB, SLA. SUSSEX – un-capped. F-c career: 32 matches; 238 runs (av 13.22); 56 wkts (av 34.67); 32 ct. HS 49 v Kent (Tunbridge Wells) 1978. BB 6–54 v Kent (Canterbury) 1976.
Turned in several useful performances, but held back by the presence of another slow left-arm spinner, Waller (who had a very good summer), in the same county.

CHILDS, John Henry, b Plymouth, Devon 15 Aug 51. LHB, SLA. GLOUCESTERSHIRE cap 1977. F-c career: 59 matches; 98 runs (av 4.90); 154 wkts (av 28.75); 25 ct. HS 12 v Derbys (Ilkeston) 1977. BB 8–34 v Hants (Basingstoke) 1978.
Last summer this most promising orthodox left-armer established himself as the number one spinner in the Gloucestershire side. He turned in several outstanding performances and promises to become a very good bowler with spin, flight, and control.

CLIFFORD, Christopher Craven, b Hovingham, Yorks 5 Jul 42. RHB, OB. WARWICKSHIRE – uncapped. Played 11 matches for Yorkshire 1972. F-c career: 22 matches; 115 runs (av 7.66); 64 wkts (av 29.46); 12 ct. HS 20 and BB 6–89 v Somerset (Weston-s-Mare) 1978.
Signed by Warwickshire on the recommendation of Boycott, and after a series of impressive performances in the 2nd XI ousted Hemmings from the 1st XI. Despite his late arrival, he could be a needed asset to his adopted county.

CLIFT, Patrick Bernard ('**Paddy**'), b Salisbury, Rhodesia 14 Jul 53. LEICESTERSHIRE cap 1976. RHB, RM. F-c career: 113 matches; 2,571 runs (av 21.07); 312 wkts (av 24.53), 1 hat-trick; 60 ct. HS 75* Rhodesia v E. Province (Bulawayo) 1972–73. BB 8–17 v MCC (Lord's) 1976.
Good new ball bowler who moves the ball late, especially in to the batsman. A dangerous striker in the lower middle-order.

CLINTON, Grahame Selvey, b Sidcup 5 May 53. LHB, occ RM. SURREY – uncapped. Played for Kent 1974–78. F-c career: 32 matches; 1,142 runs (av 24.29); 2 wkts (av 4.50); 10 ct. HS 88 Kent v Leics (Leicester) 1977. BB 2–8 Kent v Pakistanis (Canterbury) 1978.
A left-handed batsman with an application not unreminiscent of the former Kent opening batsmen, Brian Luckhurst. He is increasing his repertoire of strokes and is not worried by fast bowling.

COOK, Geoffrey, b Middlesbrough, Yorks 9 Oct 51. RHB. NORTHAMPTONSHIRE cap 1975. F-c career: 166 matches; 7,274 runs (av 27.14), 6 hundreds; 183 ct. HS 155 v Derbys (Northampton) 1978.
Sound batsman with an excellent technique.

Again consistent and could yet develop into a really fine player.

COOK, Nicholas Grant Billson, b Leicester 17 Jun 56. RHB, SLA. LEICESTERSHIRE – uncapped. F-c career: 2 matches; 33 runs (av 33.00); 3 wkts (av 27.66); 1 ct. HS 31 v Northants (Leicester) 1978. BB 1–16 v Cambridge U. (Cambridge) 1978 – on debut.
A promising slow left-arm bowler.

COOPER, Howard Pennett, b Bradford 17 Apr 49. LHB, RM. YORKSHIRE – uncapped. F-c career: 88 matches; 1,065 runs (av 14.20); 211 wkts (av 27.06); 57 ct. HS 56 v Notts (Worksop) 1976. BB 8–62 v Glam (Cardiff) 1975.
A good accurate seam bowler who gives little away and also has the happy knack of making runs when needed.

COOPER, Kevin, b Hucknall 27 Dec 57. LHB, RM. NOTTINGHAMSHIRE – uncapped, F-c career: 44 matches; 191 runs (av 5.78); 106 wkts (av 28.35); 16 ct. HS 19 v Cambridge U. (Cambridge) 1978. BB 6–32 v Derbys (Derby) 1978.
This lively seam bowler established himself as a regular member of the county XI and became the leading wicket-taker; his best season to date. Still improving.

COPE, Geoffrey Alan, b Leeds 23 Feb 47. RHB, OB. YORKSHIRE cap 1970. 3 England caps 1977–78, scoring 40 runs (av 13.33), HS 22, and taking 8 wkts (av 34.62), BB 3–102. F-c career: 216 matches; 2,206 runs (av 13.70); 631 wkts (av 23.61), 1 hat-trick; 65 ct. HS 78 v Essex (Middlesbrough) 1977. BB 8–73 v Glos (Bristol) 1975.
For the second time in his career he has been stopped from bowling because of a suspect arm action. Showed considerable courage and dedication to fight his way back into the Yorkshire XI the first time, and it would probably be asking too much to expect him to do so again. Sad that his county, the umpires, and the England selectors should have taken such a long time to realise that he was still transgressing the Law.

CORDLE, Anthony Elton, b St Michael, Barbados 21 Sep 40. RHB, RFM. GLAMORGAN cap 1967. F-c career: 285 matches; 4,906 runs (av 14.77); 635 wkts (av 27.25); 128 ct. HS 81 v Cambridge U. (Swansea) 1972. BB 9–49 v Leics (Colwyn Bay) 1969.
Fast-medium seamer who is prepared to bowl all day. Uninhibited striker in the late middle-order.

COWDREY, Christopher Stuart, b Farnborough 20 Oct 1957. RHB. KENT – uncapped. F-c career: 33 matches; 716 runs (av 24.68), 1 hundred; 2 wkts (av 55.50); 19 ct. HS 101*

v Glam (Swansea) 1977. BB 1–18.
Excellent young batsman with enormous potential. Could well emulate his father and captain Kent in the future.

COWLEY, Nigel Geoffrey, b Shaftesbury, Dorset 1 Mar 53. RHB, OB. HAMPSHIRE cap 1978. F-c career: 67 matches; 1,962 runs (av 22.81), 1 hundred; 102 wkts (av 35.82); 33 ct. HS 109* v Somerset (Taunton) 1977. BB 5–93 v Warwicks (Bournemouth) 1978.
Off-spinner and useful middle-order batsman. Hampshire have clearly found another 'bits and pieces' cricketer with a bright future.

CUMBES, James, b East Didsbury, Lancs 4 May 44. RHB, RFM. WORCESTERSHIRE cap 1978. Played for Lancs 1963–67 and 1971, and for Surrey 1968–69. F-c career: 110 matches; 303 runs (av 6.58); 267 wkts (av 27.92), 1 hat-trick; 25 ct. HS 25* Surrey v West Indies (Oval) 1969. BB 6–24 v Yorks (Worcester) 1977.
Tall, athletic soccer goalkeeper who bowls at lively fast-medium and can extract bounce from the deadest pitches. Enthusiastic outfielder.

CURZON, Christopher Colin, b Nottingham 22 Dec 58. Younger brother of J. T. RHB, WK. NOTTINGHAMSHIRE – uncapped. F-c career: 4 matches; 26 runs (av 6.50); 2 ct, 1st. HS 26 v Glos (Cheltenham) 1978.
Reserve wicket-keeper at Trent Bridge.

DANIEL, Wayne Wendell, b St Philip, Barbados 16 Jan 56. RHB, RF. MIDDLESEX cap 1977. 5 West Indies caps 1976, scoring 29 runs (av 9.66), HS 11, and taking 15 wkts (av 25.40), BB 4–53. F-c career: 66 matches; 335 runs (av 9.85); 224 wkts (av 17.52); 12 ct. HS 30* v Notts (Lord's) 1978. BB 6–21 West Indians v Yorks (Sheffield) 1976.
Extremely fast, hostile bowler who is quick enough to beat good batsmen by pace alone. Built on the lines of Charlie Griffith, he has power and enormous potential. His control has improved with Middlesex and he is one of the most feared bowlers in the world. Has signed for WSC.

DAVEY, Jack, b Tavistock, Devon 4 Sep 44. LHB, LFM. GLOUCESTERSHIRE cap 1971. F-c career: 175 matches; 918 runs (av 7.77); 411 wkts (av 28.51), 1 hat-trick; 32 ct. HS 53* v Glam (Bristol) 1977. BB 6–95 v Notts (Gloucester) 1967.
A reliable fast-medium, left-arm swing bowler. A great trier.

DAVISON, Brian Fettes, b Bulawayo, Rhodesia 21 Dec 46. RHB, RM. LEICESTERSHIRE cap 1971. F-c career: 271 matches; 15,571 runs (av 38.73), 29 hundreds; 81 wkts (av 31.18); 206 ct. HS 189 v Australians (Leicester) 1975.

BB 5–52 Rhodesia v Griqualand West (Bulawayo) 1967–68.

Especially aggressive match-winning batsman who hits the ball uncommonly .hard. Superbly athletic fieldsman who regularly stops the unstoppable and catches the uncatchable. A dynamic cricketer in every sense.

DENNESS, Michael Henry, b Bellshill, Lanarks 1 Dec 40. RHB. ESSEX cap 1977. Played for Kent 1962–76 (cap 1964, captain 1972–76). 28 England caps 1969–75 (19 as captain), scoring 1,667 runs (av 39.69), with 4 hundreds, HS 188. F-c career: 462 matches; 24,049 runs (av 33.68), 31 hundreds, 2 wkts (av 31.00); 396 ct. HS 195 v Leics (Leicester) 1977. BB 1–7.

Elegant strokemaker with a lovely stance; handsome driver off the front foot. A most attractive player to watch, especially good against spin. A fine fielder who gave Kent great service over the years and has proved a valuable acquisition for Essex.

DENNING, Peter William, b Chewton Mendip 16 Dec 49. LHB. SOMERSET cap 1973. F-c career: 160 matches; 6,601 runs (av 26.09), 4 hundreds; 1 wkt (av 70.00); 71 ct. HS 122 v Glos (Taunton) 1977. BB 1–4.

Aggressive young lefthander with a sparkling drive; especially good off his front foot and ideally suited to the needs of limited-overs cricket.

DEXTER, Roy Evatt, b Nottingham 13 Apr 55. RHB. NOTTINGHAMSHIRE – uncapped. F-c career: 8 matches; 171 runs (av 15.54); 3 ct. HS 48 v Derbys (Ilkeston) 1977.

DILLEY, Graham Roy, b Dartford 18 May 59. LHB, RFM. KENT – uncapped. F-c career: 5 matches; 42 runs (av 10.50); 8 wkts (av 27.50); 3 ct. HS 16 v Cambridge U. (Canterbury) 1977. BB 5–32 v Middx (Lord's) 1978.

D'OLIVEIRA, Basil Lewis, b Cape Town, South Africa 4 Oct 31. RHB, RM/OB. WORCESTERSHIRE cap 1965. 44 England caps 1966–72, scoring 2,484 runs (av 40.06), with 5 hundreds (HS 158), and taking 47 wkts (av 39.55), BB 3–46. F-c career: 354 matches; 18,625 runs (av 39.79), 42 hundreds; 538 wkts (av 27.38); 211 ct. HS 227 v Yorks (Hull) 1974. BB 6–29 v Hants (Portsmouth) 1968.

Learnt his cricket in South Africa and has given great service to both England and Worcestershire. A natural competitor who has the happy knack of producing his finest performances in times of crisis, he is a most effective bat. Despite his short backlift, he still manages to hit the ball extremely hard. Outstanding puller and cutter. His defence is sound, although he is inclined to be somewhat suspect at the beginning of the innings. A good medium-pace swing bowler who regularly

breaks up awkward stands. Hampered by injury in 1978 but still managed to acquire another hundred.

DREDGE, Colin Herbert, b Frome 4 Aug 54. LHB, RM. SOMERSET cap 1978. F-c career: 47 matches; 543 runs (av 13.24); 102 wkts (av 32.51); 19 ct. HS 56* v Yorks (Harrogate) 1977. BB 5–53 v Kent (Taunton) 1978.

Tall seam bowler whose somewhat slingy action enables him to generate rather more pace and lift than batsmen expect.

DOWNTON, Paul Rupert, b Farnborough 4 Apr 57. RHB, WK. KENT – uncapped. F-c career: 38 matches; 243 runs (av 11.57); 88 ct, 8 st. HS 31* v Surrey (Maidstone) 1977 – on debut.

Kept wicket well for Kent in the absence of Alan Knott. Was a surprise choice to tour Pakistan and New Zealand with England in 1977–78 for he had little first-class experience.

DUDLESTON, Barry, b Bebington, Cheshire 16 July 45. RHB, SLA, occ WK. LEICESTERSHIRE cap 1969. F-c career: 247 matches; 12,331 runs (av 33.05), 29 hundreds; 23 wkts (av 35.95); 198 ct, 6 st. HS 172 v Glam (Leicester) 1975. BB 4–6 v Surrey (Leicester) 1972.

Correct, unspectacular batsman with an admirable technique. Lately he has not been scoring the runs he should.

EALHAM, Alan George Ernest, b Ashford 30 Aug 44. RHB, occ OB. KENT cap 1970. Captain since 1978. F-c career: 257 matches: 9,247 runs (av 27.52), 5 hundreds; 2 wkts (av 49.00); 155 ct. HS 134* v Notts (Nottingham) 1976. BB 1–1.

Pressed into service as captain of Kent, this whole-hearted cricketer did a splendid job. An outstanding fieldsman with the happy knack of taking a vital catch or making a brilliant run-out when most required; a naturally aggressive batsman, especially useful in one-day cricket.

EAST, Raymond Eric, b Manningtree 20 June 47, RHB, SLA. ESSEX cap 1967. F-c career: 303 matches; 5,242 runs (av 17.76), 1 hundred; 780 wkts (av 24.80), 1 hat-trick; 196 ct. HS 113 v Hants (Chelmsford) 1976. BB 8–30 v Notts (Ilford) 1977.

Spins the ball as much, if not more, than any other left-armer in the country. He has good control while his height makes him an extremely nasty proposition on a helpful pitch. Has yet to reach his full potential. At times he suggests that he has the basic ability to develop into a genuine all-rounder and is capable of producing an off-drive of classical proportions. A splendid fieldsman, who seldom drops a catch, and a natural, often very funny, comedian.

EDMONDS, Phillippe Henri, b Lusaka, Northern Rhodesia 8 Mar 51 RHB, SLA. MIDDLESEX cap 1974. 13 England caps 1975–78, scoring 195 runs (av 16.25), HS 50, and taking 43 wkts (av 20.95), BB 7–66. F-c career: 181 matches; 4,049 runs (av 18.74), 1 hundred; 611 wkts (av 24.29); 196 ct. HS 103* T. N. Pearce's XI v West Indians (Scarborough) 1976. BB 8–132 v Glos (Lord's) 1977.

Splendid left-arm spinner with a classical action and all the ingredients needed to become an outstanding slow bowler. He made a considerable advance last year and is certainly international class. A more than useful batsman and a brilliant fieldsman, he would certainly be classified as an all-rounder at county level. His batting would be even more effective if he had more opportunities to play an innings.

EDRICH, John Hugh, b Blofield, Norfolk 21 June 37. LHB. SURREY cap 1959. Captain 1973–77. 77 England caps 1963–76, scoring 5,138 runs (av 43.54), with 12 hundreds (HS 310*). F-c career: 564 matches; 39,790 runs (av 45.47), 103 hundreds; 0 wkts; 311 ct. HS 310* England v New Zealand (Leeds) 1965.

Chunky, determined left-hander who gave England wonderful service over a long period. Not a pretty player to watch, but a great acquirer of runs who can attack as well as graft. Punches the ball strongly off his legs and drives fiercely. A fine example of a player who has learnt the value of moving in behind the line of the ball. Character and ability in his batting.

EMBUREY, John Ernest, b Peckham, Surrey 20 Aug 52. RHB, OB. MIDDLESEX cap 1977. 1 England cap 1978, scoring 2 runs (av 2.00), HS 2, and taking 2 wkts (av 20.00), BB 2–39. F-c career: 62 matches; 745 runs (av 14.90); 201 wkts (av 22.62); 66 ct. HS 48 v Warwicks (Lord's) 1977. BB 7–36 v Cambridge U. (Cambridge) 1977.

A fine off-break bowler with a high action. Has the ability to float the ball away from a right-hander, sufficient turn, and a teasing flight. His performances for Middlesex led to his being selected for England and the Australian tour.

FEATHERSTONE, Norman George, b Que Que, Rhodesia 20 Aug 49. RHB, OB. MIDDLESEX cap 1971. F-c career: 267 matches; 11,318 runs (av 29.17), 9 hundreds; 146 wkts (av 26.47); 221 ct. HS 147 v Yorks (Scarborough) 1975. BB 5–32 v Notts (Nottingham) 1978.

Strokeplayer who is always worth watching because he possesses a wide range of attacking shots. Useful off-spinner and fine fielder.

FINAN, Nicholas Hugh, b Knowle, Bristol 3 Jul 54. RHB, RM. GLOUCESTERSHIRE – uncapped. F-c career: 5 matches; 22 runs (av 11.00); 4 wkts (av 63.00); 1 ct. HS 18 v Worcs (Worcester) 1977. BB 2–57 v Sussex (Eastbourne) 1975.

FISHER, Paul Bernard, b Edmonton 19 Dec 54. RHB, WK. MIDDLESEX – uncapped. F-c career (for Oxford U.): 41 matches; 534 runs (av 9.05); 60 ct, 9 st. HS 42 Oxford U. v Warwicks (Oxford) 1975. Played in one JPL match 1978.

Reserve 'keeper, formerly in the Oxford University XI.

FLETCHER, Keith William Robert, b Worcester, Worcs 20 May 44. RHB, occ LB. ESSEX cap 1963. Captain since 1974. 52 England caps 1968–77, scoring 2,975 runs (av 40.20) with 7 hundreds, HS 216, and taking 1 wkt (av 173.00), BB 1–48. F-c career: 499 matches; 27,515 runs (av 38.59), 47 hundreds; 32 wkts (av 47.18); 467 ct. HS 228* v Sussex (Hastings) 1968. BB 4–50 MCC under-25 v North Zone (Peshawar) 1966–67.

A highly talented player who is equally adept off front and back foot. Has an unusually large repertoire of attacking strokes, but also possesses a sound technique and patience. For a player who is capable of looking so good, he can, when out of touch, appear most ordinary. A good, all-purpose fieldsman and an occasional purveyor of rather untrustworthy leg-breaks.

FLOWER, Russell William, b Stone, Staffs 6 Nov 42. LHB, SLA. WARWICKSHIRE – uncapped. F-c career: 9 matches; 23 runs (av 5.75); 10 wkts (av 55.40); 0 ct. HS 10* v Yorks (Bradford) 1978. BB 3–45 v Northants (Northampton) 1978.

A slow left-armer who came into first-class cricket from the Staffordshire League rather late and found wickets hard to obtain.

FLYNN, Vincent Anthony, b Aylesbury, Bucks 3 Oct 55. RHB, WK. NORTHAMPTONSHIRE – uncapped. F-c career: 3 matches; 21 runs (av 21.00); 4 ct, 0 st. HS 15 v Yorks (Northampton) 1978.

Reserve wicket-keeper.

FOAT, James Clive, b Salford Priors, Warwicks 21 Nov 52. RHB, occ RM. GLOUCESTERSHIRE – uncapped. F-c career: 81 matches; 2,049 runs (av 17.07), 3 hundreds; 34 ct. HS 116 v Glam (Bristol) 1975.

Brilliant cover who is invaluable in the field. Played several attractive innings and enjoyed his most impressive season.

FOWLER, Graeme, b Accrington 20 Apr 57. RHB. LANCASHIRE – uncapped. Played in one JPL match 1978 but has yet to make his first-class debut.

Apprentice batsman.

FRANCIS, David Arthur, b Clydach 29 Nov 53. RHB, occ OB. GLAMORGAN – uncapped. F-c career: 67 matches; 2,143 runs (av 21.21),

1 hundred; 38 ct. HS 110 v Warwicks (Nuneaton) 1977.

Continued to improve. He has a pleasing style and hits the ball exceptionally hard.

FRENCH, Bruce Nicholas, b Warsop 13 Aug 59. RHB, WK. NOTTINGHAMSHIRE – uncapped. F-c career: 43 matches; 454 runs (av 12.97); 65 ct, 12 st. HS 66 v Cambridge U. (Cambridge) 1978.

This diminutive wicket-keeper has become a vital part of the county team and has proved himself to be a very able practitioner of his chosen profession. His batting improved noticeably in 1978 and he could soon challenge for an England place, having already won junior honours.

GARD, Trevor, b West Lambrook 2 Jun 57. RHB, WK. SOMERSET – uncapped. F-c career: 5 matches; 12 runs (av 4.00); 7 ct, 1 st. HS 7. 2nd XI wicket-keeper.

Joel Garner: West Indies and Somerset.

GARNER, Joel, b Barbados 16 Dec 52. 6ft 8in (tallest current first-class cricketer). RHB, RFM. SOMERSET – uncapped. 7 West Indies caps 1977–78, scoring 97 runs (av 10.77), HS 43, and taking 38 wkts (av 23.23), BB 4–48. F-c career: 24 matches; 354 runs (av 16.85), 124 wkts (av 19.83); 19 ct. HS 44* Barbados v Guyana (Bridgetown) 1976–77. BB 8–31 v Glam (Cardiff) 1977.

Exceptionally tall, rather awkward-looking West Indian fast bowler who can extract surprising lift from even the most docile of pitches. Now available to play full time for his county, which must improve their chances of capturing one of the honours. Has signed for WSC.

GARNHAM, Michael Anthony, b Johannesburg, South Africa, 20 Aug 60. RHB, WK. GLOUCESTERSHIRE – uncapped. Played in one JPL match 1978 but has yet to make his first-class debut.

Looked a most promising wicket-keeper with Young England and should prove a well-above-average number two for Gloucestershire.

GATTING, Michael William, b Kingsbury 6 Jun 57. RHB, occ RM. MIDDLESEX cap 1977. 2 England caps 1978, scoring 11 runs (av 3.66), HS 6. F-c career: 77 matches; 2,975 runs (av 29.45), 2 hundreds; 52 wkts (av 23.40); 68 ct. HS 128 v Derby (Lord's) 1978. BB 5–59 v Leics (Lord's) 1978.

Exciting young batsman with plenty of strokes and a pleasing technique; he broke the three-figure barrier in first-class cricket last summer. Could well be destined for the top. A useful third or fourth seamer and brilliant fielder.

GIFFORD, Norman, b Ulverston, Lancs 30 Mar. 40. LHB, SLA. WORCESTERSHIRE cap 1961. Captain since 1971. 15 England caps 1964–73, scoring 179 runs (av 16.27), HS 25*, and taking 33 wkts (av 31.09), BB 5–55. F-c career: 493 matches; 5,408 runs (av 13.25); 1,487 wkts (av 21.57), 1 hat-trick; 243 ct. HS 89 v Oxford U. (Oxford) 1963. BB 8–28 v Yorks (Sheffield) 1968.

Fine left-arm spinner who is a natural match-winner in the right circumstances. He tends to bowl from wide of the stumps and has a rather flat trajectory, with the result that he is not easy to hit, or to cut. He never gives anything away and spins the ball rather more than most. A determined tail-ender, he has often held up the opposition with his essentially practical approach. A shrewd, thoughtful captain.

GOOCH, Graham Alan, b Leytonstone 23 Jul 53, RHB, RM. ESSEX cap 1975. 7 England caps 1975–78, scoring 301 runs (av 33.44), HS 91*. F-c career: 105 matches; 5,166 runs (av 33.11), 8 hundreds; 25 wkts (av 41.40); 72 ct. HS 136 v Worcs (Westcliff-on-Sea) 1976. BB 5–40 v

West Indians (Chelmsford) 1976.
Powerfully built batsman particularly strong off the back foot. Found opening the innings much to his taste and was picked for England in this position. Like all the great players, he appears to have plenty of time to play his shots, but it is too early to decide whether he will move into that category. Has problems against pace because of an inclination to play slightly across the line. Safe pair of hands and a handy seamer for limited-overs cricket.

GOULD, Ian James, b Slough, Bucks 19 Aug 57. LHB, WK. MIDDLESEX cap 1977. F-c career: 55 matches; 1,283 runs (av 19.73), 1 hundred; 107 ct, 17st. HS 128 v Worcs (Worcester) 1978.
Made a considerable advance both as a batsman and behind the stumps.

GOWER, David Ivon, b Tunbridge Wells, Kent 1 Apr 57. LHB, occ OB. LEICESTERSHIRE cap 1977. 6 England caps 1978, scoring 438 runs (av 54.75) with 1 hundred (111). F-c career: 58 matches; 2,307 runs (av 29.96), 4 hundreds; 3 wkts (av 20.33); 20 ct. HS 144* v Hants (Leicester) 1977. BB 3-47 v Essex (Leicester) 1977.
The most exciting English-born batsman to appear in international cricket for more than a decade. A graceful lefthander, he strokes the ball elegantly with the full flow of the bat. Plays straight and possesses an excellent temperament, but it is to be hoped that he ignores those who will advise him to cut out 'this and that' shot because of the element of risk. Better that he remembers the glittering list of West Indian batsmen who have gone on playing their attacking strokes, an approach which not only produces enjoyment but also a vast number of runs. Fine cover who moves fast without appearing to do so.

GRAVENEY, David Anthony, b Bristol 2 Jan 53. Son of J. K. R. Graveney, former Glos captain. RHB, SLA. GLOUCESTERSHIRE cap 1976. F-c career: 131 matches; 2,500 runs (av 16.89); 317 wkts (av 28.81); 64 ct. HS 92 v Warwicks (Birmingham) 1978. BB 8-85 v Notts (Cheltenham) 1974.
Tall, orthodox left-arm slow bowler who is inclined to be a shade too mechanical. His bowling fell away a little, but his batting showed a considerable improvement so that he can now be regarded as a genuine all-rounder.

GRAVES, Peter John, b Hove 19 May 46. LHB, occ SLA. SUSSEX cap 1969. F-c career: 271 matches; 11,369 runs (av 26.94), 14 hundreds; 15 wkts (av 53.13); 217 ct. HS 145* v Glos (Gloucester) 1974. BB 3-69 Orange Free State v Australians (Bloemfontein) 1969-70.
For several years this naturally aggressive lefthander has looked the part but has failed

to score the runs. Particularly good against pace bowling. A serious finger injury in May curtailed his benefit season.

GREENIDGE, Cuthbert Gordon, b St Peter, Barbados 1 May 51. RHB, occ RM. HAMPSHIRE cap 1972. 19 West Indies caps 1974-78 scoring 1,641 runs (av 48.26) with 5 hundreds, HS 134. F-c career: 217 matches; 15,159 runs (av 42.58), 35 hundreds; 16 wkts (av 26.31); 226 ct. HS 273* D. H. Robins' XI v Pakistanis (Eastbourne) 1974. BB 5-49 v Surrey (Southampton) 1971. Holds record for highest individual score in limited-overs matches: 177 in Gillette Cup 1975.
A world-class opening batsman who plays the ball very late. His defensive technique is good and his cutting superb. He is capable of taking apart any attack. Essentially a match winner, as he proved on Hampshire's John Player League campaign. A WSC signatory, he scored the fastest first-class century in 1978.

GRIFFITHS, Brian James, b Wellingborough 13 Jun 49. RHB, RM. NORTHAMPTONSHIRE cap 1978. F-c career: 36 matches; 40 runs (av 2.66); 81 wkts (av 32.20); 9 ct. HS 11 v Middx (Lord's) 1978. BB 5-66 v Surrey (Northampton) 1978. Holds world record for most (10) scoreless innings in succession in f-c matches.
Established himself as the regular opening bowler and had the satisfaction of becoming the leading wicket-taker for his county.

GURR, David Roberts, b Whitchurch, Bucks 27 Mar 56. RHB, RFM. SOMERSET – uncapped. F-c career: 37 matches; 379 runs (av 15.16); 108 wkts (av 26.75); 9 ct. HS 46* Oxford U. v Cambridge U. (Lord's) 1977. BB 6-82 Oxford U. v Warwicks (Birmingham) 1976.
Young fast bowler with a high, rather open action. He lost so much confidence that it is difficult to believe he was the same quickie who had looked so good in the University Match and at the end of the previous summer.

HACKER, Peter John, b Nottingham 16 Jul 52. RHB, LM. NOTTINGHAMSHIRE – uncapped. F-c career: 27 matches; 283 runs (av 12.86); 36 wkts (av 50.05); 6 ct. HS 35 v Kent (Canterbury) 1977. BB 3-27 v Oxford U. (Oxford) 1977.
Left-arm seam bowler who needs more control. At the moment he is proving rather expensive.

HADLEE, Richard John, b Christchurch, New Zealand, 3 Jul 51. Fourth (youngest) son of former New Zealand captain, W. A. Hadlee, and brother of D. R. and B. G. LHB, RFM. NOTTINGHAMSHIRE cap 1978. 23 New Zealand caps 1973-78, scoring 729 runs (av 19.18), HS 87, and taking 89 wkts (av 31.58), BB 7-23. F-c career: 84 matches; 2,040 runs (av 21.47),

1 hundred; 323 wkts (av 23.77), 1 hat-trick; 36 ct. HS 101* v Derbys (Nottingham) 1978. BB 7–23 New Zealand v India (Wellington) 1975–76.

World-class fast bowler with the right action, pace, and stamina. Tends to make the ball leave the right-hander and brings the odd one back off the seam. Should win a number of matches for Notts. A hard-hitting left-hand bat, but distinctly suspect against fast bowling.

HAMPSHIRE, John Harry, b Thurnscoe 10 Feb 41. Brother of A. W. Hampshire. RHB, occ LB. YORKSHIRE cap 1963. Captain 1979. 8 England caps 1969–75, scoring 403 runs (av 26.86), with 1 hundred – 107 on debut. F-c career: 451 matches; 21,530 runs (av 33.69), 34 hundreds; 29 wkts (av 54.65); 353 ct. HS 183* v Sussex (Hove) 1971. BB 7–52 v Glam (Cardiff) 1963.

One of the best batsmen in county cricket, effective and attractive, and one feels he should have become a regular Test player. Might have been a useful leg-spinner. Has an extensive knowledge of the game and a pleasing personality. Has been appointed Boycott's successor as captain and already has an excellent record as his deputy.

HANSELL, Thomas Michael Geoffrey, b Sutton Coldfield, Warwicks 24 Aug 54. LHB. GLOUCESTERSHIRE – uncapped. Played for Surrey 1975–78. F-c career: 14 matches; 319 runs (av 15.19); 2 ct. HS 54 Surrey v Notts (Oval) 1976.

A left-handed batsman who failed to establish himself in the Surrey side.

HARDIE, Brian Ross, b Stenhousemuir, Stirlingshire 14 Jan 50. RHB. ESSEX cap 1974. Played for Scotland 1970–72. F-c career: 115 matches; 5,435 runs (av 31.23), 6 hundreds; 102 ct. HS 162 v Warwicks (Birmingham) 1975.

After several seasons as a determined 'sticker' with a limited range of strokes and a rather ugly style, he blossomed forth into a much more positive and successful batsman, averaging 38 and scoring 1,000 runs. Delighted everybody; possibly even surprised himself.

HARRIS, Michael John, b St Just-in-Roseland, Cornwall 25 May 44, RHB, LB. NOTTINGHAM-SHIRE cap 1970. Played for Middx 1964–68 (cap 1967). F-c career: 301 matches; 17,262 runs (av 37.20), 39 hundreds; 79 wkts (av 42.44); 259 ct. 14 st. HS 201* v Glam (Nottingham) 1973. BB 4–16 v Warwicks (Nottingham) 1969.

Solidly built batsman with a good technique who can drive off both the front and the back foot. He can keep wicket tidily.

HARTLEY, Stuart Neil, b Shipley 18 Mar 56. RHB, RFM. YORKSHIRE – uncapped. F-c

career: 1 match; 31 runs (av 15.50); 0 ct. HS 20 v Derbys (Sheffield) 1978.

Sound young Yorkshire batsman.

HASSAN, Basharat (not 'S.B.'), b Nairobi, Kenya 24 Mar 44. RHB, occ WK. NOTTING-HAMSHIRE cap 1970. F-c career: 232 matches; 10,308 runs (av 29.36), 13 hundreds; 6 wkts (av 67.83); 205 ct, 1 st. HS 182* v Glos (Nottingham) 1977. BB 3–33 v Lancs (Manchester) 1976.

Must have the ugliest stance in first-class cricket, but he is an unconventional, cross-bat-minded striker capable of changing the whole course of a match with his far-from-textbook methods. A tremendous enthusiast. Useful stop-gap wicket-keeper and fine field.

HAYES, Frank Charles, b Preston 6 Dec 46. RHB. LANCASHIRE cap 1972. Captain since 1978. 9 England caps 1973–76, scoring 244 runs (av 15.25) with 1 hundred (106* on debut). F-c career: 194 matches; 9,566 runs (av 36.09), 18 hundreds; 144 ct. HS 187 v Indians (Manchester) 1974.

A player of polish and charm. Will score plenty of runs for Lancashire, but in international cricket he falls into that category of 'almost but not quite there'. The hook has caused his downfall rather too often, and he tends to be a poor starter, which stems from over-nervousness before going out to bat. Hoping that his second season as skipper will be rewarded by Lancashire capturing an honour.

HEAD, Timothy John, b Hammersmith, Middx 22 Sep 57. RHB, WK. SUSSEX – uncapped. F-c career: 5 matches; 105 runs (av 21.00); 14 ct, 1 st. HS 31 v Oxford U. (Oxford) 1978.

Reserve wicket-keeper who has shown much promise on his few appearances in the first team.

HEMMINGS, Edward Ernest, b Leamington Spa, Warwicks 20 Feb 49. RHB, RM/OB. NOTTINGHAMSHIRE – uncapped. Played for Warwickshire 1966 – 78 (cap 1974). F-c career: 179 matches; 4,306 runs (av 21.74); 445 wkts (av 31.90), 1 hat-trick; 87 ct. HS 85 Warwicks v Essex (Birmingham) 1977. BB 7–33 Warwicks v Cambridge U. (Cambridge) 1975.

A rather flat off-break bowler, somewhat lacking in penetration on good pitches.

HEMSLEY, Edward John Orton, b Norton, Staffs 1 Sep 43. RHB, RM. WORCESTERSHIRE cap 1969. F-c career: 166 matches; 7,137 runs (av 30.63), 8 hundreds; 67 wkts (av 34.07); 118 ct. HS 176* v Lancs (Worcester) 1977. BB 3–5 v Warwicks (Worcester) 1971.

A well-above-average middle-order batsman who, since his retirement from football, has proved himself a valuable asset to Worcestershire. Enjoyed his most consistent season in 1978.

HENDERSON, Stephen Peter, b Oxford, Oxon 24 Sep 58. LHB, RM. WORCESTERSHIRE – uncapped. F-c career: 12 matches; 237 runs (av 14.81); 6 ct. HS 52 v Northants (Worcester) 1977.

Competent batsman yet to make the grade in first-class cricket.

HENDRICK, Michael, b Darley Dale 22 Oct 48. RHB, RFM. DERBYSHIRE cap 1972. 16 England caps 1974–78, scoring 64 runs (av 5.33), HS 15, and taking 47 wkts (av 26.57), BB 4–28. F-c career: 179 matches; 1,041 runs (av 9.55); 505 wkts (av 21.12); 115 ct. HS 46 v Essex (Chelmsford) 1973. BB 8–45 v Warwicks (Chesterfield) 1973.

Seamer in the true Derbyshire tradition. Tends to move the ball away from the bat and brings the odd one back off the seam. Tall and accurate with a long – dare one say over-long – amble up to the wicket and a high action with plenty of body. Tidy and accurate, he is now considered to be the most dangerous seam bowler in the country, but has been disturbingly injury-prone. Outstanding fielder close to the wicket.

HERBERT, Reuben, b Cape Town, South Africa 1 Dec 57. RHB. ESSEX – uncapped. F-c career: 3 matches; 33 runs (av 6.60), 2 ct. HS 12 v Cambridge U. (Cambridge) 1977.

Apprentice opening bat and off-spinner.

HERKES, Robert, b Lincoln, Lincs, 30 Jun 57. RHB, RFM. MIDDLESEX – uncapped. F-c career: 1 match; 0 runs; 0 wkts, 0 ct. HS 0* Promising seamer.

HIGGS, Kenneth, b Sandyford, Staffs 14 Jan 37. LHB, RFM. LEICESTERSHIRE cap 1972. Captain 1979. Played for Lancs 1958–69 (cap 1959). 15 England caps 1965–68, scoring 185 runs (av 11.56), HS 63, and taking 71 wkts (av 20.74), BB 6–91. F-c career: 486 matches; 3,586 runs (av 11.38); 1,477 wkts (av 23.72), 3 hat-tricks; 290 ct. HS 98 v Northants (Leicester) 1977 – sharing in record Leicestershire tenth wicket partnership of 228 with R. Illingworth. BB 7–19 Lancs v Leics (Manchester) 1965.

Powerfully-built stock seam bowler who formerly did extremely well both for Lancashire and England. From a short run-up, he hits the deck sufficiently hard to jar a batsman's right hand more than many bowlers who are much quicker through the air. Tempted out of early retirement by Leicestershire, he has bowled extremely well for them. A left-handed tailender, he has used his ability to push forward with a straight bat to considerable effect on a number of occasions, including a memorable last-wicket partnership in 1977

with Illingworth, from whom he has now taken over the captaincy.

HIGNELL, Alastair James b Cambridge, Cambs 4 Sep 55. RHB. GLOUCESTERSHIRE cap 1977. F-c career: 82 matches; 3,406 runs (av 25.60), 5 hundreds; 85 ct. HS 149 Cambridge U. v Glam (Cambridge) 1977.

Cambridge double Blue and England rugby union international. Hard-hitting batsman with a rugged approach and a splendid temperament. Possesses a very safe pair of hands. Failed to live up to his talent and promise in 1978, despite two centuries for his University in the match against Surrey.

HILL, Alan, b Buxworth 29 June 50. RHB. DERBYSHIRE cap 1976. F-c career: 125 matches; 5,862 runs (av 28.18), 7 hundreds; 3 wkts (av 22.33); 49 ct. HS 160* v Warwicks (Coventry) 1976. BB 3–5 Orange Free State v Northern Transvaal (Pretoria) 1976–77.

A sound, somewhat conventional opening batsman who averaged only 22 last summer.

HILLS, Richard William, b Borough Green 8 Jan 51. RHB, RM. KENT cap 1977. F-c career: 64 matches; 840 runs (av 16.47); 131 wkts (av 26.96); 18 ct. HS 45 v Hants (Canterbury) 1975. BB 6–64 v Glos (Folkestone) 1978.

Useful 'bits and pieces' cricketer.

HOADLEY, Simon Peter, b Eridge 16 Aug 56. Younger brother of Stephen J. Hoadley (Sussex). RHB, OB. SUSSEX – uncapped. F-c career: 7 matches; 232 runs (av 19.33), 1 hundred; 4 ct. HS 112 v Glam (Swansea) 1978.

A young' opener of considerable potential who has already taken a hundred off Glamorgan.

HODGSON, Alan, b Consett, Co Durham 27 Oct 51. LHB, RFM. NORTHAMPTONSHIRE cap 1976. F-c career: 88 matches; 870 runs (av 10.11); 188 wkts (av 27.36); 27 ct. HS 41* v Glos (Northampton) 1976. BB 5–30 v Oxford U. (Oxford) 1976.

Tall (6ft 4½in), well-built fast-medium bowler with a rather ugly action.

HOGG, William, b Ulverston 12 Jul 55. RHB, RFM. LANCASHIRE – uncapped. F-c career: 18 matches; 69 runs (av 5.30); 46 wkts (av 24.82); 2 ct. HS 19 v Middx (Lord's) 1978. BB 7–84 v Warwicks (Manchester) 1978.

A most impressive young pace bowler who could well have had an outstanding season but for injury. He proved most successful in terms of wickets and cost.

HOLDER, Vanburn Alonza, b Bridgetown, Barbados 8 Oct 45, RHB, RFM. WORCESTERSHIRE cap 1970. 34 West Indies caps 1969–78, scoring 603 runs (av 14.35), HS 42, and taking

101 wkts (av 30.48), BB 6–28. F-c career: 279 matches; 3,081 runs (av 12.52), 1 hundred; 886 wkts (av 23.66); 87 ct. HS 122 Barbados v Trinidad (Bridgetown) 1973–74. BB 7–40 v Glam (Cardiff), 1974.

With his high action, control, and stamina he is an attacking fast bowler who can also be employed for long, economical spells. In county matches his pace, except for the odd ball, is a hostile fast-medium, rather than genuinely fast, but in some matches for West Indies he has shown he can be distinctly sharp. A competent tail-end bat with a highly individual technique.

HOLMES, Geoffrey Clark, b Newcastle upon Tyne, Northumberland, 16 Sep 58. RHB, RM. GLAMORGAN – uncapped. F-c career: 2 matches; 37 runs (av 18.50); 0 wkt; 1 ct. HS 17* v Warwicks (Cardiff) 1978 on debut.

Apprentice batsman.

HOPKINS, David Charles, b Birmingham 11 Feb 57. RHB, RM. WARWICKSHIRE – uncapped. F-c career: 11 matches; 56 runs (av 5.60); 10 wkts (av 48.50); 4 ct. HS 13* v Somerset (Birmingham) 1977 – on debut. BB 3–27 v Lancs (Manchester) 1978.

Tall (6ft 6½in) apprentice seam bowler.

HOPKINS, John Anthony, b Maesteg 16 Jun 53. RHB, occ WK. GLAMORGAN cap 1977. F-c career: 92 matches; 4,071 runs (av 27.32), 5 hundreds; 66 ct, 1 st. HS 230 v Worcs (Worcester) 1977.

Has developed into a mature and reliable opener who topped the Welsh batting averages and scored the most runs.

HOWARTH, Geoffrey Philip, b Auckland, New Zealand 29 Mar 51. RHB, OB. SURREY cap 1974. 14 New Zealand caps 1975–78, scoring 864 runs (av 36.00) with 3 hundreds, HS 123, and taking 2 wkts (av 54.50). F-c career: 164 matches; 8,444 runs (av 30.59), 13 hundreds; 78 wkts (av 29.79); 109 ct. HS 179* v Cambridge U. (Cambridge) 1978. BB 5–32 Auckland v Central Districts (Auckland) 1973–74.

Attractive and forceful batsman who cuts and pulls effectively. It might be said that he really came of age as a class player for New Zealand during 1978, when he at last fulfilled the promise shown when he first joined Surrey. If he continues in this vein, he should be capable of nearly doubling his usual aggregate for his county. Fine field and occasional off-spinner.

HUGHES, David Paul, b Newton-le-Willows 13 May 47. RHB, SLA. LANCASHIRE cap 1970. F-c career: 226 matches; 4,075 runs (av 18.43), 1 hundred; 510 wkts (av 28.74); 137 ct. HS 101 v Cambridge U. (Cambridge) 1975. BB 7–24 v Oxford U. (Oxford) 1970.

Left-arm orthodox bowler with excellent line and length. He is invariably tidy, but still does not spin the ball viciously enough to reap the benefits of a bad track. However, he has the knack of picking up vital wickets rather in the same way as he so often scores runs when they are most needed.

HUMPAGE, Geoffrey William, b Birmingham 24 Apr 54. RHB, WK. WARWICKSHIRE cap 1976. F-c career: 78 matches; 3,457 runs (av 32.92), 4 hundreds; 168 ct, 12 st. HS 125* v Sussex (Birmingham) 1976.

Genuine wicket-keeper/batsman. Dependable keeper and lively, pugnacious batsman.

HUMPHRIES, David John, b Alveley, Shropshire 6 Aug 53. LHB, WK. WORCESTERSHIRE cap 1978. Played for Leicestershire 1974–76. F-c career: 51 matches; 1,330 runs (av 22.16), 1 hundred; 81 ct, 14 st. HS 111* v Warwicks (Worcester) 1978.

Enjoyed his best-ever season, not only keeping most competently, despite a limited attack, but batting efficiently. Took a century off Warwickshire.

IMRAN KHAN NIAZI, b Lahore, Pakistan 25 Nov 52. RHB, RFM. SUSSEX cap 1978. Played for Worcs 1971–76 (cap 1976). 15 Pakistan caps 1971–77, scoring 503 runs (av 20.95), HS 59, and taking 62 wkts (av 32.98), BB 6–63. F-c career: 157 matches; 7,065 runs (av 31.26), 13 hundreds; 496 wkts (av 26.51); 62 ct. HS 170 Oxford U. v Northants (Oxford) 1974. BB 7–52 v Glos (Bristol) 1978.

All-rounder of outstanding potential. A lively, fast-medium bowler who moves the ball into the righthander and achieves considerable lift and movement. His batting is rich in promise, with a wealth of strokes and the time to play them. A world-class outfielder, he could well become the finest Pakistan all-rounder. Has signed for WSC.

INCHMORE, John Darling, b Ashington, Northumberland 22 Feb 49. RHB, RFM. WORCESTERSHIRE cap 1976. F-c career: 79 matches; 1,054 runs (av 14.05), 1 hundred; 206 wkts (av 27.37); 27 ct. HS 113 v Essex (Worcester) 1974. BB 8–58 v Yorks (Worcester) 1977.

A useful opening bowler who could do with a little more pace.

INTIKHAB ALAM KHAN, b Hoshiarpur, India 28 Dec 41. RHB, LB. SURREY cap 1969. 47 Pakistan caps 1959–77, scoring 1,493 runs (av 22.28), 1 hundred, HS 138, and taking 125 wkts (av 35.93), BB 7–52. Also 5 unofficial Tests for Rest of the World 1970, scoring 240 runs (av 34.28) and taking 14 wkts (av 45.50). F-c career: 445 matches; 13,301 runs (av 22.43), 9 hundreds; 1,451 wkts (av 27.64), 1 hat-trick; 217 ct. HS 182 Karachi Blues v PIA 'B'

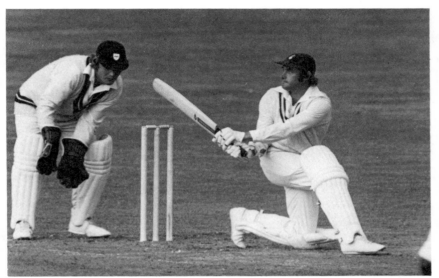

Two Davids: Worcestershire 'keeper Humphries and Hampshire's Turner.

(Karachi) 1970–71. BB 8–54 Pakistanis v
Tasmania (Hobart) 1972–73.

Cheerful cricketer and leg-break bowler. An
accurate spinner with a teasing flight, he is
usually happier on the fast pitches abroad than
at The Oval. Unlike some, he does not wilt
under pressure and will simply go on bowling.
He hits straight with remarkable power and
ferocity and is the ideal person to have coming
in down the order when quick runs are the
order of the day.

JACKMAN, Robin David, b Simla, India 13
Aug 45, RHB, RFM. SURREY cap 1970. F-c
career: 304 matches; 4,104 runs (av 16.61);
1,029 wkts (av 23.69), 3 hat-tricks; 137 ct. HS
92* v Kent (Oval) 1974. BB 8–40 Rhodesia v
Natal (Durban) 1972–73.

An ideal county all-rounder especially well
suited to the particular needs of limited-overs
cricket. An accurate fast-medium bowler who
generally moves the ball about; a determined
bat who likes to go for his shots, several of
which are unconventional and would not be
found in any coaching manual; a first-rate
field.

JARVIS, Kevin Bertram Sidney, b Dartford 23
Apr 53. RHB, RFM. KENT cap 1977. F-c
career: 78 matches; 80 runs (av 3.33); 215
wkts (av 27.25); 24 ct. HS 12* v Cambridge U.
(Canterbury) 1977. BB 8–97 v Worcs (Worcester) 1978.

A tall young fast bowler who, from time to
time, suggested he might be the pace bowler
England need.

Kevin Jarvis of Kent.

JAVED MIANDAD KHAN, b Karachi, Pakistan 12 Jun 57. RHB, LB. SUSSEX cap 1977. 13 Pakistan caps 1976–78, scoring 994 runs (av 55.22) with 2 hundreds (including 163 on debut), HS 206, and taking 15 wkts (av 34.00), BB 3–74. F-c career: 118 matches; 7,655 runs (av 44.50), 21 hundreds; 145 wkts (av 30.17); 124 ct, 2 st. HS 311 Karachi Whites v National Bank (Karachi) 1974–75. BB 6–93 Sind v Railways (Lahore) 1974–75.

Brilliant young batsman with a bright future. Although he had an unhappy time for his country in England, he refound his form with Sussex and topped their averages. Also a more than useful leg-spinner. Has signed for WSC.

JENNINGS, Keith Francis, b Wellington 5 Oct 53. RHB, RM. SOMERSET cap 1978. F-c career: 36 matches; 394 runs (av 10.94); 58 wkts (av 36.10); 24 ct. HS 49 v West Indians (Taunton) 1976. BB 5–18 v Sussex (Hove) 1978.

Young all-rounder who made a marked advance with bat and ball. Typical 'bits and pieces' player, especially well suited to the needs of limited-overs cricket.

JESTY, Trevor Edward, b Gosport 2 Jun 48. RHB, RM. HAMPSHIRE cap 1971. F-c career: 228 matches; 8,660 runs (av 27.75), 12 hundreds; 368 wkts (av 28.36); 133 ct. 1 st. HS 159* v Somerset (Bournemouth) 1976. BB 7–75 v Worcs (Southampton) 1976.

Hard-hitting batsman with a most attractive style who has the ability to drive off both front and back foot. With his medium-pace bowling he moves the ball away in the air, and he is also a splendid fieldsman.

JOHNSON, Colin, b Pocklington 5 Sep 47. RHB, OB. YORKSHIRE – uncapped. F-c career: 99 matches; 2,946 runs (av 21.66), 2 hundreds; 4 wkts (av 66.25); 49 ct. HS 107 v Somerset (Sheffield) 1973. BB 2–22 v Oxford U. (Oxford) 1971.

Fielded splendidly but did not make that hoped-for advance as a batsman, remaining a useful, but not exceptional, middle-order player.

JOHNSON, Graham William, b Beckenham 8 Nov 46. RHB, OB. KENT cap 1970. F-c career: 232 matches; 8,886 runs (av 25.24), 10 hundreds; 316 wkts (av 30.39); 188 ct. HS 168 v Surrey (Oval) 1976. BB 6–32 v Surrey (Tunbridge Wells) 1978.

His all-round performances had much to do with Kent's success. His off-break bowling was most effective in the Schweppes Championship, where he took over 50 wickets at under 19 apiece, proving an effective partner for Underwood. His batting is both correct and pleasing, but one feels he should be capable of scoring more heavily than he has done to date.

JONES, Alan, b Swansea 4 Nov 38. LHB, occ OB. GLAMORGAN cap 1962. Captain since 1976. Played one unofficial Test v Rest of the World 1970. F-c career: 532 matches; 29,716 runs (av 32.76), 46 hundreds; 3 wkts (av 109.66); 257 ct. HS 187* v Somerset (Glastonbury) 1963. BB 1–24.

Neat, competent opening bat who has given fine service to Glamorgan over the years. His consistency is shown by the fact that in 1978 he passed 1,000 runs for the 18th consecutive season. Many lesser players have represented England in official Tests. Once again led his team soundly and sensibly, though handicapped by a lack of match-winning bowlers.

JONES, Allan Arthur, b Horley, Surrey 9 Dec 47. RHB, RFM. MIDDLESEX cap 1976. Played for Sussex 1966–69 and Somerset 1970–75 (cap 1972). F-c career: 184 matches; 706 runs (av 5.38); 483 wkts (av 26.76); 42 ct. HS 33 v Kent (Canterbury) 1978. BB 9–51 Somerset v Sussex (Hove) 1972.

A distinctly lively opening bowler who came back after the injury which had kept him out for most of the previous summer.

JONES, Alan Lewis, b Alltwen 1 June 57. LHB. GLAMORGAN – uncapped. F-c career: 32 matches; 987 runs (av 18.27); 8 ct. HS 57 v Oxford U. (Oxford) 1976.

Remains one of Glamorgan's best prospects as a batsman, but the time is now right for him to translate that promise into runs.

JONES, Barry John Richardson, b Shrewsbury, Shropshire 2 Nov 55. LHB, occ RM. WORCESTERSHIRE – uncapped. F-c career: 30 matches; 675 runs (av 13.77); 17 ct. HS 65 v Warwicks (Birmingham) 1977.

Left-handed opener who failed to make the most of his opportunities.

JONES, Eifion Wyn, b Velindre 25 Jun 42. Brother of A. Jones. RHB, WK. GLAMORGAN cap 1967. F-c career: 309 matches; 6,752 runs (av 18.75), 2 hundreds; 652 ct, 73 st. HS 146* v Sussex (Hove) 1968.

Has never really received full recognition for his wicket-keeping, which has been of a consistently high standard for many years. A useful person to have in the lower order, especially during a crisis.

KALLICHARRAN, Alvin Isaac, b Port Mourant, Berbice, B.G. 21 Mar 49. LHB, occ LB. WARWICKSHIRE cap 1972. 45 West Indies caps 1972–78 (3 as captain), scoring 3,331 runs (av 48.27) with 10 hundreds, including two in his first two innings, HS 158, and taking 1 wkt (av 73.00), BB 1–7. F-c career 238 matches, 15,102 runs (av 42.30), 35 hundreds; 21 wkts (av 46.52) 165 ct. HS 197 Guyana v Jamaica (Kingston) 1973–74. BB 4–48 v Derbys (Birmingham) 1978.

Sparkling strokemaker from the Caribbean who has certainly proved himself a fine acquisition, both in the runs he has scored and the manner in which they have been made. Can bowl a useful leg-break, but length and line unreliable.

Eventually decided not to join WSC and has been rewarded by being appointed captain of West Indies. What happens when the large Caribbean Packer contingent returns makes an interesting question to be answered this summer.

KEMP, Nicholas John, b Bromley 16 Dec 56. RHB, RFM. KENT – uncapped. F-c career: 6 matches; 24 runs (av 6.00); 3 wkts (av 46.33); 1 ct. HS 14 v Lancs (Tunbridge Wells) 1977. BB 3–83 v Pakistanis (Canterbury) 1978.

KENNEDY, Andrew, b Blackburn 4 Nov 49. LHB, RM. LANCASHIRE cap 1975. F-c career: 86 matches; 683 runs (av 29.00), 4 hundreds; 2 wkts (av 29.50); 61 ct. HS 176* v Leics (Leicester) 1976. BB 2–29 v Cambridge U. (Cambridge) 1978.

After two disappointing seasons, this watchful lefthander found something approaching his true form as a sound county batsman.

Mervyn Kitchen of Somerset.

KIRSTEN, Peter Noel, b Pietermaritzburg, South Africa, 14 May 55. RHB, OB. DERBY-SHIRE cap 1978. F-c career: 62 matches; 4,077 runs (av 40.36), 12 hundreds; 23 wkts (av 32.73); 43 ct. HS 206* v Glam (Chesterfield) 1978. BB 4–51 v Notts (Derby) 1978.

Despite needing time to adjust to English conditions, this aggressive South African was able to top 1,000 runs in the Championship and gave evidence of his class with a double century against Glamorgan.

KITCHEN, Mervyn John, b Nailsea 1 Aug 40. LHB, occ RM. SOMERSET cap 1966. F-c career: 347 matches; 15,084 runs (av 26.46), 17 hundreds; 2 wkts (av 54.50); 149 ct. HS 189 v Pakistanis (Taunton) 1967. BB 1–4.

Powerful middle-order lefthander who is at his best in an attacking role.

KNIGHT, Roger David Verdon, b Streatham, Surrey 6 Sep 46. LHB, RM. SURREY cap 1978. Captain since 1978. Played for Surrey 1968–70, for Gloucestershire 1971–75 (cap 1971), and for Sussex 1976–77 (cap 1976). F-c career: 246 matches; 12,666 runs (av 31.04), 19 hundreds; 231 wkts (av 36.15); 184 ct. HS 165* Sussex v Middx (Hove) 1976. BB 6–44 Glos v Northants

Roger Knight, Surrey's captain.

(Northampton) 1974.

A fine all-round cricketer: strong front-foot driver and a useful seam bowler who tends to move the ball into the bat.

KNOTT, Alan Philip Eric, b Belvedere 9 Apr 46. RHB, WK. KENT cap 1965. 89 England caps 1967–77, scoring 4,175 runs (av 33.66), with 5 hundreds, HS 135, and making 252 dismissals – world Test record (233 ct, 19 st). F-c career: 379 matches; 14,000 runs (av 30.56), 16 hundreds; 1,032 dismissals (928 ct, 104 st); 1 wkt (av 77.00). HS 156 MCC v South Zone (Bangalore) 1972–73. BB 1–40.

Follows the tradition of those great Kent wicket-keepers of the past, Leslie Ames and Godfrey Evans. Exceptionally agile and nimble, he has already established himself as one of the great wicket-keepers of all time. His remarkable powers of concentration enable him to be as brilliant in the closing session of a long, hot, frustrating day as at the start. In addition to his value as a wicket-keeper, he is also a highly proficient, and on occasions dashing, batsman who has many outstanding innings to his credit when runs were really wanted for both Kent and England. Knott is the equivalent of another top-class all-rounder, for he is certainly worth his place in any county side for his batting alone. Did not play for Kent in 1978 because of his contract with WSC and the presence of Downton. Expects to be available for certain matches this summer.

LAMB, Allan Joseph, b Langebaanweg, Cape Town, South Africa, 20 Jun 54. RHB, occ RM. NORTHAMPTONSHIRE cap 1978. F-c career: 44 matches; 2,446 runs (av 40.76), 5 hundreds; 2 wkts (av 6.50); 32 ct. HS 109 Western Province v Rhodesia (Bulawayo) 1976–77. BB 1–1 v Derbys (Derby) 1978.

Newcomer who played some outstanding innings, including two hundreds. Came close to 1,000 runs for the season, in spite of a period sidelined because of injury, and topped the county's Championship averages.

LAMB, Timothy Michael, b Hartford, Cheshire 24 Mar 53. RHB, RM. NORTHAMPTONSHIRE cap 1978. Played for Middlesex 1974–77. F-c career: 73 matches; 761 runs (av 13.58); 171 wkts (av 27.89); 21 ct. HS 77 Middx v Notts (Lord's) 1976. BB 6–49 Middx v Surrey (Lord's) 1975.

Former Oxford Blue who, after several seasons with Middlesex, joined Northants and opened their attack with reasonable success. Great trier but lacks that extra yard or so of pace.

LARKINS, Wayne, b Roston, Beds 22 Nov 53. RHB, occ RM. NORTHAMPTONSHIRE cap 1976. F-c career: 103 matches; 3,843 runs (av 24.79), 8 hundreds; 16 wkts (av 34.62); 51 ct. HS 170* v Worcs (Northampton) 1978. BB

3–34 v Somerset (Northampton) 1976.

One of the best young batsmen in the country and rather unlucky not to go to Australia. A natural strokemaker with a wide range of handsome strokes, he had his best season for Northants; if he continues to bat in this fashion he should be in the England XI within 12 months, where he would be the most spectacular opener since that former Northamptonshire player, Colin Milburn.

LEADBEATER, Barrie, b Harehills 14 Aug 43. RHB, occ RM. YORKSHIRE cap 1969. F-c career: 145 matches; 5,307 runs (av 25.39), 1 hundred; 1 wkt (av 5.00); 82 ct. HS 140* v Hants (Portsmouth) 1976. BB 1–1.

Defensively correct opening batsman who frequently finds himself in the middle-order. Has never really fulfilled his early promise.

LEE, Peter Granville, b Arthingworth, Northants 27 Aug 45. RHB, RFM. LANCASHIRE cap 1972. Played for Northants 1967–71. F-c career: 163 matches; 647 runs (av 8.51); 531 wkts (av 24.49); 28 ct. HS 26 Northants v Glos (Northampton) 1969. BB 8–53 v Sussex (Hove) 1973.

A very good fast-medium bowler and among the most successful in the country, twice taking over 100 wickets in a season. Out of action through injury last summer.

LEVER, John Kenneth, b Ilford 24 Feb 49. RHB, LFM. ESSEX cap 1970. 13 England caps 1976–78, scoring 199 runs (av 12.43). HS 53 – on debut, and taking 44 wkts (av 24.04), BB 7–46 – on debut – the best analysis by an England bowler in his first Test innings. F-c career: 284 matches; 1,848 runs (av 10.93); 831 wkts (av 23.83); 125 ct. HS 91 v Glam (Cardiff) 1970. BB 8–127 v Glos (Cheltenham) 1976.

A well-above-average left-arm opening bowler who had to wait rather a long time before being capped by England and celebrated the event with the best-ever performance by anyone making a Test debut for England. Has a good build, pleasing approach, and a splendid body action, which enables him to move the ball in the air. Has a great record in the John Player League. Top class outfielder and useful tailender.

LILLEY, Alan William, b Ilford 8 May 59. RHB, WK. ESSEX – uncapped. F-c career: 1 match; 122 runs (av 122.00), 1 hundred; 0 ct. HS 100* v Notts (Nottingham) 1978 – on debut.

A natural; has the shots and a sound technique, while a century on his first-class debut suggests a good temperament. Clearly a name to watch out for.

LISTER, John Wilton, b Darlington, Co. Durham, 1 April 59. RHB, occ RM. DERBY-

SHIRE uncapped. F-c career: 3 matches; 137 runs (av 22.83); 1 ct. HS 48 v Warwicks (Birmingham) 1978.

Young opening batsman whose 48 against Warwickshire was decidedly encouraging.

LLEWELLYN, Michael John, b Clydach 27 Nov 53, LHB, OB. GLAMORGAN cap 1977. F-c career: 103 matches; 3,477 runs (av 23.81), 2 hundreds; 23 wkts (av 26.73); 70 ct. HS 129* v Oxford U. (Oxford) 1977. BB 4-35 v Oxford U. (Oxford) 1970 – on debut.

A most attractive lefthander who hits the ball exceptionally hard. Although he had another successful season, he might well score more runs if he was less impetuous. Too often gives his wicket away when looking set for a three-figure score.

LLOYD, Barry John, b Neath 6 Sep 53. RHB, OB. GLAMORGAN – uncapped. F-c career: 58 matches; 503 runs (av 9.86); 81 wkts (av 43.92); 31 ct. HS 45* and BB 4-49 v Hants (Portsmouth) 1973.

Still learning his difficult trade as an off-spinner and finding it rather too expensive.

LLOYD, Clive Hubert, b Georgetown, British Guyana 31 Aug 44. LHB. RM. LANCASHIRE cap 1969. 65 West Indies caps 1966-78 (29 as captain), scoring 4,594 runs (av 43.75) with 11 hundreds, HS 242*, and taking 10 wkts (av 62.10), BB 2-13. Also 5 unofficial Tests for Rest of the World 1970, scoring 400 runs (av 50.00) with 2 hundreds, and taking 6 wkts (av 20.00). F-c career 325 matches; 21,521 runs (av 49.93), 57 hundreds; 114 wkts (av 35.99); 236 ct. HS 242* West Indies v India (Bombay) 1974-75. BB 4-48 v Leics (Manchester) 1970.

Superb West Indian strokemaker who has the ability to win matches with his aggressive batting; is especially valuable in limited-overs cricket. Liable to be diffident at the start of an innings, but once established he invariably takes the initiative away from the bowlers. He is a world-class performer and a natural entertainer, the type of batsman spectators love, because he hits the ball so hard and so often. Useful medium-pace change bowler and one of the most exciting, brilliant fieldsmen the game has produced. Captained West Indies until he walked out with the other WSC players after a dispute with the West Indies Board during the series against a 'Packerless' Australia.

LLOYD, David, b Accrington 18 Mar 47. LHB, SLA. LANCASHIRE cap 1968. Captain 1973-77. 9 England caps 1974-75, scoring 552 runs (av 42.46) with 1 hundred, HS 214*. F-c career: 312 matches; 14,364 runs (av 32.27), 24 hundreds; 160 wkts (av 29.41); 278 ct. HS 214* England v India (Birmingham) 1974. BB 7-38 v Glos (Lydney) 1966.

A competent, above-average county player

with a sound technique and a pleasing stance. He possesses some attractive strokes, especially off the front foot; is not afraid to use his feet against the spinners; and has an admirable temperament. Also useful slow left-arm spinner.

LLOYD, Timothy **Andrew,** b Oswestry, Shropshire 5 Nov 56. LHB, occ RM. WARWICKSHIRE – uncapped. F-c career: 17 matches; 648 runs (av 29.45); 1 wkt (av 35.00); 15 ct. HS 93 v Worcs (Birmingham) 1978. BB 1-14.

Young lefthander who improved considerably and looks to have the ability to become a good county batsman.

LONG, Arnold, b Cheam 18 Dec 40. LHB, WK. SUSSEX cap 1976. Captain since 1978. Played for Surrey 1960-75 (cap 1962). F-c career: 420 matches; 6,436 runs (av 16.54); 856 ct, 117 st. HS 92 Surrey v Leics (Leicester) 1970. Held 11 catches in match Surrey v Sussex (Hove) 1964 to set world f-c record – equalled by R. W. Marsh for Western Australia in 1975-76.

Chirpy little wicket-keeper whose unspectacular but efficient handling of a vital job did not always receive the praise it deserved. Useful lower-order batsman. Taking over from Greig as captain he did a remarkably good job. The winning of the Gillette Cup was in no small way due to the way he got his players to perform as a team.

LOVE, James Derek, b Leeds 22 Apr 55. RHB. YORKSHIRE – uncapped. F-c career: 47 matches; 1,892 runs (av 28.23), 3 hundreds; 28 ct. HS 163 v Notts (Bradford) 1976.

A good young batsman in the best Yorkshire tradition but failed to score enough runs. This may have been due to a lack of confidence, because there is certainly no lack of ability.

LUMB, Richard Graham, b Doncaster 27 Feb 50. RHB. YORKSHIRE cap 1974. F-c career: 144 matches; 6,623 runs (av 29.83), 11 hundreds; 95 ct. HS 132 v Glos (Leeds) 1976.

Sound, competent county batsman who can be relied on to play some good innings and to average around 29.

LYNCH, Monte Alan, b Georgetown, British Guyana 21 May 58, RHB, occ RM/OB. SURREY – uncapped. F-c career: 19 matches; 621 runs (av 18.26), 1 hundred; 2 wkts (av 29.50); 7 ct. HS 101 v Pakistanis (Oval) 1978. BB 1-14.

Young batsman who is close to establishing himself in the 1st XI.

LYON, John, b St Helens 17 May 51, RHB, WK. LANCASHIRE cap 1975. F-c career: 65 matches; 703 runs (av 11.91); 129 ct, 10 st. HS 74* v Notts (Manchester) 1978.

Neat little wicket-keeper who impressed

Yorkshire's Richard Lumb: much promise in need of realisation.

some very good judges with his ability. Also a useful member of the lower order.

McEVOY, Michael Stephen Anthony, b Jorhat, India 25 Jan 56. RHB, RM. ESSEX – uncapped. F-c career: 9 matches; 296 runs (av 22.76); 0 wkts; 7 ct. HS 67* v Yorks (Middlesbrough) 1977.

Promising young batsman who did not make as much progress as had been hoped in 1978.

McEWAN, Kenneth Scott, b Bedford, South Africa 16 Jul 52. RHB, occ WK, ESSEX cap 1974. F-c career: 166 matches; 9,918 runs (av 37.85), 24 hundreds; 2 wkts (av 43.50); 175 ct, 7 st. HS 218 v Sussex (Chelmsford) 1977. BB 1–0 (with his second ball in f-c cricket).

Has strokes, class, and timing – and so inevitably scores heavily for his adopted county. Rather oddly had a disappointing season in South African cricket but was immediately among the runs when he rejoined Essex, for whom he topped the averages and hit four centuries. Although a surprising number of insipid attacks could be found among the counties, it should be noted that he consistently outscored both Fletcher and Gooch and was far more spectacular.

MACK, Andrew James, b Aylsham, Norfolk, 14 Jan 56. LHB, LFM. GLAMORGAN – uncapped. Played for Surrey 1976–77. F-c career:

15 matches; 50 runs (av 4.54); 23 wkts (av 41.52); 2 ct. HS 16 Surrey v Somerset (Westons-s-Mare) 1977. BB 4–28 v Worcs (Worcester) 1978.

Left-arm seamer from Surrey who, in his three county matches, indicated he might prove useful.

MACKINTOSH, Kevin Scott, b Surbiton, Surrey, 30 Aug 57. RHB, RM. NOTTINGHAMSHIRE – uncapped. F-c career: 14 matches; 124 runs (av 13.77); 16 wkts (av 43.31); 6 ct. HS 23* v Essex (Nottingham) 1978. BB 4–49 v Surrey (Oval) 1978.

Apprentice all-rounder.

McLELLAN, Alan James, b Ashton-under-Lyne, Lancs, 2 Sep 58. RHB, WK. DERBYSHIRE – uncapped. F-c career: 14 matches; 27 runs (av 3.00); 17 ct, 0 st. HS 11* v Surrey (Ilkeston) 1978.

Reserve wicket-keeper.

MALONE, Steven John, b Chelmsford 19 Oct 53. RHB, RFM. ESSEX – uncapped. F-c career: 2 matches; has not batted; 2 wkts (av 50.50); 0 ct. BB 1–28 v Cambridge U. (Cambridge) 1978.

Lively, but somewhat erratic, pace bowler.

MARKS, Victor James, b Middle Chinnock 25 Jun 55 RHB, OB. SOMERSET – uncapped. F-c career: 66 matches; 2,814 runs (av 26.54), 1 hundred; 119 wkts (av 34.21); 30 ct. HS 105 Oxford U. v Worcs (Oxford) 1976. BB 5–50 v Surrey (Weston-s-Mare) 1977.

An attractive batsman and much better bowler than many realise, he is one of those players likely to produce better figures than many others with more basic ability. Bowled well for his University and county, even if his wickets were at times expensive.

MARSHALL, Roger Philip Twells, b Horsham 28 Feb 52. RHB, LFM. SUSSEX – uncapped. F-c career: 24 matches; 315 runs (av 14.31); 49 wkts (av 39.32); 6 ct. HS 37 v Notts (Nottingham) 1975. BB 4–37 v Glam (Hove) 1973.

Left-arm seamer who needs to learn how to 'run the ball in' to a righthander.

MAYNARD, Christopher, b Haslemere, Surrey, 8 Apr 58. P.HB, WK. WARWICKSHIRE – uncapped. F-c career: 3 matches; 17 runs (av 8.50); 4 ct, 0 st. HS 9.

Reserve wicket-keeper.

MELLOR, Alan John, b Burton upon Trent, Staffs, 4 Jul 59. RHB, SLA. DERBYSHIRE – uncapped. F-c career: 5 matches; 19 runs (av 3.80); 9 wkts (av 33.88); 0 ct. HS 10* v Essex (Southend) 1978. BB 5–52 v Kent (Maidstone) 1978 – on debut.

Slow left-arm spinner of real promise, as he demonstrated with his five-wicket debut.

MENDIS, Gehan Dixon, b Colombo, Ceylon 24 Apr 55. RHB, WK. SUSSEX – uncapped. F-c career: 39 matches; 1,688 runs (av 27.22); 3 hundreds; 23 ct, 1 st. HS 128 v Essex (Hove) 1978.

Established himself as the regular opener with a series of sound and attractive displays which suggest he is destined for a long and successful career in county cricket.

MILLER, Geoffrey, b Chesterfield 8 Sep 52. RHB, OB. DERBYSHIRE cap 1976. 14 England caps 1976–78, scoring 398 runs (av 26.53). HS 98*, and taking 17 wkts (av 38.47), BB 3–99. F-c career: 126 matches; 4,051 runs (av 24.55); 326 wkts (av 22.97); 73 ct. HS 98* England v Pakistan (Lahore) 1977–78. BB 7–54 v Sussex (Hove) 1977.

Talented all-rounder: off-spinner; correct batsman with a fine defence; excellent field. Rather fortunate to have gained a regular place in the England side in 1978, in terms of his own performance, but the faith of the selectors could well be justified in Australia. Clearly destined for a long and successful career in both international and county cricket.

MOSELEY, Hallam Reynold, b Christchurch, Barbados 28 May 48. RHB, RFM. SOMERSET

cap 1972. F-c career: 150 matches; 1,178 runs (av 12.27); 402 wkts (av 24.13); 57 ct. HS 67 v Leics (Taunton) 1972. BB 6–34 v Derby (Bath) 1975.

Lively West Indian pace bowler who can be quite sharp. A hard, if somewhat erratic, hitter.

MOULDING, Roger Peter, b Enfield 3 Jan 58. RHB, LB. MIDDLESEX – uncapped. F-c career: 9 matches; 302 runs (av 33.55); 5 ct. HS 77* Oxford U. v Worcs (Worcester) 1978.

Apprentice batsman who topped his University's (Oxford) averages in 1978.

NASH, Malcolm Andrew, b Abergavenny, Monmouths 9 May 45. LHB, LM, SLA. GLAMORGAN cap 1969. F-c career: 265 matches; 6,137 runs (av 19.00), 2 hundreds; 790 wkts (av 25.44); 111 ct. HS 130 v Surrey (Oval) 1976 – in 119 minutes before lunch. BB 9–56 v Hants (Basingstoke) 1975.

The value to Glamorgan of this all-rounder is considerable. In addition to being a discon-certing medium-pace bowler who swings the ball very late, he also bowls cutters at a reduced pace. He is a naturally aggressive left-handed bat with enormous enthusiasm for vast sixes. Just the person to swing a match by a fierce assault.

NEALE, Phillip Anthony, b Scunthorpe, Lincs 5 Jun 54. RHB, occ RM. WORCESTERSHIRE cap 1978. F-c career: 58 matches; 2,796 runs (av 29.74), 3 hundreds; 1 wkt (av 61.00); 29 ct. HS 143 v West Indians (Worcester) 1976. BB 1–15.

Sound player who enjoyed his best season and is likely to become one of the main pillars of Worcestershire batting. Brilliant cover, as befits a natural athlete. Is also a professional footballer.

NEEDHAM, Andrew, b Calow, Derbyshire 23 Mar 57. RHB, OB. SURREY – uncapped. F-c career: 12 matches; 81 runs (av 7.36); 9 wkts (av 49.00); 3 ct. HS 21 v Sussex (Hove) 1978. BB 3–25 v Oxford U. (Oxford) 1977.

Young all-rounder yet to establish himself in the county XI.

NICHOLAS, Mark Charles Jefford, b London 29 Sep 57. RHB, occ RFM. HAMPSHIRE – uncapped. F-c career: 3 matches; 77 runs (av 25.66); 2 ct. HS 40* v Oxford U. (Oxford) 1978 – on debut.

Promising young batsman.

NICHOLLS, David, b East Dereham, Norfolk 8 Dec 43. LHB, WK, occ LB. KENT cap 1969. F-c career: 202 matches; 7,072 runs (av 22.23); 2 hundreds; 339 dismissals (326 ct, 13 st); 2 wkts (av 11.50). HS 211 v Derbys (Folkestone) 1963. BB 1–0.

Chunky left-hand bat who hits the ball hard and is at his best opening, for he is particularly partial to seam bowling. Cuts well and is strong off the back foot. Useful reserve wicket-keeper.

OLD, Christopher Middleton, b Middlesbrough 22 Dec 48. LHB, RFM. YORKSHIRE cap 1969. 40 England caps 1972–78, scoring 722 runs (av 14.15), HS 65, and taking 125 wkts (av 28.08), BB 7–50. F-c career: 242 matches; 5,582 runs (av 22.41), 6 hundreds; 698 wkts (av 21.89); 152 ct. Scored 100 in 37 minutes (second-fastest in all f-c cricket) v Warwicks (Birmingham) 1977. HS 116 v Indians (Bradford) 1974. BB 7–20 v Glos (Middlesbrough) 1969.

Tall fast bowler with a straightforward style who bangs the ball down enthusiastically, moving it away in the air, and can extract life from even the deadest of pitches. One advantage he enjoys over most of his seam bowling rivals for a place in the England side is that, at county level, he comes into the all-rounder category. Is an impressive driver, but has certain difficulty in negotiating the bouncer. Looks sounder going for his strokes, possibly because he appears fallible when playing defensively on the back foot. Fine fielder and has shown great determination in the way he has overcome a serious knee injury.

OLDHAM, Stephen, b Sheffield 26 Jul 48. RHB, RM. YORKSHIRE – uncapped. F-c career: 36 matches; 66 runs (av 5.50); 86 wkts (av 26.05); 10 ct. HS 19 v Middx (Bradford) 1976. BB 5–40 v Surrey (Oval) 1978.

A sound, dependable seamer with a League

background. Gives little away, utilises a helpful pitch, but is a shade short of pace for an easy wicket.

OLIVE, Martin, b Watford, Herts 18 Apr 58. RHB, RM. SOMERSET – uncapped. F-c career: 4 matches; 28 runs (av 4.66); 4 ct. HS 15 v Leics (Leicester) 1977.

Young apprentice batsman.

OLIVER, Philip Robert, b West Bromwich, Staffs 9 May 56. RHB, RM. WARWICKSHIRE – uncapped. F-c career: 36 matches; 816 runs (av 18.13); 11 wkts (av 102.27); 17 ct. HS 59 v Glam (Swansea) 1975 – on debut. BB 2–28 v Sussex (Birmingham) 1978.

Failed to capitalise on his potential in the three-day game but could be of value in limited-overs matches.

ONTONG, Rodney Craig, b Johannesburg, South Africa 9 Sep 55. RHB, RFM. GLAMORGAN – uncapped. F-c career: 72 matches; 2,480 runs (av 23.17), 3 hundreds; 138 wkts (av 31.05); 35 ct. HS 116* v Essex (Cardiff) 1978. BB 7–60 Border v N. Transvaal (Pretoria) 1975–76.

Hard-hitting, somewhat unconventional batsman; useful lively seam bowler and somewhat erratic off-cutter. A very enthusiastic cricketer and a natural competitor who proved a considerable asset to Glamorgan.

ORMROD, Joseph Alan, b Ramsbottom, Lancs 22 Dec 42. RHB, occ OB. WORCESTERSHIRE cap 1966. F-c career: 380 matches; 17,104

Steve Oldham, one of Yorkshire's band of steady seamers.

Rodney Ontong of Glamorgan.

runs (av 30.32), 22 hundreds; 25 wkts (av 43.00); 336 ct. HS 204* v Kent (Dartford) 1973. BB 5–27 v Glos (Bristol) 1972.

Correct, good-looking batsman with the ability to hit with a straight bat off his back foot. Always appears to have plenty of time and enjoyed another successful season. A good county player.

PARKER, Paul William Giles, b Bulawayo, Rhodesia 15 Jan 56. RHB, RM. SUSSEX – uncapped. F-c career: 60 matches; 2,993 runs (av 31.50), 5 hundreds; 7 wkts (av 43.28); 30 ct. HS 215 Cambridge U. v Essex (Cambridge) 1976 – in his third f-c match. BB 2–23 Cambridge U. v Essex (Cambridge) 1978.

Neat, correct, quick between the wickets with a pleasing style. Possesses an excellent temperament, as shown by the number of crucial innings he produced for Sussex in the Gillette Cup, and also has the concentration needed to put together a large score. Excellent fielder, fine Rugby player, and a likely future Sussex captain. Must be a serious candidate for international honours within a couple of years if he continues to improve.

PARSONS, Gordon James, b Slough, Bucks, 17 Oct 59. LHB, RFM. LEICESTERSHIRE – uncapped. F-c career: 2 matches; 10 runs (av 5.00); 0 wkts, 0 ct. HS 7.

One for the future. Talented young all-rounder who represented England Under 19 against West Indies.

PARTRIDGE, Martin David, b Stroud 25 Oct 54. LHB, RM. GLOUCESTERSHIRE – uncapped. F-c career: 12 matches; 199 runs (av 16.58); 9 wkts (av 48.00); 4 ct. HS 50 v Worcs (Bristol) 1978. BB 2–9 v Worcs (Worcester) 1977.

All-rounder who made several appearances for Gloucestershire last summer without making a real impression.

PATEL, Ashok Sitaram, b Nairobi, Kenya 23 Sep 56. LHB, SLA. MIDDLESEX – uncapped. F-c career: 2 matches; 56 runs (av 28.00); 2 wkts (av 27.50); 1 ct. HS 25* v Glos (Bristol) 1978 – on debut. BB 2–55 v Sussex (Hove) 1978.

Slow left-armer and batsman of considerable promise who might well have had more opportunities with a weaker county.

PATEL, Dipak Narshibhai, b Nairobi, Kenya 25 Oct 58. RHB, OB. WORCESTERSHIRE – uncapped. F-c career: 54 matches; 1,407 runs (av 18.76), 3 hundreds; 43 wkts (av 34.13); 25 ct. HS 107 v Surrey (Worcester) 1976. BB 5–22 v Sussex (Eastbourne) 1978.

Still young and therefore has the time, as well as the ability, to become an outstanding all-rounder in the next few years. At the moment a vital member of his county team, picking up wickets with his off-breaks and scoring runs, though possibly not quite as many as he should, in the middle order.

PAYNE, Ian Roger, b Lambeth 9 May 58. RHB, RFM. SURREY – uncapped. F-c career: 12 matches; 96 runs (av 6.85); 3 wkts (av 108.33); 10 ct. HS 29 v Kent (Oval) 1977. BB 2–41 v Cambridge U. (Cambridge) 1978.

Apprentice all-rounder.

PERRYMAN, Stephen Peter, b Birmingham 22 Oct 55. RHB, RM. WARWICKSHIRE cap 1977. F-c career: 84 matches; 563 runs (av 10.62); 213 wkts (av 27.35); 30 ct. HS 43 v Somerset (Birmingham) 1977. BB 7–49 v Hants (Bournemouth) 1978.

Good county seam bowler who moves the ball a little either way. Found his wickets harder to come by and more expensive.

PHILLIP, Norbert, b Bioche, Dominica, 12 June 48. RHB, RFM. ESSEX cap 1978. 3 West Indies caps 1978, scoring 120 runs (av 24.00), HS 46, and taking 9 wkts (av 43.44), BB 4–75. F-c career: 70 matches; 2,710 runs (av 28.63), 1 hundred; 222 wkts (av 22.97); 22 ct. HS 134 v Glos (Gloucester) 1978. BB 6–33 v Pakistanis (Chelmsford) 1978 – on Essex debut.

Ideal replacement for Keith Boyce. Another West Indian who bowls fast, hits hard, and fields well. A match-winner and an entertainer.

PHILLIPSON, Christopher Paul, b Brindaban, India 10 Feb 52. RHB, RM. SUSSEX – uncapped. F-c career: 82 matches; 1,103 runs (av 16.46); 131 wkts (av 34.51); 39 ct. HS 70 v Oxford U. (Oxford) 1978. BB 6–56 v Notts (Hove) 1972.

Has developed from a 'run of the mill' seamer into a useful, somewhat unorthodox batsman in the middle order whose determination compensates for a certain lack of style. Came to the rescue on many occasions.

PIGOTT, Anthony Charles Shackleton, b London 4 Jun 58. RHB, RFM. SUSSEX –uncapped. F-c career: 6 matches; 33 runs (av 5.50); 9 wkts (av 34.00), 1 hat-trick; 1 ct. F-c HS 11 v Kent (Hove) 1978. BB 4–62 v Middx (Hove) 1978.

Young seamer, inclined to be rather erratic; performed the hat-trick when claiming his first three wickets in first-class cricket.

PILLING, Harry, b Ashton-under-Lyne 23 Feb 43. RHB, occ OB. LANCASHIRE cap 1965. Is the shortest (5ft 3in) current British f-c cricketer. F-c career: 329 matches; 15,199 runs (av 32.40), 25 hundreds; 1 wkt (av 195.00); 88 ct. HS 149* v Glam (Liverpool) 1976. BB 1–42.

Diminutive early-order batsman who, like so many little men, is an extremely effective cutter. Has the ability to improvise, which makes him more valuable in limited-overs cricket than many big hitters.

POCOCK, Nicholas Edward Julian, b Maracaibo, Venezuela 15 Dec 51. RHB, LM. HAMPSHIRE – uncapped. F-c career: 15 matches; 445 runs (av 20.22); 1 wkt (av 73.00); 10 ct. HS 68 and BB 1–40 v Leics (Bournemouth) 1976 – on debut.

A disappointing summer; is still unable to command a place in what was not all that strong a county side.

POCOCK, Patrick Ian, b Bangor, Caernarvons 24 Sep 46. RHB, OB. SURREY cap 1967. 17 England caps 1968–76, scoring 165 runs (av 6.60), HS 33, and taking 47 wkts (av 43.04), BB 6–79. F-c career: 388 matches; 3,907 runs (av 11.69); 1,187 wkts (av 25.76), 2 hat-tricks; 135 ct. HS 75* v Notts (Oval) 1968. BB 7–57 v Essex (Romford) 1968. Took 7 wkts in 11 balls (incl. 4 in 4, 5 in 6, and 6 in 9) v Sussex (Eastbourne) 1972.

Fine off-break bowler with a deceptive dipping flight. A thoughtful, attacking bowler who gives the ball a considerable tweak, he is prepared to experiment rather more than the average English off-spinner. A rather awkward-looking tailender, he nonetheless makes some useful scores when he gets his head down.

PONT, Keith Rupert, b Wanstead 16 Jan 53. RHB, occ RM. ESSEX cap 1976. F-c career:

101 matches; 3,324 runs (av 24.08), 5 hundreds; 47 wkts (av 34.59); 56 ct. HS 113 v Warwicks (Birmingham) 1973. BB 4–100 v Middlesex (Southend) 1977.

Young all-rounder who is steadily improving. A natural attacking batsman, useful seam bowler, and good fielder. Ideally suited to the needs of limited-overs cricket.

POULTER, Stephen John, b Hornsey 9 Sep 56. RHB. MIDDLESEX – uncapped. F-c career: 3 matches; 47 runs (av 15.66); 0 ct. HS 36 v Notts (Nottingham) 1978 – on debut.

Promising young batsman who could be competing for a regular first team spot this summer.

PRIDGEON, Alan Paul, b Wall Heath, Staffs 22 Feb 54. RHB, RM. WORCESTERSHIRE – uncapped. F-c career: 70 matches; 277 runs (av 7.10); 134 wkts (av 38.29); 20 ct. HS 32 v Yorks (Middlesbrough) 1978. BB 7–35 v Oxford U. (Oxford) 1976.

With Holder absent, he was called on to do more seam bowling and responded with much improved figures, becoming the leading wicket-taker for his county. Showed greater control of line and length.

PRINGLE, Derek Raymond, b Nairobi, Kenya, 18 Sep 58. Son of Donald Pringle (East Africa). RHB, RM. ESSEX – uncapped. F-c career: 4 matches; 60 runs (av 15.00); 1 wkt (av 101.00); 1 ct. HS 50* and BB 1–31 v Cambridge U. (Cambridge) 1978 – on debut.

Big young all-rounder who could develop into an outstanding batsman and useful support seamer.

PROCTER, Michael John, b Durban, South Africa 15 Sep 46. RHB, RF. GLOUCESTERSHIRE cap 1968. Captain since 1977. 7 South Africa caps 1967–70, scoring 226 runs (av 25.11), HS 48, and taking 41 wkts (av 15.02), BB 6–73. Also 5 unofficial Tests for Rest of the World 1970, scoring 292 runs (av 48.66), HS 62, and taking 15 wkts (av 23.93). F-c career: 316 matches; 17,997 runs (av 37.41), 42 hundreds; 1,132 wkts (av 19.22), 2 hat-tricks; 266 ct. Scored hundreds in six successive innings 1970–71 to equal world record. HS 254 Rhodesia v Western Province (Salisbury) 1970–71. BB 9–71 Rhodesia v Transvaal (Bulawayo) 1972–73.

Still a world-class all-rounder, and appears to have completely recovered from a serious injury which threatened to end his career as a fast bowler. Bowls his very quick inswingers and off-breaks off the wrong foot with a very open-chested action. Just as well no purist coach tried to change him early on! Another wonderful season with both bat and ball shows that he is still one of the finest all-rounders in the world and would walk into most Test teams as either a batsman or a bowler. There must be some doubt that this would apply to Rice, Botham, or even Imran Khan. In addition he captained Gloucestershire splendidly and their lack of success is no reflection on his efforts. Has signed for WSC.

RADLEY, Clive Thornton, b Hertford, Herts 13 May 44. RHB, occ LB. MIDDLESEX cap 1967. 8 England caps 1978, scoring 481 runs (av 48.10) with 2 hundreds, HS 158. F-c career: 352 matches; 17,038 runs (av 34.63), 28 hundreds; 2 wkts (av 12.00); 358 ct. HS 171 v Cambridge U. (Cambridge) 1976. BB 1–7.

Has always been one of the most consistent run accumulators in the country. Called into international cricket late in his career he continued to score well at this level. Effective, rather than attractive, he uses plenty of right hand, cuts well, and is especially strong off his legs. However, he looks suspect against the fast lifting ball. Excellent temperament, natural fighter, and fine field.

RANDALL, Derek William, b Retford 24 Feb 51. RHB, occ RM. NOTTINGHAMSHIRE cap 1973. 16 England caps 1977–78, scoring 631 runs (av 26.29) with 1 hundred (174 in the Centenary Test). F-c career: 174 matches; 8,813 runs (av 32.40), 11 hundreds; 94 ct. HS 204* v Somerset (Nottingham) 1976.

Nottinghamshire's Derek Randall.

Bob Ratcliffe of Lancashire.

One of the best and most exciting English-born batsmen of the last decade. Although he produced a masterly century in the Centenary Test, it was noticeable that, unlike most great players, he moved around in his crease as the ball was about to be delivered; almost like a cat on hot bricks. This is probably why he has experienced several bad patches. Last summer he found his best form with Notts and was rewarded by selection for Australia, where his liking for faster pitches and more bounce should help him to be successful. One of the big attractions of his batting is that he will suddenly produce an impossibly impudent stroke to the surprise of the bowler and the delight of the spectator, but under the clowning there is both a wonderful eye and true ability. His athletic fielding in the covers is an enormous asset to any side and it would be no exaggeration to say that he often goes into bat with a bonus of 20 runs to his credit for those saved in the field.

RATCLIFFE, Robert Malcolm, b Accrington 29 Nov 51. RHB, RM. LANCASHIRE cap 1976. F-c career: 61 matches; 699 runs (av 14.56); 165 wkts (av 24.66); 20 ct. HS 48 v Middx (Lord's) 1978. BB 7–58 v Hants (Bournemouth) 1978.

A steady, accurate seamer whose pace is closer to medium than fast. He moves the ball considerably and achieves a surprising amount of lift for his pace.

REIDY, Bernard Wilfrid (sic), b Whalley 18 Sep 53. LHB, SLA. LANCASHIRE – uncapped. F-c career: 49 matches; 1,600 runs (av 25.80); 7 wkts (av 86.28); 27 ct. HS 88 and BB 2–47 v Worcs (Worcester) 1978.

Former England Young Cricketer who has still to establish himself in county cricket. He played several good innings for Lancashire last summer, but his slow left-arm bowling disappointed.

RICE, Clive Edward Butler, b Johannesburg, South Africa 23 Jul 49. RHB, RFM. NOTTINGHAMSHIRE cap 1975. F-c career: 163 matches; 8,692 runs (av 37.30), 10 hundreds; 398 wkts (av 23.81); 112 ct. HS 246 v Sussex (Hove) 1976. BB 7–62 Transvaal v W. Province (Johannesburg) 1975–76.

Outstanding all-rounder who would walk into any current Test XI. Exciting and prolific scorer of runs, he finished top of the national averages. Has all the shots, and there can be few better drivers off the front foot. Lively opening bowler and fine fieldsman. Lost the Notts' captaincy when he signed for WSC.

RICE, John Michael, b Chandler's Ford 23 Oct 49. RHB, RM. HAMPSHIRE cap 1975. F-c career: 102 matches; 2,577 runs (av 18.53); 195 wkts (av 31.69); 98 ct. HS 96* v Somerset (Weston-s-Mare) 1975. BB 7–48 v Worcs (Worcester) 1977.

Typical county all-rounder who picks up some useful wickets with his seam bowling and scores some useful runs in the lower middle order.

RICHARDS, Clifton James ('Jack'), b Penzance, Cornwall 10 Aug 58. RHB, WK. SURREY cap 1978. F-c career: 36 matches; 447 runs (av 14.90); 49 ct, 13 st. HS 50 v Notts (Oval) 1978.

Splendid young wicket-keeper who could go to the very top. Was especially impressive considering his comparative lack of experience taking the spinners. Is starting to put runs together with the bat.

RICHARDS, Gwyn, b Maesteg 29 Nov 51. RHB, OB. GLAMORGAN cap 1976. F-c career: 97 matches; 3,215 runs (av 23.63), 1 hundred; 39 wkts (av 53.66); 33 ct. HS 102* v Yorks (Middlesbrough) 1976. BB 5–55 v Somerset (Taunton) 1978.

Continued to bat in a way that suggested he should become one of the main run-getters for his county for years to come. He also picked up the occasional wicket.

RICHARDS, Ian Michael, b Stockton-on-Tees, Co. Durham 9 Dec 57. LHB, RM. NORTHAMPTONSHIRE – uncapped. F-c career: 12 matches; 155 runs (av 22.14); 7 wkts (av 25.14); 2 ct. HS 50 v Notts (Northampton) 1976. BB 4–57 v Warwicks (Birmingham) 1978.

Young left-hand bat who impressed in his appearances for the 1st XI and also picked up wickets. Could well command a regular place this summer. Exceptionally promising.

RICHARDS, Isaac Vivian Alexander, b St John's, Antigua 7 Mar 52. RHB, OB. SOMERSET cap 1974. 28 West Indies caps 1974–78, scoring 2,500 runs (av 55.55) with 8 hundreds, HS 291, and taking 4 wkts (av 58.75), BB 2–34. Set world record for most Test runs in a calendar year with 1,710 (av 90.00) in 11 Tests. F-c career: 171 matches; 13,065 runs (av 48.03), 35 hundreds; 59 wkts (av 39.94); 161 ct, 1 st. HS 291 West Indies v England (Oval) 1976. BB 3–15 v Surrey (Weston-s-Mare) 1977.

The finest strokemaker in the world. Has every shot in the book plus several of his own. Equally impressive off front and back foot against speed and spin. Hits the ball hard and yet possesses a most sound defence. A major innings by Richards is something to treasure and is liable to contain such jewels as a driven six over extra cover from a ball on the leg stump, or a good-length fast-medium delivery on the off stump sent scudding to the mid-on boundary off the back foot. Brilliant fielder and useful occasional bowler, seam or off-spin.

ROBINSON, Arthur Leslie ('Rocker'), b Brompton 17 Aug 46. LHB, LFM. YORKSHIRE cap 1976. F-c career: 84 matches; 365 runs (av 9.60); 196 wkts (av 25.13), 1 hat-trick; 46 ct. HS 30* v Glam (Cardiff) 1977 sharing in tenth wicket partnership of 144 with A. Sidebottom. BB 6–61 v Surrey (Oval) 1974.

Strongly built left-arm fast-medium bowler. Gives little away.

ROBINSON, Robert Timothy, b Sutton-in-Ashfield 21 Nov 58. RHB, RM, NOTTINGHAMSHIRE – uncapped. F-c career: 1 match; 36 runs (av 36.00); 1 ct. HS 27* v Lancs (Nottingham) 1978.

Apprentice batsman.

ROCK, David John, b Southsea 20 Apr 57. RHB. HAMPSHIRE – uncapped. F-c career: 21 matches; 754 runs (av 19.84), 2 hundreds; 0 wkts; 11 ct. HS 114 v Leics (Leicester) 1977.

A promising young batsman who experienced an unrewarding season; still has plenty of time to make the grade.

ROEBUCK, Peter Michael, b Oxford, Oxon 6 Mar 56. RHB, LB. SOMERSET cap 1978. F-c career: 69 matches; 2,880 runs (av 28.80); 4 hundreds; 38 wkts (av 45.65); 33 ct. HS 158 Cambridge U. v Oxford U. (Lord's) 1975. BB 6–50 Cambridge U. v Kent (Canterbury) 1977.

Cultured young batsman, despite a rather ungainly stance. Plays very straight with a pleasing backlift and follow-through; suggests he would do well overseas. Good temperament and sound defence. Could well be seriously challenging for a place in the England XI in the next few seasons.

ROOPE, Graham Richard James, b Fareham, Hants 12 Jul 46. RHB, RM. SURREY cap 1969 21 England caps 1973–78, scoring 860 runs (av 30.71), HS 77. F-c career: 321 matches; 15,713 runs (av 37.86), 23 hundreds; 212 wkts (av 37.63); 470 ct. 1 st. HS 171 v Yorks (Oval) 1971. BB 5–14 v West Indians (Oval) 1969.

Good county batsman who has missed out at the highest level somewhere along the line. He has always been an impressive driver off the front foot and has improved his defensive technique. A typical, rather negative, medium-pace change bowler, rather more useful in the denial of runs than the gaining of wickets. A top-class fieldsman and superb pair of hands.

ROSE, Brian Charles, b Dartford, Kent 4 June 50. LHB, occ LM. SOMERSET cap 1975. Captain since 1978. 5 England caps 1977–78, scoring 100 runs (av 14.28), HS 27. F-c career: 135 matches; 6,591 runs (av 31.08), 15 hundreds; 6 wkts (av 27.50); 62 ct. HS 205 v Northants (Weston-s-Mare) 1977. BB 3–9 v Glos (Taunton) 1975.

Good county lefthander who looks a little suspect outside the off stump and round the corner against the new ball. Might be better off at number 5 than number 1. Did well in his first season as captain, even if he will have to wait for at least another season before carrying off that long overdue honour.

ROUSE, Stephen John ('Mick'), b Merthyr Tydfil, Glam 20 Jan 49. LHB, LM. WARWICK-SHIRE cap 1974. F-c career: 108 matches; 1,582 runs (av 15.21); 246 wkts (av 29.15); 49 ct. HS 93 v Hants (Bournemouth) 1976. BB 6–34 v Leics (Leicester) 1976.

Tall, strongly built left-arm seamer who could well make a dramatic impact if he can fully master the art of moving the ball back to the right-hand batsman. A handy performer with the bat in the lower order.

ROWE, Charles James Castell, b Hong Kong 27 Nov 51. RHB, OB. KENT cap 1977. F-c career: 79 matches; 2,600 runs (av 27.36), 1 hundred; 49 wkts (av 39.38); 26 ct. HS 103 v Sussex (Tunbridge Wells) 1977. BB 6–46 v Derbys (Dover) 1976.

Extremely useful cricketer who batted well to reach 1,000 runs with a highly respectable average in the mid-30s. His off-break bowling was handicapped by lack of opportunities. Splendid fielder.

RUSSELL, Philip Edgar, b Ilkeston 9 May 44. RHB, RM/OB. DERBYSHIRE cap 1975. F-c career: 162 matches; 2,007 runs (av 12.62); 329 wkts (av 29.70); 123 ct. HS 72 v Glam

(Swansea) 1970. BB 7–46 v Yorks (Sheffield) 1976.

Medium-pace bowler who can move the ball rather more than is normally expected and can also deliver a most effective cutter. Now the county's coach.

RUSSOM, Neil, b Finchley, Middx, 3 Dec 58. RHB, RM. SOMERSET – uncapped. Played in one Gillette Trophy match 1978 but has yet to make his first-class debut.

Apprentice batsman.

SADIQ MOHAMMAD, b Junagadh, India 3 May 45. LHB, LB. GLOUCESTERSHIRE cap 1973. 34 Pakistan caps 1969–78, scoring 2,330 runs (av 38.83) with 5 hundreds, HS 166. F-c career: 259 matches; 15,923 runs (av 37.73), 32 hundreds; 181 wkts (av 30.59); 204 ct. Scored four hundreds in successive innings 1976. HS 184* v New Zealanders (Bristol) 1973. BB 5–29 PIA v Dacca (Dacca) 1964–65 and 5–29 for Karachi Blues v Lahore Greens (Karachi) 1970–71.

Diminutive left-handed opening batsman of world-class stature; has always possessed a sound defence, but is now prepared to attack the bowlers when required. Plays a wide range of attractive strokes, including a flashing hook, a delightful pick-up off his toes, and a good cover drive. A useful change spin bowler.

SARFRAZ NAWAZ, b Lahore, Pakistan 1 Dec 48. RHB, RFM. NORTHAMPTONSHIRE cap 1975. 26 Pakistan caps 1969–78. scoring 443 runs (av 14.76). HS 53, and taking 82 wkts (av 32.01), BB 6–89. F-c career: 193 matches; 3,829 runs (av 18.95); 700 wkts (av 23.37); 108 ct. HS 86 v Essex (Chelmsford) 1975. BB 8–27 (before lunch) Pakistanis v Notts (Nottingham) 1974.

A fast bowler with an ugly but powerful and effective body action. Moves the ball and is capable of producing a genuine bouncer on a placid pitch. Capable of bowling for long spells, but extremely volatile and needs careful handling. A useful striker in the middle order and has turned himself into a capable fielder. Has signed for WSC.

SAVAGE, Richard LeQuesne, b London 10 Dec 55. RHB, RM/OB. WARWICKSHIRE – uncapped. F-c career: 37 matches; 157 runs (av 6.54); 116 wkts (av 27.76); 11 ct. HS 22* Oxford U. v Worcs (Oxford) 1977. BB 7–50 v Glam (Nuneaton) 1977.

Intriguing off-spinner of around medium pace who cuts rather than spins the ball. A different and therefore exciting bowler, he might do well, or could just as easily disappear from the first-class scene.

SAXELBY, Kevin, b Worksop 23 Feb 59. RHB, RFM. NOTTINGHAMSHIRE – uncapped.

*In Kevin Sharp,
Yorkshire have one of
the brightest prospects
in English cricket.*

F-c career: 2 matches; 3 runs (av 1.50); 1 wkt (av 123.00); 1 ct. HS 3*. BB 1-32 v Leics (Nottingham) 1978 – on debut.

Promising young seamer.

SCHEPENS, Martin, b Barrow upon Soar 12 Aug 55. RHB, LB. LEICESTERSHIRE – uncapped. F-c career: 13 matches; 267 runs (av 16.68); 0 wkts; 6 ct. HS 39 v Middx (Lord's) 1976.

Another of Leicestershire's good young prospects. Extremely promising batsman.

SCOTT, Christopher John, b Swinton 16 Sep 59. LHB, WK. LANCASHIRE – uncapped. F-c career: 5 matches; 25 runs (av 6.25); 6 ct, 2 st. HS 10 v Oxford U. (Oxford) 1977 – on debut. Youngest player to keep wicket for Lancashire in f-c matches (17 years 251 days).

Reserve wicket-keeper. He has the ability and the time to develop into an exceptionally good 'keeper.

SELVEY, Michael Walter William, b Chiswick 25 Apr 48. RHB, RFM. MIDDLESEX cap 1973. Played for Surrey 1968–71. 3 England caps 1976–77, scoring 15 runs (av 7.50), HS 5*, and taking 6 wkts (av 57.16), BB 4–41 on debut. F-c career: 167 matches; 938 runs (av 9.28); 526 wkts (av 24.75); 45 ct. HS 42 Cambridge U.

v Pakistanis (Cambridge) 1971. BB 7–20 v Glos (Gloucester) 1976.

Opening bowler who moves the ball in the air and again maintained a full length. Bowled splendidly for Middlesex, finishing the season with 100 wickets, and is unlucky there is such a wealth of seam talent available in England.

SHANTRY, Brian Keith, b Bristol 26 May 55. LHB, LFM. GLOUCESTERSHIRE – uncapped. F-c career: 2 matches; has not batted; 3 wkts (av 55.66); 0 ct. BB 2–63 v Somerset (Bristol) 1978 – on debut.

Left-arm seamer who might prove to be the successor for Davey.

SHARP, George, b West Hartlepool, Co Durham 12 Mar 50. RHB, WK. NORTHAMPTONSHIRE cap 1973. F-c career: 170 matches; 3,546 runs (av 18.86); 327 ct, 62 st. HS 85 v Warwicks (Birmingham) 1976.

Probably the most under-rated 'keeper on the circuit. A quiet and efficient performer. A useful batsman.

SHARP, Kevin, b Leeds 6 Apr 59. LHB, OB. YORKSHIRE – uncapped, F-c career: 28 matches; 1,019 runs (av 25.47); 0 wkts; 9 ct. HS 91 v Middx (Bradford) 1978.

In his appearances for his county, he clearly underlined that he has the making of an outstanding batsman. Captained England Under 19 in the series against West Indies, scoring an unbeaten 260 in the second 'Test'.

SHEPHERD, David Robert, b Bideford, Devon 27 Dec 40. RHB, occ RM. GLOUCESTERSHIRE cap 1969. F-c career: 274 matches; 10,449 runs (av 24.41), 12 hundreds; 2 wkts (av 53.00); 95 ct. HS 153 v Middx (Bristol) 1968. BB 1–1.
A batsman built on heavyweight lines who regularly produces some impressive innings.

SHEPHERD, John Neil, b St Andrew, Barbados 9 Nov 43. RHB, RM. KENT cap 1967. 5 West Indies caps 1969–71, scoring 77 runs (av 9.62). HS 32, 19 wkts (av 25.21), BB 5–104. F-c career: 301 matches; 9,746 runs (av 26.19), 7 hundreds; 847 wkts (av 26.21); 227 ct. HS 170 v Northants (Folkestone) 1968. BB 8–40 West Indians v Glos (Bristol) 1969.
Fine, natural, all-round cricketer who bowls just above medium pace with a whippy action. Moves the ball a little bit off the seam either way, is accurate, and can keep going for extremely long spells. His batting has probably suffered from his representing a county with so much talent in this department. A brilliant all-purpose fieldsman and just the type of player, and person, any captain would like to have in his side. Played a leading role in Kent's Championship and Benson and Hedges Cup successes.

SHUTTLEWORTH, Kenneth, b St Helens 13 Nov 44. RHB, RFM. LEICESTERSHIRE cap 1977. Played for Lancashire 1964–76 (cap 1968). 5 England caps 1970–71, scoring 46 runs (av 7.66), HS 21, and taking 12 wkts (av 35.58). BB 5–47. F-c career: 217 matches; 2,304 runs (av 16.11); 577 wkts (av 24.01), 1 hat-trick; 110 ct. HS 71 Lancs v Glos (Cheltenham) 1967. BB 7–41 Lancs v Essex (Leyton) 1968.
At his best, an above-average. destructive fast bowler with an action reminiscent of Fred Trueman's. Has not been as successful with Leicestershire as had been hoped.

SIDEBOTTOM, Arnold, b Barnsley 1 Apr 54. RHB, RM. YORKSHIRE – uncapped. F-c career: 35 matches; 646 runs (av 17.00), 1 hundred; 45 wkts (av 32.08); 13 ct. HS 124 v Glam (Cardiff) 1977. BB 4–47 v Derbys (Chesterfield) 1975.
Useful young all-rounder whose cricket has been limited by his soccer commitments.

SIMMONS, Jack, b Clayton-le-Moors 28 Mar 41. RHB. OB. LANCASHIRE cap 1971. F-c career: 236 matches; 4,243 runs (av 21.32), 2 hundreds; 518 wkts (av 27.32), 1 hat-trick; 184 ct. HS 112 v Sussex (Hove) 1970. BB 7–64 v

Jack Simmons, Lancashire all-rounder and captain of Tasmania in the winter.

Hants (Southport) 1973.
Burly off-spinner with excellent control but a very flat trajectory and little flight. He has proved a great success in limited-overs cricket when he fires in full-length deliveries at the batsman. Competent batsman who can defend or attack according to the situation.

SLACK, Wilfred Norris, b Troumaca, St Vincent 12 Dec 54. LHB, RM. MIDDLESEX – uncapped. F-c career: 13 matches; 333 runs (av 16.65); 7 ct. HS 52 v Cambridge U. (Cambridge) 1978.
Left-hand batsman who averaged 15 in his 15 innings for his county. Needs to establish himself in first-class cricket within the next two years and to do that he will have to score many more runs.

SLOCOMBE, Philip Anthony, b Weston-s-Mare 6 Sep 54. RHB. SOMERSET cap 1978. F-c career: 75 matches; 3,452 runs (av 30.82), 5 hundreds; 40 ct. HS 132 v Notts (Taunton) 1975. First Somerset player to score 1,000 runs in season of f-c debut.
Returned to his best form, hitting three Championship centuries and making more than 1,100 runs; was second only to Richards

in the averages. Probably the soundest of the young batsmen in a county who might be said to possess a surfeit of them.

SMEDLEY, Michael John, b Maltby, Yorks 28 Oct 41. RHB. NOTTINGHAMSHIRE cap 1966. Captain since 1975. F-c career: 348 matches; 16,131 runs (av 31.44), 28 hundreds; 249 ct. HS 149 v Glam (Cardiff) 1970.

Good-looking upright middle-order batsman who has tended to promise rather more than he has produced. Especially impressive off the back foot. Took over the captaincy again after Rice had been sacked and did his usual efficient job.

SMITH, David Mark, b Balham 9 Jan 56. LHB, RM. SURREY – uncapped. F-c career: 56 matches; 1,397 runs (av 21.82), 2 hundreds; 21 wkts (av 52.61); 28 ct. HS 115 v Hants (Portsmouth) 1978. BB 3–40 v Sussex (Oval) 1976.

Steadily improving left-hand batsman. Played several impressive innings, including a century against Hampshire.

SMITH, Kevin Brian, b Lewes 28 Aug 57. LHB, SLA. SUSSEX – uncapped. F-c career: 4 matches; 90 runs (av 12.85); 1 ct. HS 43 v Kent (Hove) 1978.

SMITH, Kenneth David, b Jesmond, Northumberland 9 Jul 56. RHB. WARWICKSHIRE cap 1978. F-c career: 63 matches; 3,008 runs (av 30.08), 5 hundreds; 16 ct. HS 135 v Lancs (Manchester) 1977.

Considered by many to have the potential to become an international batsman, scoring over 1,100 runs and hitting three centuries in his third season with the 1st XI. Already an above-average county cricketer.

SMITH, Michael John, b Enfield 4 Jan 42. RHB, SLA. MIDDLESEX cap 1967. F-c career: 398 matches; 18,622 runs (av 31.56), 35 hundreds; 57 wkts (av 32.35); 214 ct. HS 181 v Lancs (Manchester) 1967. BB 4–13 v Glos (Lord's) 1961.

Tall, effective opener, though his on-the-move technique must make him suspect against top-class bowling. Like his captain and opening partner, he struck, for no obvious reason, a long and most uncharacteristic bad patch.

SMITH, Neil, b Dewsbury, Yorks 1 Apr 49. RHB, WK. ESSEX cap 1975. Played for Yorks 1970–72. F-c career: 133 matches; 2,438 runs (av 17.92), 2 hundreds; 281 ct, 42 st. HS 126 v Somerset (Leyton) 1976.

Has proved to be a highly efficient performer behind the stumps. Also batted with considerable skill and determination when runs were really needed.

SOUTHERN, John William, b King's Cross, Middx 2 Sep 52. RHB, SLA. HAMPSHIRE cap 1978. F-c career: 79 matches; 448 runs (av 9.14); 230 wkts (28.56); 22 ct. HS 51 v Glos (Basingstoke) 1978. BB 6–46 v Glos (Bournemouth) 1975.

Tall left-arm slow bowler who really came into his own last summer when he found conditions very much to his taste. He sent down more overs than anybody and was Hampshire's leading wicket-taker. Has become a very good county spinner.

SPELMAN, Guy Dennis, b Westminster (Middx) 18 Oct 58. LHB, RM. KENT– uncapped. Played in 3 JPL matches 1978 (taking 3–39 v Derbys) but has yet to make his first-class debut.

Promising seamer.

SPENCER, John, b Brighton 6 Oct 49. RHB, RM. SUSSEX cap 1973. F-c career: 190 matches; 2,576 runs (av 13.70); 507 wkts (av 26.02); 69 ct. HS 79 v Hants (Southampton) 1975. BB 6–19 v Glos (Gloucester) 1974.

Ideal stock bowler; an accurate seamer who depends on movement rather than pace for his wickets.

STEAD, Barry, b Leeds, Yorks 21 Jun 39. LHB, LFM. NOTTINGHAMSHIRE cap 1969. Played for Yorks 1959. F-c career: 232 matches; 2,166 runs (av 12.30); 653 wkts (av 28.05), 1 hat-trick; 59 ct. HS 58 v Glos (Bristol) 1972. BB 8–44 v Somerset (Nottingham) 1972.

Hampshire's Bob Stephenson.

Useful county opening bowler for many years. He improved in the early 1970s when he discovered how to move the ball late in its flight.

STEELE, David Stanley, b Bradeley, Staffs 29 Sep 41. Brother of J. F. Steele (Leics). RHB, SLA. DERBYSHIRE cap 1979. Captain 1979. Played for Northants 1963–78 (cap 1965). 8 England caps 1975–76, scoring 673 runs (av 42.06), with one hundred (106), and taking 2 wkts (av 19.50), BB 1–1. F-c career: 358 matches; 17,375 runs (av 33.09), 27 hundreds; 272 wkts (av 23.26); 407 ct. HS 140* Northants v Worcs (Worcester) 1971. BB 8–29 Northants v Lancs (Northampton) 1966.
Has gradually developed from an average county batsman into one of the more consistent and dependable players. Dogged and determined, he should provide Derbyshire with stability and backbone. These characteristics were at last recognised by the selectors against Ian Chappell's Australians and the 1976 West Indians, but his brief, valuable international career would now appear to be over. With the departure of both main spinners from his county he came into his own as a slow left-arm bowler last summer.

STEELE, John Frederick, b Brown Edge, Staffs 23 Jul 46. Brother of D. S. Steele (Derbys). RHB, SLA. LEICESTERSHIRE cap 1971. F-c career: 223 matches; 9,746 runs (av 29.35), 14 hundreds; 310 wkts (av 26.65); 254 ct. HS 195 v Derbys (Leicester) 1971. BB 7–29 Natal B v Griqualand West (Umzinto) 1973–74.
Dedication and enthusiasm have made this talented all-rounder an integral part of the Leicestershire side. Originally a grafting bat, he is now more eager to play his strokes. His trajectory when bowling is inclined to be too flat but he is difficult to score runs against, hence his success in limited-overs cricket.

STEPHENSON, George Robert, b Derby, Derbys 19 Nov 42. RHB, WK. DERBYSHIRE cap 1969. Captain 1979. Played for Derbys 1967–68. F-c career: 232 matches; 4,144 runs (av 17.05), 1 hundred; 534 ct, 72 st. HS 100* v Somerset (Taunton) 1976.
A neat, diminutive wicket-keeper who has secured a large haul of dismissals in the past seasons. Useful batsman with an unusually upright stance. Takes over the captaincy from Gilliat at a difficult period of adjustment for the county.

STEVENSON, Graham Barry, b Ackworth 16 Dec 55. RHB, RM. YORKSHIRE cap 1978. F-c career: 63 matches; 1,437 runs (av 21.77); 155 wkts (av 27.77); 30 ct. HS 83 v Derbys (Chesterfield) 1976. BB 8–65 v Lancs (Leeds) 1978.
Bouncy young all-rounder who looks to

have the ability, confidence, and that little extra fire which make all the difference. Lively seamer, batsman with a keen eye, and a dashing field. His bowling improved considerably but he should have scored more runs.

Yorkshire's Graham Stevenson.

STEVENSON, Keith, b Derby 6 Oct 50. RHB, RM. HAMPSHIRE – uncapped. Played for Derbys 1974–77. F-c career: 68 matches; 485 runs (av 8.36); 154 wkts (av 30.53); 23 ct. HS 33 Derbys v Northants (Chesterfield) 1974. BB 7–68 Derbys v Warwicks (Chesterfield) 1977.
A seamer with a pleasing body action.

STOREY, Stewart James, b Worthing 6 Jan 41. RHB, RM. SUSSEX – uncapped. Played for Surrey 1960–74 (cap 1964). Played no first-class cricket 1975–77. F-c career: 332 matches; 10,776 runs (av 25.06), 12 hundreds; 496 wkts (av 26.56), 1 hat-trick; 325 ct. HS 164 Surrey v Derbys (Oval) 1971. BB 8–22 Surrey v Glam (Swansea) 1965.
Experienced all-rounder who turned in several useful performances for his new county with bat and ball. Plays very straight. Bowls a useful leg-cutter at medium pace and safe slip.

STOVOLD, Andrew Willis-, b Bristol 19 Mar 53. RHB, WK. GLOUCESTERSHIRE cap 1976. F-c career: 113 matches; 5,474 runs (av 28.36), 5 hundreds; 1 wkt (av 23.00); 125 ct, 25 st. HS 196 v Notts (Nottingham) 1977. BB 1–0.
Has developed into a most attractive, fast-

scoring opener with a wide range of attacking strokes. He has the ability to hit boundaries off his back foot with straight-bat strokes on both sides of the wicket. A competent performer behind the stumps with a safe pair of hands.

STOVOLD, Martin Willis-, b Bristol 28 Dec 55. Younger brother of Andrew. LHB. GLOUCESTERSHIRE – uncapped. Played in one JPL match 1978 but has yet to make his first-class debut.

STUCHBURY, Stephen, b Sheffield 22 Jun 54. LHB, LFM. YORKSHIRE – uncapped. F-c career: 1 match; has not batted; 2 wkts (av 30.00); 0 ct. BB 2–39 v New Zealanders (Leeds) 1978.
Left-arm fast-medium bowler.

SURRIDGE, Stuart Spicer, b Westminster, (Middx) 28 Oct 51. Son of W.S. Surridge. RHB, WK. SURREY – uncapped. F-c career: 1 match; 2 runs; 1 ct, 0 st. HS 2*.
Reserve wicket-keeper.

SUTCLIFFE, Richard John, b Rochdale 18 Sep 54. RHB, RFM. LANCASHIRE – uncapped. F-c career: 1 match; 10 runs; 1 wkt (av 37.00); 0 ct. HS 10* and BB 1–37 v Essex (Southport) 1978.
Apprentice seamer.

SWARBROOK, Frederick William, b Derby 17 Dec 50. LHB, SLA. DERBYSHIRE cap 1975. F-c career: 214 matches; 4,696 runs (av 20.50); 467 wkts (av 29.62); 133 ct. HS 90 v Essex (Leyton) 1970. BB 9–20 v Sussex (Hove) 1975.
Orthodox left-arm spinner, tenacious bat, and good fighting cricketer who has been consistently under-rated. Failed to do himself justice last season in conditions that should have suited him.

SWART, Peter Douglas, b Bulawayo, Southern Rhodesia, 27 Apr 46. RHB, RFM. GLAMORGAN – uncapped. F-c career: 99 matches; 3,210 runs (av 23.77); 5 hundreds; 235 wkts (av 26.04); 56 ct. HS 115 v Oxford U. (Oxford) 1978. BB 6–85 Western Province v Natal (Pietermaritzburg) 1971–72.
Useful all-rounder from Rhodesia. Although he had a good first season, he did not return the figures one expects from an imported cricketer.

TAVARE, Christopher James, b Orpington 27 Oct 54. RHB, occ RM. KENT cap 1978. F-c career: 75 matches; 3,819 runs (av 34.71), 5 hundreds; 1 wkt (av 48.00); 93 ct. HS 124* v Notts (Canterbury) 1977. BB 1–20.
In his first full season with Kent this graceful young batsman impressed everybody with his batting. He looked as good as Woolmer, who would have been in the England team but for his WSC associations, which suggests he

will be playing Test cricket shortly. Probably should have been picked for Australia. Technically a sound and attractive stroke-maker with plenty of time for his shots, he has a very bright future.

TAYLOR, Derek John Somerset, b Amersham, Bucks 12 Nov 42. Twin brother of M. N. S. Taylor (Notts and Hants). RHB, WK. SOMERSET cap 1971. Played for Surrey 1966–69 (cap 1969). F-c career: 221 matches; 5,639 runs (av 22.02), 4 hundreds; 463 ct, 60 st. HS 179 v Glam (Swansea) 1974.
Highly competent wicket-keeper and extremely useful batsman.

TAYLOR, Leslie Brian, b Earl Shilton 25 Oct 53. RHB, RFM. LEICESTERSHIRE – uncapped. F-c career: 14 matches; 29 runs (av 5.80); 43 wkts (av 27.44); 4 ct. HS 15 v Kent (Canterbury) 1978. BB 4–32 v Derbys (Derby) 1978.
Strong fast bowler who is still improving. Handicapped to some extent by the large number of useful bowlers on his county's staff.

TAYLOR, Michael Norman Somerset, b Amersham, Bucks 12 Nov 42. Twin brother of D. J. S. Taylor (Somerset). RHB, RM. HAMPSHIRE cap 1973. Played for Notts 1964–72 (cap 1967). F-c career: 344 matches; 7,257 runs (av 20.04), 3 hundreds; 794 wkts (av 26.45), 1 hat-trick; 202 ct. HS 105 Notts v Lancs (Nottingham) 1967. BB 7–23 v Notts (Basingstoke) 1977.
Typical modern all-rounder – accurate medium-pace seamer; pleasant-looking, attacking bat; fine outfielder.

TAYLOR, Robert William, b Stoke, Staffs 17 Jul 41. RHB, WK. DERBYSHIRE cap 1962. Captain 1975–76. 13 England caps 1971–78, scoring 202 runs (av 15.53), HS 45, and making 39 dismissals (36 ct, 3 st). F-c career: 479

matches; 9,306 runs (av 16.88); 1,108 ct, 133 st. HS 97 International Wanderers v South African Invitation XI (Johannesburg) 1975-76.

Extremely efficient, undemonstrative wicketkeeper of Test calibre who maintains the highest standard day after day. A competent tailender with plenty of determination. Only the presence of Alan Knott prevented him from gaining numerous caps for England, and following the defection of the Kent 'keeper to Packerland his selection for England was automatic and highly successful.

TERRY, Vivian **Paul,** b Osnabruck, West Germany, 14 Jan 59. RHB, RM. HAMPSHIRE – uncapped. F-c career: 2 matches; 16 runs (av 5.33); 0 ct. HS 8.

Young opening batsman.

Leslie Taylor of Leicestershire.

THOMAS, David James, b Solihull, Warwicks 30 Jun 59. LHB, LFM. SURREY – uncapped. F-c career: 16 matches; 84 runs (av 5.60); 21 wkts (av 48.76); 5 ct. HS 14 v Lancs (Oval) 1977 – on debut. BB 4–47 v Pakistanis (Oval) 1978.

Young fast bowler who failed to build on an impressive performance in the Sunday League when he captured the first four Sussex wickets for one run.

THOMAS, Gary Philip, b Birmingham 8 Nov 58. RHB, occ RM. WARWICKSHIRE – uncapped. F-c career: 1 match; 5 runs (av 2.50); 0 ct. HS 4.

Apprentice batsman.

TODD, Paul Adrian, b Morton 12 Mar 53. RHB. NOTTINGHAMSHIRE cap 1977, F-c career: 85 matches; 3,770 runs (av 26.18), 3 hundreds; 63 ct. HS 178 v Glos (Nottingham) 1975.

Now firmly established as a correct, competent, opening bat with a good defence and an equable temperament.

TOLCHARD, Roger William, b Torquay, Devon 15 Jun 46. RHB, WK. LEICESTERSHIRE cap 1966. 4 England caps 1976–77, scoring 129 runs (av 25.80), HS 67 on debut. F-c career: 367 matches; 11,192 runs (av 31.35), 9 hundreds; 1 wkt (av 20.00); 701 ct, 97 st. HS 126* v Cambridge U. (Cambridge) 1970. BB 1–4.

Lively, aggressive, agile 'keeper, he is also a a pugnacious fast-scoring batsman and an outstanding runner between the wickets. He is especially valuable when runs are needed quickly and is not afraid to hook fast bowling.

TOMLINS, Keith Patrick, b Kingston upon Thames, Surrey 23 Oct 57. RHB, RM. MIDDLESEX – uncapped. F-c career: 14 matches; 296 runs (av 17.41); 9 ct. HS 94 v Worcs (Worcester) 1978.

Young apprentice.

TREMLETT, Timothy Maurice, b Wellington, Somerset 26 Jul 56. Son of M. F. Tremlett. RHB, RM. HAMPSHIRE – uncapped. F-c career: 8 matches; 202 runs (av 20.20); 9 wkts (av 29.44); 2 ct. HS 50 v Glos (Basingstoke) 1978. BB 2–25 v Yorks (Southampton) 1978.

Young seamer whose batting suggested that he could become an all-rounder.

TRIM, Geoffrey Edward, b Openshaw 6 Apr 56. RHB, occ LB. LANCASHIRE – uncapped. F-c career: 2 matches; 36 runs (av 9.00); 0 ct. HS 15 v Notts (Nottingham) 1976.

A diminutive apprentice opening bat.

TUNNICLIFFE, Colin John, b Derby 11 Aug 51. RHB, LFM. DERBYSHIRE cap 1977. F-c career: 56 matches; 445 runs (av 9.88); 117 wkts (av 30.47); 23 ct. HS 82* and BB 4–22 v

Middx (Ilkeston) 1977.

Dependable opening bowler; has good line and length and moves the ball off the seam.

TUNNICLIFFE, Howard Trevor, b Derby, Derbyshire 4 Mar 50. RHB, RM, NOTTINGHAM-SHIRE – uncapped. F-c career: 33 matches; 937 runs (av 22.30); 20 wkts (av 45.15); 14 ct. HS 87 v Derbys (Nottingham) 1974. BB 3–48 v Leics (Nottingham) 1975.

Still trying to establish himself as a recognised county batsman but may be running out of time.

TURNER, David Roy, b Chippenham, Wiltshire 5 Feb 49. LHB, occ RM. HAMPSHIRE cap 1970. F-c career: 241 matches; 10,569 runs (av 28.79), 17 hundreds; 2 wkts (av 67.50); 142 ct. HS 181* v Surrey (Oval) 1969. BB 1–4.

Small, neat lefthander who is very quick on his feet and a good county batsman, having at one time promised rather more. A fine fielder, he again served his county splendidly.

TURNER, Glenn Maitland, b Dunedin, New Zealand 26 May 47, RHB, occ RM/OB. WORCESTERSHIRE cap 1968. 39 New Zealand caps 1969–77 (10 as captain), scoring 2,920 runs (av 45.62) with 7 hundreds. HS 259. F-c career: 373 matches; 27,128 runs (av 48.27), 73 hundreds; 5 wkts (av 37.80); 342 ct. HS 259 New Zealand v West Indies (Georgetown) 1971–72 and 259 New Zealanders v Guyana (Georgetown) 1971–72. BB 3–18 v Pakistanis (Worcester) 1967.

World-class opening batsman from New Zealand with the pedigree one expects from an outstanding player. Was playing Test cricket and making runs in his early 20s, and in 1973 scored a thousand runs before the end of May. He plays straight, and with this and a sound ultra-defensive technique as the vital base, he has blossomed forth so that he can adjust his tempo to suit the requirements. Possesses a temperament and singleness of purpose that have given him an insatiable appetite for records and runs.

TURNER, Stuart, b Chester, Cheshire 18 Jul 43. RHB, RM. ESSEX cap 1970. F-c career: 243 matches; 6,203 runs (av 21.68), 3 hundreds; 580 wkts (av 25.41) 1 hat-trick; 164 ct. HS 121 v Somerset (Taunton) 1970. BB 6–26 v Northants (Northampton) 1977.

Good county all-rounder and a natural for limited-overs cricket. He is an accurate fast-medium bowler – a shade nippier than he looks – an attacking batsman, and a splendid fieldsman.

UNDERWOOD, Derek Leslie, b Bromley 8 Jun 45. RHB, LM. KENT cap 1964. 74 England caps 1966–77, scoring 824 runs (av 11.94), HS 45* and taking 265 wkts (av 24.90), BB 8–51. F-c career: 447 matches; 3,266 runs (av 9.14);

1,734 wkts (av 19.55), 1 hat-trick; 191 ct. HS 80 v Lancs (Manchester) 1969. BB 9–28 v Sussex (Hastings) 1964.

A world-class bowler; on a pitch giving any assistance at all, he is most devastating. His pace is close to medium, so he gives batsmen few opportunities to use their feet. On perfect pitches he can be employed as a stock bowler because his accuracy always makes him difficult to score against, and he has an outstanding record in limited-overs games when the denial of runs is all-important. It is noticeable that he is less effective against lefthanders, and he could do with a well-disguised slower ball that turns as much as his normal delivery. He can bat with great tenacity when the situation demands. As he signed for Packer he was not considered for the Tests; the outcome – 110 wickets at 14.49 apiece and Kent won the Schweppes Championship.

WALLER, Christopher Edward, b Guildford, Surrey 3 Oct 48 RHB, SLA. SUSSEX cap 1976. Played for Surrey 1967–73 (cap 1972). F-c career: 126 matches; 811 runs (av 8.62); 323 wkts (av 27.13); 65 ct. HS 47 Surrey v Pakistanis (Oval) 1971. BB 7–64 Surrey v Sussex (Oval) 1974.

This slow left-armer really came into his own in 1978 and has probably never bowled better. Flights the ball well, runs it on with his arm and imparts sufficient spin. Not flat enough for limited-overs cricket, especially on a small ground.

WALTERS, John, b Brampton, Yorks 7 Aug 49, LHB, RFM, DERBYSHIRE – uncapped. F-c career: 19 matches; 545 runs (av 24.77); 17 wkts (av 35.05); 2 ct. HS 90 v Hants (Bournemouth) 1978. BB 3–70 v Hants (Derby) 1978.

WARD, Alan, b Dronfield, Derbyshire 10 Aug 47. RHB, RF. LEICESTERSHIRE cap 1977. Played for Derbyshire 1966–76 (cap 1969). 5 England caps 1969–76, scoring 40 runs (av 8.00), HS 21, and taking 14 wkts (av 32.35), BB 4–61. F-c career: 163 matches; 928 runs (av 8.43); 460 wkts (av 22.81); 51 ct. HS 44 Derbys v Notts (Ilkeston) 1969. BB 7–42 Derbys v Glam (Burton upon Trent) 1974.

Genuine fast bowler who has continually been held back by injuries.

WATSON, Gregory George, b Gulgong, NSW, Australia, 29 Jan 55. RHB, RFM. WORCESTERSHIRE – uncapped. F-c career: 28 matches; 384 runs (av 14.76); 65 wkts (av 34.20); 10 ct. HS 38 v Somerset (Taunton) 1978. BB 6–45 v Sussex (Eastbourne) 1978.

Australian fast bowler who had a reasonable, but far from exceptional, first season with Worcestershire. Not quite quick enough and inclined to be erratic.

WATSON, William Kenneth, b Port Elizabeth, South Africa 21 May 55. RHB, RFM.

NOTTINGHAMSHIRE – uncapped. F-c career: 33 matches; 234 runs (av 11.70); 109 wkts (av 26.38); 8 ct. HS 28* v Cambridge U. (Cambridge) 1978. BB 6–102 v Kent (Nottingham) 1978.

South African fast bowler who made little impact in county cricket. Opportunities limited in a side with several imports.

WATTS, Patrick James, b Henlow, Beds 16 Jun 40. LHB, RM. NORTHAMPTONSHIRE cap 1962. Captain 1971–74 and since 1978. F-c career: 343 matches; 13,906 runs (av 28.49), 10 hundreds; 255 wkts (av 25.61); 255 ct. HS 145 v Hants (Bournemouth) 1962. BB 6–18 v Somerset (Taunton) 1965.

Returned to captain the county once again. A dependable lefthander with a marked preference for the front foot, he plays straight, has a fluent off-drive, and is difficult to remove.

WELLS, Colin Mark, b Newhaven 3 Mar 60. RHB, RM. SUSSEX – uncapped. Played in 3 JPL matches 1978 but has yet to make his first-class debut.

Sussex ground staff.

WESSELS, Kepler Christoffel, b Bloemfontein, South Africa, 14 Sep 57. LHB, OB. SUSSEX cap 1977. F-c career: 44 matches; 2,725 runs (av 41.28), 4 hundreds; 3 wkts (av 26.33); 27 ct. HS 146 Northern Transvaal v Western Province B (Cape Town) 1977–78. BB 1–4.

Brilliant young South African batsman who played only on a few occasions because of his National Service. Everything suggests that he will become an outstanding player. Signed for WSC.

WHITE, Robert Arthur, b Fulham, Middx 6 Oct 36. LHB, OB. NOTTINGHAMSHIRE cap 1966. Played for Middx 1958–65 (cap 1963). F-c career: 411 matches; 12,442 runs (av 23.29), 5 hundreds; 682 wkts (av 30.86); 188 ct. HS 116* v Surrey (Oval) 1967. BB 7–41 v Derbys (Ilkeston) 1971.

Formerly only an occasional off-spinner who modelled his action on that of Fred Titmus, he was pressed into service so often by Nottinghamshire that he became a mainline bowler. Accurate but does not turn the ball much. Also a useful batsman.

WHITEHOUSE, John, b Nuneaton 8 Apr 49. RHB, occ OB. WARWICKSHIRE cap 1973. Captain since 1978. F-c career: 149 matches; 7,344 runs (av 31.93), 14 hundreds; 5 wkts (av 74.80); 107 ct. HS 173 v Oxford U. (Oxford) 1971–on debut. BB 2–55 v Yorks (Birmingham) 1977.

Right-handed bat with an open stance and a tendency to play across the line, but he times the ball well and has a good eye. Although his appointment as skipper coincided with a disastrous season with the bat, he should be back among the runs in 1979.

WHITELEY, John Peter, b Otley 28 Feb 55. RHB, OB. YORKSHIRE – uncapped. F-c career: 9 matches; 14 runs (av 7.00); 22 wkts (av 21.59); 6 ct. HS 8. BB 4–14 v Notts (Scarborough) 1978.

Found himself in the Yorkshire side when Cope was banned from bowling because of his action and performed creditably.

WILKINS, Alan Haydn, b Cardiff 22 Aug 53. RHB, LFM. GLAMORGAN – uncapped. F-c career: 41 matches; 236 runs (av 8.13); 93 wkts (av 28.67); 15 ct. HS 70 v Notts (Worksop) 1977. BB 5–58 v Hants (Portsmouth) 1977.

Left-arm seamer who still needs to learn to move the ball into the righthander. Like other members of the Welsh attack, found wickets hard to obtain and too expensive.

WILLEY, Peter, b Sedgefield, Co Durham 6 Dec 49. RHB, RM. NORTHAMPTONSHIRE cap 1971. 2 England caps 1976, scoring 115 runs (av 28.75), HS 45. F-c career: 241 matches; 8,584 runs (av 25.47), 10 hundreds; 323 wkts (av 27.46); 102 ct. HS 227 v Somerset (Northampton) 1976. BB 7–37 v Oxford U. (Oxford) 1975.

One of the best home-born strokemakers. His striking of the ball off his back foot is especially impressive and he always has enough time to give himself room to play his shots. Although very open when playing, he can still drive well through the covers but is slightly suspect against the ball leaving him sharply. Has become an efficient off-break bowler.

WILLIAMS, Richard Grenville, b Bangor, Caernarvons 10 Aug 57. RHB, OB. NORTHAMPTONSHIRE – uncapped. F-c career: 41 matches; 966 runs (av 17.88); 14 wkts (av 44.21); 18 ct. HS 64 v Oxford U. (Oxford) 1974. BB 4–48 v Derbys (Northampton) 1978.

Young all-rounder who has not lived up to the early promise of his debut in 1974.

WILLIAMS, Stephen, b Swindon, Wiltshire, 11 Mar 54. RHB, LB. GLOUCESTERSHIRE – uncapped. F-c career: 1 match; 0 runs; 0 ct.

Ground staff.

WILLIS, Robert George Dylan, b Sunderland, Co Durham 30 May 49. RHB, RF. WARWICKSHIRE cap 1972. Played for Surrey 1969–71. 41 England caps 1971–78, scoring 328 runs (av 13.12), HS 24*, and taking 151 wkts (av 24.19), BB 7–78. F-c career: 183 matches; 1,413 runs (av 14.27); 572 wkts (av 23.30), 2 hat-tricks; 88 ct. HS 43 v Middx (Birmingham) 1976. BB 8–32 v Glos (Bristol) 1977.

Tall, rather open-chested fast bowler. Hits the deck and achieves lift even on a placid pitch. Does not move the ball much, either in the air or off the wicket, but makes batting uncomfortable and is the main strike bowler in the England XI. Is prepared to keep going for long periods. Occasionally inaccurate, owing to an action which is not smoothly grooved. His speed is the result of sheer effort. Useful tailender who does not reckon to play back more than once a season. Fine field.

WILSON, Peter Hugh L'Estrange, b Guildford 17 Aug 58. RHB, RFM. SURREY – uncapped. F-c career: 9 matches; 9 runs; 11 wkts (av 32.27); 1 ct. HS 9* and BB 4–56 v Hants (Oval) 1978.
Promising young seamer.

WINCER, Robert Colin, b Southsea, Hants, 2 Apr 52. LHB, RFM. DERBYSHIRE – uncapped. F-c career: 10 matches; 43 runs (av 7.16); 19 wkts (av 35.78); 5 ct. HS 16* v Hants (Bournemouth) 1978. BB 4–42 v Leics (Derby) 1978 – on debut.
Promising seamer.

WOOD, Barry, b Ossett, Yorks 26 Dec 42. RHB, RM. LANCASHIRE cap 1968. Played for Yorkshire 1964. 12 England caps 1972–78, scoring 454 runs (av 21.61), HS 90. F-c career: 272 matches; 13,117 runs (av 33.29), 22 hundreds; 243 wkts (av 27.58); 214 ct. HS 198 v Glam (Liverpool) 1976. BB 7–52 v Middx (Manchester) 1968.
Tough, gutsy little opener with a penchant for fast bowling. A good cutter and hooker, he is also prepared to take on a sheet-anchor role. Certain deficiencies in technique can lead to his downfall against top-class spin, as was seen in India. A more than useful county medium-pace seam bowler who wobbles the ball about. Brilliant field and born competitor.

WOOLMER, Robert Andrew, b Kanpur, India 14 May 48. RHB, RFM. KENT cap 1970. 15 England caps 1975–77, scoring 920 runs (av 36.80) with 3 hundreds, HS 149, and taking 4 wkts (av 74.75), BB 1–8. F-c career: 244 matches; 10,028 runs (av 32.77), 19 hundreds; 385 wkts (av 25.54), 1 hat-trick; 171 ct. HS 149 England v Australia (Oval) 1975. BB 7–47 v Sussex (Canterbury) 1969.
For several years with Kent he was regarded as a steady seam bowler and handy number 8 batsman but has now blossomed forth into primarily a batsman. He has an impressive repertoire of strokes and plenty of time to make them, as he showed for both Kent and England. Has a fine pair of hands and is a useful bowler on a green wicket or in limited-overs cricket. Has joined WSC. His regular presence in the Kent team played a considerable part in their success.

WORSICK, Alan, b Rawtenstall 13 Aug 43. RHB, RFM. LANCASHIRE – uncapped. Played in one JPL match 1978 (taking 4–26 v Essex) but has yet to make his first-class debut.
Apprentice seamer.

WRIGHT, John Geoffrey, b Darfield, New Zealand 5 Jul 54. LHB. DERBYSHIRE cap 1977. 5 New Zealand caps 1978, scoring 223 runs (av 22.30), HS 62. F-c career: 63 matches; 3,332 runs (av 31.73), 4 hundreds; 42 ct. HS 164 v Pakistanis (Chesterfield) 1978.
Sound, unspectacular opening bat with plenty of patience and an excellent temperament. He was much missed by his county while on duty with the New Zealand team.

YARDLEY, Thomas James, b Chaddesley Corbett, Worcs 27 Oct 46. LHB, occ WK. NORTHAMPTONSHIRE cap 1978. Played for Worcestershire 1967–75 (cap 1972). F-c career: 190 matches; 6,065 runs (av 25.37), 4 hundreds; 167 ct, 2 st. HS 135 Worcs v Notts (Worcester) 1973.
Solid lefthander with a limited range of strokes.

ZAHEER ABBAS, Syed, b Sialkot, Pakistan 24 Jul 47. RHB, occ OB. GLOUCESTERSHIRE cap 1975. 26 Pakistan caps 1969–77, scoring 1,583 runs (av 34.41) with 3 hundreds, HS 274. F-c career: 262 matches; 19,804 runs (av 49.75), 61 hundreds; 20 wkts (av 32.05); 197 ct. HS 274 Pakistan v England (Birmingham) 1971. BB 5–15 Dawood Club v Railways (Lahore) 1975–76. Only batsman to score a double-century and a century in a match on three occasions – all six innings were not out.
A strokemaker of very high class. His graceful style, combined with his ability to hit the ball on the rise along the ground, make him a delight to watch and a menace to bowl against. Although he has a wide variety of off-side strokes he is especially devastating to leg. Once he has established himself at the crease he has, like all great players, the appetite to go on and on. Has joined WSC.

FIXTURES 1979

ICC Trophy

Tuesday 22 May
PICKWICK − ARGENTINA V SINGAPORE
WARWICK − CANADA V MALAYSIA
WELLINGTON − DENMARK V FIJI
WOLVERHAMPTON − EAST AFRICA V PAPUA NEW GUINEA
ENVILLE − GIBRALTAR V HOLLAND
BLOSSOMFIELD − ISRAEL V USA

Thursday 24 May
COVENTRY & N.W. − ARGENTINA V EAST AFRICA
WATER ORTON − BANGLADESH V FIJI
STOURBRIDGE − BERMUDA V PAPUA NEW GUINEA
KIDDERMINSTER − DENMARK V MALAYSIA
BANBURY 'TWENTY' − HOLLAND V ISRAEL
NORTHANTS SAINTS − SRI LANKA V USA

Tuesday 29 May
BANBURY − ARGENTINA V PAPUA NEW GUINEA
LICHFIELD − BANGLADESH V CANADA
FORDHOUSES − BERMUDA V SINGAPORE
KENILWORTH WARDENS − FIJI V MALAYSIA
HINCKLEY TOWN − GIBRALTAR V SRI LANKA
LEAMINGTON SPA − HOLLAND V USA

Thursday 31 May
OLD HILL − ARGENTINA V BERMUDA
WALSALL − BANGLADESH V MALAYSIA
KNOWLE & DORRIDGE − CANADA V DENMARK
SHREWSBURY − EAST AFRICA V SINGAPORE
ASTWOOD BANK − GIBRALTAR V ISRAEL
MOSELEY − HOLLAND V SRI LANKA

Monday 4 June
KINGS HEATH − BANGLADESH V DENMARK
BOURNVILLE − BERMUDA V EAST AFRICA
SOLIHULL − CANADA V FIJI
OLTON & W. WARWICKS − GIBRALTAR V USA
KENILWORTH − ISRAEL V SRI LANKA
W. BROMWICH DARTMOUTH − PAPUA NEW GUINEA V SINGAPORE

Wednesday 6 June
BIRMINGHAM ⎫
BURTON UPON TRENT ⎭ **Semi-Finals**

Thursday 21 June
WORCESTER − **Final**
        − Losing semi-finalists play-off

Prudential Cup

Saturday 9 June
LORD'S − AUSTRALIA V ENGLAND
NOTTINGHAM − NEW ZEALAND V ASSOCIATE 'A'
LEEDS − PAKISTAN V ASSOCIATE 'B'
BIRMINGHAM − WEST INDIES V INDIA

Wednesday 13 June
NOTTINGHAM − AUSTRALIA V PAKISTAN
MANCHESTER − ENGLAND V ASSOCIATE 'B'
LEEDS − INDIA V NEW ZEALAND
THE OVAL − WEST INDIES V ASSOCIATE 'A'

Saturday 16 June
BIRMINGHAM − AUSTRALIA V ASSOCIATE 'B'
LEEDS − ENGLAND V PAKISTAN
MANCHESTER − INDIA V ASSOCIATE 'A'
NOTTINGHAM − WEST INDIES V NEW ZEALAND

Wednesday 20 June
MANCHESTER ⎫
THE OVAL ⎭ **Semi-Finals**

Saturday 23 June
LORD'S − **Final**

Indian Tour

All matches 3 days unless otherwise stated
* Includes play on Sunday

JUNE
Wednesday 27 NORTHAMPTON − Northamptonshire
Saturday   30 LORD'S − MCC

JULY
Wednesday 4 SOUTHAMPTON − Hampshire
Saturday   7 *LEICESTER − Leicestershire
Thursday   12 BIRMINGHAM − ENGLAND 1st Test (5 days)
Wednesday 18 v county not in Gillette Cup 2nd Round
Saturday   21 BRISTOL − Gloucestershire
Wednesday 25 SWANSEA − Glamorgan
Saturday   28 *TAUNTON − Somerset

AUGUST
Thursday   2 LORD'S − ENGLAND 2nd Test (5 days)
Wednesday   8 CANTERBURY − Kent
Saturday   11 *CHELMSFORD − Essex
Thursday   16 LEEDS − ENGLAND 3rd Test (5 days)
Wednesday 22 MANCHESTER − Lancashire
Saturday   25 *NOTTINGHAM − Nottinghamshire
Thursday   30 THE OVAL − ENGLAND 4th Test (5 days)

Test Matches played for the Cornhill Insurance Trophy.
County matches played for the Holt Products Trophy.

Sri Lankan Tour

All matches 3 days unless otherwise stated

MAY
Saturday   12 NOTTINGHAM − Nottinghamshire

JUNE
Wednesday 27 DERBY – Derbyshire
Saturday 30 CANTERBURY – Kent

JULY
Wednesday 4 v County not in B & H Semi-Finals
Saturday 7 DUBLIN – Ireland
Wednesday 11 WORCESTER – Worcestershire
Saturday 14 SWANSEA – Glamorgan
Wednesday 18 GLASGOW – Scotland
Wednesday 25 HORSHAM – Sussex

Schweppes County Championship

*Includes play on Sunday

Wednesday 2 May
DERBY – Derbyshire v Leicestershire
CHELMSFORD – Essex v Kent
SOUTHAMPTON – Hampshire v Glamorgan
LORD'S – Middlesex v Warwickshire
NOTTINGHAM – Nottinghamshire v Lancashire
HOVE – Sussex v Gloucestershire
WORCESTER – Worcestershire v Somerset
MIDDLESBROUGH – Yorkshire v Northamptonshire

Wednesday 9 May
SWANSEA – Glamorgan v Worcestershire
BRISTOL – Gloucestershire v Sussex
MANCHESTER – Lancashire v Surrey
LORD'S – Middlesex v Essex
TAUNTON – Somerset v Northamptonshire
BIRMINGHAM – Warwickshire v Leicestershire
LEEDS – Yorkshire v Derbyshire

Wednesday 16 May
CHESTERFIELD – Derbyshire v Essex
CARDIFF – Glamorgan v Yorkshire
LORD'S – Middlesex v Kent
NOTTINGHAM – Nottinghamshire v Leicestershire
TAUNTON – Somerset v Surrey
HOVE – Sussex v Lancashire
BIRMINGHAM – Warwickshire v Northamptonshire
WORCESTER – Worcestershire v Hampshire

Saturday 26 May
DERBY – Derbyshire v Nottinghamshire
BRISTOL – Gloucestershire v Somerset
CANTERBURY – Kent v Hampshire
MANCHESTER – Lancashire v Yorkshire
LORD'S – Middlesex v Sussex
NORTHAMPTON – Northamptonshire v Glamorgan
THE OVAL – Surrey v Essex
BIRMINGHAM – Warwickshire v Worcestershire

Wednesday 30 May
ILFORD – Essex v Glamorgan
MANCHESTER – Lancashire v Gloucestershire
LEICESTER – Leicestershire v Hampshire
THE OVAL – Surrey v Northamptonshire
BIRMINGHAM – Warwickshire v Somerset
SHEFFIELD – Yorkshire v Nottinghamshire

Saturday 2 June
ILFORD – Essex v Lancashire
LEICESTER – Leicestershire v Kent
LORD'S – Middlesex v Gloucestershire
NOTTINGHAM – Nottinghamshire v Glamorgan
TAUNTON – Somerset v Hampshire
HOVE – Sussex v Derbyshire
WORCESTER – Worcestershire v Northamptonshire
BRADFORD – Yorkshire v Surrey

Saturday 9 June
DERBY – Derbyshire v Middlesex
CHELMSFORD – Essex v Leicestershire
SWANSEA – Glamorgan v Warwickshire
PORTSMOUTH – Hampshire v Northamptonshire
CANTERBURY – Kent v Sussex
THE OVAL – Surrey v Lancashire
WORCESTER – Worcestershire v Gloucestershire

Wednesday 13 June
DARTFORD – Kent v Somerset
LORD'S – Middlesex v Nottinghamshire
NORTHAMPTON – Northamptonshire v Derbyshire
BIRMINGHAM – Warwickshire v Essex
WORCESTER – Worcestershire v Lancashire

Saturday 16 June
*CHESTERFIELD – Derbyshire v Lancashire
GLOUCESTER – Gloucestershire v Kent
BOURNEMOUTH – Hampshire v Nottinghamshire
LEICESTER – Leicestershire v Glamorgan
LORD'S – Middlesex v Surrey
NORTHAMPTON – Northamptonshire v Yorkshire
BATH – Somerset v Essex
HOVE – Sussex v Warwickshire

Wednesday 20 June
CHELMSFORD – Essex v Derbyshire
GLOUCESTER – Gloucestershire v Hampshire
TUNBRIDGE WELLS – Kent v Middlesex
LEICESTER – Leicestershire v Sussex
NOTTINGHAM – Nottinghamshire v Northamptonshire
BATH – Somerset v Glamorgan
BIRMINGHAM – Warwickshire v Yorkshire

Saturday 23 June
CARDIFF – Glamorgan v Surrey
TUNBRIDGE WELLS – Kent v Essex
MANCHESTER – Lancashire v Middlesex
LEICESTER – Leicestershire v Nottinghamshire
NORTHAMPTON – Northamptonshire v Gloucestershire
HOVE – Sussex v Hampshire
WORCESTER – Worcestershire v Yorkshire

Wednesday 27 June
TAUNTON – Somerset v Worcestershire
THE OVAL – Surrey v Warwickshire

Saturday 30 June
BRISTOL – Gloucestershire v Glamorgan
SOUTHPORT – Lancashire v Worcestershire
NOTTINGHAM – Nottinghamshire v Sussex
THE OVAL – Surrey v Leicestershire
HARROGATE – Yorkshire v Somerset

Saturday 7 July
CHESTERFIELD – Derbyshire v Yorkshire
SOUTHEND-ON-SEA – Essex v Sussex
SWANSEA – Glamorgan v Somerset
SOUTHAMPTON – Hampshire v Gloucestershire
MAIDSTONE – Kent v Lancashire
NORTHAMPTON – Northamptonshire v Warwickshire
NOTTINGHAM – Nottinghamshire v Worcestershire
THE OVAL – Surrey v Middlesex

Wednesday 11 July
SOUTHEND-ON-SEA – Essex v Nottinghamshire
CARDIFF – Glamorgan v Gloucestershire
BASINGSTOKE – Hampshire v Derbyshire
MAIDSTONE – Kent v Leicestershire
LORD'S – Middlesex v Yorkshire
NORTHAMPTON – Northamptonshire v Lancashire
TAUNTON – Somerset v Warwickshire
HOVE – Sussex v Surrey

Saturday 14 July
LIVERPOOL – Lancashire v Derbyshire
LEICESTER – Leicestershire v Somerset
NOTTINGHAM – Nottinghamshire v Gloucestershire
THE OVAL – Surrey v Kent
WORCESTER – Worcestershire v Sussex
BRADFORD – Yorkshire v Hampshire

Saturday 21 July
CHESTERFIELD – Derbyshire v Kent (†*29 August*)
BIRMINGHAM – Warwickshire v Glamorgan (†*15 August*)
† *Alternative date if either County in B & H Final.*

Wednesday 25 July
DERBY – Derbyshire v Gloucestershire
BOURNEMOUTH – Hampshire v Essex
MANCHESTER – Lancashire v Warwickshire
LEICESTER – Leicestershire v Middlesex
NORTHAMPTON – Northamptonshire v Kent
WORKSOP – Nottinghamshire v Yorkshire
GUILDFORD – Surrey v Worcestershire

Saturday 28 July
COLCHESTER – Essex v Gloucestershire
SWANSEA – Glamorgan v Lancashire
FOLKESTONE – Kent v Nottinghamshire
LEICESTER – Leicestershire v Worcestershire
NORTHAMPTON – Northamptonshire v Sussex
THE OVAL – Surrey v Derbyshire
NUNEATON – Warwickshire v Hampshire
SCARBOROUGH – Yorkshire v Middlesex

Wednesday 1 August
BURTON UPON TRENT – Derbyshire v Northamptonshire
COLCHESTER – Essex v Middlesex
BRISTOL – Gloucestershire v Leicestershire
SOUTHAMPTON – Hampshire v Somerset
FOLKESTONE – Kent v Surrey
EASTBOURNE – Sussex v Glamorgan
WORCESTER – Worcestershire v Nottinghamshire
SHEFFIELD – Yorkshire v Warwickshire

Saturday 4 August
CHESTERFIELD – Derbyshire v Warwickshire
CARDIFF – Glamorgan v Hampshire
MANCHESTER – Lancashire v Somerset
NORTHAMPTON – Northamptonshire v Middlesex
NOTTINGHAM – Nottinghamshire v Surrey
EASTBOURNE – Sussex v Kent
WORCESTER – Worcestershire v Essex
BRADFORD – Yorkshire v Leicestershire

Saturday 11 August
CHELTENHAM – Gloucestershire v Yorkshire
PORTSMOUTH – Hampshire v Surrey
CANTERBURY – Kent v Worcestershire
LORD'S – Middlesex v Glamorgan
WELLINGBOROUGH – Northamptonshire v Leicestershire
NOTTINGHAM – Nottinghamshire v Derbyshire
WESTON-SUPER-MARE – Somerset v Sussex
BIRMINGHAM – Warwickshire v Lancashire

Wednesday 15 August
CHELTENHAM – Gloucestershire v Worcestershire
PORTSMOUTH – Hampshire v Middlesex
CANTERBURY – Kent v Yorkshire
LEICESTER – Leicestershire v Derbyshire
WESTON-SUPER-MARE – Somerset v Nottinghamshire
THE OVAL – Surrey v Sussex
BIRMINGHAM – Warwickshire v Glamorgan (*if not played on 21 July*)

Saturday 18 August
DERBY – Derbyshire v Worcestershire
CARDIFF – Glamorgan v Leicestershire
CHELTENHAM – Gloucestershire v Surrey
MANCHESTER – Lancashire v Hampshire
LORD'S – Middlesex v Somerset
NORTHAMPTON – Northamptonshire v Essex
HOVE – Sussex v Yorkshire

Saturday 25 August
CHELMSFORD – Essex v Surrey
SWANSEA – Glamorgan v Derbyshire
BOURNEMOUTH – Hampshire v Kent
LEICESTER – Leicestershire v Northamptonshire
TAUNTON – Somerset v Gloucestershire
HOVE – Sussex v Middlesex
WORCESTER – Worcestershire v Warwickshire
LEEDS – Yorkshire v Lancashire

Wednesday 29 August
CHESTERFIELD – Derbyshire v Kent (*if not played on 21 July*)
CHELMSFORD – Essex v Northamptonshire
BOURNEMOUTH – Hampshire v Sussex
LORD'S – Middlesex v Worcestershire
BIRMINGHAM – Warwickshire v Nottinghamshire

Saturday 1 September
CARDIFF – Glamorgan v Kent
BRISTOL – Gloucestershire v Warwickshire
BLACKPOOL – Lancashire v Nottinghamshire
LEICESTER – Leicestershire v Essex
TAUNTON – Somerset v Derbyshire

Wednesday 5 September
BRISTOL – Gloucestershire v Northamptonshire
MANCHESTER – Lancashire v Leicestershire
NOTTINGHAM – Nottinghamshire v Middlesex
THE OVAL – Surrey v Hampshire
HOVE – Sussex v Somerset
BIRMINGHAM – Warwickshire v Kent
WORCESTER – Worcestershire v Glamorgan
SCARBOROUGH – Yorkshire v Essex

Other First-Class Matches

*Includes play on Sunday

Saturday 21 April
*LORD'S – MCC v Kent
CAMBRIDGE – Cambridge U. v. Essex

Wednesday 25 April
CAMBRIDGE – Cambridge U. v. Leicestershire
OXFORD – Oxford U. v Glamorgan

Wednesday 2 May
CAMBRIDGE – Cambridge U. v Surrey

Wednesday 9 May
CAMBRIDGE – Cambridge U. v Nottinghamshire
OXFORD – Oxford U. v Hampshire

Wednesday 16 May
CAMBRIDGE – Cambridge U. v Gloucestershire

Wednesday 23 May
OXFORD – Oxford U. v Gloucestershire

Saturday 2 June
OXFORD – Oxford U. v Warwickshire

Saturday 9 June
CAMBRIDGE – Cambridge U. v. Yorkshire
OXFORD – Oxford U. v Somerset

Wednesday 13 June
CAMBRIDGE – Cambridge U. v Sussex
OXFORD – Oxford U. v Leicestershire

Saturday 16 June
OXFORD – Oxford U. v Worcestershire

Wednesday 20 June
CAMBRIDGE – Cambridge U. v Lancashire
OXFORD – Oxford U. v Surrey

Saturday 23 June
*BATH – Somerset v Cambridge U.

Wednesday 27 June
PAGHAM – Sussex v Oxford U.

Wednesday 4 July
†LORD'S – Cambridge U. v Oxford U.
†*At* ARUNDEL *if Middlesex at home in B & H Semi-Final.*

Saturday 28 July
DUBLIN – Ireland v Scotland

Saturday 1 September
SCARBOROUGH – T. N. Pearce's XI v MCC

John Player League

Sunday 29 April
DERBY – Derbyshire v Hampshire
CARDIFF – Glamorgan v Worcestershire
BRISTOL – Gloucestershire v Lancashire
NOTTINGHAM – Nottinghamshire v Middlesex
THE OVAL – Surrey v Somerset
HOVE – Sussex v Northamptonshire
BIRMINGHAM – Warwickshire v Essex
MIDDLESBROUGH – Yorkshire v Leicestershire

Sunday 6 May
CHELMSFORD – Essex v Derbyshire
MAIDSTONE – Kent v Warwickshire
LEICESTER – Leicestershire v Sussex
LORD'S – Middlesex v Hampshire
NORTHAMPTON – Northamptonshire v Glamorgan
WORCESTER – Worcestershire v Gloucestershire

Sunday 13 May
SWANSEA – Glamorgan v Sussex
SOUTHAMPTON – Hampshire v Essex
MANCHESTER – Lancashire v Leicestershire
NOTTINGHAM – Nottinghamshire v Yorkshire
TAUNTON – Somerset v Warwickshire

Sunday 20 May
BRISTOL – Gloucestershire v Derbyshire
MANCHESTER – Lancashire v Northamptonshire
LORD'S – Middlesex v Leicestershire
NOTTINGHAM – Nottinghamshire v Essex
HORSHAM – Sussex v Surrey
WORCESTER – Worcestershire v Somerset
HUDDERSFIELD – Yorkshire v Kent

Sunday 27 May
DERBY – Derbyshire v Nottinghamshire
BRISTOL – Gloucestershire v Leicestershire
CANTERBURY – Kent v Hampshire

MILTON KEYNES – Northamptonshire v Middlesex
THE OVAL – Surrey v Essex
BIRMINGHAM – Warwickshire v Worcestershire
BRADFORD – Yorkshire v Glamorgan

Sunday 3 June
ILFORD – Essex v Lancashire
LEICESTER – Leicestershire v Kent
LORD'S – Middlesex v Gloucestershire '
NOTTINGHAM – Nottinghamshire v Glamorgan
GLASTONBURY – Somerset v Hampshire
HOVE – Sussex v Derbyshire
WORCESTER – Worcestershire v Northamptonshire
HULL – Yorkshire v Surrey

Sunday 10 June
CHESTERFIELD – Derbyshire v Middlesex
SWANSEA – Glamorgan v Warwickshire
CANTERBURY – Kent v Northamptonshire
BRISTOL – Somerset v Gloucestershire
THE OVAL – Surrey v Lancashire

Sunday 17 June
GLOUCESTER – Gloucestershire v Kent
SOUTHAMPTON – Hampshire v Nottinghamshire
LEICESTER – Leicestershire v Glamorgan
LORD'S – Middlesex v Worcestershire
NORTHAMPTON – Northamptonshire v Yorkshire
BATH – Somerset v Essex
HOVE – Sussex v Warwickshire

Sunday 24 June
EBBW VALE – Glamorgan v Surrey
MANCHESTER – Lancashire v Middlesex
LEICESTER – Leicestershire v Nottinghamshire
TRING – Northamptonshire v Gloucestershire
NUNEATON – Warwickshire v Derbyshire
WORCESTER – Worcestershire v Yorkshire

Sunday 1 July
LONG EATON – Derbyshire v Northamptonshire
CHELMSFORD – Essex v Kent
BRISTOL – Gloucestershire v Glamorgan
PORTSMOUTH – Hampshire v Leicestershire
MANCHESTER – Lancashire v Worcestershire
LORD'S Middlesex v Warwickshire
NOTTINGHAM – Nottinghamshire v Sussex
SCARBOROUGH – Yorkshire v Somerset

Sunday 8 July
SOUTHEND-ON-SEA – Essex v Sussex
SWANSEA – Glamorgan v Somerset
BASINGSTOKE – Hampshire v Gloucestershire
MAIDSTONE – Kent v Lancashire
THE OVAL – Surrey v Middlesex
BIRMINGHAM – Warwickshire v Nottinghamshire

Sunday 15 July
MAIDSTONE – Kent v Surrey
MANCHESTER – Lancashire v Derbyshire
LEICESTER – Leicestershire v Somerset
LUTON – Northamptonshire v Essex
NOTTINGHAM – Nottinghamshire v Gloucestershire
WORCESTER – Worcestershire v Sussex
LEEDS – Yorkshire v Hampshire

Sunday 22 July
CHESTERFIELD – Derbyshire v Kent
COLCHESTER – Essex v Yorkshire
PORTSMOUTH – Hampshire v Glamorgan
YEOVIL – Somerset v Northamptonshire
BYFLEET – Surrey v Warwickshire
HASTINGS – Sussex v Lancashire
WORCESTER – Worcestershire v Nottinghamshire

Sunday 29 July
COLCHESTER – Essex v Gloucestershire
CARDIFF – Glamorgan v Lancashire
FOLKESTONE – Kent v Nottinghamshire
LEICESTER – Leicestershire v Worcestershire
THE OVAL – Surrey v Derbyshire
BIRMINGHAM – Warwickshire v Hampshire
SCARBOROUGH – Yorkshire v Middlesex

Sunday 5 August
CHESTERFIELD – Derbyshire v Yorkshire
MANCHESTER – Lancashire v Somerset
NORTHAMPTON – Northamptonshire v Warwickshire
NOTTINGHAM – Nottinghamshire v Surrey
EASTBOURNE – Sussex v Kent
WORCESTER – Worcestershire v Hampshire

Sunday 12 August
CHELTENHAM – Gloucestershire v Yorkshire
BOURNEMOUTH – Hampshire v Surrey
CANTERBURY – Kent v Worcestershire
LORD'S – Middlesex v Glamorgan
WELLINGBOROUGH – Northamptonshire v Leicestershire
WESTON-SUPER-MARE – Somerset v Sussex
BIRMINGHAM – Warwickshire v Lancashire

Sunday 19 August
DERBY – Derbyshire v Worcestershire
CHELTENHAM – Gloucestershire v Surrey
MANCHESTER – Lancashire v Hampshire
LEICESTER – Leicestershire v Essex
LORD'S – Middlesex v Somerset
NORTHAMPTON – Northamptonshire v Nottinghamshire
HOVE – Sussex v Yorkshire

Sunday 26 August
CHELMSFORD – Essex v Middlesex
SWANSEA – Glamorgan v Derbyshire
SOUTHAMPTON – Hampshire v Sussex
TAUNTON – Somerset v Kent
THE OVAL – Surrey v Northamptonshire
BIRMINGHAM – Warwickshire v Leicestershire
BRADFORD – Yorkshire v Lancashire

Sunday 2 September
CARDIFF – Glamorgan v Kent
MORETON-IN-MARSH – Gloucestershire v Warwickshire
MANCHESTER – Lancashire v Nottinghamshire
LEICESTER – Leicestershire v Surrey
LORD'S – Middlesex v Sussex
TAUNTON – Somerset v Derbyshire
WORCESTER – Worcestershire v Essex

Sunday 9 September
DERBY – Derbyshire v Leicestershire
CHELMSFORD – Essex v Glamorgan
BOURNEMOUTH – Hampshire v Northamptonshire
CANTERBURY – Kent v Middlesex
NOTTINGHAM – Nottinghamshire v Somerset
THE OVAL – Surrey v Worcestershire
HOVE – Sussex v Gloucestershire
BIRMINGHAM – Warwickshire v Yorkshire

Benson and Hedges

Saturday 28 April
DERBY – Derbyshire v Hampshire
CARDIFF – Glamorgan v Worcestershire
BRISTOL – Gloucestershire v Minor Counties (S)
NOTTINGHAM – Nottinghamshire v Middlesex
THE OVAL – Surrey v Combined Us
EASTBOURNE – Sussex v Northamptonshire

BIRMINGHAM – Warwickshire v Leicestershire
LINCOLN – Minor Counties (N) v Kent

Saturday 5 May
SOUTHPORT – Lancashire v Warwickshire
LEICESTER – Leicestershire v Derbyshire
LORD'S – Middlesex v Minor Counties (N)
NORTHAMPTON – Northamptonshire v Essex
TAUNTON – Somerset v Glamorgan
WORCESTER – Worcestershire v Gloucestershire
BRADFORD – Yorkshire v Nottinghamshire
OXFORD – Combined Us v Sussex

Saturday 12 May
BRISTOL – Gloucestershire v Somerset
BOURNEMOUTH – Hampshire v Warwickshire
CANTERBURY – Kent v Middlesex
LEICESTER – Leicestershire v Lancashire
THE OVAL – Surrey v Essex
NEWCASTLE UPON TYNE – Minor Counties (N) v Yorkshire
HIGH WYCOMBE – Minor Counties (S) v Worcestershire
CAMBRIDGE – Combined Us v Northamptonshire

Saturday 19 May
CHELMSFORD – Essex v Combined Us
SWANSEA – Glamorgan v Gloucestershire
MANCHESTER – Lancashire v Hampshire
NOTTINGHAM – Nottinghamshire v Minor Counties (N)
TAUNTON – Somerset v Minor Counties (S)
HOVE – Sussex v Surrey
BIRMINGHAM – Warwickshire v Derbyshire
LEEDS – Yorkshire v Kent

Wednesday 23 May
CHESTERFIELD – Derbyshire v Lancashire
CHELMSFORD – Essex v Sussex
SOUTHAMPTON – Hampshire v Leicestershire
CANTERBURY – Kent v Nottinghamshire
LORD'S – Middlesex v Yorkshire
NORTHAMPTON – Northamptonshire v Surrey
WORCESTER – Worcestershire v Somerset
WATFORD – Minor Counties (S) v Glamorgan

Wednesday 6 June – Quarter-Finals
Wednesday 4 July – Semi-Finals
Saturday 21 July – Final (LORD'S)

Gillette Cup

Wednesday 27 June – First Round
HIGH WYCOMBE – Buckinghamshire v Suffolk
DURHAM CITY – Durham v Berkshire
SWANSEA – Glamorgan v Kent
BRISTOL – Gloucestershire v Hampshire
MANCHESTER – Lancashire v Essex
LEICESTER – Leicestershire v Devon

Wednesday 18 July – Second Round
CHESTER-LE-STREET/READING – Durham/Berkshire v Yorkshire
CARDIFF/CANTERBURY – Glamorgan/Kent v Lancashire/Essex
LEICESTER/TORQUAY – Leicestershire/Devon v Worcestershire
LORD'S – Middlesex v Gloucestershire/Hampshire
NORTHAMPTON – Northamptonshire v Surrey
TAUNTON – Somerset v Derbyshire
HOVE – Sussex v Buckinghamshire/Suffolk
BIRMINGHAM – Warwickshire v Nottinghamshire

Wednesday 8 August – Quarter-Finals
Wednesday 22 August – Semi-Finals
Saturday 8 September – Final (LORD'S)